T0281796

THE DUEL

JOHN IBBITSON

The Duel

Diefenbaker, Pearson, and the
Making of Modern Canada

SIGNAL

McCLELLAND
& STEWART

Signal and colophon are registered trademarks of Penguin Random House Canada Limited.

Library and Archives Canada Cataloguing in Publication
Title: The duel : Diefenbaker, Pearson, and the making of modern Canada / John Ibbitson.
Names: Ibbitson, John, author.
Description: Includes index.
Identifiers: Canadiana 20230159265 | ISBN 9780771003264 (hardcover) | ISBN 9780771003271 (EPUB)
Subjects: LCSH: Diefenbaker, John G., 1895-1979. | LCSH: Pearson, Lester B. | LCSH: Prime ministers—Canada—Biography. | LCSH: Canada—Politics and government—1945-1980. | CSH: Canada—Politics and government—1957-1963. | CSH: Canada—Politics and government—1963-1968. | LCGFT: Biographies.
Classification: LCC FC616.D53 I23 2023 | DDC 971.064/2092—dc23

Jacket design by Kate Sinclair
Jacket art: Mario Geo / Contributor / Getty Images
Typeset in Sabon LT Pro by M&S, Toronto
Printed in Canada

Published by Signal,
an imprint of McClelland & Stewart,
a division of Penguin Random House Canada Limited,
a Penguin Random House Company
www.penguinrandomhouse.ca

3   4   5   6   27   26   25   24   23

For the poker table.

Contents

Acknowledgements

The Right Honourable Jean Chrétien, twentieth prime minister of Canada, agreed to speak with me at length about the years when he was a newly arrived MP watching Lester Pearson and John Diefenbaker face off across the floor of the House of Commons. I am grateful for his time and his insights. I am grateful as well to the Right Honourable Joe Clark, sixteenth prime minister, for confirming that memorable story of Diefenbaker's funeral. The Honourable John Baird, who served in Ontario and federal cabinets, including as minister of foreign affairs, and who describes himself as a "lifelong Diefenbaker geek," reviewed the manuscript, offering many valued corrections and suggestions.

Throughout the writing of *The Duel*, three books were never far from my side: *Rogue Tory: The Life and Legend of John G. Diefenbaker*, by Denis Smith, and John English's two-volume biography of Lester B. Pearson: *Shadow of Heaven* and *The Worldly Years*. I am greatly indebted to Professor English for his meticulous review of the manuscript, and to the distinguished Canadian historian Robert Bothwell, who offered his own enlightening review. Antony Anderson, author of *Diplomacy: Lester Pearson and the Suez Crisis*, reviewed not only the section devoted to that event, but the entire manuscript as well, for which I am most grateful. My thanks to historian Michael Stevenson of Lakehead University, both for his contributions to understanding Diefenbaker's foreign policy and for his review of that portion of the manuscript. University of Saskatchewan professor emeritus John C. Courtney graciously provided me with an advance copy of *Revival and Change: The 1957 and 1958 Diefenbaker Elections.* His analysis of those elections enriched my own.

While writing this book, I had many lunches with retired senator Marjory LeBreton, who worked in Diefenbaker's office during his years in opposition and who shared many insights. William Macadam, who was Diefenbaker's associate and friend, went through the manuscript carefully and I gratefully incorporated many of his suggestions, along with his anecdote about Diefenbaker, Churchill, and a bottle of cognac.

I owe a particular debt to Tim Hutchinson, assistant dean of University Archives and Special Collections at the University of Saskatchewan's library, who greatly assisted my research both before and during my time there. As well, university president Peter Stoicheff and other senior officials made me most welcome on campus. And I am greatly beholden to Amber Lannon, Carleton University's librarian, and Chris Trainor, head of Carleton's Archives and Special Collections, for providing access to Lester Pearson's correspondence.

A special mention: Throughout its long history, the *Globe and Mail* has supported those journalists who choose to work on books. In the case of *The Duel*, editor-in-chief David Walmsley came to my rescue when I was facing a particularly daunting deadline, providing the time and resources needed to meet it. To David, to publisher and CEO Phillip Crawley, to Ottawa bureau chief Robert Fife, and to all my colleagues at the *Globe*, past and present, thank you for providing me with the opportunity to work with you at one of the world's great newspapers.

This is my fifth book with Douglas Pepper, publisher of Signal Books at McClelland & Stewart/Penguin Random House Canada, who edited the manuscript. That partnership has deeply enriched my life as a writer, as has the friendship and advocacy of my agent, John Pearce. To both of you, once again, my deepest thanks. This is the third time that Tara Tovell has copy-edited one of my manuscripts, and for the third time I am in her debt. And I am very grateful to Lloyd Davis for his meticulous proofreading of the manuscript. For any errors or omissions that got through I alone am responsible.

Throughout the four years it took to write this book, my husband Grant Burke was, as always, my inspiration, partner, and best friend. *The*

Duel tested his forbearance more than anything that had come before, though he never—well, hardly ever—let on.

In the spring of 1987, I started playing poker with some fellow students at Western University's Graduate School of Journalism. More than three decades later, the annual poker weekend with Andy, Dave, Hugh, Joe, Kevin, Larry, Stephen, and Vince has become a touchstone of my life. Guys, this book is for you.

OTTAWA
April 8, 2023

Preface

On Sunday, August 19, 1979, just before the beginning of the state funeral in the nation's capital for John George Diefenbaker, a senior official came to Prime Minister Joe Clark with news of a bomb threat. It might be necessary, he was advised, to evacuate 1,200 politicians, judges, ambassadors, and other dignitaries from Christ Church Cathedral and cancel the service. The decision was the prime minister's to make. Clark looked around at the rows of political eminences. He pointed to the casket. "The only one who wants us all dead is lying right there. Let's carry on."[1]

Diefenbaker had spent three years planning his funeral, which included his casket taking a three-thousand-kilometre train ride, escorted by friends and family and reporters, back to Saskatoon, where Canada's thirteenth prime minister would be buried. Although the only scheduled stops were at Sudbury, Winnipeg, and Prince Albert, people gathered along the route to mark his passing: sometimes just a few at a dirt road crossing, or a family at harvest in a field, standing silently in tribute. "Workmen holding hard hats in their hands as the train went by," the *Globe and Mail*'s Joan Hollobon wrote. "Old men standing at attention. Women waving. Young people."[2]

But also crowds, lining the track as the train passed through towns and cities. Ten thousand waited past midnight in Winnipeg. Canada's first and most populist prime minister was resented by the leadership of both the Liberal and Progressive Conservative parties, and the feeling was mutual. But he was still loved by the people he had fought for, who welcomed him home.

John Diefenbaker has been unfairly treated by history. His governments launched major reforms to health care, immigration, and the justice system. On his watch, First Nations obtained the right to vote and the federal government began to open up the North. He established Canada as a leader in the struggle against apartheid in South Africa, and took the first steps in making Canada a leader in the fight against the proliferation of nuclear weapons. And Diefenbaker's Bill of Rights laid the groundwork for the Charter of Rights and Freedoms (which might not have been needed had the Supreme Court not disregarded Diefenbaker's bill).

These and other achievements were obscured by his baffling conduct, by his suspicion and vanity and vendettas, and by a cadre of historians and journalists who are always more comfortable when Liberals are in charge. "To work, gentlemen, we have a government to bring down," *Toronto Star* reporter Val Sears memorably declared in the press gallery on the day of the 1963 election call.[3] That same year, the journalist Peter C. Newman considerably advanced his career with *Renegade in Power: The Diefenbaker Years*, a brilliantly written but vicious assault.

Despite the personal demons that he battled, Diefenbaker set in motion many of the achievements credited to his successor, Lester B. Pearson. Pearson, in turn, gave coherence to Diefenbaker's piecemeal reforms. He also pushed Parliament to adopt a new, and now much-loved, Canadian flag against Diefenbaker's fierce opposition. Pearson understood that in the postwar world, Canada's attachment to Great Britain must give way to the reality of American power—that if Canada were to be taken seriously as a nation, it needed to develop a stronger sense of self. Diefenbaker's parochial vision remained rooted in nostalgia for the Empire. He raged as Canada grew beyond the limits of his imagination. Both men grappled with Quebec's Quiet Revolution; neither truly understood it.

Pearson was superbly prepared for the role of prime minister: decades of experience at External Affairs, the respect of leaders from Washington to London to Delhi to Tokyo, the only Canadian to win the Nobel Peace Prize. And Pearson possessed none of Diefenbaker's paranoia. He was a decent and honourable man.

Diefenbaker was the better politician, though. If Pearson walked with ease in the halls of power, Diefenbaker connected with the farmers and small-town merchants and others left outside the inner circles. Diefenbaker was one of the great orators of Canadian political life; Pearson spoke with a slight lisp. And though Pearson thought he could better manage relations with the United States during the tumultuous 1960s, he ended as estranged from Lyndon Johnson as Diefenbaker became from John F. Kennedy.

Most of Diefenbaker's and Pearson's biographers have focused on foreign affairs, scandals, the struggle for national unity, and the enmity of each toward the other. But while the Bomarc missile crisis and the Gerda Munsinger affair have faded from popular memory, public health care, an enlightened immigration policy, pensions, and civil rights define the social fabric of this country. These are the true legacies of Diefenbaker and Pearson, the things for which both prime ministers deserve to be praised and remembered.

Their growth was Canada's growth. Both were born in small-town Ontario, one the son of a teacher, the other of a preacher, when Canada was a semi-colonial backwater with no voice in the world. While the Pearsons remained rooted in Southern Ontario—however much they moved around within it—the Diefenbakers migrated to Saskatchewan when John was still a boy, a cleavage that defined his life.

Both served in the First World War—why neither saw combat makes for two fascinating tales—and prospered in a post-war, post-Prohibition Canada where women had the vote and a maturing dominion took greater control over its own affairs.

Diefenbaker first came to public notice as a crusading attorney: Diefenbaker for the Defence, champion of the little man or woman caught in a legal vise and desperately in need of a good lawyer. *R. v. Olson*, *R. v. Bajer*, *R. v. Emele*, the fight over Grey Owl's estate. Most famous of all: the defence of John Atherton, a telegraph operator accused of negligence leading to a train wreck and the death of twenty-one men. Diefenbaker won acquittal by arguing that the railway was the true culprit, though in other cases victory meant saving his client from the gallows.

Pearson at first seemed fated to spend his life playing and coaching sports well and teaching history indifferently. But he caught the attention of the men who were shaping Canada's first true department of foreign affairs. As the Roaring Twenties gave way to Dust Bowl and Depression and then to yet another great war, he rose to prominence as a masterful diplomat, the embodiment of a new country that had earned its place on the battlefield in the councils of nations: ambassador, undersecretary, minister, peacemaker. Everyone knew he was destined to be prime minister. But in 1957, destiny took a detour.

Then they faced each other, *Diefenbaker v. Pearson*, across the House of Commons, leaders of their parties, each determined to wrest and hold power, in a decade-long contest that would shake and shape the country.

Here is a tale of two men, children of Victoria, who led Canada into the atomic age: each the product of his past, each more like the other than either would ever admit, fighting each other relentlessly while together forging the Canada we live in today.

Their story is the story of Canada's transformation from a rural, religious appendage of the British Empire to an urban, multi-ethnic middle power embracing its Centennial year. To understand our times, we must first understand theirs.

ONE

The Teacher's Son; the Preacher's Son

(1895–1918)

I

John George Diefenbaker and Lester Bowles Pearson were born only two years and 135 kilometres apart, but they had very different names and very different parents.

John Diefenbaker came into this world on September 18, 1895, in Neustadt, a German-settled village in Grey County in Central Ontario. He described his forebears as "dispossessed Scottish Highlanders and discontented Palatine Germans."[1] His grandfather, George M. Diefenbacker (other variations included Diefenbach and Diefenbacher), immigrated from Baden to Upper Canada in the 1850s, where he did well as a farmer and wagon-maker. Diefenbaker's father William was one of seven children.

William started out as a teacher, acquiring his professional qualifications in 1891 after one year at the Model School in Ottawa, where he spent much of his time watching the young Wilfrid Laurier dazzle everyone, including William, in the House of Commons. (Prime Minister John A. Macdonald was in decline, and in any case, William didn't approve of his drinking.) A dreamy, impractical man, William Diefenbaker's greatest gift to his son

John might have been transmitting this love for the House of Commons—a stage upon which Diefenbaker would perform for much of his adult life—along with a Whiggish view of history that celebrated a humanity largely under the sway of beneficent Britain. These noble islanders had from Saxon times nurtured a devotion to freedom under the rule of law, or so the story went: the story of Alfred and Magna Carta and Parliament and the Glorious Revolution, of rights and liberties bequeathed to the British colonies in North America—thirteen of which proved to be ungrateful—and now to the world through an empire on which the sun never set. Though the wars and other traumas of the twentieth century would shatter this pleasant myth, John Diefenbaker never lost faith in it.

His mother Mary was descended from Campbells on her mother's side and Bannermans on her father's. The defeat of Bonnie Prince Charlie at Culloden in 1745 killed off much of the clan; the enclosures that robbed poorer Scots of their grazing lands drove the rest south to England or, in the case of Mary's ancestors, west to the New World—across the Atlantic in 1813 on a disease-ridden ship to Hudson Bay, eventually reaching a settlement along Manitoba's Red River that had been sponsored by Lord Selkirk.

The trek was brutal and deadly, and the settlement unwelcoming. In 1815, the Bannermans joined a brigade of about 130 who travelled mostly by canoe and on foot to Upper Canada. Imagine the strength of will needed to survive the crossing, the long journey from Hudson Bay to the Red River settlement, and then the endless trek across what is now Northern Ontario, through forest and muskeg and swamp, down rivers and across lakes and along the storm-swept shorelines, swarmed by mosquitos while on land, at constant risk of being swamped while on water, with no other soul for so many miles, death only a slip on a wet rock or an infected cut away. Eventually they reached Elgin County, and then Holland Landing, and finally Bruce County, on the shores of Lake Huron.

They were archetypically stubborn Scots. Diefenbaker's maternal great-grandfather, who hated the Toronto Tory pseudo-aristocracy known as the Family Compact as much as his family had hated the English and Scottish lairds, joined William Lyon Mackenzie in the rebellion of 1837—no small irony since William Lyon Mackenzie King, the rebel's grandson, and John

Diefenbaker would become fierce political opponents. Mary was born in Bruce County, and there she met and married William, the itinerant teacher. As stern and practical as her husband was unfocused and spendthrift, Mary wasn't always able to hide her impatience. And her contempt for the English was as strong as William's devotion to the Empire. (When William delivered the news to the family that Victoria had died, he wept.) John inherited a Scottish crofter's sense of grievance at overlords who trampled on the rights of others and treated the less fortunate as worthless. That anger propelled him to become a crusading attorney, a politician, and ultimately prime minister.

After the marriage, the young couple moved to the village of Neustadt, in next-door Grey County, where John was born. The region had a long and turbulent history. French missionaries had ministered to the Hurons there in the early 1600s, until both were massacred by the Iroquois. But English settlers did not penetrate the rolling hills stretching south from Georgian Bay until the 1830s. There was good reason for the delay.

British loyalists fleeing the former American colonies after the Revolution, and soldiers retiring from the army, found the soils of southern and south-western Upper Canada rich and profitable. Displacing the fur trade that had sustained the Indigenous population, and taking their land, they grew and sold wheat to feed Britain when the Napoleonic wars closed off the continental market. To grind and transport the wheat, they built grist mills on every navigable river—which is why so many Ontario towns are centred on local waterfalls or rapids—and large brick houses to mark their success, which they attributed to the grace of the Almighty while quietly thinking it was really due to their own hard work. The Family Compact dominated the cities, especially York—which reverted to its original name, Toronto, in 1834—governing in cahoots with whichever aristocrat London sent to take charge of the colony, while prosperous Methodist farmers fumed. But though the 1837 rebellion was a bust, the Tory elites heard the message and accepted government that was responsible to the will of the legislature. All sides eventually joined in a coalition with their Lower Canadian counterparts and together with the separate colonies of New Brunswick and Nova Scotia forged the Dominion of Canada in 1867. Upper Canada, which had been renamed Canada West, was now the Province of Ontario, part of a self-governing dominion with aspirations that stretched *a mari usque ad mare.*

By now the best soil had been tilled. The settlers who eventually pushed their way into the lands south of Georgian Bay found hilly terrain and cooler temperatures that made the region less inviting. They did the best they could. David Winkler, who had emigrated as a child from Dreisbach in the Grand Duchy of Baden, was still a young man when he dammed Meaux Creek in 1856 and built a sawmill, naming the settlement Neustadt ("New Town"). Those who followed were also mostly German.

German settlers—industrious, artisanal, insular—had been part of Upper Canada's mix since the late 1700s, when Mennonites, Hessian mercenaries, and other German-speakers left Pennsylvania in search of religious tolerance and cheap land. Many of them staked their claims along the banks of the Grand River in Waterloo County, with the manufacturing town of Berlin (renamed Kitchener during the Great War) their unofficial capital. German veterans who had fought for the British in the revolutionary war joined them, along with later German-speaking immigrants from Europe. Most were Lutheran (though, like the Diefenbakers, many became Methodist), but there were also substantial Mennonite and Catholic populations; German was the language at home and in church; they co-existed with, but remained outside, the dominant British culture of the colony and the province.

Though German settlers who farmed to the south and west of Neustadt—such as those surrounding Guelph, Stratford, and Berlin—did well, their cousins in Grey County struggled with the hilly, rocky land. Grey County's population declined by a third between the 1880s and the 1910s. Neustadt, located on a minor local road, could not keep up with the competition of nearby villages and towns. At Diefenbaker's birth, its population was already dwindling from a peak of five hundred; the brewery that dominated the local economy would be out of business by the time of the First World War. John Diefenbaker was born into the quiet resentment of decline.

William was an able teacher, counting among his students several future members of Parliament. He was devoted to the works of Shakespeare and proficient on the organ. His son inherited no love of music and was far from devout. "Father was an unusual person," John remembered, carefully, in his memoirs. "He was not a driver in any sense of the word, but a dreamer who loved books."[2] The lack of respect is palpable. But along with a love for politics and history, William taught John how to fish, which became a lifelong passion: a form of solace and a means of escape. "There is a pleasure and, above all, a peace to be enjoyed in fishing beyond anything else I know."[3] He showed no particular interest in team sports, then or later. John Diefenbaker was a solitary boy who became a solitary man, a man who preferred fishing alone or with a few close friends to anything involving a ball or a puck or a crowd.

This may have been because he was bullied at school. William the father was also William the teacher, who didn't want to be accused of playing favourites, and who was particularly hard on his son. And once the family left Neustadt, his German name stood out. "I used to get quite upset when my schoolmates teased me about my name," he recalled in his memoirs. The Diefenbakers had been in Canada for as long as most of his classmates' families, but Toronto and environs were overwhelmingly British. Though it seems remarkable today, Diefenbaker's name would be an encumbrance throughout his political life.

The family's straightened circumstances also marked him. Local school boards often struggled to pay a teacher's meagre salary, and William lacked the discipline to live within his modest means. Young John chafed at the swells who drove by in their newfangled automobiles, never condescending to offer him a ride; when they broke down he would taunt the drivers, enjoying the curses they hurled back in return. He remembered one family whose children "had everything money could buy. They had Shetland ponies and two-wheeled carts in which the poor were not allowed even the shortest ride." John and his younger brother Elmer dreamed of oatmeal in a box; theirs came in a bag. The distinctions of wealth and class infuriated him. He would note in his memoirs, "At an early age I developed a consciousness of injustice that has never left me."[4] And a sense of resentment and inferiority that never left him, either.

II

Lester Bowles Pearson, the middle son of Edwin Pearson and Anne (Bowles) Pearson, inherited no grievances of any kind. He was born in the Methodist parsonage in Newtonbrook—then a small village north of Toronto, now a suburban neighbourhood centred on Yonge Street and Finch Avenue. Ed, as everyone called him, was a minister and a minister's son; Annie was the daughter of Thomas Bowles, who had been made the sheriff of Dufferin County to compensate for several close defeats in his efforts to become a Liberal member of the federal or provincial parliaments. Both the Bowleses and the Pearsons were of Anglo-Irish stock, and both were staunch Methodists. The Pearsons, who had prospered as linen drapers, fled decaying and disease-ridden Dublin in 1847—"Black '47"—the peak of the Irish famine. They settled first in New York, then two years later moved north to Canada, where Marmaduke Pearson established a successful dry goods store in Toronto; his son, Marmaduke Jr., became an ordained minister. As for the other side of the family, their Protestant religion might have helped prompt Charles Bowles to emigrate from Killarney to Canada in 1826, ultimately settling in Peel County, where the family prospered as farmers, except for Thomas, who was attracted to business and politics and town life.[5]

The Pearsons were every bit as devoted to the Tory cause as the Bowleses were to the Grits. But neither side was unreasonable about it. Lester later recalled, "My grandfather once agreed in a family discussion that if a Liberal candidate were honest, God-fearing, a good Methodist, and a prohibitionist, while the Tory was a rascally, hard-drinking Episcopalian, he would be morally obliged to vote for the foe, if he voted at all. He refused, however, to admit that such a situation should arise."[6]

Ed Pearson met Annie Bowles at a church event one Sunday afternoon in Orangeville, northwest of Toronto. Their Methodist faith had long since lost the reformist rigour of the church's founder, John Wesley; Methodism and Methodist churches in Ontario were generally less ostentatious than their Anglican counterparts, but more respectable than the Baptists. When Ed and Anne were married in Orangeville in 1892, the wedding was mentioned in the Toronto papers.

That city, and the province surrounding it, seemed to be changing by the day. Demand for wheat had slackened with the opening of the American, and then Canadian, prairies, but farmers simply switched their focus to other grains, such as oats and barley, or to beef and dairy, although marginal land was already starting to fall out of cultivation. Those farmers and farmworkers who couldn't make a go of it migrated to the cities. After decades of low growth, the mid-1890s saw a sustained expansion as Central Canada's industrial revolution accelerated.

There was an energy to Ontario at the turn of the century that would rarely be equalled after. The population had grown steadily from 1.6 million at Confederation to 2.5 million in 1911. The National Policy of high tariffs might have stifled competition and efficiency—many factories, from Singer Sewing Machine to Gillette, were branch plants intended to circumvent tariff barriers—but it also boosted nascent industries in Southern Ontario, especially in farm implements. The merger of the Massey and Harris companies in 1891 produced a continental giant that lasted, in one form or another, for almost a century.

But not everyone prospered. Thousands of men and women worked in sweatshops. Twelve-hour days were common, as well as sixty-six-hour work weeks and child labour. The 1871 census revealed that 25 per cent of boys and 10 per cent of girls ages eleven to fifteen were working. Little more than a century after the first pioneer settlers arrived in Ontario, Canada had its own proletariat. Meanwhile, one report claimed that fifty men controlled one third of Canada's wealth.

While a student, Ed had joined in the turmoil rocking the Methodist Church as it tried to accommodate its mission to the social stress of the industrial revolution. But the reform-minded student soon settled down, earning a reputation as a calm, sensible, and well-liked minister, stronger at pastoral care than at preaching, perhaps, an "outgoing, friendly, easygoing man." When Victoria College awarded him an honorary Doctor of Divinity in 1927, the citation praised his "well-balanced mind . . . sanity of judgment," his "warmth of heart" and "genial and winning personality," that in combination made him "in many respects the ideal Christian Minister."[7] Lester adored him.

For the children of a Methodist minister, cards and dancing were forbidden and the cinema discouraged. But unusually for a cleric, Ed was an enthusiastic sportsman, with baseball his particular love. His sons inherited his passion, and a passion for nature as well, which was always just beyond the edge of the small towns to which Ed ministered. Lester's mother Annie was often unwell—though she outlived her husband by three decades—but soldiered on nonetheless. She provided a safe and secure home for the three boys—she always regretted that there had never been a girl—made her own bread and her own soap, drew water from a well and attended to the many social responsibilities of a minister's wife. Lester adored her, too.

The Pearsons, despite their Christian concern for the plight of the poor, revelled in the galloping progress of the age. Everywhere, everything was new. Trains and the telegraph were well established, but now there was also the telephone—Alexander Graham Bell made the world's first long-distance telephone call from Brantford to nearby Paris, Ontario, on August 10, 1876—and the automobile. Ford opened its first Canadian plant, across the river from Detroit, in 1904, a year after the Wright brothers made the world's first controlled, heavier-than-air flight. Hamilton inaugurated Canada's first incandescent street lighting system in 1883. The next year, Parliament became one of the first government buildings in the world equipped with incandescent lighting. In 1906, with the harnessing of the Niagara River, hydro arrived fully in Ontario.

There were common threads in the backgrounds of John Diefenbaker and Lester Pearson. Both fathers were itinerant, moving their families from town to town every few years. In John, this bred solitary independence; in Lester, the ability to make new friends and to settle quickly into whatever environment he found himself. Both men received an above-average education, both were well read, and both parents had to make do with modest incomes.

But there were large differences as well. A minister was one of the few university-educated men in a small town. (Women rarely attended university.) Lester grew up in a succession of solid brick manses, with little of the financial worry that attended the Diefenbaker household. Most important, he was of Anglo-Irish descent and Methodist background, comfortably ensconced within the middle class, and with a clear path to the next level of affluence and accomplishment, if he was willing to work for it. His home life, if probably less idyllic than he painted it in his memoirs, was comfortable and supportive. "No one we knew suffered from tensions," as he put it.[8] From the moment of his birth, Lester B. Pearson belonged.

John Diefenbaker never belonged: constant stress at home between a strong, stern mother and a weak, distracted father who was held in something approaching contempt within his own family; barely enough money to get by, made worse by his father's irresponsible fondness for buying on credit; the outsider status of a German background—these would mark John Diefenbaker for life.

The two young men bounced around Southern Ontario—parsonage to parsonage, school district to school district—for years. Then, for John, there came a break—a cleavage, really—that would define his future. Without it, he would probably never have been who he became. In 1903, when he was eight, the Diefenbakers headed out west.

III

That year, William Diefenbaker experienced some form of medical crisis. "More devoted to his duties in my opinion than was necessary, Father suffered a breakdown in health in the spring of 1903," Diefenbaker wrote in his memoirs. "Doctors warned he was on the brink of 'galloping consumption,'" an aggressive form of tuberculosis.[9] Highly contagious and almost invariably fatal, tuberculosis was a leading cause of death at the turn of the century. Conventional medical wisdom held that clean, dry air could help prevent and treat the disease, so the doctors recommended that William move to the Prairies for his health. He applied for and received a posting to a school in rural northern Saskatchewan, as we know it today.

The doctors were wrong. The tuberculosis bacterium is airborne, passing from one person to the other through talking or coughing or sneezing, as with the flu virus. While a cool, dry climate is generally better for anyone's constitution than a hot, humid one, climate can neither prevent nor cure the disease, which was only treated effectively with the arrival of antibiotics in the 1950s. In any case, William's health crisis might not have been physical. Poorly paid and in debt, his love of literature and Empire and Parliament unappreciated at home, his self-worth under assault, William's mental health might have been at risk. The shame of what used to be called a nervous breakdown might have spurred the family to leave Ontario and head west.

Still, it was an enormous undertaking. The Riel rebellion had been suppressed less than twenty years before. The North-West Mounted Police kept order, and new settlers cohabited with the First Nations and Métis peoples, but the Diefenbakers would be moving from heartland to frontier.

What is now Saskatchewan and Alberta was then still part of the Northwest Territories, governed by a local legislative assembly and executive council, but with Ottawa still having the final say. Tensions were growing between the distant capital and local politicians who demanded provincial status so that the legislature could raise taxes and take on debt to pay for the schools and roads and other improvements required by the burgeoning population, which had more than doubled in a decade, reaching 159,000 in 1901.

The population had swollen because of the federal government's aggressive immigration policy, aimed at filling the prairie lands with settlers to prevent American annexation. Any settler was entitled to 65 hectares, also known as a quarter section, upon payment of ten dollars and the commitment to live on and work the land. The opportunity of a new start was irresistible for those living in poverty and sometimes persecution in places such as Germany, what is now Poland, Ukraine, and other parts of Eastern Europe. It also offered a fresh start for the Diefenbakers, whose name would no longer stick out so much.

By the time they were ready to leave, William had changed his mind, but Mary was determined. "Once you have your hand to the plough, you don't turn back," she told her husband.[10]

With their furniture sent on ahead, the family departed August 15, travelling third-class. Unfortunately, William had placed the family's food and bedding on the wrong train. Though other passengers—mostly immigrants and field hands—pitched in when they learned of the family's troubles, the first part of the journey was tough. The boys didn't have a proper meal till they reached Fort William (part of Thunder Bay, today). They sat on hard wooden benches, with Elmer and John strapped onto a shelf above the bench for sleeping. "Mile, after endless mile, Elmer and I learned something of the meaning of eternity," Diefenbaker would later recall.[11]

At Fort William, William tried but failed to convince his wife to turn back. The family was carrying on, she told him; if he returned to Toronto, he would do so alone.

At Winnipeg, John had "the most enjoyable meal of my life" for thirty-five cents, at a restaurant outside the train station. By the time they reached Saskatoon, population five hundred, the family had $1.75 to their name.

They left the train, finally, at Rosthern, a booming town about 60 kilometres north of Saskatoon, after a journey of more than 2,700 kilometres.

Two days later, they set out by wagon along the trail—there were no roads—that would take them to the school district of Tiefengrund ("deep ground," named in praise of its topsoil) twenty-seven kilometres northwest of Rosthern. The settlers were mostly Mennonites who had come over from East Prussia in the 1890s, only a few years before. The living quarters were attached to the school: three rooms and a kitchen.

The Battle of Duck Lake, part of the Métis rebellion, had been fought only a few kilometres away. Gabriel Dumont, Riel's ablest fighter, still lived nearby, and Diefenbaker, who became a lifelong admirer, would see him from time to time. Members of the local Cree population would drop by the school, and Diefenbaker said that from a young age he felt a kinship with Indigenous people, and indignation at their second-tier status within Canadian society. (Though he might have been reinventing his history, it was John Diefenbaker who, as prime minister, secured the federal vote for First Nations.)

John loved the West—the vast sweep of the sky, the loneliness of a coyote's howl, the dancing Northern Lights, the gently rolling land that emerged out of the prairies north of Saskatoon. And the family as a whole seemed to take to this new land—even William, who, after two years of teaching, decided his future lay in farming. William and John travelled by horse and buggy to inspect the new sections that were to be opened for settlement. By August 1905, the Diefenbakers had their own quarter section, near the new village of Borden. John was eleven years old and in grade seven. He was still not terribly popular. Esther Bradshaw, who went to school with the Diefenbaker boys in Saskatchewan, remembered John as a loner who walked around with his hands in his pockets, though Elmer was more outgoing and played in their games.[12]

Life, especially by today's standards, was brutally hard. William and John and Elmer cleared more than a hectare of rocks and trees each year, planting wheat in the newly tilled soil. Mary churned and sold butter, and tried but failed to turn a profit raising turkeys. William continued to teach school, as did his brother Ed, who had moved to the district and started his own, adjacent, farm. Ed was thin and sallow like his brother, and also had his head in the clouds—he too was devoted to Shakespeare and studied philosophy throughout his life—but he and John took to each other in a way not given to father and son. In every season except winter, they would walk together the five kilometres to school, talking about everything and nothing. When there wasn't school, there were chores or threshing at harvest time. The winters were endless and hard, with temperatures never climbing past minus twenty-five degrees Celsius for days on end. One year, the sleds were still in use in May. Another year, they had frost every month. And then there was the terrible night that John and Ed got lost in a blizzard while returning to the farm from a community event. They were forced to stay in their cart overnight, and by the time Ed got them home, John's legs were frozen to the knees, as he told it. It took several weeks, but he fully recovered.

And yet, though William never cleared more than $150 a year from that farm, the land provided a sense of purpose and pride, and the boys had time for devilment, including attaching Mary's parasol to a cart, installing the dog as a pilot, and then sending the contraption off the roof of the barn, in hopes of emulating the Wright brothers' breakthrough. The parasol was destroyed and the dog didn't return for days.

Young as John was, he bristled at socio-economic unfairness as he learned of the unscrupulous practices of the wheat barons, whose agents would declare the farmers' wheat wet or seedy when it wasn't, and then discount the price they were willing to pay. "While the lords of the grain trade lived in opulence in Winnipeg," he wrote many years later, "the farmers were subjected to practices that soured their thinking and seared their souls."[13]

Hearing the farmers' complaints of being cheated and mistreated by the powerful interests instilled in Diefenbaker a youthful sense of righteous anger—heated as well, perhaps, by the class envy he felt when growing up in Ontario. He had devoured the thousand-page encyclopedia that William had purchased, taking a particular interest in the heroic struggle for English liberty and the characters who had led that struggle, from Alfred the Great to William of Orange. Shakespeare was in the house, and the King James Bible, and Gibbon and Macaulay—prose that would one day shape the cadence of his oratory. He was also a devoted admirer of Abraham Lincoln, the country lawyer who led the American republic through its civil war. He recalled that he was only eight or nine years old when he declared to the family, "Someday I am going to be prime minister." Mary didn't think much of the idea at first, but Ed offered support.

The Diefenbakers spent five years on that farm before moving to Saskatoon so that John and Elmer could complete their education. But that wasn't the only reason. Though they had lived on the farm long enough, and cleared enough land, that William was finally able to take full title, the truth was that William was no better at making a living as a farmer than as a teacher. They never got any real money out of it.

William was done with teaching, too, and found a job as a clerk in the provincial land office. The low pay left Mary unimpressed. They kept a cow and planted a garden and John sold newspapers, was a delivery boy, and also worked as a janitor. Diefenbaker loved to tell about the time in 1910 that he met Prime Minister Wilfrid Laurier, who was standing alone outside the special train he travelled on, taking the early morning air. The two chatted, and as Diefenbaker recalled in his memoirs, Laurier later told the crowd at a rally that the young newspaper boy had dismissed him by saying, "Sorry, Prime Minister, but I can't waste any more time on you. I've got work to do."[14] A statue in Saskatoon commemorates the event, which may or may not have occurred.

Two million people flooded into Canada's Plains region between 1896 and 1914, the greatest influx in this country's history. In 1913, 400,870 people came to Canada, when the population was less than 8 million. (In the 2020s, immigration targets once again pushed past 400,000, but by then Canada's population had topped 38 million. In proportional terms, there will never again be a year like 1913.) Most of them, like William, broke the land; for many, like William, the land broke them. As the Canadian Museum of Immigration later noted, "British immigrants displayed a general ineptitude on rural farming enterprises, [but] many other desirable immigrant groups succeeded in Prairie agriculture. The Americans, Poles, Dutch, Germans, Finns, and Scandinavians all proved to be prosperous settlers."[15] (Many of the Americans were themselves immigrants from Eastern Europe.) But though the period was unusually wet—creating false expectations that would be cruelly disappointed in the years to come—the quality of the soil was variable, the grain merchants were tough customers, and some people were just not born to farm. Like William, they gave up and migrated to town, looking for work. Prairie cities grew exponentially in those years—Winnipeg's population went from less than 8,000 in 1881 to almost 180,000 in 1921. Many of those new arrivals were unskilled workers or settlers who had given up on their land.

The British who were already in place resented the exotic new arrivals, with their foreign languages and strange customs. The territorial government resented them as well, because of the financial burden they imposed. But looking back, we can see that the Laurier government's generous immigration policies created the Prairie provinces of today and laid the foundation for multiculturalism—the uniquely Canadian condition of encouraging newcomers to preserve their faith, language, and culture as part of the patchwork quilt of ethnicities that Canada would become.

With settlement and the need for schools and other services came increased demand for responsible government, championed by Frederick William Alpin Gordon Haultain, a father of Confederation equal to any who met in Charlottetown in 1864. Born in England, his family immigrated to Peterborough, Ontario, when he was three. After receiving his law degree, Haultain, like many other ambitious young men at the time, headed west to make his fortune, establishing his law office in Fort Macleod in 1884. Politically ambitious as well, he represented Macleod in the North-West Council and then the legislative assembly that replaced it. He was appointed president of the Executive Council, or premier, in 1897, while also serving as attorney general, treasurer, commissioner of public instruction, and commissioner of education. But Haultain wanted provincehood for the territory and campaigned relentlessly to force Ottawa to agree to create a new province of Buffalo. The Laurier government, fearing a large Western province could challenge Ontario and Quebec for dominance, instead created two provinces, Alberta and Saskatchewan. Many thought Haultain should be Saskatchewan's first premier, but he was a Conservative, and that wouldn't do. The Laurier government appointed a Liberal instead, inaugurating decades of virtually unbroken rule.

Laurier met Diefenbaker because the prime minister was in Saskatchewan to celebrate the creation of Canada's newest provinces and the success of his government's policy of aggressively recruiting the immigrants who were filling the land. But Ottawa had given the Prairie provinces less than full provincial powers. Unlike the founding provinces, Manitoba, Saskatchewan, and Alberta entered Confederation without control over natural resources. The political and business powers in Toronto, Montreal, and Ottawa saw the Prairie provinces as colonies of Central Canada in all but name. The resentments born of Laurentian Canada's arrogance toward the West would span the generations.

But none of this mattered to John as the family made the move to Saskatoon. What really mattered was finishing secondary school and going to university. When William came home with news that he had found a job for John at a local bank, Mary scotched the idea. She and her son both had bigger plans. A compact had formed between the two of them; his advancement was all that mattered now. John wanted to become a politician. And he had noticed that many politicians started out as lawyers. In June 1912, John graduated from the Saskatoon Collegiate Institute. Three months later, he began undergraduate studies at the University of Saskatchewan, which that year opened its first building in what remains the heart of the campus today.

IV

It must have been hard, at times, for Annie Pearson, her own health uncertain, to raise three sons on the modest salary of a Methodist minister. But for the family, these were happy days. "Certainly, for her children, they were very happy," Pearson remembered toward the end of his life. "We lacked nothing that was important, although I longed for a bicycle, a boy scout uniform, and a pair of genuine tube hockey skates."[16]

The family moved every three years or so from one town to another, one parsonage to another. They spent a few years in Toronto itself, a rapidly expanding city of banks and slaughterhouses, the horse-drawn streetcar from Yorkville to the waterfront only recently replaced by the city's first electric service. The new Trader's Bank Building, at Yonge and Colborne, soared fifteen stories toward the sky, the tallest building in the British Commonwealth. Bay Street already had some of the buildings found there today, including a new city hall at Bay and Queen streets that dominated the avenue. The new city hall was one of the first buildings to encroach on the Ward, as everyone called it—a slum in the heart of the downtown where newly arrived immigrants, many of them Chinese or Jewish or Italian, or Black people who had fled the United States, huddled in unplumbed tenements, six people to a room. No respectable person ventured into the Ward, unless it was to minister to the poor or in search of what couldn't be found elsewhere. Outside the Ward, all was confident optimism at what lay ahead—and inside the tenements, too, if you looked hard enough. Though a fire devastated much of the commercial district in 1904, the city of two hundred thousand quickly rebuilt. Everything was new, first, tallest, best. The future.

But Pearson spent most of his childhood in small towns, including Peterborough (his favourite) to the east of Toronto and Chatham to the southwest. Each parsonage was like the other: a solid brick home surrounded by elms or oaks or maples, beside a modest but well-built church near a main street that invariably included a greengrocer, a butcher shop, and a "department store" that sold everything from women's dresses to shotguns, with the merchandise literally piled to the rafters. The storefront windows were vinegar-and-water spotless, the wood floors pleasantly pungent after they'd been oiled, the street itself usually unpaved and redolent of horse dung.

"There were advantages and disadvantages in moving around so much," Pearson later wrote. "There was hardly any time to take root or become attached to a house and community. But against that there were new scenes, new people, new experiences." He acquired the valuable skill of quickly making friends, learning to get along, counting on baseball or hockey to forge and cement comradery. Pearson's passion for team sports and Diefenbaker's love of the solitary pursuit of fishing say much about how their childhoods shaped their futures.

Although the Dominion was flourishing—especially Southern Ontario—politics had become tumultuous. After fifteen years in power, sunny Wilfrid Laurier was losing his touch. The British wanted financial support from Canada to help fund the naval arms race against Germany. Laurier responded by creating a Canadian navy that could be put at the service of the Empire in an emergency. Britishers in English Canada considered a Canadian navy disloyal; Quebecers considered it a waste of money. But what broke Laurier was his proposed reciprocity (trade) agreement with the United States. Though farmers welcomed an open border, manufacturers feared the competition, and Conservatives raised the ancient fear of annexation. Laurier called an election on reciprocity and lost to Robert Borden. The Conservatives were back in charge.

The Pearson boys hardly noticed. They played sports, got into scrapes—Lester's older brother Marmaduke was suspected but not convicted of belonging to a cabal that wrote rude words on the walls of the school basement—and studied at school, completing their homework each night under Ed and Annie's watchful and encouraging eye. The family was in Hamilton when Lester entered high school, where teachers took note of a scholastically exceptional young man. But his passion for athletics, and a marked but appropriate fondness for girls, saved him from being labelled a sissy. "Thus, growing for me was a healthy, happy, untroubled process."[17]

Of course, he went to Victoria College, the Methodist bastion at University of Toronto. As Lester was a bit quieter and more studious than his older and younger brother, his father and mother hoped he might join the family trade and become a man of the cloth. He roomed with Duke—as people called Marmaduke, sensibly—at the newly built Burwash Hall, where the dean of residence was a young Vincent Massey, scion of the farm equipment giant and someone who would be part of Lester Pearson's life for decades to come. At the end of his first year, Lester was top of his class in history, though math and science were a struggle. His father had found him a summer job, and he was having a fine time playing with the Regiment Baseball Team of Chatham's City League, when Archduke Franz Ferdinand, heir-presumptive to the Austro-Hungarian throne, was assassinated in the city of Sarajevo by a Serbian nationalist.

After centuries of fragmentation, Germany was united, restless, and belligerent, led by a fool-king, Kaiser Wilhelm II. The Austro-Hungarian Empire sought to hold its seething, multi-ethnic conglomeration together by ruthlessly suppressing dissent. Everywhere, as industry expanded and new inventions connected the world, workers demanded better pay and a greater say. The twentieth century had arrived in a Europe that still ran on political assumptions in place since the Congress of Vienna, now almost a century gone by. The Kaiser and his advisers wanted a war, both to put their rivals in their place and to distract the restless masses, who were drifting toward socialism. Vienna, out for blood in the wake of the assassination, made impossible demands on Serbia, which appealed to Russia for help. Berlin backed Vienna, of course. The Russians invoked their alliance with France. Britain warned Germany to leave Belgium out of it. Germany invaded Belgium. Britain was at war, which meant Canada was at war.

No one thought of Canada as a nation among nations. London conducted its foreign policy. And as it always had been and always would be, Canada was a land of solitudes. Quebec was governed as much by the Catholic Church as by any politicians in Quebec City, and even less by Ottawa. English Canada was fiercely British in its loyalties, even among those who weren't British. Tensions between French—not so much pacifist as simply indifferent to the Empire—and English would threaten to tear the Dominion apart, as the Conservative government of Robert Borden moved to impose conscription in 1917. But at the beginning of the war, with the slaughters of Ypres and the Somme unimagined, thousands of young men rushed to join the cause. Lester Pearson and John Diefenbaker served as well. Both would be marked by the war, though neither would see combat. For both, the mental stress of facing death would prove more than they could bear.

V

At first, Diefenbaker was in no rush to enlist. "As a young boy, I had set my mind on becoming a lawyer," he later related, and he had no intention of allowing a war to get in the way. Law was the path to redressing wrongs against the weak—including the Prairie settlers he had grown up among—by the mighty. It was also the path to a life in politics. Although he combined a diffident shyness with a combative streak—challenging his teachers in class on the one hand, struggling to make it through a short speech on the other— and although his marks were generally undistinguished, Diefenbaker flourished at the University of Saskatchewan, obtaining both a bachelor's and then a master's, while also taking courses in law. Slowly, the shy, bullied boy began to give way to the confident young man. He joined the debating society, got himself elected to the Student's Representative Council, and ended up leading the Conservative Party, the official opposition in the university's Mock Parliament. People had begun to notice: the fierce, accusing blue eyes, the shock of wavy hair that he plastered down with difficulty, the rakish good looks, marred only by a less-than-forceful chin inherited from his father. Most of all, they noticed that rolling, beautifully modulated baritone voice that he was already shaping into a powerful instrument, able to reach the farthest corner of the largest hall, as ambition gradually triumphed over reserve, the lawyer and politician new-born.

For summer jobs he worked on a farm one year, taught school the next, and sold books door-to-door the third. Still, there was a war on, and it was time to make his contribution. In the spring of 1916, John travelled to Winnipeg to take the officers' training course. At first, there didn't appear to be a great demand for his services; he fretted about languishing at home, articling for his law degree while those with better connections went overseas. But on July 1, the British and French launched the Somme offensive, one of the most horrific battles in human history. More than nineteen thousand British troops died on the first day, including seven hundred members of the Newfoundland regiment, Newfoundland then being separate from Canada. Over the next four months, the British threw four Canadian divisions at the enemy. Any gains were limited, and resistance fierce. By the time the offensive staggered to its inconclusive end in November, twenty-four thousand Canadians had been killed, wounded, or captured, or recorded as missing.

On September 7, First Lieutenant Diefenbaker of the 196th (Western Universities) Battalion reported for duty at Camp Hughes in Manitoba, where the homesick young officer recorded in his diary: "the most lonesome ever have been."[18] Ten days later, the battalion departed for Halifax, leaving port on September 23 on the *Lapland* of the White Star Line. By Canadian Thanksgiving, the 196th was at Shorncliffe Camp in Kent, training for the front. The next five months were the most mysterious of Diefenbaker's life.

There are three versions of events. The future prime minister recorded in his memoirs that, at the end of a day of practising trench-digging, someone threw an entrenching tool, a combination of pickaxe and shovel, into the seven-foot ditch, hitting Diefenbaker on the back. The wound bled severely. He tried to avoid hospitalization, fearing he would not be sent into action, but the bleeding continued, internally as well as externally, and before long he was hospitalized. "The impact on my back caused my heart to be moved out of alignment," he wrote.[19] Eventually Diefenbaker was sent back to Canada and, after several further examinations, declared permanently unfit for service, despite his efforts to re-enlist. He refused the proffered pension, even though his injury required surgery in the 1920s, and he suffered bouts of hemorrhaging for years after.

Diefenbaker's own diary of the time tells a different story. He enjoyed life in England. There were frequent trips to London for sightseeing and theatre. The Charing Cross Hotel was a particular favourite. He even managed to snag a ticket to the galleries of the House of Commons. On November 18, he records a medical examination, which he passed "with weak heart and eyesight."[20] But he was hospitalized for further tests, though there were also more trips to London. By mid-December, the army was determined to send him back to Canada. There is a diary entry in which, for the first time, he mentions spitting blood. He spent January in limbo, but on February 20, the SS *Grampian* sailed for Canada, with him on it. No mention of a back injury. No real explanation for what ailed him.

Medical Board reports of the time tell a third story. The reports say Lieutenant Diefenbaker experienced episodes of shortness of breath and a racing heart. Medical examination revealed an enlarged heart and a "marked systolic murmur."[21] After several bouts of hospitalization, he was discharged due to a "Disordered Action of the Heart," a vague term used at the time to record apparent physical distress for which no physiological cause could be found.

As for his claim to have rejected a proffered pension, a record in his files suggests the very opposite. On April 9, 1918, the Board of Pension Commissioners wrote to him, advising: "Owing to the fact that you are suffering from no disability which was due to or was incurred during your military service, it has been decided that you are not entitled to pension," which proves there never was an accident with an entrenching tool.[22]

Diefenbaker well knew the fate that awaited him in France. Fully 17 per cent of the British officers who served in the Great War died, compared to 12 per cent of enlisted men. Lieutenants leading their men over the top into No Man's Land during an offensive were the first to fall. Diefenbaker recalls one veteran officer advising the young lieutenants, "Sixty-five per cent of you will be pushing up daisies within three months." The day they signed up in Regina, his friend Allan Macmillan had told him, "Well, that's the end of my life." He was killed at the front.[23]

It is possible that Diefenbaker suffered the symptoms described in the report, that they were sufficiently grave he was sent back to Saskatchewan to recover, that once he was feeling better he was nonetheless discharged because there was no local position requiring his services. This is what the report suggests, and it is true that for years afterward he suffered bouts of intense internal discomfort. But the symptoms might also have indicated a psychiatrically induced nervous order. That is certainly what the letter from the Board of Pension Commissioners suggests. Diefenbaker's biographer, Denis Smith, concluded that the conditions listed in the medical reports "justified an officer's honourable discharge, while suggesting discreetly that a basic physical disability had not necessarily been demonstrated."[24]

Such situations were not uncommon among those in the service. The high risk of injury or death could send troops waiting to go the front into depression, and could generate genuine symptoms of illness. But the shame of being invalided out of the service for what used to be called "nerves" may have caused Diefenbaker to concoct the story of a trenching accident that over time he convinced himself was true. That, at least, would explain why he never destroyed his war diary, which flatly contradicts his remembrance of events in his memoirs.

In any case, Diefenbaker's illness saved him from likely injury or death. Had he not been invalided out, he might never have become prime minister. This was also true of Lester Pearson.

VI

The Pearsons were Conservative and pro-British, like most of Ontario at the time, and so when war began there was not a doubt in the world that the boys would sign up. After a summer at the Bowles family farm in Chinguacousy Township, Duke and Lester enrolled in the University Officers Training Corps, commanded by Vincent Massey, with Lester his orderly. But there was no rush, for everyone assumed the war would end quickly, with England victorious. By February 1915—when it was clear nothing would end quickly, and victory was far from certain—Pearson was pressing his parents to be permitted to enlist. Duke had already signed up.

As the pace of war quickened, and Lester grew out of adolescence, his religious convictions waned. He went to shows, was obsessed with sports, and slept in on Sundays, though he still observed his temperance pledge. His marks were high, despite days filled with participating in or watching every game played by every college or university team. But the university was emptying out. Canadians were fighting, choking on tear gas, and dying at the Battle of Ypres. The casualty lists filled the newspapers. On April 23, 1915, Lester turned eighteen. That same day, he enlisted. The University of Toronto Hospital Unit was about to deploy and had a vacancy. Pearson volunteered to fill it. By the middle of May, he was on his way to England. "Pretty homesick," he confessed to his diary, and pretty seasick, too.[25] Throughout his life, travel by sea and by air would not agree with Pearson's stomach.

For the Allies, the war was going badly. The Germans, having advanced as far as they could, dug their trenches and dared the British and French to dislodge them. Hundreds of thousands died in the futile effort. In the east, the Russians suffered crushing defeats, while the scheme of Winston Churchill, First Lord of the Admiralty, to open a front in the Balkans failed disastrously at Gallipoli. Soon, Private Pearson was at Shorncliffe, the same camp where Lieutenant Diefenbaker would arrive a year later, emptying bedpans and chafing at the monotony. Like Diefenbaker, Pearson got away as often as he could to sample the delights of London, a city impossibly large and sophisticated for a boy from Upper Canada.

Duke went to the front, but Lester and his hospital crew were shipped much farther east, stopping in Malta and Alexandria, which the priggish Lester found squalid and dirty and somehow immoral, and ending up at Salonika, about as far from the Western Front as you could get and still be in Europe. The general purpose of the Allied forces in Macedonia was to separate Bulgaria from its German ally, but there was little fighting, compared to the carnage of the Western and Eastern fronts, and more men ended up in hospital with frostbite than from combat wounds. There he languished, anxious to get to the action, until his father pulled some strings and Pearson was transferred back to England in February 1917. The three brothers met briefly in March by Duke's bedside, for he was back in England recovering from wounds. Corporal Pearson, as he was now ranked, found himself in a unit of various colonials, commanded by the future poet and author Robert Graves. He ended up a lieutenant, deciding to join the air force, along with Duke.

There could not have been a more life-limiting decision. It had been little longer than a decade since Kitty Hawk; airplanes were primitive and dangerous to fly. They had value for reconnaissance, however, and as the war ground on, both sides developed fighter aircraft to shoot down other aircraft. By 1917, fighters came equipped with machine guns, which tore into the wood-and-fabric frames and the bodies of the pilots. The planes themselves were unreliable and temperamental, and the six-week training program utterly inadequate. Almost as many pilots died from accidents, especially training accidents, as died in combat. The life expectancy of a pilot in action was ten weeks.

Pearson's squadron commander thought "Lester" too sissified and gave him a new name, Mike, which he happily embraced for the rest of his life. By November, Mike Pearson was in training; on December 15, he took his first solo flight.

As Pearson explained in his memoirs, he was in London one night, just before Christmas, when the air raid sirens sounded. Because he was away from his base without permission, Pearson hopped on a bus to get back before being detected. The bus was running without lights—standard procedure during an air raid—and when a bomb landed some ways off, the driver stopped and ordered everyone off. Crossing the road from behind the bus, Pearson was hit by another bus operating without lights. "A London bus is no mean battering ram," Pearson observed, and "my active service, though I didn't know it then, had ended, and ingloriously."[26]

The medical records suggest something else. Any bus accident he might have been in caused little physical injury. Rather, the Medical Board reports, Pearson suffered from "nervous debility." There is reference to a "crash when flying with subsequent motor injury." Another report refers to "incapacity due to impaired function of nerves," and "crash while flying and subsequently knocked down by a motor omnibus." There is reference to a six-week stay in hospital, and to "incapacity due to partial loss of the nervous system."[27] It seems clear that Pearson was invalided home after his plane crashed during a training flight, which brought on a mental health crisis. Today we would call it post-traumatic stress disorder.

Neither Pearson nor Diefenbaker ever fired a weapon in anger in the First World War. Both were invalided out—in Pearson's case after almost three years of non-combatant duty in the service; in Diefenbaker's case after less than a year—for reasons more psychological than physical. Both would concoct stories to cover what, for them, must have been a source of shame. Over the years, perhaps, those stories became their personal truth. In the wars of the twentieth century, men were put to tests that few have faced today. Those most willing to judge are least qualified.

TWO

Love and Purpose

(1919–1928)

I

Mike Pearson and John Diefenbaker returned to a Canada utterly transformed by war. A self-governing dominion within the British Empire with a population of just under 8 million had sent 430,000 men overseas. The first battalions were absorbed into the British ranks, but by 1917, the four divisions of the Canadian Corps had their own commander, Arthur Currie. The sheer scale of the carnage seems even harder to grasp today than it was at the time: almost 61,000 killed and 172,000 wounded. Every village and town, and every city neighbourhood, counted the sons and brothers lost. Their names line the cenotaphs to this day. In contrast, the Canadian mission in Afghanistan, the largest deployment of Canadian Forces overseas since the Korean War, had taken the lives of 165 soldiers and civilians by the time it ended in 2014. Then there were the uncounted casualties of the Great War: men who saw and suffered, and brought that suffering home, hidden inside.

To compound the carnage, the Spanish flu, the mother of all pandemics, struck in 1918. Over the next year, it infected one third of the world's population, taking between fifty million and one hundred million lives. Scientists still debate why the flu was particularly vicious among healthy adults. An 1889 flu outbreak might have partially immunized older people; the crowded and unsanitary conditions of the troops might have been a factor; the disease might have provoked a response in immune systems that was more deadly if the immune system was stronger. Regardless, the flu took up to fifty thousand Canadian lives, only ten thousand fewer than were killed by the war.

Canadians fought gallantly, earning a reputation among both the Allies and the Germans for fierceness and tenacity. Some historians believe this country came of age when the Canadian Corps captured Vimy Ridge in April 1917. In any case, what was a semi-colonial British dominion in 1914 signed the Treaty of Versailles in its own right in 1919 and became a founding member of the League of Nations, an intergovernmental organization created to prevent future wars through dialogue and collective security.

In the midst of the war, Conservative prime minister Robert Borden had sought to fill the thinning Canadian ranks by imposing conscription—a move popular among the British loyalists in Ontario, but less popular with immigrants from Eastern Europe and anathema to the French in Quebec. To preserve unity, Borden invited Wilfrid Laurier to join him in a coalition government. But the Liberal leader believed the country would be lost if anti-conscription Quebecers had no voice in Parliament. His decision to stay in opposition split the party, guaranteeing Borden victory in the 1917 election—a victory partly rigged by ensuring that soldiers overseas and women serving on the home front got the vote while immigrants from enemy countries lost it. That split would benefit Conservatives in one election and benefit Liberals—the voice of Quebec; the voice of new Canadians—for generations to come.

To pay for the war, the Borden government had implemented an income tax in 1917. The temporary tax became permanent, a substantial but insufficient source of funds aimed at helping to reintegrate veterans who came home to a country struggling with inflation and recession as the war industries demobilized. And a man couldn't even have a drink for solace, because Canada was dry. Women who were campaigning for the vote campaigned as well for prohibition: the complete ban on the sale of alcohol—which, they rightly argued, contributed to violence against women in the home. In the late 1800s, legislation allowed local municipalities to declare themselves dry. Prince Edward Island became the first dry province in 1900; other provinces gradually followed suit, and the Borden government enacted a national ban in 1918, arguing that scarce resources should not be wasted on fermentation. Women made huge gains in the war, capably filling the factory and office jobs that only men were thought able to manage. After the war, the men took the factory jobs back, but women became, for the first time, a permanent presence in the office. The percentage of clerical jobs filled by women more than doubled from 9 to 19 per cent between the 1911 and 1921 censuses, and the number of women professionals doubled, too. By 1917, women had the vote in every province west of the Ottawa River. In 1918, they received the federal franchise, although Quebec held out provincially until 1940, and held out as well against temperance, enacting the measure in 1919 but repealing it within a year.

In the wake of war came unrest. Troops impatient to return home rioted in England; rising unemployment and inflation stoked protests at home, with political and business leaders fearful that communism, which had arrived in Russia via revolution in 1917, might come to Canada as well. Strikes and demonstrations became a widespread and permanent part of the social landscape. Canadians had always been divided by class as well as by language and geography. Now those divisions were open and ugly.

All this turmoil had little impact on Mike Pearson and John Diefenbaker, invalided home before the war was over and ready to get on with life. Like hundreds of thousands of other young men, they would profit from their status as veterans, launching successfully into the world of work: two talented, ambitious up-and-comers on their way to making something of themselves. And for both men, love was in the air.

II

Everyone agreed that men who had been away at war for up to four years— in Europe, no less, which offered them the delights of Paris and London as well as the dank trenches of Belgium and France—could not simply take up where they had left off. Universities, for example, found ways to accelerate their students toward graduation. Both Diefenbaker and Pearson benefited.

Because he enlisted before the academic year was over, Diefenbaker received his master's degree in absentia. Once back, he put in a few intense months of study, which were sufficient for him to receive a law degree in May 1919, and he was exempted from any further articling requirements by reason of his war service. This was just as well. Diefenbaker's efforts to fit in at other law firms as an articling student had all ended in failure. "He was always running around, into politics," recalled one lawyer who took Diefenbaker on. "So we soon parted ways."[1] On June 30, 1919, John George Diefenbaker became a member of the Law Society of Saskatchewan and a practising lawyer; the very next day, he opened a practice in the town of Wakaw.

The move was classic Diefenbaker. The conventional route for a talented young lawyer just starting out was to sign on as a junior associate in one of the Saskatoon firms. But Diefenbaker found it hard to work for others as a subordinate. In any case, he was determined to have his own practice from the get-go, and to accumulate courtroom experience as quickly as possible. He wanted to be a barrister—a courtroom lawyer—not a solicitor drawing up documents. As a high school student in Saskatoon, he had often slipped into courtrooms to watch the legal giants of the day, including future prime minister R.B. Bennett, argue their cases. This theatre of the courtroom was his stage, and he intended to figure prominently on it.

Wakaw was, it turned out, a smart choice. Located on the belt of parkland that separates the southern prairie from the northern boreal forest, the town had a population of only four hundred, but it was surrounded by densely populated—for Saskatchewan—townships, and was on the district circuit, being midway between Saskatoon and Prince Albert, with both road and rail access. And having reviewed court dockets in a number of communities, Diefenbaker found that in Wakaw, "the people were particularly litigious."[2] There was a problem: the town already had a lawyer, and the local businessmen weren't in the mood to welcome another. Diefenbaker had to build his own law office, with the help of a carpenter. It resembled, and in fact was, a two-room shack, nine paces long by six paces wide with an anteroom that included a counter and bookcase and a tiny office in the back just big enough for a desk and chair, another chair for clients, and a wood stove. (A replica still exists in the town.) He took in an articling student, which was a bit much since the lawyer knew little more than the student. But Michael Stechishin spoke Ukrainian, which was what mattered for attracting clientele in this part of Canada.

Within a month, Diefenbaker had a major case: John Chernyski had shot and wounded a young man who was crossing his land. The farmer claimed he mistook the trespasser for a wolf or a coyote that his dogs were attacking, but it mattered not. Chernyski was charged with attempted murder. Diefenbaker took on the case at the request of Chernyski's wife, who offered the substantial fee of six hundred dollars. There was bad blood between the families of the victim and the accused, offering motive for the shooting, but Diefenbaker emphasized that the events had occurred in failing light. Emmett Hall, Diefenbaker's friend from university—and the future jurist and author of the report that gave Canada medicare—was articling in Humboldt at the time. He discovered in a conversation with Chief Justice James Thomas Brown of the Saskatchewan Court of King's Bench that the judge liked Diefenbaker's presentation and found the testimony of the victim contradictory and unconvincing. However, the judge thought Diefenbaker was overplaying the darkness angle. Hall passed along this informal advice, if that's what it was, to his friend and colleague. Diefenbaker adjusted his argument, darkness turned to dusk, and the jury acquitted.

He was a very serious young lawyer, typically dressed in a dark suit with vest, striding purposefully through town, the glowering face and piercing eyes beneath the waves of hair—an intimidating sight. He was also awkward and almost anti-social, at community dances standing ramrod straight, off to the side, incapable of and uninterested in small talk. But what mattered most was that Diefenbaker was a good lawyer, even at twenty-four. He had already won an acquittal on a case with high profile, at least as far as Wakaw, Saskatchewan, was concerned. And with his next major case, he would become known in legal circles throughout the province.

Although the British North America Act protected the rights of minority language groups—principally anglophones in Quebec and francophones outside it—provincial governments often succumbed to the intolerance of the majority. There were, in the 1880s, four French-language Catholic high schools in what would become Saskatchewan, until a new law in 1888 required that English be the only language of instruction. Despite a slight weakening of the ban in 1892, the Loyal Orange Lodge—a fraternal order as anti-French as it was anti-Catholic—successfully pressed the new provincial government to suppress minority language rights, though if parents wanted their children educated in French, provincial officials often turned a blind eye.

But that wasn't sufficient for William Mackie, of the Ethier School District, who hired A.E. Stewart, the other lawyer in Wakaw, to file a complaint against two of the board's trustees for permitting French-language instruction in local schools. A justice of the peace found for Mackie and fined the trustees. Diefenbaker took up the case on the behalf of the trustees on appeal.

In May 1922, district court judge A.E. Doak found that, indeed, some schools were teaching their students almost entirely in French, violating the provincial prohibition. He strongly suspected that the trustees knew this to be so, and noted, "I am more than a little suspicious that it was being done with their connivance."[3] But the judge accepted Diefenbaker's technical argument that trustees could not be held liable for what went on in a classroom, and overturned the conviction on that technicality. The province's francophone association was so relieved that it took up a subscription to pay Diefenbaker's legal fees.

He could, of course, have argued that the Saskatchewan law banning French-language instruction violated constitutionally protected minority language rights. But at that time, and at his age, it would have been an argument too far. What mattered was that French-language education carried on. The province's francophone community was grateful, and Diefenbaker started to develop a reputation as a champion of minority rights.

Although there were ups and downs, the young barrister flourished in Wakaw. The other lawyer eventually left town, and Diefenbaker chased away any others who tried to move in. He was prosperous, successful, a member of the town council—his first electoral victory—and was already starting to develop a reputation provincially as a fine defence attorney. By 1924, it was already time to move on. He made another lawyer partner in the Wakaw office and headed up the road to Prince Albert.

III

Mike Pearson was not in good shape when his parents met him at Toronto's Union Station in April 1918. The Medical Board, to which he still reported, noted a tremor and stuttering speech. He slept badly and had nightmares of crashing his plane. As the symptoms eased, Mike spent the final months of the war teaching aerial navigation to students who knew they would never need it. The German front had collapsed and the fighting was clearly about to end, along with Pearson's military service. It was time to finish his degree.

Pearson, like Diefenbaker, benefited scholastically from his war service. Returning as a veteran to the University of Toronto, his third-year requirements were waived, and after four months he sat for his fourth-year exams—passing, he believed, with the help of a generous and understanding examiner. In June 1919, he graduated with an honours bachelor of history. The all-important question was: What next? "I was restless, unsettled and had no answers," he remembered later.[4] More than unsettled. We will never know how long the trauma of Pearson's wartime service lingered. We only know that, for two years, he couldn't stick to anything, which is hardly unusual for a young man who had lived through so much in so little time.

The course of least resistance was to proceed to a degree in law. But a few weeks of reading Anson's *Law of Contracts* sufficed to convince the young graduate that the law held no appeal. After a happy summer playing inter-county-league baseball in Guelph, where his parents now lived, he decided to climb the rungs of the corporate ladder, using family connections to land a job with Armour and Company, a meat-packing firm. The bottom rung—stuffing sausages at a plant in Hamilton—was a very low rung indeed, though at least Pearson could later claim personal experience with both ends of Bismarck's maxim: "If you like laws and sausages, you should never watch either one being made."

Even being promoted to sales clerk in the company's Chicago head office did not convince Pearson that he was cut out for the corporate world. And though he was fascinated by the juxtaposition of high culture and brutal street life of Chicago during the bootlegging era of Al Capone, he also decided he was a Canadian who wanted to make his way in Canada. So if not the law and not business, what then would be his way forward? He considered the federal public service, but at the time it was such a small and exclusive entity that the capital's entire workforce could be accommodated among the buildings on Parliament Hill and the Langevin Block across the street. For Pearson, the only obvious alternative to law, business, and public service was academia. But to become a respectable university professor in Ontario between the wars, one generally required a degree from Oxford or another elite British university—no small feat and very expensive. And then there was the question of how his kindly Uncle Edson, who had gotten him the job at Armour and who was now president of the company, would react to such a betrayal. As it turned out, he needn't have worried on either count. His uncle was not unhappy to see him go, declaring, "I don't think you were cut out for business, anyway."[5] And Vincent Massey, who supervised the Massey Foundation Fellowship for aspiring scholars, once again entered Pearson's life, this time approving his application. An army friend put in a good word at Oxford, and in September 1921, Lester Bowles Pearson arrived for his first term at St. John's College.

England in the early 1920s grappled with the grim realities of a declining empire abroad and class warfare at home. This state of affairs was not apparent to most people at the time. After all, not only had Britain been on the winning side of the First World War, its empire had expanded—thanks to League of Nations "mandates"—to five hundred million souls, with new additions in Africa and the Middle East. But the peoples of the Empire seethed with discontent. The suicidal carnage of the First World War made the assertion of white superiority seem ludicrous to many. A global post-war economic slump damaged colonial economies, leading to riots and demonstrations from Ceylon to the West Indies. Ireland was in a full-fledged civil war, as Sinn Féin turned to violence in its campaign for a united and independent republic, and Ulster unionists retaliated in defence of the United Kingdom and the Protestant faith. The Empire at its peak was also at great risk. One general warned that the military was "spread all over the world, strong nowhere, weak everywhere."[6]

Things were just as precarious at home. On the one hand, governments had increased the age for free and mandatory education to fourteen and introduced unemployment insurance and rudimentary public health insurance for the working class. Among the upper classes, the beautiful young things flitted in their motor cars from one country house to the next, the most discerning among them debating the merits of E.M. Forster and Virginia Woolf, Ralph Vaughan Williams and Gustav Holst, Gertrude Lawrence, and the Barrymore family. It was the era of the flapper, of exposed legs and easy—or at least easier—sex, as survivors of the war partied and tried to forget.

But behind the glitter, life was grim. The war had practically bankrupted Britain, and the post-war slump brought such severe unemployment that one cabinet minister wrote to his colleagues, "The almost complete absence of civil disorder is remarkable."[7] Whether through blinkered incompetence or lack of capital, or both, industrial managers failed to modernize their factories; an economy built on exports fell farther and farther behind the competition, especially the American juggernaut, which any intelligent observer recognized was now the world's greatest power, its isolationism notwithstanding. Beneath it all throbbed the wound of the war: almost 900,000 dead. At Oxford, 90 of 350 alumnae of Corpus Christi College were killed in the fighting, the equivalent of more than four consecutive years of enrolment. Oxford men were automatically made lieutenants, which meant they were the first to die. The carnage ended with a peace treaty so flawed and harsh that the economist John Maynard Keynes warned that another war was almost inevitable because of "the shifting by the victors of their unbearable financial burdens on to the shoulders of the defeated."[8] Most people with a solid understanding of the geopolitics of the Continent feared he might be right.

Change was in the air at Oxford. Women were granted full admission to the university in 1920. (A decision by Cambridge not to grant admission produced a celebratory riot by male students.) And scholarships were available for working-class students of exceptional ability. But this was also the era of the Aesthetes, as the band of Oxford bohemians called themselves. They studied little but revelled in glorious, alcohol-fuelled parties and brazen homosexual escapades, all of it immortalized in *Brideshead Revisited*, written by their most famous alumnus, Evelyn Waugh.

Mike Pearson seems to have been blissfully unaware of any of this when, in the fall of 1921, he arrived at St. John's, where he asked the porter to take his bags to his room, not realizing he was in fact speaking to the senior tutor.

They both got over it. Pearson loved Oxford—"I simply revelled in every-thing from the first day," he recalled many years later—and loved St. John's: studying and talking and arguing before the fire that cast too little heat in the four-hundred-year-old suite of rooms that he shared with an American student; the informal approach to studies, in which attendance at lectures was optional, a senior tutor providing whatever guidance was needed to prepare for essays and examinations; and the devotion to sports, which Pearson embraced with such enthusiasm that it seriously interfered with his studies.⁹ He played rugby and hockey and lacrosse. The lacrosse team acquitted itself well on an American tour, and the hockey team was stellar by European standards of the day. In one match, with Pearson's Oxford playing Cambridge in Switzerland, the game was called off at the end of the second period, with Oxford up 27-0.

His tutor, W.C. Costin, was mildly alarmed by Pearson's devotion to sports over studies, but the two became good friends nonetheless. (Costin eventually became president of St. John's, and he followed Pearson's prog-ress with pride, eventually noting in a 1963 telegram that "with Dean Rusk (St. John's) Secretary of State in Washington, Michael Stewart (St. John's) Foreign Secretary in London and Mike Pearson (St. John's), Prime Minister of Canada, all's well with the world.")¹⁰

Pearson's friendship with Costin, the many interventions of Vincent Massey on his behalf, his love for and success at sports, even his preference for "Mike" over "Lester," speak to one of his greatest strengths: the ability to fit in. This son of an itinerant Methodist preacher from Southern Ontario embraced Oxford and Oxford embraced him, not because he had mastered the airs of the English upper class, but because people of power and influ-ence liked him and were impressed by him and enjoyed his company. He had an easy laugh and a wicked, but not cruel, sense of humour. He was obviously intelligent—sharp, even—but his deep passion for sports spoke to his willingness to be part of a team—a man to be trusted in a world of powerful men in which trust counted above all other currencies. From class president and Delta Upsilon fraternity member back at Vic to president of the Colonial Club and even a member of Oxford's exclusive King Charles Club—which always ended its dinners with an inebriated toast to "King Charles and his bounteous graciousness in sending Prince Rupert to dwell among us"—Mike Pearson won the confidence of people who mattered. A man with such qualities could go far.

The club that most influenced his thinking might have been the Sophists, whose members gathered weekly to debate everything from capital punishment to nationalism to birth control. We do not know what stand Pearson took on any of these issues, but we do know, from articles he sent home to the *Christian Guardian*, that he had become aware of the growing class-fuelled tensions in England and that he rejected both the socialist dogmas of the Labour Party and the Conservatives' indifference toward the poor (beyond a certain sense of *noblesse oblige*), adhering instead to the reforming but pragmatic tendencies of Liberal prime minister David Lloyd George. Indeed, Pearson admired Lloyd George as much as Diefenbaker did, and admired, as well, what many called the civilizing mission of the British Empire, though he had also developed a strong interest in the League of Nations and other mechanisms designed to preserve the post-war peace.

Although Pearson failed to get a first in modern history after two years of study, he managed a strong second-class degree, which was enough, coupled with his personal attributes and connections, to earn him an invitation from Professor George Wrong (a friend of Vincent Massey's, of course) to teach history at University of Toronto. At twenty-six, he was willing to experiment with academic life, but with no intention of ever becoming a cloistered professor. He would teach for a few years and see what happened. Maybe he would make a career of it. Maybe something else would come along. Mike Pearson was ready to take on the world, whatever that world might be.

IV

"I have spent my years on the side of the individual against the powerful establishments of our nation, whether public or private," John Diefenbaker asserted, late in life. "One never had to worry about who was looking after the interests of the powerful; they had minions without number. The individual, uncertain of his rights, with limited means, too often frightened by the pomp and panoply of the courtroom, required not only every advantage that counsel could obtain for him but, most of all, the belief that justice would be done him." Diefenbaker defined himself through this myth, and did indeed practise his preaching, while also acquiring a comfortable income and a reputation that would help his long-planned launch into politics.

He hung his shingle in Prince Albert in May 1924. The town had seen more than its share of bad luck, some of it self-induced. Over-cutting had done in the local lumber industry, and a failed hydro-electric project had left the town on the brink of insolvency. In 1918, with business at a standstill after the Great War and the population less than half of its boom-time peak of fourteen thousand, the schools were only able to open when the mayor pledged his personal assets. Roads went unpaved and other improvements had to be postponed, as taxpayers struggled to meet the bondholders' steely demands. The final debentures weren't paid off until the 1960s. But then as now, the town boasted a substantial main street of two- and three-storey stores and offices, with pleasant neighbourhoods on a ridge overlooking the downtown. There was a federal penitentiary and a provincial jail, which meant guaranteed work for criminal lawyers, including John G. Diefenbaker, LLB, with all of five years' experience before the bar. Most of the casework was petty, involving suits and countersuits where honour mattered more than money. Diefenbaker represented a Mrs. Kuneruk, who alleged that a Mrs. Gawliuk had called her a *masch ty publica*, which questioned the plaintiff's chastity. The defence argued that the defendant only meant to call the plaintiff a troublemaker, but Diefenbaker won on cross-examination.

With a dozen lawyers in town, a man needed to do everything possible to stand out. In Diefenbaker's case, this included wearing an enormous, five-gallon black hat. More substantially, it meant winning an acquittal for Anthime Bourdon, accused of killing Peter Champagne in a drunken dispute. Diefenbaker raised the possibility that the shooting was in self-defence, and the jury agreed. In other cases, victory took the form of saving the convicted murderer from the gallows, often by proving he had a diminished mental capacity. Each victory, complete or partial, further cemented Diefenbaker's reputation as a top-flight defence attorney, prone to eviscerating the slapdash work of police officers and raising questions about who might be the real culprit, other than the accused.

Still, he was a strange sight. "John Diefenbaker, tall, stiff, formally dressed even by the standards of Prince Albert's business and professional group, was an anachronism as he strode to his office on Central Avenue," wrote the Saskatchewan lawyer Garrett Wilson.

> The sidewalks on either side of the unpaved street were filled with men of the outdoors. The lawyer passed trappers outfitting for their fall migration to the North, bush pilots and policemen, farmers and fishermen. Cree Indians, some lumbermen still, prospectors, railwaymen, goldminers dredging the alluvial deposits of the Saskatchewan River and its tributaries, prison guards, sportsmen drawn by the fish and game of the North—all passed the doors of the Bank d'Hochelaga Building. The stairs up to the second floor led to the law offices of Diefenbaker and Co.

Prince Albert, Saskatchewan, and all of Canada were in a state of contradiction born of transition. Manual labour was giving way to farm machinery. Saskatchewan had the highest number of cars of any province, per capita, on its slowly improving roads. But police heading out into the bush still used dog teams and sleds. With the men back from war, women retreated to home and hearth. But at least they benefited from a wave of innovation that made housework less burdensome, such as washing machines and iceboxes. Manufacturing the new machines brought jobs to factories and nurtured a growing middle class. And new jobs emerged: in offices, to handle the paperwork of burgeoning industries; in the new dealerships and gas stations that accompanied mass production of automobiles; in construction of the new, hard-surfaced roads that drivers demanded; in credit services and advertising and all the other infant industries spawned by twentieth-century industrialization. The opening of the Panama Canal in 1914 created opportunities for British Columbia businesses to export to Europe. As the global economy recovered, Western farmers pooled their resources in cooperative ventures that helped stabilize prices. But the Roaring Twenties roared only for some. By one calculation, "it is likely that more than half of all Canadians were never anything but poor."[11] At the end of the 1920s, only 2 per cent of Manitoba farm homes had running water.

A tectonic shift in religiosity was underway. The spread of automobile ownership made it easier to drive to church, causing many small parishes to consolidate into fewer large ones. In 1925, the Methodist, Congregational, and (most of the) Presbyterian churches merged into the United Church of Canada. But with evolution and other scientific theories increasingly being taught in the classroom, religious faith began to wane among the better-educated, and many of those who had been raised on readings from the Bible grew less devout. Mike Pearson was no longer a teetotaller. And John Diefenbaker liked to tell off-colour jokes, though he insisted he was only repeating what so-and-so had told him.

As the post-war slump gave way to rising prosperity, the ambitious young man in his twenties gave way to the increasingly well-known lawyer in his early thirties. And with maturity, new priorities arose. Diefenbaker had already served on the Wakaw town council, but that was a non-partisan municipal appointment. The time had come to leverage his growing reputation in law to launch a career in politics. But first, he needed to choose a political party.

The choice seemed obvious. The Liberals bestrode Saskatchewan. The government of Wilfrid Laurier had created the province; agents of his interior minister, Clifford Sifton, had beaten the bushes of Eastern Europe for immigrants to populate its lands. The Ukrainians and Germans and many thousands of other new arrivals gratefully voted for their patron party, putting Liberals in power election after election, often by embarrassingly large margins, although Liberals are not easily embarrassed. Besides, Diefenbaker's father was probably a Liberal: not only had William worshipped Laurier, he readily secured a position in the Saskatchewan public service after giving up the farm, which suggests he had ties to the Liberal Party. For an ambitious young politician in the province, the biggest challenge was to get noticed by the party machine, something Diefenbaker had already accomplished with his courtroom successes. The path was clear. Yet he chose otherwise.

The Davis family was part of the reason. T.O. "Tommy" Davis had established a machine in Prince Albert that in its manipulation of patronage to advance the interests of Liberals in general, and the Davises in particular, would have earned the admiration of Tammany Hall. After his death in 1919, his son, T.C. "Tommy" Davis, inherited the machine, which made him mayor of Prince Albert and eventually attorney general under premier

Jimmy Gardiner. But early on, the Davises and Diefenbaker clashed, when Tommy tried to install his brother, Clifford Sifton (!) Davis, as a lawyer in Wakaw. Diefenbaker complained to the Law Society that the younger Davis could not operate the office because he was only an articling student. The Law Society agreed, and the office was forced to close. Tommy was not amused. Still, most everyone assumed that Diefenbaker would run as a Liberal, and there were efforts to recruit him. Riding officials approached him federally in 1921 and provincially in 1925, a testament to his growing reputation. But on both occasions he turned them down. Instead, three weeks after the 1925 provincial election, which the Liberals won by a breathtaking fifty-one seats to the Conservatives' three, Diefenbaker declared his candidacy for the Conservatives in the upcoming federal election. As it turned out, he was a Tory after all.

The Conservative attachment to Britain had something to do with it. Diefenbaker was passionate in his love for the Empire. Liberal opposition to conscription during the war had rankled him. The Tories opposed free trade and so did he, viewing it as some unholy conspiracy to sell Canada out to the Americans. But the principal reason was that Diefenbaker was an outsider who enjoyed tilting at vested interests, and there was no interest more vested than the Liberal Party of Saskatchewan in the 1920s. Advancement would mean making peace with—really, sucking up to—Tommy Davis and his machine. He was destined by temperament more than political philosophy to oppose the Liberals for the same reason that he chafed at the swells who drove around in their automobiles and lorded it over him when he was a lad in Ontario. He had his own car now—a gleaming Maxwell that he used to visit his parents in Saskatoon each weekend—and had made his own way without need of Liberal patronage. As far as John G. Diefenbaker was concerned, the Grits knew where they could go.

"In a matter of one day he turned Tory, when there were no issues and no election," Davis marvelled, but he understood why as well as anyone. "He changed because a prominent friend of mine, a good Tory, told him that he had better switch as I would always be in his road in the Liberal Party."[12] That friend was Sam Donaldson, a local liveryman and political foe of Davis, who had succeeded him as mayor of Prince Albert and who had served in the legislature as well. Donaldson convinced Diefenbaker that although the Conservative pond was small, the young lawyer would be a very big fish in it. Donaldson became such a mentor that at one point Diefenbaker boarded with him.

There was, at the time, an alternative: the Progressives, a short-lived political movement that grew out of the turbulence of the late war years and early twenties. Internal divisions over conscription had split the Liberal Party federally. But the federal Conservatives had their own troubles. The Prairies had entered a dry spell, which would have reduced profits regardless. But with recession and the end of war, the Americans raised new tariff walls, which combined with Canadian tariffs to hurt farmers across the country, but especially in the West. The farmers saw the Conservatives as the party of Big Business and high tariffs, and distrusted the Liberals as too lukewarm on progressive issues and on tariff reduction. They responded by creating their own United Farmers and Progressive parties. The cities were in turmoil, too. Change, even revolution, was in the air as post-war demobilization reduced demand for agricultural and industrial output, which led to falling wages, prices, and recession. Revolution in Russia offered a stark alternative, one that some workers embraced and all employers and establishment politicians feared. On May 15, 1919, the Winnipeg Trades and Labour Council called for a general strike. Although only twelve thousand workers were unionized, thirty thousand took to the streets and picket lines. The Winnipeg General Strike was copycatted across the country, terrifying provincial governments and the Borden federal government, which sent in the North-West Mounted Police. On Bloody Sunday, June 21, the Mounties fired on protesters, killing two and injuring many others. The leaders of the strike capitulated, but resentment between workers and employers would define Western politics for decades to come, and would contribute to the founding of the Labour and then Cooperative Commonwealth Federation parties. Yet it was the farmers, not the urban proletariat, who had the political clout. The United Farmers, an agrarian protest party, won power provincially in Ontario and Alberta, as did the agrarian Progressive Party in Manitoba. And in the 1921 federal election, the Progressive Party, led by former Borden cabinet minister Thomas Crerar, took 58 of 235 seats in the House, despite the lack of any proper political organization.

Notwithstanding the rise of the populist Progressives, the political tide federally was turning Liberal. Conservative prime minister Robert Borden was tenacious: he had fought off enemies within and without to lead the Conservative Party from defeat (1904) to defeat (1908) to victory (1911) and to victory again (1917). He was principled: he banished patronage from much of the public service and risked breaking apart the Dominion because he believed so firmly in the need for conscription. He was politically skilled: able to cobble together a coalition of Conservatives and Liberals who supported conscription, which brought victory in the 1917 election. He was a proud Imperialist: his attachment to Britain took him out of the Liberal Party and over to the Conservatives in 1891 over the issue of reciprocity. And he was a proud Canadian: he insisted that Canada have its own seat at the table during the Treaty of Versailles negotiations. He was also, by 1920, exhausted, and so retired from government. His successor, Arthur Meighen, lacked Borden's political good sense and, in any event, the Union government had lost its purpose with the end of the war. In 1921, the Conservatives were defeated by the Liberals under the leadership of Laurier's young successor, William Lyon Mackenzie King, perhaps Canada's most successful, and certainly its strangest, prime minister.

Strange because of his lifelong devotion to seances, numerology, and other lines of communication with the dead, including his beloved Laurier, his even more beloved mother, and his dogs, all of them Irish terriers named Pat. Successful, at least in part, because he was keenly insightful, especially about the weaknesses of his enemies. He understood and manipulated the members of his often-fractious cabinet better than they ever knew. And he understood the country, which he realized was best governed incrementally, in small steps. If he was often reluctant to intervene on behalf of the common folk, he ultimately served them and the rest of his country well: introducing old-age pensions and unemployment insurance, guiding Canada through the Depression and the Second World War, and presiding over a country that, when he became prime minister, was still not fully sovereign and that, when he left office, was a charter member of the Western alliance.

In any case, the crisis over conscription had made the Conservative Party persona non grata in Quebec; in 1921, King was able to form government with the help of MPs from that province and from the Western-based Progressives, who concluded that their best hope for lower tariffs lay with the Liberals. By 1925, however, King's promises of lower tariffs someday, maybe, had worn thin. Meighen had worked hard to rebuild the Conservative Party; in the 1925 election, the Conservatives won Ontario and the most seats in the House; the Liberals were strong in Quebec and parts of the West, with the Progressives once again holding the balance of power. King had not only lost the election (or so it seemed), he had even lost his own seat.

Diefenbaker hadn't a hope of winning the riding of Prince Albert, and he knew it. The natural gratitude of Saskatchewan immigrant farmers toward Clifford Sifton's Liberals had been reinforced by the noxious law passed by the Borden government that stripped the vote from naturalized citizens who came from countries with which Canada was at war. Over the years, the Liberals had created a powerful political machine that could deliver votes, and no one looked too closely at how those votes were delivered. Progressives had done well in Saskatchewan in the 1921 election and would do well again in 1925. But the Conservatives were bound to be virtually shut out. They almost always were. Years later, Diefenbaker would joke that the only thing protecting Conservatives in Saskatchewan in those days were the game laws. To make matters worse, Meighen campaigned against subsidized freight rates for Prairie farmers and against the completion of the Hudson Bay railway to Churchill, which would make it easier for Saskatchewan farmers to sell their grain to Europe. Diefenbaker campaigned against his own party in support of the railway, but it was no use. He placed third and lost his deposit. And things were about to get much worse.

King's feral will to power kept him clinging to it long after others would have surrendered. Despite losing his North York seat and placing second in the seat count, he resolved to meet the House, counting on the support of the skittish, cantankerous Progressives. Meighen and Lord Byng, the governor general, were appalled by King's ruthlessness, but there was nothing they could do. To get back into the House, King first delayed the return of Parliament, then went looking for a safe Liberal seat whose incumbent would gracefully step aside, allowing King to enter the House through a by-election. Charles McDonald, who had defeated Diefenbaker in Prince

Albert, agreed to make the sacrifice. (He was eventually appointed to the Senate, but died before taking up the post.) The Conservatives didn't contest the seat—a traditional courtesy when the leader of the governing or Opposition party seeks to enter Parliament—and King became a Saskatchewan MP. If Diefenbaker contested Prince Albert again, he'd be facing off against the prime minister.

That difficult choice arrived in less than a year. The House had barely returned before the Liberals found themselves consumed by one of the worst corruption scandals in Canada's history.

Prohibition had always been a half-hearted affair. By the 1920s, it was on the retreat in most parts of Canada. Quebec never really bothered with it at all. Even at Prohibition's peak, brewers and distillers were allowed to continue exporting into the American market, where Prohibition had been enacted through the Eighteenth Amendment to the Constitution in 1919. A lucrative cross-border trade brought substantial revenues, at the cost of systemic corruption. In Canada the customs department was so corrupt that one minister arranged for the release of a rum-runner from prison because his talents were needed to secure Liberal votes in New Brunswick. Such revelations left the Progressives with no choice but to vote against the government on a confidence motion. King appeared finally to have run out of rope.

The prime minister asked Governor General Byng to dissolve Parliament and call an election. Had Byng agreed, King probably would have lost the election and been relegated to history as one of the Liberal Party's least successful leaders. But Byng believed that King should never have formed a government in the first place and thought that fair play demanded Arthur Meighen be given a chance. Byng asked Meighen to form a government. This, constitutional historians have concluded, was a mistake: once an administration has survived a vote of confidence in the House of Commons, it is the prime minister's will, not the governor general's, that decides whether Parliament should be prorogued or dissolved. In any event, the Progressives had no intention of allowing Conservatives to take charge. Meighen's government fell within days, and now Byng had no choice but to permit an election.

King ran on a platform that consisted of a single question: Who governs Canada? Meighen, who was brilliant and austere—"Whatever people may expect of me, they shouldn't expect emotion," he often said—was also politically naive. He refused to take King's constitutional posturing seriously. Even worse, as far as Diefenbaker was concerned, Meighen retained his opposition to freight subsidies and the Churchill railroad and attacked the new plan for old age pensions that the King government had brought in to secure the votes of J.S. Woodsworth and A.A. Heaps, two MPs representing the Labour Party. If that weren't bad enough, the Ontario Conservative press happily reprinted diatribes excoriating King for fleeing to a region, as one Tory stalwart put it, of "garlic-stinking Continentals, Eskimos, bohunks and Indians."[13] The constituents of Prince Albert did not take this well. On election night, King defeated Diefenbaker in Prince Albert by more than four thousand votes. And nationally, he whupped the hapless Meighen, who was the one who lost his own seat this time, and resigned.

No one held Diefenbaker's electoral losses against him. He was a Conservative in Saskatchewan and he was running against the Liberal leader: what did you expect? In 1926, he spoke at the British Columbia Conservative convention, where he attracted the attention of an up-and-coming young journalist, Bruce Hutchison. "He was tall, lean, almost skeletal," Hutchison wrote, "his body motions jerky and spasmodic, his face pinched and white, his pallor emphasized by metallic black curls and sunken, hypnotic eyes. But from this frail, wraithlike person, so deceptive in his look of physical infirmity, a voice of vehement power and rude health blared like a trombone."[14]

John Diefenbaker had made a name for himself in the courtroom. Now he was making a name for himself on the hustings. He was a successful failure in a party where failure was a fact of life. And he was making progress on another front as well.

By now there had been several women in Diefenbaker's life, despite his visible discomfort at social functions, his bore-right-through-you stare, and his single-minded ambition. Years earlier, Olive Freeman, the daughter of a Methodist minister, had caught his eye. But she was only a teenager, and when the family moved to Brandon, Manitoba, that was that. Then there was Beth Newell, a cashier at the Massey Harris company, who lived with her parents and who was as shy as he. Only a few people knew that they were seeing each other, although by early 1921, they were secretly engaged. She loved to hear him talk about his plans and ambitions, and to encourage him—qualities, it seems, Diefenbaker needed in his romantic partners. They would have married, but in the summer of 1923 Newell fell ill, and later that year was diagnosed with tuberculosis. The relationship ended several months before she died in the spring of 1924. Diefenbaker may have fled once he realized she had the disease.

Diefenbaker's own health had been uncertain ever since he got back from the war. He was off work for two months in 1923, taking to his bed and being nursed by his mother. He feared tuberculosis, especially after Beth Newell's diagnosis, going so far as to check himself into a sanitarium. But the problem lay elsewhere. In November 1923, he visited the Mayo Clinic in Rochester, Minnesota, and was operated on for a gastric ulcer. He immediately felt better, though there were occasional flareups in subsequent years. He cut back even further on drink and rich food—no one would ever accuse Diefenbaker of intemperance.

In the summer of 1927, he began to date Edna May Brower. Like John, Edna had grown up on a farm near Saskatoon and had already been in a relationship or two. Slender, witty, attractive, high-spirited, she worked as a schoolteacher; wore flapper-era dresses; enjoyed coffee klatches, bridge games, and parties in general; and was informally engaged to someone twenty years her senior. But soon after they started dating, John Diefenbaker and Edna Brower became devoted to each other. Edna admired his political ambition and thought she could temper his sometimes off-putting intensity. John's mother Mary reluctantly accepted the relationship, without ever intending to cede pride of place in her son's affections. The parents chaperoned a car trip to California that John took with Edna, unable to be apart from her for any length of time. By the time they returned to Saskatchewan, it was clear that Edna Brower would one day become Edna Diefenbaker. The two were besotted.

V

Mike Pearson arrived at the University of Toronto in 1923 with first-hand knowledge of America's rambunctious energy, via Chicago and Armour and Company, along with the glories, even if they were already fading, of the British Imperial and intellectual tradition, via Oxford. But he was an all-Canadian: a small-town boy making good thanks to his smarts, winning personality, and passion for sports. And he arrived at University of Toronto's history department at an ideal time and place. George Wrong and his successor, Charles Martin, believed that Canada needed to define itself, and that the history department at the University of Toronto could play an important role in that mission. Though he might not have known it at the time, Pearson was not retreating to the cloistered irrelevancies of academia; he was at the very centre of oncoming change. Besides, at two thousand dollars a year (plus free accommodation), the pay wasn't bad for a young man who was single.

He gave his first lecture, on English constitutional history, on September 26, 1923. In the tutorial was a third-year student, Maryon Moody, the middle of three children of Arthur Moody, a distinguished Winnipeg physician, and his wife Elizabeth—a "prosperous, Methodist and devoutly Conservative" family, as Pearson's biographer, John English, described them.[15]

Until 1884, women were prohibited from attending lectures at the University of Toronto. Common wisdom in North America and Europe held that their smaller brains made women unable to compete with men academically. Even if they could keep up, their weaker bodies could not stand the stress of academic life. And if somehow a woman could complete an academic program successfully—well, what was the point? Her mission in life was to make a home for her husband and to bear and raise his children. Even after the ban was lifted, women struggled to fit in at U of T and elsewhere. In the early years, the number of women on campus could be counted on the fingers of one hand. But women students and graduates pushed, prodded, protested, provoked. Clara Martin, who graduated from U of T with an LLB in 1899, became the first woman lawyer in the British Empire. In 1920, Annie Laird and Clara Benson became the first women professors—in the Faculty of Household Science—at the university. Women students at Victoria College in the 1920s weren't unheard of, though they were still in a minority, and they were still expected to eventually marry and settle down. Maryon understood this, however little the idea appealed to her. "It's no use pretending I *like* being a woman," she wrote a male friend while at university. "I have always thought my great misfortune . . . was being born a girl." Still, "one *does* resign oneself, since one must."[16]

Throughout their lives together, Maryon Pearson would support and encourage her husband, while chafing at her surrendered independence.

While beating off the advances of other men, Maryon mentioned in a couple of letters that she had attended this or gone to that with the "awfully nice" Mike Pearson, back from Oxford. By March, they were secretly engaged—even then, the idea of professors dating students was frowned upon. By the end of term, the engagement was official, with the wedding set for the summer of 1925. "Oh I just *can't* believe that I am actually going to be married," she marvelled. "*I* who always thought myself immune—and meant to have a career."[17] Mike gave his fiancée a first in history—she earned a first in English as well, so the mark was no doubt deserved. Having graduated, Maryon returned to Winnipeg, to wait and to prepare for the wedding. She worked on cooking and sewing, and was thrilled when Mike came to visit in the summer of 1924, charming her parents. But it was a long and dreary autumn and winter before they were finally able to be together, marrying in a double ceremony with Mike's friend Norman Young and his bride, Maryon's sister Grace, at Broadway United Church, Winnipeg, in August 1925. Ed Pearson did the honours.

Some young couples are fortunate enough to enjoy a halcyon period after marriage, when they live happily together, entertaining their friends, looking forward to the future, but fully alive in the moment. There isn't much money, but prospects are encouraging, and until the first child arrives, at least, they are able to have fun. Mike and Maryon Pearson enjoyed such an interlude. They took a third-floor flat in a fine Victorian house—later acquired by the journalist and then governor general Adrienne Clarkson and her husband, the philosopher and writer John Ralston Saul—on Admiral Road in the Annex, the leafy neighbourhood due north of the University of Toronto, less affluent then than now, a place that a young couple on a lecturer's income could afford. They revelled in each other, their friends, and the burgeoning city of Toronto.

Though no Montreal—in the 1920s still Canada's largest and most important city, both culturally and as a manufacturing and financial centre—Toronto had a population of five hundred thousand, with 80 per cent of its residents British. The university and the city bore a certain resemblance to what's there today, especially in the area surrounding U of T—the original wing of the Royal Ontario Museum on Bloor Street, the red-bricked Royal Conservatory of Music just to the west, University and Trinity and Victoria and St. Michael's colleges anchoring the university campus. There was the new Union Station to the south, with the Royal York Hotel, the largest in the British Empire, going up across the street, the Manhattanish office buildings lining Bay Street, Eaton's and Simpson's facing off against each other at Yonge and Queen. Many of Mike's chums were in town: Roly Michener, back from Oxford and practising law; Billy Dafoe, a fellow jock who was now a doctor (he would become one of Canada's leading obstetricians); Frank Underhill, a friend and fellow academic who was ideologically well to the left of Mike; the sharp-tongued Hume Wrong, son of George Wrong, who had brought both his son and his daughter Margaret—the department's first woman teacher—to the University of Toronto history department at the same time as Mike; brother Vaughan and other Pearsons and Bowleses. The university had achieved international fame when Frederick Banting and his supervisor, J.J.R. Macleod, won the Nobel Prize for the discovery of insulin. For two blissful years, Mike and Maryon socialized with their friends, went often to the movies—the first talkie arrived in Toronto in 1928—ate and drank and were merry. Mike's only disappointment was that he could not get Maryon interested in athletics. He was not only teaching a full course load, he was coaching or playing virtually every imaginable sport, from hockey to baseball to football to lacrosse. She resisted coming to the games.

Maryon had dreamed of a career in writing or journalism or even diplomacy. Instead, she increasingly found herself hemmed in as the wife of Mike Pearson, history professor and jock. Her personality might have begun its transformation in these early years, from sharp but high-spirited to unforgiving and tart. Many of Pearson's senior advisers in later years disliked Maryon, finding her rude and nagging and unpleasant. They may have been reacting to a woman who, while she loyally supported her husband's ambitions, resented surrendering her future for him. "Behind every successful man there stands a surprised woman," Maryon Pearson famously said. There is bitterness there.

As a history professor, Pearson made a good hockey coach. The historian Charles Stacey, who took one of Pearson's history courses, recalled a professor with "a cheerful sort of adolescent charm," who sometimes came to his classes demonstrably unprepared. Paul Martin, another Pearson student and a future cabinet colleague (his son, Paul Martin Jr., would become Canada's twenty-first prime minister), found him entertaining but not academically challenging. Donald Fleming, who would be John Diefenbaker's finance minister, thought that, but for his academic gown, Pearson was "more like a student than a professor."[18]

Pearson taught British history and constitutional history. He remained enthusiastic about the Empire, though he acknowledged that colonization "has often introduced not Christian ethics and regular government, so much as European diseases, European vices, European firearms and European race slavery." Still, better the contradictions of British civilization than the "crushing curse of sameness, the destruction of individuality, the dead level of mechanical mediocrity" that he equated with the American melting pot.[19] In the mid-twenties, progressive thought, abhorring the blinkered nationalism that drove European nations into the Great War, pushed for greater independence, and a more clearly defined identity, for Canada. Pearson embraced both impulses in his teaching. But as he probably surmised, his future as a historian at the University of Toronto was limited. Despite the resistance of George Wrong and others in the old guard, the Oxbridge tradition of gentlemanly tutorials centred on key readings and self-directed research was giving way to the more structured scholarship coming out of American universities. Pearson was surrounded by students and young faculty who would embrace that new tradition—not least the brilliant young student Donald Creighton, future biographer of John A. Macdonald. Rigorous post-graduate research was probably outside Mike Pearson's interest, though not beyond his abilities.

Proof came in 1926, when Pearson visited Ottawa to pursue archival research for a planned book and Ph.D. on the United Empire Loyalists. Instead of burying himself in the stacks, he sat in the gallery of the House of Commons, entranced, as the King–Byng affair raged. (His sympathies lay not with King but with the put-upon governor general.) At a dinner at the Ottawa Country Club, he found himself seated beside O.D. Skelton, the former dean of arts at Queen's University who was now undersecretary of state in the External Affairs office. It was now clear to all knowledgeable observers that achieving full control over foreign affairs, along with a much expanded foreign service, was only a matter of time and detail for Canada, along with the other self-governing dominions of South Africa, Australia, New Zealand, and the Irish Free State (as it was then known). Skelton— imperious, demanding, careless of others' feelings or needs, but a brilliant mind who clearly foresaw Canada's role in the world as an independent middle power—must have made note of his dining companion, for when a professor at U of T recommended Pearson for a position in the new department, and when Pearson himself wrote to ask if something might be available, Skelton's response was encouraging.

In the spring of 1928, the position of first secretary came open. Skelton was determined that the new Canadian foreign service would be constructed on merit, not patronage, so Pearson would have to take the foreign service exams. When Mike formally applied in May, University of Toronto presi-dent Robert Falconer provided one of the letters of reference, which sug-gests there were some in the academy who saw a future for Pearson beyond it. In late June, Pearson sat the exams—which concentrated on international affairs, modern history, and international law—over four days, obtaining the highest mark of any who took them that year; no mean feat since he was competing with fellow applicant Norman Robertson, who would become a major figure in Canadian foreign policy in his own right. But Skelton wasn't completely convinced. He consulted Vincent Massey, who had been appointed Canada's first envoy to Washington with full diplomatic creden-tials. Skelton agreed when Massey observed "there is something curiously loose-jointed and sloppy about his mental makeup which, as a matter of fact, is reflected in some measure in his physical bearing." The patrician Massey may never have gotten over Pearson's easy amiability and small-town roots. But however loose-jointed he might have been, Pearson had bested the competition in the exams, suggesting there was more to him than athlete and academic pretender. On August 10, 1928, Skelton wired Pearson, offering him the job of first secretary and asking him to report to Ottawa the following Monday.

Despite Falconer's letter, the university made a pitch to keep Pearson, who was a double threat as professor and coach. He was offered a pay raise that would have put his salary above what Skelton was offering, along with the title of full professor, athletic director, and coach. But Mike and Maryon both knew that his future lay beyond a Victoria College classroom or the Varsity Stadium sidelines. Besides, Geoffrey Pearson had been born to them on Christmas Day 1926 (actually, he entered the world at 11:58 p.m. on Christmas Eve, but Billy Dafoe, the attending obstetrician, obligingly altered the birth certificate to create a Christmas baby), and Maryon quickly became pregnant again. Pearson was thirty. It was time for him to make his way in the world.

THREE

Becoming Somebody

(1929–1940)

I

Edna Brower's father Chauncey was so unwell from what the doctors called "progressive paralysis" that she almost cancelled the trip to California with the Diefenbakers. Urged on by her mother Maren—as much a stern matriarch to the Browers as Mary was to the Diefenbakers—she went anyway, but by the time she returned it was clear Chauncey was near the end. Father and daughter spent all their time together on his farm in Langham and at the hospital in Saskatoon, with Edna helping to feed and care for him. Other family members came home to say farewell. Chauncey had a life-long dream of seeing the Pacific Ocean, and the Browers decided to honour that wish. At the end of September 1928, Edna said goodbye to her father as he left for the coast, accompanied on the train ride by his daughter-in-law, who was a nurse. He died in Victoria on October 28.

With Chauncey no longer there to walk his daughter down the aisle, John and Edna decided to be married in Toronto, home to her brother Edward who was both wealthy (he gave his sister the money she needed for her trousseau) and powerful (he was the vice-president of the Detroit and

Windsor Subway Company). John was hoping that Edward would introduce him to Conservatives Who Mattered in the East.

They were married on June 29, 1929, at Walmer Road Baptist Church, a substantial, neo-Gothic pile, with a small reception at the home of Edward and his wife Mabel. (Though the Diefenbakers were Methodists, the Bannermans were Baptist, and John was raised in his mother's denomination.) John adored his new wife. "I have never known anyone with the purity of mind Edna has," he enthused. "She is always optimistic and sees the best in everyone." This included her husband, whom some considered driven and humourless. "If anyone can make John a success, it will be Edna," people told each other.[1] Their honeymoon was a boat trip on the Great Lakes that also helped get them back to Prince Albert, where they stayed in a hotel until the house they would live in for the next two decades—a two-bedroom stucco bungalow—was finished.

Outside the protective walls of a home filled with the intensity of a young couple in love, things were getting darker by the day. Drought had arrived, a searing dryness that evaporated shallow lakes and streams and withered crops. What could be grown could not be sold, for the New York Stock Market crashed in October, taking both the American and Canadian economies with it.

But John George Diefenbaker was one of Saskatchewan's most successful attorneys, with two other lawyers and eight secretaries and a net personal income of more than $4,500 a year. As the hard times dragged on, the firm pulled back a bit, but Diefenbaker was never in any kind of financial trouble. Neither was Mike Pearson, whose family lived comfortably as his career advanced in tandem with the growth of the department. Both families were insulated from a decade dominated by poverty, unrest, and the thrum of approaching war.

II

Oscar Douglas Skelton "seemed a man apart—contained, solitary, abrupt even, not readily looking a person in the eye."[2] He walked awkwardly, wore three-piece tweed suits and stiff white shirts even in the heat of summer and, as he aged, gazed diffidently at the world through ever-thicker glasses. But the well informed knew better than to overlook the undersecretary of state for external affairs. Intellectually confident—at times overconfident, in the judgment of his biographer, Norman Hillmer—and a master of navigating treacherous political currents at Queen's University and then in Ottawa, O.D. Skelton was a proud contrarian, happiest when championing the unconventional, which included his conviction that Canada should speak with a stronger voice in the world, even if that voice weakened Imperial unity. He and Mackenzie King seduced each other—each at times reluctant, at times eager—into having King appoint Skelton number two at External Affairs (King served as his own foreign minister), which Skelton helmed from 1925 until his death in 1941, with a mandate to gradually untangle the skein of Canadian dependence on Great Britain, preferably without making too much of a fuss. Skelton came to exercise so much influence that he was often referred to, though always behind his back, as the deputy prime minister.

External Affairs had been established in 1909, principally to ease communication between Ottawa and London. The department consisted of an undersecretary, two clerks, and four other employees, and was initially housed over a barber shop on Bank Street, in Centretown (the name given to the neighbourhood stretching south from Parliament Hill). In 1912, External was folded into the Prime Minister's Office and helmed by Sir Joseph Pope. He had served John A. Macdonald, was now of great age, and firmly believed that Canada should have no foreign policy other than complete fealty to the Empire. But by the end of the Great War, the Dominion was increasingly speaking in the world on its own behalf. Skelton was with King at the 1926 Imperial Conference when the obstreperous South Africans demanded a statement acknowledging the full independence of the dominions, even as the British stressed unity and mutual obligations. In what would become something of a trademark, Canada proposed a compromise that all sides could live with. The Balfour Report*—named after former prime minister Arthur Balfour, who chaired the conference—acknowledged that Great Britain and the self-governing dominions "are autonomous

---

* As opposed to the Balfour Declaration of 1917, which declared British support for a "national home for the Jewish people" in Palestine.

Communities within the British Empire, equal in status, in no way subordinate to one another in any aspect of their domestic or external affairs, though united by a common allegiance to the Crown, and freely associated as members of the British Commonwealth of Nations." This was as close to a declaration of independence as Canada would ever get. The Empire was now the Commonwealth, and Canada was a fully equal and autonomous member within it.

In the wake of the Balfour Report, External would need to expand in size and improve in competence. King asked Skelton to manage the job. Determined that his department would be both independent and meritocratic, Skelton instituted the examinations for prospective officers that Pearson aced. Skelton also convinced King that Canada should establish permanent legations in the United States, France, and Japan, all outside the orbit of the British Empire. External Affairs, on his watch, would assert an independent voice.

If Skelton was a skilled diplomatic and geopolitical strategist, he was a ramshackle administrator. Pearson and others chafed at the paternalism and neglect that characterized the former dean of arts's management style. Still, the young men he recruited respected and, in their way, grew to love their aloof but devoted chief. All of those serving in the senior ranks of External Affairs as the 1920s gave way to the 1930s shared Skelton's conviction that Canada needed to assert an independent voice within a united British Commonwealth. If those priorities were ever in conflict, it was the task of any good diplomat to reconcile such contradictions.

Pearson arrived in Ottawa in August 1928, just as Skelton and King were leaving for Paris to attend the conference that culminated in the Kellogg–Briand Pact, named after American secretary of state Frank Kellogg and French foreign minister Aristide Briand, which renounced war as an instrument of national policy. Derided then and later as a meaningless gesture—principally because there was no enforcement mechanism—the document nonetheless represented the high-water mark of the time in hopes for peace. And there was good reason to hope. The treaty marked the re-emergence of the United States onto the international stage after the isolationism that had followed the Senate's rejection of the League of Nations. The League itself was grounds for hope—Canada had become a non-permanent member of its council in 1927—and many hoped Germany, now a democratic republic that had emerged from the horrors of hyperinflation, would help safeguard the peace along with France and Great Britain. Had it not been for the Depression, who can say whether those hopes might have been realized.

Ottawa has always been a modest capital, and in the 1920s there was much to be modest about. Its lumber town roots re-emerged each spring, as the log drives on the Ottawa and Gatineau rivers converged at the capital. Factories occupied the banks of the Ottawa River and the islands linking Ottawa on the Ontario side to Hull on the Quebec side. Rail lines ran beside the Rideau Canal. But aspects of the modern capital were emerging as well, such as Union Station, designed to complement the French gothic revival style of the Château Laurier Hotel across the street, so central to the social life of the political class that it became jokingly known as the Third House of Parliament. The Peace Tower that anchored the new Centre Block on Parliament Hill—grander but less attractive than the one that had burned during the war—dominated the city of low-rise buildings from its completion in 1920. Liberals and Conservatives fought over the cost of a new memorial to honour the war dead, though it would take more than a decade to complete the cenotaph and beautify the area surrounding it.

But the city's finest feature, then as now, were the neighbourhoods that had emerged in the late 1800s: the Glebe, south of Centretown; Sandy Hill to the east; French-speaking Lowertown to the east of the bustling ByWard Market; and New Edinburgh to the northeast, surrounding the grounds of Government House. Mike rented the apartment of a departing colleague, while Maryon packed the house—the first of many moves she would be expected to manage over the years. With the arrival on March 9, 1929, of Patricia Pearson, the quartet was complete: husband and wife; daughter and son. The Pearsons were a close-knit family, though Mike later lamented that work too often kept him from being with his children when they were growing up. Neither Geoffrey nor Patricia ever complained, at least in public. By the time Patricia came along, the Pearsons were living on Russell Avenue in Sandy Hill, a brisk walk or short streetcar ride to the stifling, freezing, bat-infested attic on the third floor of East Block that Mike shared with Hugh Keenleyside—also a Methodist minister's son and also newly arrived—who remembered his colleague as a vigorous and athletic thirty-year-old, "cheerful, amusing, keenly interested in his work, ambitious for the service and for himself."[3]

Though his starting salary at External Affairs was a respectable $3,900—the average wage at that time for someone with a job in manufacturing was $1,900—the job was uninspiring at first. Pearson worked up a report on the appropriate nomenclature for causes of death. And there was the task of analyzing which British Imperial treaties should apply to a sovereign Canada. But he also pitched in on a case in which an American schooner had sunk a Canadian vessel, an alleged rum-runner, in the open seas. The experience taught him three vital lessons: the Americans could be aggressive and heavy-handed, but no more than you would expect from a major power; it was foolish to respond with petulance; and quiet, behind-the-scenes negotiations yielded better results than diplomacy by newspaper headline.

Probably as a reward, though it could as easily have served as punishment, Pearson was sent to the Washington office in the summer of 1929 to substitute for Vincent Massey, Canada's man in D.C., and his aide, Hume Wrong, who had both fled the city's oppressive heat and humidity. But he was back in Ottawa after Labour Day, not knowing that the world, and Canadian politics, were about to upend.

III

To this day, economists debate the causes of the Great Depression, and why it lasted so long. Global monetary policies certainly had something to do with it: pegging currencies to the price of gold distorted national economies and trade balances. Excess speculation led the U.S. stock market to crash over several days, culminating in Black Tuesday, October 29, 1929. With good intent but little understanding, President Herbert Hoover sought to keep wages high and the budget balanced, culminating in mass unemployment. The Smoot–Hawley Tariff Act sought to protect wages and jobs through sharp increases in tariffs, which strangled global trade. As conditions worsened, people lost confidence in business, in the banking system, in government itself. But the American and Canadian governments eventually learned some important lessons: they stimulated demand and allowed government deficits to grow, protected workers through unemployment insurance, and supported those too old to work through government pensions. They failed, though, to learn other lessons, worsening unemployment through efforts to maintain wage levels and cutting back on stimulus too quickly, which brought the bad times back. Only the mass mobilization of the workforce and economy during the Second World War extinguished the Depression, leaving planners wondering whether hard times would return at war's end.

Although the Depression was global, Canada and the United States were hit harder than other countries, in part because of the viciousness of the Dust Bowl. Unusually wet summers in the early 1900s hid the truth that it was highly risky to try to farm in the Palliser's Triangle of southern Alberta and Saskatchewan. The drought that had arrived in the twenties worsened during the thirties, year after unrelenting year. Poor farming practices, such as single-crop farming, left thin topsoil vulnerable to erosion. Windstorms stripped the soil and whipped it into vast clouds that coated every surface. For decades after, survivors of those times turned their teacup over in their saucer, to keep the dust out. Crashing commodity prices brought on by the Depression added to the misery. A final tragic coda: the protein composition of drought-stressed wheat is attractive to grasshoppers, which arrived in such swarms that they carpeted streets and trains lost traction because the insects' crushed bodies coated the rails.

With neither hope nor topsoil, farmers in the south left the province or moved to the parkland, where there was at least a chance of harvesting a decent crop. But many never owned another farm, instead settling in town and working for others. The migration further disrupted the traditional lands and lives of the First Nations and Métis living in the northern regions of Saskatchewan. Everyone suffered. In northern and remote communities, whole families were wiped out through malnutrition after the Hudson's Bay Company cut off credit. In Depression-era Canada, people starved to death.

John and Edna Diefenbaker were largely insulated from these hardships. Their pleasant new stucco bungalow in Prince Albert had a large living and dining room, divided by an arch, and two bedrooms, one of which was intended for a nursery and which also contained a desk for when John worked at home. They acquired a gentle German shepherd named Max, who wandered freely about town. Edna's fashionable clothes—complemented by her buoyant charm—dazzled the local ladies and delighted the men. While John and Edna were very much in love, they were also very unalike: John stern, introverted, often resentful of others; Edna full of laughter and life. He was known as practically a teetotaller, though he could be talked into a glass of sherry now and then; she liked to party. Edna reluctantly joined the Baptist Church, a grim denomination for such an effervescent young woman. She bristled at her husband's habit of calling his mother every day. Mary remained the matriarch of the family and had the final, often disapproving, say. But in the early years, at least, the young couple's love and genuine affection for each other smoothed over the contradictions. In the meantime, John's prominence as a crusading defence attorney continued to grow, case by case.

Everyone agreed that Anthime Bourdon, who farmed in the French district of Domremy, north of Wakaw, was upstanding and hardworking. Everyone also agreed that Peter Champagne, a farm labourer, was wild and dangerous: women lived in fear of him. So people were shocked when police charged Bourdon with having murdered Champagne after a day in which both men had been drinking. Bourdon's many explanations for shooting Champagne—it was in self-defence; no, it was an accident; Champagne had choked him; Champagne had come at him with an axe—did the accused no favours. But in Diefenbaker's first murder trial, he won a clean acquittal for his client by focusing on inconsistencies and contradictions of the police investigation, though it's possible the jury was simply relieved that Peter Champagne was no longer in the world.

In other cases, success was measured not by acquittal but by the survival of the accused, sometimes against terrifying odds. One autumn morning in 1928, defence lawyer Bert Keown was summoned to the Prince Albert courthouse with instructions to represent one Ernest Olson, whom he had never met. Olson had been accused of murder and his trial was to begin that day. The defendant was "feeble minded," in the opinion of a psychiatric report; nonetheless, the Crown asked and a jury agreed that he be tried as sane. By 2 p.m., the trial was underway. Olson was charged with killing a farmer he had worked for. The farmer's wife had left the marriage and moved in with Olson, before abandoning that relationship as well. She told the jury that

Olson had confessed to her that he was behind the house fire that killed the farmer and his housekeeper. The judge declared from the bench that her testimony was true. The jury took two hours to reach a verdict of guilty. The judge sentenced Olson to be hanged. Keown, overwhelmed by this whirlwind of a trial, turned to Diefenbaker for help. At the appeal hearing, he stressed the judge's interjection from the bench, the possible guilt of the farmer's wife, and the state of mind of the accused. The judges upheld the sentence but urged Diefenbaker to appeal to cabinet for leniency. He did, and on February 1, 1929, the federal cabinet commuted Olson's sentence to life in prison.

Then there was *R. v. Pasowesty*. Someone shot and killed the farmer Nick Pasowesty as he walked the path from the cattle pasture to his home. Police arrested his son John, who confessed but later tried to recant, saying his mother had shot his father and convinced him to confess in her stead. Police arrested Anne Pasowesty as well. Diefenbaker failed to get the confession of a seventeen-year-old boy given without legal counsel thrown out; he failed to convince the jury the mother might have been involved. The boy was angry that he had been forced to give up a car he had bought by selling his father's cattle, the Crown alleged. Surely that was sufficient motive.

But Diefenbaker never gave up. "John Pasowesty had nothing to gain by the death of his father, not only nothing to gain but much to lose. Where is the motive for murder in that?"[4] The jury struggled for many hours before reaching a verdict of guilty. Appellate judges rejected Diefenbaker's efforts from the bench. He then summoned a psychiatrist, who said the condemned man was mentally deficient. That was enough for cabinet to commute the sentence to life in prison. "Gallows Cheated of Youth," the *Daily Herald* headline blared in disappointment.[5]

One of his most famous cases concerned the very complicated estate of Grey Owl. The famed conservationist focused national and international attention on exploitation of the environment, especially of the beaver, which was on the verge of extinction. Grey Owl's books and lectures helped mobilize the environmental movement in the early twentieth century. He was only fifty when he was found unconscious on the floor of his cabin in Prince Albert National Park in April 1938. He died of pneumonia a few days later.

But Grey Owl, as the public soon discovered, was a fraud. He was born Archie Belaney, in Hastings, Sussex. He had not a drop of Indigenous blood. He also drank heavily, and philandered. After he died, two women claimed to have been his wife. Diefenbaker represented Yvonne Perrier, whom Belaney married in 1936, and represented as well Shirley Dawn, his daughter from another relationship; they were the principal beneficiaries of Archie's fairly substantial estate. But Angele Belaney said she had married Archie in 1910, only to have him desert her, leaving Angele to raise their three children on her own. The judge concluded that Angele Belaney was entitled to a third of the estate, though he made a point of saying Diefenbaker acted responsibly in defending Perrier and Dawn.

Through it all, the firm prospered, though Diefenbaker and his law partner split in a dispute over money. He pleaded with his landlord, the Banque Canadienne Nationale, for a rent reduction from sixty dollars a month to fifty dollars—"business is only half what it used to be"—but the bank was unmoved, perhaps with good reason. In 1933, both income and revenue were down only 10 per cent from 1930 levels. Diefenbaker cleared more than four thousand dollars that year. Meanwhile, men clamoured for relief in front of city hall. There was no work and little to harvest.

In 1929, remarkably, Diefenbaker missed his first real opportunity for a career as a politician and narrowly skirted a stigma that could have eliminated all hopes of high office. The Ku Klux Klan arrived in Saskatchewan in the late 1920s, its growth fuelled by the resentment of British and German Protestants toward the Catholic, Eastern European settlers who had flooded the province. Jews and French Canadians were lumped in as well. Things started badly for the Klan when the original promoters absconded with a hundred thousand dollars in membership fees. But J.J. Maloney arrived from Ontario to take charge, and under his leadership the movement grew to include as many as forty thousand members; thousands of hooded men met at rallies with burning crosses. That said, it was a very Canadian Klan: no night riders, and certainly no lynchings. Most of their anger, in concert with the much more established Loyal Orange Lodge, focused on the peripheral presence of French in the school system. The Conservative Party of Saskatchewan also opposed French-language instruction, providing the opportunity for a tempting, but extremely dangerous, political alliance.

Catholics were purged from the provincial party's executive, and Diefenbaker helped with the purging. At a provincial convention, delegates approved a motion banning the presence of any religious symbol in a public school. Critics complained that the Lodge and the Klan now dominated the Conservative Party in Saskatchewan, and the critics weren't wrong. There were Klan members at the convention, and everyone knew it.

Liberal premier Jimmy Gardiner decided that tarring the Conservatives with the brush of being Klan sympathizers was the key to re-election. But the Liberals had been in power for two and a half decades, with a patronage machine that ensured the lowliest clerk or road worker didn't get the job until his Liberal bona fides were in order, supervised by the local party boss, which in Prince Albert was the attorney general and Diefenbaker nemesis T.C. Davis. Then there was the question of corruption, especially the blind eye the Liberals turned to bootlegging. The Grits were beyond long in the tooth.

In 1928, Gardiner called a by-election for Arm River, a rural riding halfway between Regina and Saskatoon. The battle was between the Liberals on the one side and the Conservatives and Progressives and the Orange Lodge and the Klan on the other, and it was singularly unpleasant. The Liberals' opponents focused on the government's reluctance to prosecute bootleggers, especially Harry Bronfman, who also happened to be Jewish. The Anglican bishop of Prince Albert openly declared that "Jews defile the country by engaging in disreputable pursuits."[6] Conservatives also campaigned on keeping religion out of schools, by which they meant the Catholic religion. The leader of the right wing of the Conservative Party, a Regina lawyer named James Fraser Bryant, warned the citizens of Arm River that "within five years, or ten at the most, under present political conditions, Roman Catholics will be the majority in Saskatchewan, and the French will control the political destinies of Quebec, Saskatchewan, and all of Canada."[7] Everyone knew Bryant was in tight with the Klan. In the final days of the campaign, Diefenbaker went down to Arm River, where he shared a stage with Bryant. The lawyer who had defended minority language rights was now the politician campaigning against them. At one event—a rally for Gardiner that he crashed—Diefenbaker complained of "nuns in religious garb" teaching in what were supposed to be public schools, where "the crucifix is hung on the wall," though he also took pains to point out, "I am not a member of the Ku Klux Klan."[8]

The Liberals held on to Arm River, but by only fifty-nine votes in a once-safe seat. Gardiner complained to Mackenzie King that the Klan had planted men dressed as priests at polling stations, to make it look as though the Catholics were manipulating the vote.

It was natural for new Canadians from countries where their church ran the school systems to seek similar practices in their local schools. Many saw no harm in it, at least in those schools where immigrant children dominated. But for Diefenbaker and many Conservatives, the issue was one of keeping sectarian influences out of education. "Ask any Catholic, is it fair?" Diefenbaker asked at one rally. "Would you send your child to a school presided over by an Orangeman in regalia or a Klansman in a nightshirt?" Emotions ran high as Gardiner called a general election for June 6, 1929. Diefenbaker took on T.C. Davis in Prince Albert. Davis's brother Sifton— who had been forced to close the Davis law firm in Wakaw due to Diefenbaker's protest—accused the Conservative candidate of links to the Klan. "It is only necessary to go into Mr. Diefenbaker's committee rooms and you will find the heads among them there."[9] Diefenbaker was silent in response, which suggests he didn't want to draw attention to who was helping him. Though there was never any evidence John Diefenbaker consorted with the Klan, rumours and insinuations would dog him for years.

On election day, the Liberals held a plurality of seats, but the Conservatives under leader James Anderson knew they could form a majority with the help of the Progressives, and said so. Gardiner held on, hoping against hope, until he was forced in September to summon the legislature, where his government was promptly defeated on a motion of non-confidence.

Diefenbaker narrowly lost Prince Albert to Davis—the luckiest defeat of his political career. The Klan soon burned out in Saskatchewan, but Conservatives in government were tainted by it, and Diefenbaker would have been, too. In any case, the Saskatchewan Conservatives came to power as drought descended on the Prairies and the stock market crashed. A flare-up of internal bleeding forced Diefenbaker to sit out the 1930 federal campaign that brought to power R.B. Bennett, the Alberta lawyer and businessman (though he was originally from New Brunswick). Both Conservative governments would suffer the unhappy fate of parties that governed in the early years of the Depression. Diefenbaker was better off outside both the Anderson and Bennett governments than in them.

Instead, as the winds howled and the economy crashed, the young defence attorney continued to make a name for himself in the province's courtrooms. He was more famous, and better off, there than in any legislature.

IV

Although Canada increasingly spoke with its own voice after the First World War, Britain still hoped to be the deciding voice on matters of Imperial foreign policy—unity with diversity, Pearson called it—and many pro-Empire Canadians hoped so, too. The tension resolved steadily in Canada's favour, with the country refusing to commit to joining Britain in a threatened war with Turkey in 1922; the approval of the Balfour Report in 1926; and the passage of the Statute of Westminster in 1931, in which Britain gave formal recognition to that declaration. Canada was an independent and sovereign nation.

Sort of.

The country's constitution was still an act of the British Parliament (and would remain so until its patriation in 1982). The mechanisms of independence lagged behind the Balfour Report's principles. Canada's highest court, the Judicial Committee of the Privy Council, still resided in London. Canadians were British subjects: there would be no such thing as a Canadian citizen until the Canadian Citizenship Act of 1947, and many Canadians—especially English Canadians, especially the descendants of settlers, and especially Conservatives, including John Diefenbaker—celebrated the Empire and Canada's place within it. When Mike Pearson joined External Affairs in 1928, the department was evolving from a glorified post office, handling correspondence between Ottawa and London, into a true department of foreign affairs. And Canada's foreign policy was constrained by the hesitations and machinations of Mackenzie King, who was fundamentally an isolationist, in Pearson's view, and who feared that too bold a Canadian stand on the world stage would offend French nationalism in Quebec. These vacillations frustrated Pearson, who was as ambitious for his country as he was for himself, though many years later he would come to appreciate the subtle wisdom that lay beneath King's hesitations.

Pearson returned from his brief stint holding the fort at the new Washington legation to a Canada traumatized by the Depression and tired of the scandal-ridden and unpopular King government, which clearly had no proposed solution to the rising unemployment. Though O.D. Skelton was a devoted Liberal and the department quietly rooted for King, Canadians chose differently, awarding a majority government in August 1930 to R.B. Bennett, the lawyer whom Diefenbaker had watched in court as a teenager.

Bennett was the complete opposite of King. He personified the open frankness of the West: good-humoured unless crossed, then thunderous. Pearson employed that meteorological metaphor in comparing the two prime ministers: Bennett's "storms were rough, but they were usually of short duration and often cleared the air. I do not recall that Mr. King ever stormed. When he felt that he had been badly used or not adequately or wisely served, the weather become sultry and overcast. For those around the presence at these times, a fan was more useful than an umbrella."[10]

The young men Skelton had recruited would form the spine of the Canadian foreign service for decades: the acid-tongued Hume Wrong, assisting Vincent Massey in Washington; Hugh Keenleyside, like Mike, a young university professor turned diplomat; Kenneth Kirkwood, who had been a close friend of Maryon, which is probably why he and Pearson didn't get along; Thomas "Tommy" Stone, who had been a friend of Pearson's since boyhood; Norman Robertson, who joined in 1929 and would become Pearson's boss—these and several others were Skelton's first and finest recruits, though they were stronger on academic experience than business, and not one of them was francophone. (Pearson always regretted that he never learned French, and would have good reason for that regret.)

Mike was young, fit, obviously capable, a pleasure to be around. Esprit in the fledgling department was high. "Robertson admired French novels, Tommy Stone French wines, Kirkwood wrote poetry, Keenleyside read it, and Wrong bitched about their lot brilliantly," John English summarized. While the others soon headed out for posts abroad—Tokyo, as well as Washington, London, Paris, and the League headquarters in Geneva—Skelton kept

Pearson at home. The young diplomat chafed at not being sent overseas, but close proximity to his boss and to the prime minister served Pearson well. It made, rather than impeded, his career.

Bennett meant to fire Skelton, but in the opening weeks of his administration the prime minister had other things on his plate, and he soon came to appreciate the ability and advice coming from his undersecretary. Pearson, too, got on well with the hands-on, action-oriented Westerner. The department was small enough, and Pearson able enough, to ensure he advanced rapidly. He was an extremely minor figure at the London Naval Conference of 1930, one in a series of conferences that tried, but ultimately failed, to secure agreement by the major powers to limit the size of their fleets—though he was able to bring Maryon with him, and the two took in the sights. The conference was the first in a series of engagements in which Pearson came to appreciate the necessary brick-by-brick process of establishing and broadening international conventions and laws, and the futility of utopian dreams of eternal world peace. Nonetheless, he continued to work on disarmament issues, even as Japan savagely invaded China in 1931 and Nazi street thugs disturbed the always-shaky peace in Berlin.

Edwin Pearson died suddenly in 1931, the result of a misdiagnosed appendicitis attack. The death shocked and saddened Mike, who admired his father, a man gentle in word and deed. The Pearsons had always been a close-knit family who viewed the world with Ed's pragmatic optimism. Ed's death came as Mike was about to head to Geneva to represent Canada during talks at the League. Those who worked with him at the Palais de Justice there said he was uncharacteristically moody and ill-tempered. He was a long way from Southern Ontario and his family, in every sense. Mike Pearson would extol Ed Pearson as the ideal father for the rest of his life.

But the son was now a father as well, growing in both ambition and confidence as a Canadian diplomat in tumultuous times. Bennett, who like King was his own foreign minister, seconded Pearson from the department to work on two royal commissions, one on grain futures and one on price spreads (the difference between what producers received for their commodities and what consumers paid for them). The commissions' work sent Pearson to the Prairies, where he witnessed first-hand the drought and economic devastation. Grain futures were a topic far removed from his work at External, but Pearson was in direct contact with the prime minister on important files, which is never a bad thing for a public servant's career. Though everyone in the department had taken a 10 per cent pay cut, deflation had actually improved Pearson's standard of living. Maryon was able to hire someone to help with the house and children, and they had all the gadgets, including an electric refrigerator—just the latest thing. His work on the royal commission on price spreads, which recommended steps to limit profiteering, earned such high praise that Bennett gave Pearson an $1,800 bonus, took his young aide with him to the celebration of King George V's Silver Jubilee in 1935, and recommended him for the Order of the British Empire, to Mike's embarrassment and his friends' amusement.

In the summer of 1935, it was time for Maryon to pack again. Bennett wanted Pearson in London as attaché, second-in-command to High Commissioner Howard Ferguson, a former Conservative premier of Ontario and a staunch Imperialist. Mike and Maryon both looked forward to living in the centre of civilization, even as Europe careened toward war. And Mike was convinced that actions taken in London, not Ottawa, would shape Canada's fate in the years ahead. But not long after the Pearsons arrived that summer, the appointment was put in doubt. Although in the latter years of his government Bennett had begun to embrace the activism of Franklin Roosevelt's New Deal, the conversion came too late, and much of what Bennett proposed was struck down by the British high court. He was, at least up till then, Canada's most hated prime minister. Bennett Buggies referred to cars that had been converted into carriages by having their engines removed, so that they could be pulled by horses. (In the U.S., they were called Hoovermobiles, after the hapless President Herbert Hoover.) Unemployed young men were sent to remote relief camps to work for twenty cents a day. Communist organizers soon stirred things up, and in 1935 militants and the simply desperate began a trek called "On to Ottawa." Bennett, fearing insurrection, ordered the police to break up the marchers. Two were killed when police fired on three thousand protesters in Regina on July 1, 1935. The voters had had enough. Bennett's government suffered a devastating defeat in the election on October 14, 1935, winning only 39 of 245 seats. William Lyon Mackenzie King, back from the politically dead—and communing regularly with the literal kind—was prime minister again. He chose Vincent Massey to replace Howard Ferguson in London, and decided to leave Pearson where he was. Mike's imperious mentor had become a constant presence in his life, if a sometimes irritating one.

Pearson found London stripped of illusion. The Depression seemed relatively mild in Britain only because growth had been so weak in the twenties, in part because of the U.K.'s foolish insistence on tying the pound to the gold standard. London still glittered, for those who could afford to shine, but the mood was grim. First Benito Mussolini in Italy through a coup, then Adolf Hitler in Germany through elections, and finally Francisco Franco in Spain through civil war had displaced democracies. The Nazis were particularly vicious. All talk of disarmament was over. Europe was remilitarizing with a new generation of weapons: the tank, the bomber, the fighter. Everyone assumed chemical warfare would join the list of horrors.

For a moment in 1935, the League seemed able and willing to push back against the militarizing tide. Mussolini was determined to annex Ethiopia, for no good reason other than that he could. British leaders, goaded by public opinion that backed the Abyssinian underdog, began talking about economic sanctions. Though Skelton opposed any Canadian involvement, High Commissioner Ferguson and Pearson were convinced Canada had to take a stand. They voted with the U.K. and other nations to impose sanctions on Italy, and joined the committee charged with designing them. But when King replaced Bennett, that was it for Canada's brave stand. Worse, crossed wires led the Canadian delegation in Geneva to suggest a suite of sanctions that became known as "the Canadian proposal." Horrified, King and Skelton disowned the document, angering the British and leaving the Canadians looking like fools. It all proved moot, for France and Britain lost their nerve, and Il Duce triumphed over both the Ethiopians and the League, leaving Pearson thoroughly disillusioned. His foreign policy principles in those years were as confused as Canada's: embracing collective security to prevent aggression, but not if it meant Canada going to war, even though Pearson and Massey and King all knew that if Britain went to war, Canada would almost certainly follow. Outside Quebec, the country was still overwhelmingly Anglophilic. Mike Pearson had become a deeply cynical diplomat, with little respect for the will or ability of Britain and its allies to contain the rising tyrants on the Continent.

In the deteriorating months that followed, Pearson, like Canada, was mostly a bystander, including during the crisis that led King Edward VIII, who loved the divorcee Wallis Simpson, to abdicate in favour of his brother, King George VI. In 1936, Hitler occupied the Rhineland—demilitarized under the Treaty of Versailles—and Spain disintegrated into civil war, while Britain and France did nothing. For all intents and purposes, the League was finished. The only question now was whether Germany could be contained.

Morale sank among the young men at External Affairs. Pearson respected Vincent Massey, and fully understood his great debt to the quasi-aristocrat, but the small-town minister's son had liked Ferguson better, just as he preferred Bennett's openness to King's guile. Pearson and his friends chafed at Canada's timorous foreign policy under King and Skelton: say nothing, do less. No commitments, no entanglements, no risks. Pearson was unhappy and frustrated and bored. And so when an offer arrived in 1937 from the new Canadian Broadcasting Corporation, created by Bennett—the broadcaster and the Bank of Canada would be his most his lasting legacies—Pearson was definitely intrigued.

Mike liked reporters and reporters liked him. They shared a mutual fondness for gossip over a drink. (Pearson had long since abandoned his Methodist teetotaller pledge.) He saw little prospect for advancement in the service, and he had long advocated the need for a public broadcaster. (He had made broadcasts and formed friendships at the BBC.) But in the end, he stayed. Massey had come to greatly admire Pearson, going so far as to lend Mike and Maryon paintings by David Milne for their walls. Skelton fought hard to keep him, citing his "intellectual capacity and fine educational background," his industriousness and sound judgment, and his "marked ability in getting on well with people."[11] It would be "a great calamity to lose Pearson from our service," he wrote, and King agreed. Pearson got a raise—he and Maryon were already making enough to hire a cook and maid and driver, even a nanny, helped by the fact the Canadian diplomats overseas paid neither tax nor rent—more responsibility, and affirmation from everyone from the high commissioner to the prime minister. Anyway, the Pearsons had gotten used to evenings in the West End, dinner at the best restaurants, and weekends in the country. Maryon increasingly preferred the theatre, cocktail parties, and the attention of handsome men to the drudgery of housework; Mike's wide-open grin and ease with everyone made him a valuable addition at any table. To give up all that for Ottawa or Toronto . . .

Besides, by 1937 everyone knew that war was likely. And if you were a diplomat, that meant London was the place to be.

V

The cases that increased John Diefenbaker's fame as a defence attorney testify to the misery of the underclass in Depression-era Saskatchewan. By the middle of the decade, travelling from the province's central parkland to the Palliser's Triangle "was like moving from the Garden of Eden to the Dead Sea," Diefenbaker recalled.[12] Windstorms blew dunes that almost buried telephone poles. "The land simply dried up and blew away." In the northern regions, rust was a blight. Crop revenues fell by two thirds. And even if a farmer could get grain or cattle to market, shipping charges wiped out any profit. For two years, from 1931 to 1933, Saskatchewan reported a negative income from agriculture.

But townsfolk and city folk were no better off. Single men shuffled in lines at soup kitchens. Employed women were forced out of their jobs, so that men would have work. In British Columbia, Asian Canadians were only eligible for half the level of relief of white people. In Calgary, they weren't eligible at all, until the Communist Party successfully came to their defence. No wonder populist movements of both the left and right proliferated, and unions finally began to wage successful strikes.

For the already poor, the uneducated, those with addictions, those who were "slow," as they used to say, things were always hard and sometimes desperate. After her husband abandoned her, Nadia Bajer survived, barely, in a one-room shack on the edge of Wakaw, where she tried to provide for her two small children. She took in washing and cleaned houses, including the house of Stanley Lepine, who'd pay her an extra fifty cents or sometimes a dollar—a day's wage for the poor—to sleep with him. She became pregnant. Lepine gave her pills that he said would induce an abortion—illegal and sinful and often life-threatening. When she refused, he abandoned her. One day, people noticed Bajer was no longer pregnant. She finally admitted to police the baby had been born but she had later accidentally dropped the infant, which hurt its head and died. She said she had placed a cloth in its mouth so people wouldn't hear it crying. After Bajer showed officials where she had buried the baby, a physician examined the exhumed body and ruled the child had died of suffocation. Bajer was charged with murder. The one-day trial began October 9, 1930. Diefenbaker led the defence. He cross-examined the physician and called his own medical experts, raising serious doubts about asphyxiation as the cause of death. The baby may have bled to death from complications associated with the birth, they testified.

Diefenbaker's summation was masterful. As Nadia Bajer sat sobbing at the table, he described the hovel in which she and her children lived, the shame of an illegitimate childbirth, the men who had abandoned and abused her. Lepine "gave her *pills*," he spat out. "Pills, when she needed succour, food, clothing. Pills, when she needed honour and protection." The baby could have died of natural causes, and the Crown had failed to prove otherwise, he maintained. The accused had buried the body to hide her shame. The jury took only fifteen minutes to find Bajer not guilty of murder but guilty of concealing a childbirth. On the latter count, the judge suspended sentence so that the young mother could go back to caring for her children.

Diefenbaker received little or no compensation for such cases—though he demanded payment up front for those who could pay—but the firm prospered nonetheless, despite the hard times, and especially after Diefenbaker took on Jack (John M.) Cuelenaere as an articling assistant in 1933. Cuelenaere had met Diefenbaker six years earlier, as a grade-twelve student, at a political meeting. The teenager declared he was going to be a lawyer and Diefenbaker should hire him. Sure, the young attorney agreed, and then promptly forgot about it, until Cuelenaere showed up asking Diefenbaker to honour his pledge. In 1933, Diefenbaker was trying to reduce his staff, not increase it, but a promise was a promise. "There's your desk," he pointed. Called to the bar in 1935, Cuelenaere served as assistant and then partner for more than two decades, complementing Diefenbaker's skills in the courtroom with his own in legal research. Through hard work and careful management, the firm was able to pay Diefenbaker more than four thousand dollars a year, which was enough for John and Edna to acquire a live-in housekeeper in the fall of 1936.

Cuelenaere was also a devoted Liberal, who eventually became mayor of Prince Albert, a member of the provincial legislature, and then minister of natural resources in the 1960s under Premier Ross Thatcher. But Diefenbaker maintained that he never held a man's political persuasions against him. "Partisanship has its place and is necessary in maintaining the political health of our society," he wrote in his memoirs. "But there is a line that is crossed at one's peril; if one allows the battles of the hustings and the House to carry over into the other aspects of his life, he will invariably be the loser." It seems a strange thing for such a partisan warrior to say, but politics was less brutal a blood sport back in the day, even though corruption and patronage could determine everything from major contracts to getting a job in the post office. As Diefenbaker noted, the fact that T.C. Davis was his arch-enemy on the hustings and in the courtroom "did not stop me from liking him."[13]

The stern, dashing accusatory lawyer with the flashing blue eyes was now known as the finest defence attorney in Saskatchewan, maybe the finest the province had ever seen. He won case after case, or at least had the sentence reduced. One typical, and prominent, case involved the Fouquette family. Ernest Fouquette, a prosperous farmer of Métis stock, was so unpleasant that his wife Annie moved out, preferring to live in a shack with her nine children than in a farmhouse with him. Annie retained Diefenbaker to win child support, but Fouquette defied the subsequent court order. On the morning of Sunday, July 28, 1935, Fouquette was found with his head bashed in. Suspicion fell on seventeen-year-old Napoleon Fouquette, Annie's son, though police thought Annie herself might be behind the killing. Diefenbaker exploited that confusion to win an acquittal. And in *R. v. Harms*, though it took a trial, an appeal, and a second trial, he secured a manslaughter conviction for John Harms, who had shot a fellow trapper in the head—a crime stoked by cabin fever in the long, dark northern night. Diefenbaker convinced the jury Harms was so drunk when he fired the gun that murder was a conviction too far.

Meanwhile, the young attorney advanced within the Conservative Party of Saskatchewan, even as its fortunes ebbed. When the Anderson government came to power in 1929, Diefenbaker replaced T.C. Davis as the master of patronage in Prince Albert, a responsibility he wielded with relish. He was made King's Counsel, a mostly ceremonial but still coveted title. And he was appointed junior counsel for the commission of inquiry into alleged political interference in provincial police by the Gardiner Liberals. (The commission simply proved what everybody already knew.)

He also entered, impulsively and at almost the last minute, the race for mayor of Prince Albert in 1933, on a platform of reducing the town debt. In a fight that Diefenbaker described as "particularly bitter,"[14] with the heaviest turnout of any municipal election in Prince Albert up to that time, Diefenbaker lost by forty-eight votes to Harold John Fraser. "It was probably the closest mayor's race we ever had here," observed the *Prince Albert Daily Herald*.[15]

In the meantime, the Anderson government was on the ropes, riven between moderates who thought government should support those most in need and "true-blue conservatives." In any case, by 1934 the Prairie governments were effectively bankrupt. In May 1934, the Conservatives went down to defeat; Jimmy Gardiner returned as premier, and all was right with the world. Although he knew better than to run for a seat in the 1934 election—it was clear long before then that the party's unhappy fate was sealed—Diefenbaker did secure election as party vice-president in 1933, and was appointed acting president in 1935. By then, the party had been reduced to a clutch of lawyers and some stalwart volunteers. Diefenbaker won the leadership of the party in 1936, mostly because all of the other contestants dropped out: no one wanted to drink from that chalice.

As the 1938 provincial election approached, Diefenbaker's life was as politically grim as it was professionally successful. He had enough money to travel to Europe in 1936 to witness the unveiling of the Vimy Memorial and attend the 1936 Olympics. By one account, he came back filled with admiration for Adolf Hitler and the discipline he had imposed on the chaos of the fallen Weimar Republic. The prejudice he had experienced because of his German name might also have made Diefenbaker partial toward anyone who could advance the German cause. In any case, Edna quickly warned him never to say such things, for Hitler's abuses toward minorities had already made him unpopular in Prince Albert and elsewhere.

Edna was indispensable to John. When they were out and about, she walked slightly behind him so that she could whisper into his ear who was approaching and suggest, for example, that he should ask about the latest sporting achievement of their son. John eventually mastered the art, but Edna was his teacher. They travelled everywhere together, with Edna an irreplaceable helpmate and aide. But there were tensions. John's mother Mary continued to dominate the family, leaving Edna always feeling as though she had to compete for John's affections, a competition she often lost. Edna wanted to go back to teaching; John wouldn't hear of it. Then there was Elmer, John's brother. He was, by all accounts, a pleasant man who failed in several attempts at careers. John spent a great deal of his own money making good the debts Elmer had incurred as a failed insurance agent. Orest Bendas, who worked in Diefenbaker's law firm, remembers Elmer as hopelessly disorganized as a real estate agent—John kept his books for him—but also "the kindest man, very talkative, and he idolized John."[16] Elmer was part of Team John, led with fierce determination by Mary, dedicated to fulfilling the ambitions of her first born. Emmett Hall remembers Mary as "autocratic" and "domineering." William, on the other hand, was "a gentlemanly, a scholarly man, but with no initiative . . . he was totally submerged by his wife."[17]

When the two brothers proposed Elmer move in, Edna put her foot down, and got her way. But she never got her way on the question of children. John was too busy and too ambitious—and perhaps had too little love to give—to become a father. Later, when he decided he was ready, Edna told him she was too old.

The Depression had spawned movements of populist protest throughout North America and the world. In the stricken Prairies, evangelical populism and class tensions brought forward two movements, each far more benign than anything happening in Europe or the United States. Labour and United Farmer members of Parliament allied with left-wing intellectuals and social activists to form the Co-operative Commonwealth Federation (CCF) in 1932, under the leadership of J.S. Woodsworth, a Labour MP and Methodist minister. The CCF blamed the Depression on the ills of capitalism, with socialism the promised cure. Social Credit sprang from the same resentment and religious fervour. Its founder, the evangelical preacher William "Bible

Bill" Aberhart, used the power of radio to preach a message of righteous anger at politicians and other sinners, mixed with inexplicable monetary theories that amounted to giving every citizen money to spend, thus stimulating demand. The Socreds won the 1935 election in Alberta, and they aimed to break through in Saskatchewan as well. They and the CCF alarmed the monied interests in Ontario and Quebec, who sent cheques to the Liberal Party to keep the socialists and Social Credit at bay. Diefenbaker never forgot or forgave their abandonment. Destitute of funds, many potential Conservative candidates withdrew because they couldn't afford to lose their deposit. Diefenbaker spent his own money where he could, and campaigned flat out as party leader, but with the Liberals receiving the cash and Social Credit splitting the vote, the Conservatives were wiped out in the election, winning not a single seat. Diefenbaker was defeated this time in Arm River, the central Saskatchewan riding of the infamous 1928 by-election, where he had made a name for himself among the party faithful.

John was devastated. He couldn't win election to the legislature even as leader of a provincial party. "The election was lost in the last two days, when money flowed into the province to buy the electorate," he wrote a supporter, bitterly. "The Eastern financial interests became panic-stricken, and went so far as to instruct their provincial officials to support Liberal candidates so as to withstand the Social Credit threat. . . . " It was "most discouraging to work for over a year and a half and then be wiped out of existence."[18]

This marked his fifth straight election loss: twice at the federal level in Prince Albert, twice now at the provincial level, and in the contest for mayor. He was finished with politics, he vowed. He might also have been worried about his marriage. Edna had thrown herself into her husband's campaign, and took the loss as badly as he did—perhaps worse. She experienced chronic insomnia, and the sleeping pills the doctor prescribed may have led to dependence. In any case, Edna felt increasingly claustrophobic within the marriage. In 1937, she had moved into a separate bedroom and was known to go out dancing at night. There were rumours about how late she stayed out and who she left with. In both his personal and political life, John Diefenbaker was on his way to rock bottom. Until William Lyon Mackenzie King stepped in and saved him.

Though Canada had gone to war automatically in 1914, as part of the British Empire, King made it clear, in both word and deed, that Canada would decide for itself whether to join Britain in any future conflict. As war with Germany approached in 1939, isolationist sentiment was strong enough in Quebec and even parts of English Canada that King George VI and his wife Queen Elizabeth embarked on a royal tour—the first visit of a British monarch to the Dominion—largely to shore up support. Whatever John Diefenbaker might originally have thought of Germany under Adolf Hitler, the Nazis were clearly seeking to reverse the outcome of the war that did not end all wars. After occupying the Rhineland, Germany annexed Austria, then forced the dismemberment of Czechoslovakia, only to then absorb what was left. In August 1939, Germany and the Soviet Union shocked the world by signing a non-aggression pact, leaving Hitler free to attack Poland. The Wehrmacht crossed the frontier on September 1. Having failed to counter Hitler's previous aggressions, Britain and France reluctantly declared war on September 3. Though the outcome was never in doubt, King consulted Parliament before declaring war on September 10.

Not much happened in the following months of what people called the Phoney War. In Quebec, Maurice Duplessis, a strong-arm, pro-rural, anti-union nationalist, saw opposition to conscription as a distraction from the economic mismanagement of his government and as the path to a second term. The opposition Liberals, led by Adélard Godbout, also opposed conscription. But the federal Liberals supported their provincial counterparts, and Ernest Lapointe, King's lieutenant, warned voters that a win by Duplessis's Union Nationale would force federal Liberal cabinet ministers to resign, bringing Conservatives to power in Ottawa and ensuring conscription. Duplessis went down to defeat.

Mitchell "Call Me Mitch" Hepburn learned no lessons from Duplessis's defeat. The populist Liberal premier of Ontario—also pro-rural, also anti-union—loathed King and sought to embarrass the prime minister by arranging passage of a motion in the Ontario legislature condemning the federal government's prosecution of the war. King seized the opportunity to call a general election on the grounds that his government required a war mandate. He confronted the utterly hapless Robert Manion, a former cabinet minister in the Meighen and Bennett governments, who talked a good game but lacked, his many critics felt, seriousness of purpose and sound judgment. Manion had sought to build bridges within Quebec by courting Duplessis. When Duplessis went down, so did Manion's hopes in Quebec. But his Duplessis-wooing stand against conscription poisoned pro-British voters in the rest of Canada. Manion called for the creation of a government of national unity. The best way to achieve that, King rebutted, was to vote Liberal. On March 26, 1940, the briefly renamed National Government Party took 39 seats to the Liberals' 179. Manion was defeated in his own riding. The Tories were routed from coast to coast. But not in the Saskatchewan riding of Lake Centre.

Diefenbaker had been playing cat and mouse in the federal riding, which roughly corresponded with Arm River, for months. He might accept the nomination if it was offered to him, he suggested, but only if no local candidate was willing. Meanwhile, his supporters lined up the votes. On nomination night, lo and behold, there were four local candidates. Diefenbaker promptly withdrew and left to sit with Edna in their car. The winning candidate then withdrew himself, and the meeting unanimously endorsed Diefenbaker. Someone went out to the car to let him know. Diefenbaker feigned surprise.

Though he worked hard through the summer of 1939 to organize the riding, the nominee for Lake Centre wasn't expecting a winter election call. He was arguing a case in Ottawa before the Supreme Court when King visited the governor general. And when Diefenbaker returned to Saskatchewan in February, he found himself in the midst of another murder case. That case, however, was his political salvation.

Henry Emele was vile. The farmer had twice assaulted his wife Isobel. But he needed her around, and after she threatened to leave him—and briefly did—the beatings stopped. They lived on a farm north of Prince Albert in a state of constant tension, which worsened as war approached, for Henry was also a committed Nazi, and Isobel, of Northern Irish stock, a proud daughter of the Empire. When Hitler invaded Poland, Henry promised Isobel that Canada would be next. "Hitler will run this country and you'll learn to like it," he gloated.[19] On September 18, she approached two hunters in the woods, distraught, wearing only a slip. Her husband had been shot, she said. "She gave me the works," Emele told the men, before dying on the way to the hospital. At first, Isobel said her husband had killed himself. Eventually she confessed. When Diefenbaker read her statement, he smiled. "We shouldn't have much trouble crying our way out of this," he predicted. And he was right.

Henry Emele was a member of the Bund, a Nazi support group. He was a miser. He was autocratic and cruel. He was violent. As for Henry's dying accusation and Isobel's confession, Diefenbaker got both thrown out. He was that good. He also made the ballistics evidence look questionable. And where were her fingerprints on the gun? Reasonable doubt, members of the jury, reasonable doubt.

The jurors enjoyed dinner before declaring a verdict of not guilty. On hearing that verdict, spectators in the courtroom burst into applause. Diefenbaker had convinced everyone that, whatever happened on that farm, Isobel Emele was no murderer, she was a war hero. Five weeks later, in the midst of a national rout for the Conservatives, John George Diefenbaker finally won an election.

He was the luckiest man who ever lost five elections—almost six, for the provincial riding of Prince Albert finally opened up when Tommy Davis was given a seat on the Saskatchewan Court of Appeal. Had Diefenbaker not already been committed federally to Lake Centre, he would probably have run in Prince Albert, again, and lost again, for the riding ended up going Liberal by acclamation. But after years of having doors slammed in his face, he had won a ticket to Ottawa, in part as a reward for his years representing little people caught in the maw of the justice system. Progress in politics, as in life, is often a matter of luck. But looking back, this stroke of luck seemed only fair.

FOUR

Ascent

(1940–1946)

I

The Union Club was built in the Greek Revival style—so, lots of columns—in the 1820s, as part of London's new Trafalgar Square, a beautification project that came to dominate Westminster, anchored by Nelson's Monument, the National Gallery, and the Church of St. Martin-in-the-Fields. After the federal government acquired the building in the 1920s, it became the heart of Canada in Britain, and dominated Lester Pearson's life as the nations of Europe rushed, on the part of Germany, or dragged themselves, on the part of France and Britain, toward war.

Much of Pearson's job consisted of saying no to Jews, Czechs, and Germans who were fleeing from Hitler and seeking refuge in Canada. The Depression and anti-Semitism combined to keep them out. The government maintained that, unless the applicant could work in agriculture, they were not needed in Canada. Most of those fleeing Nazi persecution were merchants, academics, or other urban professionals. The agricultural requirement was implemented specifically to exclude them. Jews were especially unwelcome. Ernest Lapointe, King's minister of justice and Quebec lieutenant, feared a backlash in Quebec from Jewish immigration. "None is too many," Frederick Blair, director of the immigration branch, later declared when asked how many Jews should be admitted to Canada.[1] King, while lamenting the terrible persecution of the Jews, believed nothing could, or should, be done. "My own feeling is that nothing is to be gained by creating an internal problem in an effort to meet an international one," he wrote in his diary in 1938.[2] From 1933 to 1945, the United States brought in more than 200,000 Jewish refugees. Canada accepted 5,000, one quarter of the U.S. rate, per capita, and one of the worst acceptance rates among Western countries. Though O.D. Skelton regretted the policy, he personally communicated the government's decision to reject the plea for asylum from 937 Jewish passengers on board the ocean liner *St. Louis*. The ship was sent back to Europe, and the passengers to their fates. Two hundred and fifty-four of them died at the hands of the Nazis.

It fell on Mike Pearson to reject the applications of desperate Jewish and other refugees in his official capacity at Canada House. "I have some pretty pathetic interviews these days with refugees who want to go to Canada," he wrote his mother and his brother Vaughan. "I wish we were a little more generous to them. It's distressing having to tell so many of them you can do nothing for them."[3] He completely rejected the arguments of Vincent Massey and other Anglo- and French-Canadian elites that Jews would never integrate into Canadian society. "But even if this were true, who is responsible for this tendency?" he asked during a dialogue on the BBC. "It wasn't so many centuries ago . . . when Jews were forbidden to be anything but Jews, no matter how long they'd lived in a country."[4]

Depressed by the darkening times and the King government's unwillingness to face them, Mike and Maryon left England with their children at the end of June 1939 for a summer vacation. They took refuge in a large farmhouse on Lac du Bonnet, 120 kilometres northeast of Winnipeg, which they shared with Norman and Grace Young, as the extended Moody family celebrated the fortieth wedding anniversary of Maryon's parents. The clear and unconcerned prairie air was thousands of kilometres removed from Europe's gathering storm. But even here there were newspapers, and one day in August, after Pearson had gone into town, he saw a headline: Germany threatens Poland over Danzig corridor. Having allowed Hitler's Germany to absorb Austria and Czechoslovakia, Britain and France had guaranteed to protect Poland. There would be war.

Abandoning Maryon and the children, Pearson travelled by train to Ottawa, where he convinced a skeptical Skelton and King—who thought he was overreacting to Hitler's threats—to let him become the first Canadian official to fly from North America to Europe, using the newly inaugurated Pan Am Clipper service from New York to Southampton.

He was firmly ensconced in London in September 1939 when Germany invaded Poland, France and Britain declared war on Germany, and King took Canada to war over Skelton's objections. He felt Canada was surrendering its hard-won independence.

With the departure of Georges Vanier—a lawyer who became a soldier with distinguished service in the Great War and who later entered the diplomatic service—to become Canada's representative in Paris, Pearson was now the number two in the high commission. He quickly learned he had to be as much a diplomat within the department as he was for his country. Skelton and Massey disliked and distrusted each other: Skelton chafed at Massey's aristocratic airs and hawkish tone; Massey considered Skelton an uninformed appeaser. War ended that debate, but Ottawa remained guarded about the strength of its commitment during the phoney war in the autumn of 1939 and winter of 1940. Canada did, however, successfully lobby for and implement a plan to become the centre for the Commonwealth pilot training program. The idea was Massey's; Pearson helped a bit with the early stages, before King and British dominion affairs secretary Anthony Eden took over. Pearson's diplomatic skills were put to a greater test when Hume Wrong arrived from Geneva to take up an undefined post at Canada House. The strong-willed Wrong, who considered virtually everyone his intellectual inferior—the fact that this was almost always true didn't help—had clashed with Massey when the two were in Washington. Now Wrong was in the house again, with a huge ego and nothing specific to do. To make matters even worse, Massey made it clear that, although Wrong was senior to Pearson within External Affairs, Mike was number two at the high commission. Pearson defused what could have been an explosive situation by taking Wrong golfing, to shows in the West End, and home for dinner. The Wrongs and the Pearsons became fast friends, though Wrong's role remained ambiguous.

Pearson and Wrong became part of a brilliant, tightly knit circle of diplomats and other Canadian ex-pats anchored at Canada House. The elegant, amusing, and amorous Charles Ritchie had taken up duties just before the beginning of the war, and George Ignatieff arrived in 1940 to help out. The Ignatieffs were well-born Russian refugees who had fled to Canada after the revolution, and who embraced their new homeland with enthusiasm. Ignatieff and Pearson became so close that George named his son Michael—the future leader of the Liberal Party—after his friend. Pearson, Wrong, Ritchie, and Ignatieff formed the future aristocracy of the Canadian foreign and public service. They golfed together, played cards and tennis, gossiped endlessly, and waited for the real war to begin. They didn't have to wait long.

On April 9, 1940, Germany invaded Norway and Denmark. Britain and France were still searching for a proper response when, on May 10, the Wehrmacht invaded Belgium and France. Hitler had rightly concluded that the best way to eliminate the French line of defensive fortresses known as the Maginot Line was to go around them, through the Ardennes Forest. In six short weeks of Blitzkrieg—lightning war—German tank divisions smashed through the French lines, occupied Paris, and surrounded the British Expeditionary Force (BEF) at Dunkirk. The hapless Neville Chamberlain gave way to a new administration led by Winston Churchill, who ordered the rescue of the BEF. A flotilla of fishing and pleasure vessels assisted the Royal Navy. The soldiers came back disarmed, but British factories, now firmly on a war footing, rapidly replaced their kit.

Throughout that long, gloriously sunny, deadly summer, the Royal Air Force fought to prevent German mastery of the skies over England and the English Channel, as Hitler prepared to invade the island. Fortunately, British technology and tactics—especially their skilful use of the new radar—were as superior to the Germans' in air war as they were inferior in ground war. Frustrated, Hitler turned to bombing London and other cities. The Blitz would do great damage and cost many civilian lives, but it meant Germany had given up on invasion.

Many of those who lived through those months looked back on them fondly. Britons of all classes found solidarity, at least for a moment, as they huddled in Underground stations while the bombs thudded above. American journalists, most famously CBS's Edward R. "This Is London" Murrow, told of the stoic grit of Londoners, especially those in the working-class East End, which took the brunt of the bombing in the first weeks. To endure the Blitz required a certain aplomb. Pearson remembered a golf game in which, "just as I was about to tee off, Joyce's caddy, a Dickensian old boy, advised me to slice well over to the right, 'farther over than usual, sir, because there's a time bomb over on the left side of the fairway.'"[5] He preferred his upstairs bedroom to the safety of the coal cellar, but night after night the sirens sent him hustling down to the basement, though he was reluctant to stop working every time the siren sounded. "Mummy and granny think it is very silly of you not going to an air raid shelter as soon as you can," Patsy chided in a letter. "Work is important, but I think your life is more important to us."[6] Charles Ritchie's flat was demolished, but he was in Aldershot that night. (Ritchie slept in many different beds.) "I have lost everything I own," he wrote in his diary. "That is not a tragedy but a bore."[7] Pearson arrived at work one morning to discover the West End had been heavily damaged. Piccadilly Circus was "destroyed," he wrote Maryon, Leicester Square "smashed up," and his favourite restaurant "a rubble heap," though "a bomb landed in Trafalgar Square and didn't even break my windows. Freakish things, bombs." The Canucks of Canada House ate together, drank together, sometimes did more together, all of it in high spirits while cocking a snoot at the Luftwaffe.

In those critical months, Pearson continued to sort out the swelling stream of people desperate to come to Canada. "Canada House has been bedlam," Mike wrote Maryon, "thronged with Canadians who want to be sent back home at once, with people who say they are Canadian and with hundreds of English people who drift in and calmly announce they have two children whom they are willing to allow a suitable Canadian family to keep for the duration." Friends and strangers begged him to intercede with the authorities "so that they can leave England for our suddenly discovered to be alluring Canada."[8]

He helped Canadian military officials untangle the skein of British bureaucracy and endure the Brits' infuriating condescension. At times, he almost lost patience, declaring that if England surrendered, Canada should withdraw from the war and become a republic. But England endured, and Pearson was invaluable in helping A.G.L. McNaughton, commander of the

First Canadian Division, get along with his British counterparts. He found it amusing to be consorting with high-ranking Canadian and British officers, "unlike the last war, when my only pals were Privates," as he told his brother Duke.⁹ Andy McNaughton so admired Pearson that he asked him to become his special assistant, but Pearson wisely declined: while he admired McNaughton's blunt, brusque approach to dealing with the British toffs, and his dedication to maintaining a well-equipped, united army under Canadian command, Pearson knew his future lay outside the military.

Although King had made it abundantly clear to the British that Canada would not be imposing conscription, economic cooperation was a different matter. Because the issues were so complex, and the British so suspicious of Canada's willingness to fight, King sent Graham Towers, governor of the Bank of Canada, to handle the talks. The Towerses and the Pearsons were already friends from their Ottawa days; that friendship grew even closer, for although Graham personified the buttoned-down city banker during the day, he liked to party at night. Maryon and Graham were close; he liked a drink and a dance; so did she, more than Mike. They were bawdy and flirtatious. Did it go farther than that? Some people thought there were signs that Mike resented the closeness of the friendship between Graham and Maryon.

As German tanks rolled through France, Mike convinced Maryon, who had joined him in London, to return to Canada to be with the children. Maryon agreed, assuming the other wives of the mission would also be returning to the safety of Canada's shores. When she realized that others had stayed, she was furious. In the meantime, the Vaniers were back, refugees from fallen Paris. At a dinner to welcome them, Alice Massey was so venomous toward the French that Pauline Vanier burst into tears, before fiercely counterattacking. As Mike wrote Maryon afterward, "I broke in by saying I despised beyond words the French govt & some of their military leaders but I wouldn't say *one* word against the French people. Whereupon Mrs. M whispered 'disloyal' in my ear and I felt like strangling her."¹⁰

Despite the times, and perhaps because of the rising tempers, Pearson felt underused in London, consigned to extinguishing diplomatic fires and managing the flow of paperwork while King and Churchill or their deputies made all the important decisions. (Carping by diplomats when their political masters go over their heads was as chronic a complaint then as it is now.)

Mike's most memorable, and maddest, assignment was to secure some stones from Westminster Hall, which had been bombed the night before, for Kingsmere. King had assembled a collection of stone relics at his estate in Gatineau and craved this addition from the mother of Parliaments.

But Pearson's role and life were about to change. On Monday, January 27, 1941, as O.D. Skelton drove down O'Connor Street on his way back to Parliament Hill from lunch, the undersecretary suffered a massive, fatal heart attack. The car drifted along, finally bumping into a streetcar on Sparks Street.

His death shook the government. As the first true undersecretary for external affairs, Skelton had built Canada's foreign service: hired the men who staffed it, shaped its policies and priorities, influenced—though never controlled—the thinking of his prime minister. He could be careless and demanding, and his isolationism drove the impatient young diplomats mad with frustration. But they were used to him, trusted him, took him for granted, perhaps, but depended on him more than they knew. "It's only when you start taking inventory that you begin to realize what a range of responsibilities he took," Norman Robertson wrote to Pearson, "and how we all lived and worked secure in the shadow of a great rock."[11] Pearson learned of Skelton's death by reading about it over breakfast in the *Times*, "and it gave me almost a physical blow, it was so horrible and sudden."[12]

King, who interpreted Skelton's death as a sign that he, alone, must now be responsible for the prosecution of the war, nonetheless moved swiftly to make Robertson acting undersecretary, simply because he was the most senior member of the department residing in Ottawa. Pearson was not happy. "I could do the job better myself and I'm naturally pretty disappointed at being passed over," he complained to Maryon. With the talented but disorganized Robertson in charge, "things will go on in the same old impossible way."[13]

He was even unhappier when Robertson, trying to be helpful, suggested Pearson might want to consider becoming ambassador somewhere in South America, which was far too far removed for someone who wanted and expected to be at the centre of the action. In the end, King summoned Pearson back to Ottawa to serve in an undefined role. He felt "no enthusiasm for going back to the Department in some vague position which will, in fact, if I take it, mean that Norman will be in charge—and get all the most interesting work, while I, as usual, have to do all the dirty work," he wrote Maryon.[14] He offered to serve in the military, but the offer was refused. There was nothing for it. After a series of farewell parties, Lester Pearson departed for home in June.

II

Moving to Ottawa in the spring of 1940 helped the Diefenbakers' marriage. John's mother was now 3,200 kilometres away. Edna's husband had finally fulfilled his lifetime dream of winning a seat in Parliament. Now they were both dedicated to the even bigger dream of him leading the Conservative Party and becoming prime minister. And in John's bid to eventually realize that dream, Edna was, once again, indispensable.

"Edna was a wonderful person; she gave her all for John," one fellow MP later recalled. "She was his secretary, his research staff, and his telephone answering service, all rolled into one."[15] Also his press agent: courting reporters, tipping them to something important her husband was going to say in the House, scanning newspapers and clipping any articles that mentioned John, hosting off-the-record parties for politicians and journalists. As one friend recalled, "Edna did everything for John. She taught him to play bridge; she taught him to dance; she taught him to enjoy life. She was always gay and happy herself, and able to lift him out of his depression."[16]

Though some found Edna a bit pushy in advancing her husband's interest, most were charmed, including Mackenzie King, who was once seen engaged in a long conversation with her outside the House. Saskatchewan MP Tommy Douglas, a Baptist minister, social crusader, and rising star inside the CCF, adored her. "You know, Edna," he once said, "if John and I got along as well and you and I, we would make a real country out of this place."[17]

Members of Parliament earned four thousand dollars a year and were given a free railway pass. John also had revenue coming in from his law practice, so while many MPs endured crowded rooming houses, the Diefenbakers enjoyed a room at the Château Laurier, a three-minute walk from Parliament Hill. It was good that they could afford a hotel, because the city was in the midst of a housing shortage. Ottawa had been transformed by war, its population of a little over one hundred thousand swollen by 50 per cent. Lansdowne Park had become an army depot; there were temporary wooden office buildings and barracks on Sussex Drive and behind the Parliament Buildings (some of the latter would survive into the twenty-first century). The city's factories were converted into making bomb bay doors and other war materials, with women increasingly working the lines because the men had gone to war. Women served as secretaries as well, inside and outside the armed services, and as machinists and drivers. Others, operating out of a well-guarded office on the Central Experimental Farm, worked at intercepting enemy transmissions, which were then sent to Bletchley Park in England, where Alan Turing was developing what would become a war-changing machine that could decode German messages.

Canada had transitioned from a country struggling through the sluggish aftermath of the Depression to a workhouse of war. Unemployment disappeared as the assembly lines ran around the clock cranking out war materiel, such as the tiny corvettes that were intended to protect merchant ships from enemy submarines. (Their record, at first, was dismal, but with improved training, equipment, air support, and intelligence they eventually helped turn the tide in the Battle of the Atlantic.) The poorest benefited from finally being able to work, though middle-class taxpayers endured both high taxes and the dreary business of rationing. Canadian exports not only fed Canada's army overseas but provided much of the British diet as well. The challenge was to ensure there were enough calories to go around in both Canada and the U.K. Every household had its ration card: one cup of sugar, a stick of butter, and twenty-four tea bags per adult per week. Tripe, kidney, tongue, and liver replaced roasts and steaks. Spam, a form of canned ham, was also popular, if that's the right word. Worried about people's nutrition, the government began recommending minimum portions from different food groups—today we call it Canada's Food Guide. Tomato soup cake (the soup replaced milk) was a typical example of the new diet. People donated fat and bones to the war effort—fat provided glycerine for ammunition, for example—and grew victory gardens that provided fresh vegetables. Even city folk mastered the art of canning to preserve food for the winter months. And, of course, not only food was rationed. Everything from rubber tires to nylon stockings was no longer available. In the Depression, people had no money. In the war, they had money enough but there was nothing to spend it on. People grumbled but made do in an economy where everything, including wages and prices and rent, was strictly controlled.

The mood in the capital was sombre, even depressed, when the Diefenbakers arrived at Ottawa's Union Station. Although the election was held during the quiet of the phoney war, Parliament met during the Blitzkrieg. As Chief Justice Sir Lyman Duff read the Speech from the Throne on May 15, panzer divisions were sweeping through France and the Low Countries.

"You have been summoned to the first session of a new parliament at a time of the greatest conflict in the history of mankind," Duff declared, without exaggeration. ". . . Unless the evil powers, which threaten the very existence of freedom, are vanquished, the world itself will inevitably be reduced to a state of international anarchy."[18] But Diefenbaker, as he later admitted, wasn't listening. He was dreaming of the day when he would be in the chair to the right of the Senate Speaker, reserved for the prime minister during the Speech from the Throne. He looked up into the packed gallery. Edna smiled back. It was her dream, too.

Because Manion had failed to win his own seat, the party would need someone to lead their paltry thirty-nine members in the House—someone who might well become party leader. Remarkably, senior figures in the party were throwing around Diefenbaker's name, even though he was only a rookie. His rhetorical skills were well known, and his breakthrough in Saskatchewan was a rare bit of good news. But Diefenbaker's own mother warned against allowing his name to be put forward. While Mary was confident in her son's ability, she advised, "You should think it over very carefully, you know the jealousy here in this world." She worried about his health and, most important, "the ones that has been there for years will be wild and might not work with you," she warned, in her semi-literate style of writing.[19] Diefenbaker agreed. "I refused to let my name stand for leadership," he wrote her, once he discovered "everything was pretty well cut and dried." And he added, in a foreshadowing of his future estrangement from his own party, "Between us, there is more logrolling here in a day than there is elsewhere in a year."[20] The day he arrived in Ottawa, caucus chose Richard Burpee Hanson, a competent if hardly charismatic lawyer from

New Brunswick, as what we today would call interim leader. Mary urged her son to rise above partisan politics. "You people down there have a wonderful opportunity to do good," she wrote. "If you would only forget politics and try to do some service for your country."[21]

Diefenbaker at first resolved to lie low and watch how things were done. But that was not in his nature. Before long he was on his feet, criticizing King and his government with increasing effectiveness. One admiring profile described a speaker who, at the beginning of any address, seemed uncertain, his voice high-pitched, "almost like a schoolboy. This is sheer nervousness. But when he gets his hands on his hips, and leans forward, he really goes to town. He bends over toward the Grits, truculently, takes a hand from his hips to cock a menacing indicating finger, and the listeners fear that any minute he'll jump over his bench and offer combat."[22]

There was more to it than rhetoric. The Liberals were using the War Measures Act to massively retool the Canadian economy and society by converting industry to war production. Much of the transformation was led by the brilliant but autocratic industry minister, C.D. Howe, who did not welcome criticism. He received a great deal of it from the member for Lake Centre, who would pore over the new regulations through the night and pounce on the unsuspecting government the next day. Howe hated it. King hated it. The Tory backbench didn't think much of it either. "He annoyed many in his own party," Tommy Douglas later recalled. "The old stalwarts thought he was too pushy. They were used to taking life pretty easy."[23]

In the early weeks, Diefenbaker obsessed over traitors to Canada. It was no secret, he alleged, that there were Nazi sympathizers, especially among more recent arrivals, especially in the German and Eastern European communities. Why, there were such people even in his beloved Saskatchewan, and the government was doing nothing about it.

On the contrary, the government was probably doing too much about it. The War Measures Act gave the King government virtually unlimited power to detain without judicial review, and officials were happy to lock up suspects, often for no good reason. Yes, some were Nazis, but others simply had the wrong last name. Camp 33 in Petawawa, 140 kilometres to the north of Ottawa, housed 645 German and Italian detainees. (Italy entered the war on the side of the Axis powers in June, once Mussolini was sure which side would win the Battle for France.) Tens of thousands more were forced to register. By far the worst action was forcing twenty-one thousand Japanese Canadians out of their homes after Japan attacked the United States on December 7, 1941. Both Canada and the United States unconscionably transported thousands of loyal citizens to internment camps, while stripping them of their property. The governments of both countries later apologized and offered restitution. But the Japanese internment remains a dark stain on this country's past.

Diefenbaker showed scant sympathy for those who might have been unfairly interned, and with good reason. Being fiercer than anyone else in condemning disloyalty, real or perceived, might help inoculate him against prejudice toward his last name, which remained a millstone, creating suspicion and blocking advancement. Though he maintains in his memoirs that he opposed the Japanese internment, he in fact initially supported it. He demanded greater restrictions on the press, on speech, and on anyone who might be deemed disloyal. The future author of the Bill of Rights cared little for rights in the early years of the war. He was hardly alone. As chief justice of the U.S. Supreme Court in the 1950s, Earl Warren championed the rights of minorities. But as California attorney general in the 1940s, he was a leader in the campaign for the Japanese internment.

The greatest personal highlight of that time for Diefenbaker was being briefly introduced to Winston Churchill on December 30, 1941, after the British prime minister addressed Parliament and had his portrait famously taken in the Speaker's Office by Yousuf Karsh. (Churchill told Parliament that when Britain declared it would fight on after France fell in 1940, French generals predicted "'in three weeks England will have her neck wrung like a chicken.' Some chicken. Some neck." As for the famous Bulldog portrait, Churchill was scowling because Karsh had yanked his cigar away.)

By early 1942, the member of Parliament for Lake Centre was becoming increasingly prominent in the debate over conscription, which once again divided the nation and threatened to tear it apart. As in the Great War, many Quebecers saw no need to risk their lives in yet another imperialist conflict. Even the fall of France didn't budge them. Pierre Trudeau, who gave the war a pass, later remembered, "If you were a French-Canadian in Montreal in the early 1940's, you did not automatically believe that this was a just war. We still knew nothing of the Holocaust, and we tended to think of this war as a settling of scores among the superpowers."[24] But for most English Canadians, the war was a struggle, not just to protect Britain but to rid the world of Hitler. King took Canada to war with a public pledge never to invoke conscription. But as the situation in Europe deteriorated in 1940, Parliament passed the National Resources Mobilization Act, which permitted conscription for home defence. By 1941, the Conservative Party had come out in favour of conscription for overseas service, and King was beginning to feel boxed in. He asked the Canadian public to release him from his pledge through a plebiscite. Quebec voted 73 per cent No; the rest of Canada, 80 per cent Yes. That was enough for King to conclude he had a mandate to call for, as he put it during the debate over the plebiscite, "not necessarily conscription, but conscription if necessary."[25]

Diefenbaker argued strenuously in the House for the mobilization of all available troops and "unity of effort" in both English and French Canada, while also berating the government for ignoring the ancient privileges of Parliament and governing by decree. He got under King's skin. Diefenbaker understood that his opponent's greatest weakness was his vanity—including his resentment of Churchill for receiving more credit than King received for prosecuting the war.

But Diefenbaker covertly admired King's ability to dominate Parliament, later recalling, "Throughout the years, he did all he could to destroy his political opponents, sometimes not excluding those within his own party, while all the time clasping his hands in pretence that he would never do anything unfair or unjust. No more sublime actor have I ever known."[26] In any case, by 1942, Diefenbaker's attention was more firmly fixed on his own party's troubles than on anything happening on the other side of the House, two swords' length distant.

From the beginning, Diefenbaker was on the outs with the Conservative leadership. He considered caucus's abrupt dismissal of Manion after the election—which took the leader completely by surprise—callous and ungrateful. He fought, successfully, against the party's decision not to contest a by-election in Saskatchewan; there was no money for it, the leadership insisted, but Diefenbaker convinced them to scrape some funds together and run a candidate, who won. And now he watched as the party once again self-immolated over who should be Manion's successor.

Hanson was a capable voice in the House, but not one to inspire. With a convention out of the question in wartime, caucus and a few other party leaders decided that Arthur Meighen should return as leader. The problem was that Meighen was a senator, and the leader of a political party typically sat in the House. An obliging member gave up his seat so that Meighen could parachute in through a by-election. Following custom, the government of the day did not contest the seat. But King loathed Meighen and wanted him outside the House at all costs. The Liberals aided and abetted the CCF candidate, who won. Out of the Senate, and shut out of the House, Meighen abandoned his last bid for the Conservative leadership in disgust.

Diefenbaker watched and learned and seethed. Nothing had changed from his time as a poor kid on the outskirts of Toronto. The Conservative Party was the party of the business class, especially the business class in Toronto. It cared nothing for the pioneer settlers of the West. The party's ruling clique was insular, walled off from much of the caucus, much of the party membership, and much of the country. And it was a leadership accustomed to defeat at the hands of the Liberals, with little real interest in internal reform. There was no place for a man like John Diefenbaker in its ranks. If he was to advance within the party, it would have to be from outside the oligarchy that controlled it. But that was fine: John George Diefenbaker was always happiest being on the outside.

III

When Lester Pearson returned to Ottawa in June 1941, Mary Greey returned as well. This may not have been a coincidence.

In 1940, sisters Mary and Elizabeth Greey were flatmates in London with Alison Grant, a niece of Vincent Massey—part of the tight, even incestuous community of Canadian expats who hung together in London during the Blitz. Alison later married George Ignatieff. Mary probably had an affair with Mike.

Although the Pearsons had a successful marriage, they were also cosmopolitan, and war upends conventional behaviour. Mike and Maryon were separated by an ocean. There were rumours about Maryon and Graham Towers. She sometimes drove with him to a cottage he and his wife Molly owned in Murray Bay, Quebec. Tongues wagged.

Mary Greey, according to Alison Grant, was powerfully attractive. "When she looks limpidly through her blue eyes, people go absolutely weak."[27] It's almost certain she and Pearson became romantically involved, which may have continued when he returned to Ottawa. Alison's brother, George Grant, who was studying theology on a Rhodes Scholarship at Oxford, wrote his mother about Mary's return to Ottawa, remarking, "If you have ever seen Mary and Mike together you would know how absolutely suited they are for each other and how each adores the other. They are both far too fine to ever let it interfere with his children and wife, but please try to understand it and make it a natural, easy thing." William Christian, George Grant's biographer, declared Mike and Mary had an affair. The writer and journalist Andrew Cohen, in his biography of Pearson, agreed. Both writers attributed Grant's later animosity to Pearson, which reached its epitome in his famed 1965 polemic *Lament for a Nation*, to Grant's animus toward Pearson over his treatment of Mary Greey. "Grant's hostility was personal as much as intellectual," Cohen concluded,[28] while Christian wrote that Grant never forgave Pearson, who Grant believed had "strung Mary along, and treated her execrably" after her return to Canada.[29] Whatever happened, Mary Greey went back to England in 1945 and married Gerald Graham, a much-respected historian. The Pearsons' marriage endured.

Pearson returned to a greatly energized Department of External Affairs. With Mackenzie King distracted by domestic considerations, Norman Robertson was evolving into a de facto minister of foreign affairs. Though skilled, even brilliant, in defending Canada's interests before both the British and Americans, he was no better at administration than Skelton had been. Part of Pearson's job as deputy undersecretary was to bring order to the department. To the extent he succeeded, it was more by encouraging people to work together than through any mastery of flow charts.

External's job was critically important to Canada's role in the war and to the country's future. While still in London, Pearson had represented

Canada's interests in negotiations in which Britain leased fifty destroyers from the still-neutral United States in exchange for long-term American leases on British bases in the West Indies, Bermuda, and Newfoundland. The Americans clearly had their eyes on Newfoundland, which was still a British colony, and Canada had to push hard to get both sides to acknowledge Canada's interests. At the signing of the agreement, which Pearson witnessed, Churchill paced about, smoked his cigar, drank champagne, and swore. "There's no use deceiving ourselves because the world over here is collapsing and victory over the Nazis can't prevent it," Mike wrote to Maryon afterward. "England will never get back to the old complaisant Rolls Royce long weekend existence of yesteryear. The last war began the process, this one will complete it."[30] It was clear to Pearson that destroyers-for-bases was the first instalment in the liquidation of the British Empire, with the United States rising to take its place. The job of the diplomats at External was to assert Canadian interests in an Anglo-American dialogue in which the smaller Commonwealth country was often overlooked.

It was not only External that had been transformed by war. A whole new management class had arrived, the dollar-a-year men, seconded from private industry to Ottawa, principally to oversee the Ministry of Munitions and Supply, and the Wartime Prices and Trade Board. The companies paid their salaries; the government paid their expenses. Their job was to equip and sustain an army, a navy, and an air service that could contribute its share to winning the war. They did, and when the war ended, some of them stayed. Partnered with the mandarins brought in by O.D. Skelton in the 1930s—the "Ottawa men," the historian J.L. Granatstein later dubbed them—they formed the backbone of a new, expanded, and highly professional public service. Many of them were Conservatives: Henry Borden, chairman of the Wartime Industries Control Board, was Robert Borden's son. But none of them paid much attention to partisan politics, and most of them came to adore Howe.

Though not everyone could see it at the time, two events sealed the fate of the Axis powers that year. In June 1941, Hitler invaded Russia, determined to win "living space" for his people by occupying of the fertile lands to Germany's east. German tanks surrounded Leningrad—formerly and today St. Petersburg—plunged toward Crimea, and almost reached Moscow before the cold and bitter Russian winter intervened, as fatal to Hitler's ambitions as to Napoleon's. The German slaughter of civilians was horrific.

Pearson was at the office on the morning of December 7, 1941 when General Henry Crerar, chief of the Defence Staff, dropped in on the Pearson home. While waiting for Maryon to come downstairs, Patty Pearson made small talk, asking Crerar what he thought about the news on the radio that the Japanese had bombed Pearl Harbor. Crerar cried out in amazement and bolted out the door, making for his headquarters, where, Pearson surmised in his memoirs, he "no doubt arranged for summary court martials for his high-ranking intelligence officers who had allowed a child to 'scoop' them."[31]

Although Germany continued to occupy much of western Russia, and Japan raged unchecked in the Pacific, the Allies were convinced that they would win the Second World War. No combination of powers on earth could withstand an alliance that included Russia, the United States, and the British Empire. In May 1942, through a combination of luck and code-breaking, American aircraft carriers surprised Japanese carriers near the mid-Pacific island of Midway, sinking four of them and effectively ending Japan's offensive capability in the Pacific. Meanwhile, the United States and Britain prepared to go on the offensive in North Africa, which led to a small sideshow that much irked Pearson and the Canadian government.

Like Britain, Canada recognized the Free French government-in-exile of the brave but temperamental General Charles de Gaulle. The Free French even had representation in Ottawa. But the Americans were courting the Vichy regime that the Germans had permitted to exist in the southern half of France, hoping to secure acquiescence for the Allied occupation of French North Africa. So the Americans were somewhat annoyed when the "so-called Free French," as Secretary of State Cordell Hull called them, occupied the French islands of St. Pierre and Miquelon in the Gulf of St. Lawrence on Christmas Eve 1941. The Americans wanted the Canadians to expel the occupying forces. The Canadians had no intention of kowtowing to American pressure over the islands or changing their recognition of the Free French. Robertson crafted Canada's formal response, which Pearson delivered in off-the-record language that forcefully reminded the American head of mission in Ottawa that Canada was an independent nation that did no one's bidding.

It was perfectly clear to Pearson, and to Robertson, and to Wrong, and to King, that Canada's relationship with the United States was taking precedence over its relationship with Britain. Back in August 1940, with Britain's survival in doubt, King had met Roosevelt in Ogdensburg, New York, where the two powers agreed on a joint defence of North America in the event of invasion. The rapidly expanding mesh of linkages between the two countries made it even more urgent to fix the shemozzle that the Canadian delegation in Washington had turned into. Loring Christie, Canada's envoy in the American capital, had died of a heart attack at the age of fifty-six in April 1941. King replaced him with Leighton McCarthy, an elderly businessman whose only qualification for the post was that he and Franklin Roosevelt were friends. McCarthy was one of many, many people who clashed with the imperious Hume Wrong, back as the number two in Washington after his brief London stint. In late winter 1942, Pearson sent a long memorandum to Robertson urging a restructuring of the D.C. legation that would have been career-limiting had it gotten out, since it caustically said that the U.S. paid no attention to the legation or to Canada itself, "except when [Ontario premier Mitchell] Hepburn accuses the American Navy of hiding from the Japs and we fiddle over a plebiscite while Singapore and Java burn."

Like Diefenbaker, Pearson clearly thought that Canada should be doing more in the war effort, and by doing more he meant conscription. Neither of them understood King's patient, devious, but in the end masterful manipulation of the issue, not only as a tactic to foil his political enemies but as the way to preserve national unity. Pearson acknowledged as much years later, though in his defence he noted how difficult it was for anyone, even those within his own bureaucracy, to understand the "subtleties and apparent hesitations" of King. "This understanding was not made easier by his enigmatic and contradictory personality, with that combination of charming friendliness and self-centred calculation, of kindness and ruthlessness, of political vision and personal pettiness which so many who worked for him found disconcerting."[32]

In any case, Pearson's proposal—that McCarthy be recalled—was never going to happen. Instead, Wrong was recalled and Pearson sent in his place. In some ways, the timing was unfortunate. Pearson had enjoyed his months in Ottawa: the children were in school; Mike appreciated the opportunity to reconnect with his friends for tennis, dinner, fishing; he and Maryon had just bought a house in tony Rockcliffe Park. John English, in his biography of Pearson, citing confidential sources, says, "Mike and Maryon also needed the time together after their wartime separation, a separation that some feel created strains in their relationship."[33] But Mike had to go to D.C., and wanted to go, even if he would be playing second fiddle, once again, to an envoy at least partially disengaged from the mission. As Pearson knew better than most, Washington had become the centre of the world. After his years in London, it was the best possible posting for an ambitious young diplomat.

The summer of 1942 was pretty typical, weatherwise, in D.C.: daily highs averaging thirty-two degrees Celsius, lows of around twenty-one. The humidity was brutal, which is why anyone who could manage it typically fled the capital in the summer. But not in the summer of 1942, the first summer of the U.S. at war with both Germany and Japan. Along with everyone else, the Pearsons endured. Because air conditioning was virtually unheard of for homes, people shuttered their windows in the morning to keep out the heat, opening them later in the day. They drank iced tea on their verandas, took afternoon naps. But again, there was no time for naps in 1942.

Top secret preparations were underway for Operation Torch, the Allied landings in French North Africa slated for late 1942. In the Pacific, the Americans recaptured Guadalcanal in the Solomon Islands in August. For the next four months, the Japanese would throw everything they had at the Americans, in an effort to retake the island. But although losses were fearsome, the Marines hung on. By December, after three land and seven naval battles, the Japanese had given up, the first step in their long, slow, bloody retreat across the Pacific.

The population of the American capital had nearly doubled during the war, reaching eight hundred thousand. Tens of thousands of workers typed and sorted and filed in temporary office buildings thrown up along the National Mall and around the Washington Monument, while Defense workers moved into the first wedge of the Pentagon, the world's largest office building, still under construction. The White House grounds, once open to the public, were closed off and guarded. (They would never reopen.) Housing was nearly impossible to find, but the Pearsons got lucky. Charles Drury—everyone called him Bud—was leaving his post as a military attaché for active service and the Pearsons gratefully took over his pleasant house. (Drury would later serve as a minister under Pearson and Pierre Trudeau.)

As minister-counsellor of the legation, Pearson was once again effectively running the shop, just as he had in London. Even more than Vincent Massey, McCarthy was mostly absent from day-to-day affairs. His real job, one that King valued highly, was to reach out to his good friend Franklin when needed. Though Pearson privately chafed at his boss's absence—six hours a day, four days a week was as much as he could handle, Wrong had noted—the situation served him well. For at a critical time in the life of Canada–U.S. relations, Pearson was, for all intents and purposes, Canada's voice in Washington.

The country needed that voice. In the councils of total war, Britain and the U.S. spoke directly to each other, often ignoring Canadian concerns, even when Canadian interests were at stake. During the destroyers-for-bases negotiations, Pearson had witnessed the waning power of Britain first-hand. The new global powers were the United States, a country endlessly fascinated with itself and historically indifferent to everyone else, and Josef Stalin's Soviet Union, which in 1942 remained an enigma. As Canada struggled to find its place in the emerging new world order, Pearson fought two simultaneous, though contradictory, American assumptions: that Canada was part of the British Empire, whose interests would be looked after by London; and that Canada was a semi-autonomous extension of the United States and could be told what to do. "The American authorities often tend to consider us not as a foreign nation at all, but as one of themselves," Pearson wrote in a memorandum to McCarthy. "Suspended, then, somewhat uneasily in the minds of so many Americans between the position of British Colony and American dependency, we are going to have a difficult time in the months ahead in maintaining our own position and standing on our own feet."[34]

Part of that task could be accomplished by getting to know people. At this, Mike Pearson was unequalled. His charm, intelligence, and easy good humour made him immensely popular, allowing him to form friendships that stood him and his country in good stead for decades to come. Two friendships, especially, stood out. One was with James "Scotty" Reston, a young reporter at the New York Times who would become one of the most influential voices in American journalism. (Pearson's comradery with journalists would serve him well in the years to come.) The other was with Dean Acheson, then assistant secretary of state. Acheson's mother was a Gooderham, once a prominent family in the Canadian distilling business. The Achesons and the Pearsons became good friends—they both loved to gossip, and the information exchanged could be valuable—though that friendship eroded as each man grew more powerful.

As Pearson had noted, to the Americans, Canada was either a tributary of the waning British Empire, and so could be ignored, or a tributary of the rising American empire, and so could be ignored. The trick in the post-war world would be to navigate between the rising and waning superpowers. But Canada's prime minister seemed to his aides more interested in getting into photographs with Churchill and Roosevelt than in being in the room when decisions were made. In reality, King often helped explain Churchill and Roosevelt—both of whom he'd known before the war—to each other.

The country had earned a seat at the tables of the powerful. Canada's factories churned out materiel, its aerodromes trained thousands of pilots. Almost a thousand Canadians had died at the ill-fated raid on Dieppe. (One of them was Pearson's brother-in-law, Norman Young. The two couples had been married together and the Pearsons were staying with the Youngs when Mike saw the newspaper headline about Poland. Mike and Maryon felt the loss deeply.) Canadian ships protected half the convoys crossing the Atlantic. Canadian troops fought in the grinding battles that were slowly liberating Italy.

Through it all, military and civilian staffs in Washington, London, and Ottawa bargained and brokered and bickered. To navigate these tempestuous diplomatic waters, Hume Wrong, Norman Robertson, and Lester Pearson developed a foreign policy that became known as "functionalism." Simply put, Canada would assert its interests in any forum that affected those interests, based on its substantial contribution to the war and its stature as a responsible middle power. In practice, this meant arguing for a seat at the table. Often, it meant compromise. Canada expected to play a major role in the post-war reconstruction of Europe, and it sought a seat at the Central Policy Committee of the United Nations Relief and Rehabilitation Administration (UNRRA). That request was rebuffed, but Pearson did get to chair the Supply Committee, and to sit in on meetings of the Policy Committee. UNRRA meetings occupied almost half his time from 1943 to 1946, and they took him to Europe, where he witnessed the devastation of Berlin and where, after an absence of ten years, he was asked by the porter at the Geneva hotel where he had stayed for League meetings if he would like his old room.

The idea of functionalism was Hume Wrong's. As undersecretary, Robertson embraced it as departmental policy. Pearson executed the policy in Washington. The three men, all close friends, had become a powerful and tightly knit troika, effectively responsible for Canadian foreign policy as King grappled with the conscription crisis and a plethora of other concerns. The aging prime minister willingly ceded day-to-day control of foreign affairs to the three men, whom he had come to trust. "Wrong was the best intellect, cool and quick, a polished technician and a supremely organized man," J.L. Granatstein wrote of them, "but Robertson also had a deep and splendid mind, even if he was no administrator. . . . Pearson was ambitious and charming, adept with the press. His abilities suffered only in comparison with Wrong and Robertson. The three friends reinforced each other's strengths and compensated for their weaknesses; together, they changed the country's course."[35]

One stand taken by Pearson, Robertson, and Wrong, as Canada struggled for representation on joint Anglo-American boards, was to reject a British proposal that Canada act as representative of the Commonwealth. "This [offer] amounts to the revival of the old concept of diplomatic unity of the Commonwealth," Wrong wrote. Canada was an independent country with interests distinct from those of Australia, South Africa, and other Commonwealth members. With this statement of fact, British hopes of leading a united Commonwealth came to an end. And in an even more muscular display, Wrong et al. pointed out that Canada sent billions of dollars' worth of food and military supplies to Britain without asking for payment. If the British were unwilling to respect Canada's interests, that policy might have to be reviewed. Canada got the seat it wanted on several boards. And it was Canada, through whose airspace planes would fly to and from North America and Europe after the war, that the Allies chose as host country for the temporary and then permanent headquarters, in

Montreal, of what would become the International Civil Aviation Organization.

In May 1943, hundreds of delegates gathered at Hot Springs, West Virginia—whose waters Roosevelt loved to take, wrongly thinking they strengthened his withered limbs—to talk about post-war food aid in a world of shattered nations and supply chains. As one of the world's great food exporters, and with much of Europe and Western Russia in ruins, Canada was expected to play a vital role in feeding the post-war world, which is why Pearson was there. He initially didn't think much of the woolly-minded rhetoric around ending the scourge of malnutrition among the world's poor, especially since the British aims were so modest and the Americans' so grandiose but unfocused. Before long, though, he found himself negotiating a consensus, impressing both the Americans and the British, who agreed to make him chairman of the Interim Commission. It cost Pearson his summer vacation, but the result was the charter of the Food and Agriculture Organization, the first organization under the auspices of the new United Nations.

On June 6, 1944, in the largest amphibious assault in history, five Allied armies landed at Normandy: two American, two British, one Canadian. Canada was now the fourth largest military power in the alliance.

The battles for Caen in the summer of 1944 and the Scheldt in the autumn were brutal, with the Canadian First Army's casualty rate approaching 50 per cent, even as the First Canada Corps ground its way up the Italian peninsula. The telegrams arrived by the thousands across the country: "We deeply regret to inform you . . . ." Defence Secretary James Ralston threatened to resign from cabinet unless King sent over sixteen thousand zombies, as the men conscripted for home defence were called. But the Quebec cabinet ministers fiercely opposed conscription, and so did Maurice Duplessis, back in office as Quebec premier. Passions ran so high between English and French that King feared civil war. To prevent it, he fired Ralston, replacing him with General Andrew McNaughton, who opposed conscription. His successful efforts to keep the cabinet and the country together in the face of the crisis may have been King's greatest political achievement as prime minister. But losses reached the point that the government eventually had no choice but to send zombies overseas in November 1944, though only about two thousand of them saw action, with sixty-nine killed.

Earlier that year, Ottawa had upgraded its legation in Washington to an embassy, making Leighton McCarthy Canada's first ambassador to the United States. A year later, at McCarthy's urging, Pearson took over the job. By now, he was one of the best-known Canadians in the world, a name in headlines that editors assumed readers would recognize.

On April 30, 1945, as Allied armies closed in from the east and west— but mostly from the east—Hitler committed suicide in his Berlin bunker. Three months later, the U.S. shocked the world by releasing a horrifying new weapon. One atomic bomb devastated Hiroshima; the other, Nagasaki. American scientific ingenuity and industrial might knew no bounds: by the end of the war, the United States was launching three Liberty cargo ships every two days. Three hundred thousand aircraft and almost ninety thousand tanks had rolled off the line. And while the Germans and Japanese abandoned their atomic-weapon research as unfeasible, the Americans perfected both a uranium-based and a plutonium-based bomb. Unsure which would work, or work better, they built both. At the end of the Second World War, there was no power on earth that could challenge the United States, though Soviet spies had stolen much of the American atomic research and were busily working away on a bomb of their own. On a Potomac cruise with the new president, Harry S. Truman, Pearson futilely argued that the United States should surrender its atomic power to international oversight.

Although Pearson didn't play much of a role in creating the United Nations—in those negotiations, Wrong and Robertson represented Canada's interests—when the time came to appoint the organization's first secretary general, his work on UNRRA and the UN's Food and Agriculture Organization made Pearson the Americans' first choice. The Soviets would have none of it, seeing Canada as a proxy for the U.S. Still, "You are becoming a very important person in the international world," Georges Vanier observed.[36] Indeed he was.

War has a tendency to reward competence. When Germany invaded Poland in 1939, Dwight Eisenhower was a lieutenant colonel in the tiny American army; four years later he was Supreme Allied Commander in Europe. Pearson went from being Vincent Massey's aide in London to being a candidate for secretary general of the United Nations in six not-very-short years.

By 1946, foreign policy was too important, and Mackenzie King too feeble, for the prime minister to also serve even as titular minister of foreign affairs. King had recruited Louis St. Laurent, one of Quebec's most prominent and talented lawyers, as his justice minister and Quebec lieutenant in 1941, after the death of Ernest Lapointe. On September 4, 1946, St. Laurent became effectively the first secretary of state for external affairs who was not also prime minister (though a Liberal MP had had served briefly in that role under Laurier). One of St. Laurent's first acts was to ask Pearson to come back to Ottawa as undersecretary. Mike, enjoying the high life of a famous Canadian diplomat in Washington, did not welcome the thought of returning to dull, quiet Ottawa. But, of course, he went. Undersecretary had always been his ambition. And he had reason to suspect even greater things might lie in store.

IV

Edna Diefenbaker was increasingly unhappy and unwell. Few men in the 1940s understood menopause or cared about its effects on the mental health of some women. Edna felt those effects severely. She was obsessed with preserving her figure and her looks, lest John stop finding her attractive. But her chestnut hair was coming out in clumps, forcing her to wear a turban, leaving her feeling increasingly insecure. Dieting to preserve her figure stressed her will and her body. Now that she could no longer have a child, she longed for one, if only for companionship. The press of political life, especially the need to appear with her husband in front of crowds, wore on her. When she complained, John ignored her, self-absorbed and consumed by his work. She had few friends in Ottawa, and when the couple returned to Prince Albert, Mary would visit, more imperious than ever, making the house, making life itself, intolerable. John doted on his mother and she on him. Alvin Hamilton, who served as a (largely unpaid) political aide to Diefenbaker in the 1930s, and who Diefenbaker regarded as protégé, once visited Diefenbaker's home and found him lying with his head in his mother's lap "as though he were a six-year-old kid or something."[37]

In the later years of his life, Diefenbaker intimated that Edna was drinking or taking pills, though her friends hotly denied the accusation when asked by Edna Diefenbaker's biographer, Simma Holt. There were rumours that Edna would go out dancing at night and would sometimes accept the offer of a ride home with a man. At other times she would take long walks through town, or visit her mother. Maren Brower was also demanding, but at least she would listen to her daughter's woes. John Diefenbaker's wife felt lonely and boxed in and unappreciated by a neglectful and yet possessive husband who wanted her to be with him constantly, both for companionship and to serve his needs.

They fought. While waiting for an elevator at the Château Laurier, one reporter heard her lash out at him: "You are not even a man! You could not even produce a baby."[38] John raged when Edna threw out his moth-eaten army uniform. Visitors to the home found the mood tense, Edna's gaiety forced, her endless talkativeness a strain on everyone. And, of course, there was the war. News that her niece's husband had been killed at Caen struck Edna hard.

Through it all, the Conservative Party struggled to find a voice. Following Meighen's humiliating by-election loss, a group of young Conservative Turks met at Port Hope, a town on the shores of Lake Ontario east of Toronto, to draft a new manifesto for the party. While embracing free enterprise and supporting conscription, the Port Hopefuls, as they were dubbed, also called for full employment, respect for labour, low-cost housing, and even government-financed health care. The Liberals were already making similar plans. No one wanted to repeat the hard times that followed the First World War, or to relive the Great Depression. The federal government had amassed enormous deficits by putting more than a million men and women into uniform and building an independent Canadian army, navy, and air force, all while contributing secretly to the Manhattan project that produced the atomic weapons. But Ottawa was able to service the debt, and the war had proven that government could sustain the operations of a mobilized economy. If Big Government could win the war, maybe Big Government could better manage the peace. The veterans would want homes to live in, a shot at a decent education, jobs that paid a living wage. The new technologies of war had transformed aviation and ground transportation, communications, energy, and medicine. Planners in Washington and London and Ottawa envisioned a government-directed economy and state-supported services. The

Conservatives, while emphasizing the need to preserve market forces in peacetime, were also ready to launch what would become known as the welfare state.

But both the Liberals and Conservatives were shifting left for another reason: fear of the CCF, which had broken the grip of the Liberal Party in Saskatchewan. Tommy Douglas, whose energy and passion for social justice animated his wiry frame, took more than half the vote in the June 15, 1944, provincial election, reducing the Liberals to five seats. Both national parties decided that the only way to beat the socialists was to steal the most digestible parts of their platform. The Conservatives were willing to go so far as to change the name of the party, turning it into an oxymoron.

Arthur Meighen was privately skeptical of the progressive bent of the Port Hopefuls. But he realized that the Conservative Party needed to move in a different direction and expand its appeal beyond the establishment class in Ontario. The party would need a new leader, and Meighen settled on the premier of Manitoba, John Bracken, who he calculated would unite Ontario and the West in a new, governing, Conservative coalition. There was a problem: Bracken wasn't a Conservative. His governing party called itself Liberal-Progressive. Like so many, he had been born in Ontario but moved out west to seek his fortune, which in Bracken's case meant becoming an agronomist and eventually president of the Manitoba Agricultural College, before stumbling into the premiership of his province. In 1922, the United Farmers of Manitoba captured a majority of seats in the provincial election, shocking everyone, including the United Farmers of Manitoba, which hadn't even bothered to choose a leader. After several potential candidates turned the job down, Bracken agreed to step in. For more than two decades he had provided his province with competent, cautious, pragmatic government. A non-ideological populist at heart, Bracken called himself a Progressive until the party merged with the Liberals; by 1942 his wartime government included members of the Conservative, CCF, and Social Credit parties.

Meighen arranged for the party to hold a leadership convention in Winnipeg on December 9–11, 1942. The zeitgeist seemed to have settled on the need for a leader from the West, to exploit the growing sense of Liberal vulnerability in the region. Diefenbaker was part of the mix. He objected to Meighen and the party establishment's efforts to engineer the leadership. He was, by common consent, the most brilliant debater in the House—on top of every file and possessed of the ability to infuriate the Liberals across the aisle, not least King and Howe. But he also annoyed members of his own caucus by grandstanding in front of the press or popping into committee hearings to upstage the caucus critic with a pithy quote that invariably made it into the papers. He was admired and despised in equal measure, though for many the biggest problem was his strange, German-rooted name. Canada was at war with Germany, after all. Nonetheless, Diefenbaker put his name in. Though he lacked any real organization or base of support, Bracken still hadn't made up his mind, the convention was wide open, anything might happen.

Except Bracken did finally decide to run, Meighen's cabal engineered the change of party name to Progressive Conservative, and despite five candidates vying for support, Manitoba's premier won handily on the second ballot. Diefenbaker wasn't particularly upset. Bracken was a Westerner and they shared the same outlook, which in turn aligned with the agenda of the Port Hope crowd: capitalism and free enterprise, leavened with social supports for those in need. "I have no fear of the CCF if we stand for something," Diefenbaker declared in his speech to the convention. More disappointing was losing his bid to become house leader. Since the new Conservative leader did not intend to enter the House anytime soon, House leader was an important post, but Bracken decided to let the caucus members decide who should lead them. Diefenbaker lost by one vote to Gordon Graydon, MP for Peel, just west of Toronto. He might have had only himself to blame. It was considered honourable in such contests for a candidate to vote for their opponent. But according to one account, "John voted for Gordon and Gordon voted for himself. This is a swell set."[39]

The months that followed were hard: Elmer, always at loose ends, moved back in with his parents. (He had become John's eyes and ears in Lake Centre, and watched over the parents.) William died on February 12, 1943, of a heart attack, and Edna's mental health was deteriorating. The new Progressive Conservative Party was moribund. Bracken by his own admission was a dull debater, and unwilling in any case to risk disgrace by losing a by-election. He was never accepted by the Ontario wing of the party, which had been transformed provincially under the leadership of George Drew, a powerful lawyer with a solid reputation for managerial competence, who, by fair means and foul, suppressed the CCF in Ontario, in part by absconding with its policies. Drew became premier in 1943, inaugurating what would become forty-two unbroken years of Conservative rule in Ontario. Grits in Ottawa; Tories at Queen's Park. Ontario voters seemed to like it that way.

In the spring of 1945, with Germany defeated, Holland liberated by the Canadian First Army—at the cost of more than 7,600 Canadian lives—and the Allies planning for the invasion of Japan, King decided it was time for a general election. The Liberals should have been vulnerable. Despite rescuing Britain from defeat and helping lead it to victory, Winston Churchill's Conservatives had been trounced by Labour in an election that year. Franklin Roosevelt had won a fourth term in 1944, but he died only weeks after the inauguration, making Harry Truman president. King was the last of the triumvirate still in office. People were sick of war and wanted a peace that spread prosperity across all classes. The Progressive Conservatives were offering modest social reforms. And King had been in power, with the exception of the Bennett hiatus, since 1919. He was an old and tired man. Surely it was time for a change.

No, it wasn't. The merger of business, bureaucracy, and the Liberal Party of Canada was virtually complete, both in Ottawa and in the minds of many Canadians. The Ottawa men had won the war; the Ottawa men would ensure a prosperous peace. The government had already instituted a scheme for direct payments to families with children: known as the family allowance, most people called it the "baby bonus." Though Diefenbaker supported the family allowance program, other Conservatives in caucus opposed it, and George Drew railed against a measure that he said would take money from Ontario taxpayers and give it to the fecund families of Quebec, whose sons had not even volunteered to fight.

King watched the internal Tory strife with delight, even as his party made plans to promote full employment and improve health care. For millions of Canadians, having an all-powerful, corporate, professional Liberal Party in charge just seemed natural, almost inevitable. Especially when contrasted with the hapless Progressive Conservatives.

The party was in as much conflict as its new name suggested. J.W. Dafoe of the *Winnipeg Free Press* spotted the contradiction soon after Bracken was chosen leader. The leader might be a Progressive, he wrote, and the party might now have the word "Progressive" in its name, but the base remained unchanged. "I cannot see Bracken mouthing the Tory-Orange-Imperialist slogans," he wrote. And he was right. Conservative leaders, Progressive or otherwise, did not remake the party in their image. Instead, the party broke the will of its leaders.

Whatever he might have envisioned for Canada at peace, Bracken was bound by the Tory orthodoxy of supporting conscription in war. The Conservatives promised, if elected, to employ conscription to raise an army that would be part of the invasion of Japan, which all sides expected would be a bloody business that could take years and cost hundreds of thousands of Allied lives. King was prepared to commit only a single division to the invading force. By promoting conscription, Bracken was writing off Quebec and pushing the Progressive Conservatives well to the right.

On election day, June 11, the Liberals won a weak majority government, dependent on eight "Independent Liberals" who had opposed conscription. The Conservatives increased their seat count from thirty-nine to sixty-seven, winning a majority of Ontario ridings along with a smattering of seats in British Columbia and an even smaller smattering on the Prairies, where the CCF dominated. But the socialists were largely shut out of Ontario, Quebec, and the Maritimes. Diefenbaker held on in Lake Centre, in part by defying his party on conscription for the Japan campaign—many farmers had opposed conscription because young workers were needed in the fields.

The Liberals would have yet another four years. Bracken had finally made it into the House, but he was under assault by the powerful Ontario machine, which had engineered a smashing majority-government victory for Drew even as the federal election was underway. Diefenbaker was still in the House—a place he had grown to love more than his own home—but within a dispirited and disunited caucus. At least the conscription issue was laid to rest with the surrender of Japan on August 15, following the atomic bombing of Hiroshima and Nagasaki. But the Conservative Party was an anachronism: weak, divided, out of touch with the times. Those times would witness unheard-of prosperity and unrelenting fear.

On September 5, 1945, after learning that he and his family were about to be transferred back to Russia, Igor Gouzenko, an intelligence officer at the Soviet embassy in Ottawa, left the embassy with a briefcase crammed with Russian code books. At first, he couldn't get anyone to pay attention, but the RCMP eventually examined the briefcase, and Gouzenko was spirited off to a secret facility for interrogation. His revelations of the Soviets' success in stealing Western secrets and in planting sleeper agents shocked both Ottawa and Washington.

A great, horrible global war had ended. A new cold war that threatened to turn at any moment into a nuclear holocaust was already underway. Both Mike Pearson and John Diefenbaker would be in the thick of it.

FIVE

Power and Grief

(1947–1951)

I

On the morning of November 21, 1950, Bill Tindill and Harry Patterson were loading poles at a railroad siding at Canoe River, British Columbia, 320 kilometres north of Kamloops, deep in the Canadian Rockies. They looked up as they heard the whistle from Canadian National Railways (CNR) Passenger Extra No. 3538 West, a troop train taking three hundred men on their way to fight in the Korean War. Suddenly, another passenger train came around the curve on the same track: CNR's transcontinental train number 2, the *Continental Limited*. Tindill waved a frantic warning to the transcontinental. The fireman, smiling, waved back. The two locomotives collided with such force that they leapt into the air before exploding, killing the crews on both trains. Passenger cars derailed or telescoped. Five hundred feet of train were compacted into 130 feet. While the cars on the transcontinental were steel-sided, protecting the passengers, many of the cars on the troop train were wooden-sided, crushing or impaling men with wood and glass. It took hours for medical and rescue crews to reach the site. Twenty-one men, seventeen of them passengers on the troop train, died, and dozens were injured. Apart from the engine crew, there were no fatalities on the transcontinental.

At Red Pass junction, eighty kilometres to the east, Jack Atherton's face went pale when he heard the news. He was the telegraph operator who had handed the crew of the troop train the instructions he had received by phone from the dispatcher in Kamloops. He scanned the instructions: the train was to proceed to Gosnell, then wait at a siding for train number 2, the transcontinental, and another train, number 4, to pass. But two days later, as he was grilled by the RCMP, a discrepancy emerged. The dispatcher at Kamloops had ordered the train to wait for the transcontinental at the Cedarside siding, and then for the number 4 at Gosnell. Those two words, "at Cedarside," were missing from the instructions Atherton had handed the crew of the troop train. Those two missing words had killed twenty-one men.

Atherton swore he had never heard "at Cedarside." Phone lines sometimes faded out, which is why operators repeated their instructions back to the dispatcher. How had neither of them caught the mistake? The RCMP didn't particularly care. It was clear to them that Atherton, who was only twenty-two and new on the job, had improperly taken down the instructions. They charged him with manslaughter. Atherton had been raised in Saskatoon, so it wasn't surprising that his parents asked—begged, pleaded with—John Diefenbaker to take the case. Edna joined in their plea. It was her dying wish.

The post-war years were hard on John Diefenbaker. He experienced disappointment and loss on every front, personal and political. Through much of that time, Edna was in treatment for one illness or another. Each needed the other's support; neither could fully provide it. And the Progressive Conservative Party was moving away from Diefenbaker, making him even more of an outcast in his own caucus. When Jack Atherton's parents came to him, he was at the lowest ebb of his personal and political life.

II

There has never been a morning like the post-war years, and there never will be again. A decade of depression followed by history's most devastating war should have left the world exhausted and in despair. Reality turned out to be the very opposite.

The United States, Canada, Australia, and New Zealand—all former British colonies and so all English-speaking—had fought and won the war without the war coming to them. No one had invaded them; their cities were intact. These four countries now possessed much of the wealth of the world. The United States alone accounted for half of the global gross domestic product. During the war, many economists feared that peacetime would bring mass unemployment, as tens of millions of men returned from the front looking for work. But that never happened, for two reasons: the war had generated technological miracles the likes of which none had imagined, and governments had learned from the mistakes they had made after the Great War and during the Depression and resolved not to repeat them.

First and foremost, they protected the worker. The U.S. Congress passed and Franklin Roosevelt signed the Servicemen's Readjustment Act in June 1944. The G.I. Bill, as everyone called it ("general infantryman" was government-speak for a soldier) offered low-interest mortgages and free education to those who had served in the war. For the first time, working-class men and women were able to learn more than the basics of reading and writing, and able as well to own their own home. Veterans received free health care, and governments built a network of hospitals to provide that care. Unemployment insurance supported those looking for work, but mass unemployment never returned. Pretty much anyone who wanted a job could find one.

Canadian programs, known as the Veterans Charter, mirrored the American. More than a million men and women had worn the uniform by war's end. Discharge payments gave them seed money to plan for the future. The Veterans Land Act helped them purchase land or houses, many of them bungalows designed in Cape Cod vernacular, known as wartime housing. There were grants for university or vocational training, grants to help start businesses, pensions for the spouses of those killed in war.

War had unleashed wonderous technological advances. There were still biplanes in air forces in 1939; by 1945 there were jet aircraft. Advancement begat advancement. Consider the automobile. The need for more powerful airplane engines in war translated into more powerful and reliable automobile engines in peace. Power steering and automatic transmission migrated from tanks to station wagons. Wartime scarcities drove innovation in plastics, which created new possibilities for car seats and dashboards. Wartime needs even influenced peacetime aesthetics. Inspired by the vertical stabilizers used on the Lockheed P-38 Lightning, Harley Earl, chief designer at General Motors, introduced tail fins on the 1948 Cadillac, which started a craze.

Take automotive innovation and apply it across any field: The arrival of penicillin to treat infections and pneumonia on the battlefield launched a medical revolution of wonder drugs, accompanied by surgical innovations. Energy had gone nuclear. Commercial aviation allowed people who had sailed around the world before the war to fly around it after. Kitchen appliances transformed housework. Scientists and businessmen were just beginning to grasp the potential of the new computing machines. In the public sector, take the G.I. Bill or the Veterans Charter and apply it across the whole of government: health insurance, unemployment insurance, public education.

Then put it all together: A young couple leave their cramped downtown apartment. He, finally home from the war, has landed a good job, thanks to the technical diploma he earned with government support. She didn't mind working while he studied; she'd spent the war on an assembly line, after all. But now they have a car, which they drive on wide new roads to the biggest post-war invention of them all: the suburb, dominated by swathes of identical, affordable homes. Critics would complain about blight and sprawl. The critics had forgotten that some of the people living in that sprawl had been raised in tenements or on dirt-poor farms. They forgot about the transformation in living standards suburbia represented, the miraculous decrease in infant mortality and increase in life expectancy. Stability, prosperity, babies. Lots and lots of healthy babies. The baby boom.

Under American leadership, much of the world prospered. At the Mount Washington Hotel in Bretton Woods, New Hampshire, in July 1944, the Allied nations had signed a series of accords that stabilized exchange rates and created the International Monetary Fund and the World Bank. The United States came to the aid of a shattered Europe in 1948 with the Marshall Plan, which poured billions of dollars of aid and investment into France, West Germany, Italy, and other Continental nations in need that were at risk of voting in communist governments. The Germans called the transformative growth that followed the *Wirtschaftswunder*, the "economic miracle." And the American-led United Nations offered the promise of a world that might finally be spared the carnage of war. If the UN failed to live up to its ideals, it wasn't for want of American trying.

The U.S.S.R. had borne the brunt of the fighting, with up to twenty-seven million military and civilian casualties. Josef Stalin had no intention of contributing to a post-war world under America's sway. With Germany and Japan defeated, the capitalist powers of the West represented the only real threat to communist expansion. Meeting that threat meant acquiring atomic weapons and the means of delivering them to American cities. And it meant control of Eastern Europe, both as spoils of war and as a buffer against Western forces.

George Kennan, a U.S. diplomat in Moscow, in what became known as the Long Telegram, argued that the Soviet Union was, in reality, a neurotic and insecure empire, and should be treated like one. The U.S. and its allies should recognize the U.S.S.R.'s sphere of influence—principally Eastern Europe—but should seek to contain any expansion beyond that sphere. The Truman administration embraced this doctrine of containment. The world was at Cold War.

Mackenzie King was no longer part of this world. He was seventy-one when the war ended, but there was more to it than his age. Apart from the R.B. Bennett interregnum and Arthur Meighen's brief hours in the sun, he had been prime minister for a quarter of a century, through the Roaring Twenties and the Dirty Thirties and the second Great War. His instinct, with the return of peace, was to return Canada to its traditionally cautious role: avoiding entanglements, regardless of who sought to entangle; navigating between the competing vortexes of Great Britain and the United States; bringing the books back into balance (which would not prove difficult); and holding together a nation that had been fractured once again by conscription. He was not averse to expanding the power of the state through entitlements—he had always seen himself as a crusading reformer, even when he wasn't, which was mostly—but he could not possibly embrace the zeitgeist of a nation galvanized by millions of young men and women released from war and eager to make up for the lost years any more than he could embrace the energetic and outward-looking diplomacy of Pearson, Wrong, Robertson, and the new generation of foreign service officers who sought to emulate them. The future was in a hurry, and he was tired to the point of exhaustion—"over-fatigued and bedraggled"[1]— as he complained in September 1945. He and everyone else knew that the June 1945 election had been his last.

It took three long years, however, for him to leave. Like many who came before and after, King had convinced himself that he was indispensable, the only one who could keep the country together and moving forward. It isn't much of an exaggeration to say that, from 1945 to 1948, Mackenzie King's advisers and ministers governed by going around the wishes of an obstinate, cantankerous, and increasingly irrelevant prime minister.

King had already let go of External Affairs. The department that once operated over a barber shop on Bank Street had burgeoned into the foreign service of a major middle power. Between 1944 and 1948, External had more than doubled in size, from under 500 workers to more than 1,200. In choosing Louis St. Laurent to be the first independent secretary of state for external affairs, King knew he was also appointing his successor. Pearson replaced Norman Robertson—who had grown weary of trying to ride herd over the department's burgeoning bureaucracy and King's infuriating self-absorption and hesitancy—as undersecretary. Robertson departed for London, and Wrong returned to Washington—this time, finally, as head of mission. Already, in the halls and restaurants of power in Ottawa, there was talk of Pearson one day becoming prime minister.

Mike and Maryon settled into a gabled, peak-roofed former farmhouse with a pleasant porch on Augusta Street in Sandy Hill—not nearly so refined a neighbourhood as Rockcliffe Park, but only a brisk, fifteen-minute walk to the East Block, where External Affairs was still headquartered. The walk was no hardship; Pearson was remarkably fit for a man of fifty—the mop of sandy hair receding but still intact, his skill at tennis so formidable that he had once beaten a Canadian champion. Journalists still described him as youthful, even calling him "Boy Wonder." With Patricia and Geoffrey at private schools, the Pearsons lived alone: a middle-aged couple, he distracted by work, careless with his attire, with a marked preference for bow ties; she waspy and tart, known to wear veils and sunglasses, devoted to Mike but chary with her affection. Patsy once admitted that she was afraid of her mother. "There was no praise," she remembered later. "She was a very, very critical person . . . she could cut you off at the knees."[2] The Pearsons had always moved in cosmopolitan circles in London and Washington, and they did the same in Ottawa, to the extent such a thing was possible in a city of two hundred thousand that still bore traces of its mill-town past. They liked to party, to drink (she more than he) and to dance (she more than he). The children had been raised by nannies and boarding schools. But they never complained—about their father, at least.

Pearson, Robertson, Wrong, and Escott Reid—a former academic (of course) whose strong left-wing views had kept him out of External Affairs until the war, after which he rose rapidly within it—all believed that Canada could and should play a prominent role in post-war diplomacy as a helpful fixer: a country that knew both Britain and the United States intimately, without being in thrall to either, a country that could join and promote alliances while being trusted as a neutral arbiter when one was needed. "If there is one conclusion that our common experience has led us to accept, it is that security for this country lies in the development of a firm structure of international organization," St. Laurent declared in the Gray Lecture, a speech he gave at the University of Toronto in 1947, which laid out Canada's post-war foreign policy.[3] Canada would become a nation of joiners. Although Pearson was complaining about the ineffectiveness of the UN as early as 1946, he led the successful charge to win a temporary seat on the Security Council for Canada in 1948 and 1949.

As an international diplomatic celebrity, Pearson played a key role in projecting Canadian influence in parts of the world that it had never engaged with before. One was the Middle East. Prior to the Second World War, Canada had no foreign policy to speak of, and certainly no interest in the Levant. But six million Jews had died in the Holocaust, some of whom could have been saved had Canada and other Western nations not closed their doors to Jewish refugees. Now the survivors flooded into Palestine, determined to make a country where they could defend themselves. But Palestine was already occupied, by Arabs. To create a homeland for the Jews could mean evicting Arabs from their homes.

By 1947, as tension and violence escalated, Britain declared its intention to end its mandate over Palestine. The Americans favoured the creation of Arab and Jewish states, which Britain opposed. King wanted nothing to do with any of it, but both Pearson and St. Laurent saw an opportunity for Canada to mediate between the U.S. and the U.K., as well as between Arabs and Jews. Pearson also had to overcome differing opinions within External Affairs. His strong support for a Jewish state brought sneers from pro-Arabs and some anti-Semites inside the department, who called Pearson "King of the Jews" behind his back. But with American support, Canada was one of the member states on the UN committee that recommended the creation of separate states for Jews and Arabs, and that chaired a four-nation working group on the terms of their creation. King was unimpressed: Pearson "likes keeping Canada at the head of everything," he lamented in his diary, "in the forefront of connection with UN affairs." He did not mean it as a compliment.

But if King could not deter the energetic undersecretary's meddling in the Middle East, he put his foot down on an adventure on the other side of the world when Pearson agreed to an American request that Canada join the United Nations Temporary Commission on Korea, a nine-nation commission charged with unifying the peninsula—once occupied by Japan, now divided into American and Soviet zones of occupation—and arranging free elections. King ordered Pearson to tell President Harry Truman that Canada would not be on the committee. Pearson and St. Laurent hotly protested, but King prevailed. "Pearson, with his youth and inexperience, and influenced by the persuasion of others around him, had been anxious to have Canada's External Affairs figure prominently in world affairs, and has really directed affairs in New York [at the UN] when he should have been in Ottawa, and without any real control by Ministers of the Crown," King complained.[4]

But by the summer of 1948, King was no longer Liberal leader, St. Laurent was preparing to become prime minister, and Pearson was the golden boy, recognized and feted around the world for his tireless energy and diplomatic skill.

III

On September 24, 1945, Edna Diefenbaker entered the Homewood Sanitorium in Guelph, a private facility for people with addictions and mental health issues. She entered voluntarily, after consultations with her doctor in Saskatoon and a specialist in Toronto. Both John and Edna's brother Jack were mystified by her condition. She worried obsessively about her hair falling out, and about losing her figure, although obviously there was more to it than that. All parties agreed that a period of private treatment offered the best hope for improvement.

Despite public education campaigns, far too many people today still view mental illness through a lens of shame or ignorance. In the 1940s, the stigma was far, far greater. John was embarrassed by his wife's illness, becoming evasive whenever anyone asked where Edna was, and was doubtless far from being the supportive, understanding husband she needed. The doctors said his wife required treatment at a sanitorium; very well. The doctors advised that electroconvulsive therapy offered the best hope for a cure; very well. Though she entered voluntarily, Edna quickly came to loathe Homewood, abhorred the doctors and the drugs she was forced to take, and was soon begging John to let her come home. "This is just a place for people who can afford to keep their relations out of mental hospitals," she wrote her husband in a letter almost incoherent in its desperation. " . . . if you don't come—I'm going to leave I'll try home Ottawa or any place but there is nothing conducive to health here they are really tough, John. . . . Please tell me you will come soon otherwise I'll go clean crazy and disgrace you. . . . Come soon & try & find if I can have shock and get well."[5] But he followed the doctors' advice and insisted she stay. Without treatment, he was advised, her "obsession" over her looks, her problems at home and with her husband would get worse.

Diefenbaker missed Edna, was lonely without her. He was as relieved as she when he visited the sanitorium for the last time, March 26, 1946, to take her home. But she was bitter, and on the train ride back to Prince Albert accused him of forcing her to undergo useless and painful procedures. He, in return, insisted he had only done what medical professionals recommended. And he told her a remarkable story. His ancient political rival, Jimmy Gardiner, former Liberal premier in Saskatchewan and now

Mackenzie King's minister of agriculture, approached John in the parliamentary dining room, the sixth-floor restaurant where MPs, senators, and journalists ate well, with the taxpayer footing much of the bill. He had heard that Edna was receiving treatment and urged John to make sure she got the best of care. His own wife had recently committed suicide upon learning that their son, missing in action, had been confirmed dead. Diefenbaker's hated political foe broke down in tears as they talked. Edna said then, and often, that if political husbands "would stop for a moment" and consider the needs of their wives, life would be better for all concerned.[6]

In public they were happy, and there was some element of happiness privately, as well, now that they were together again. They rejected one ridiculous piece of medical advice: that Edna have a child so that she could devote her energies to it. John was fifty and she was forty-six and in menopause. (The doctors must have been referring to adoption.) They did agree to another recommendation: leave the Château Laurier and find an apartment so that Edna would feel more at home when in Ottawa.

But at root, each of them wanted what the other could not give. John was lonely in Ottawa, isolated even from some members of his own caucus. They found him arrogant and pushy; he found them lazy and far too content with life in opposition. He wanted a companion who would make him the focus of her life without interfering in his political work, someone to look after the house and offer moral support whenever needed, and physical companionship whenever he needed that, too. Edna was willing to offer that support, but she had come to hate the back-biting world of Ottawa and often remained in Prince Albert. "If I were well enough to go somewhere and get away from worry and too much responsibility but [Ottawa] isn't the place," she wrote him in February of 1947. "I have such an inferiority complex over myself with everyone down there looking their best. I just can't face it."[7] She cried when John turned down an offer to become legal counsel for a large company at five times his parliamentary salary. She dreamed of escaping Prince Albert and Mary's domineering presence, of a comfortable home and life in Toronto or Montreal or Vancouver. But John wanted none of that. He was devoted to his wife, his mother, and his life as a politician, but not in that order. Things were destined to continue as before, each of them trying to find whatever happiness they could.

The 1945 election had not been entirely disastrous for the Tories. There was new blood on the opposition benches, many of them veterans from the war: First Lieutenant Donald Fleming, a sharp-tongued former Toronto city councillor; Major E. Davie Fulton, a British Columbia lawyer; J.M. (Jim) Macdonnell, a businessman from Toronto who had been awarded the Military Cross; veteran officers George Pearkes and Cecil Marritt, both of whom had won the Victoria Cross; and the Calgary oilman A.L. Smith. Many of the new crew gravitated to Diefenbaker, despite his unpopularity with much of the rest of the caucus. For both Diefenbaker and the rookies, the party was too beholden to Toronto business interests and too tempted to make common cause with the Union Nationale in Quebec, two forces that pushed the party to the right. Diefenbaker was progressive in outlook, Western in orientation, populist in his bones. And he had become a perpetual thorn in the side of the Liberals, who were evolving from a conventional political party into an institution of government. That institution was comfortable with control: over finances, infrastructure, social policy, business. A professional, managerial class had emerged in Ottawa to help win the war; why not let the same men, exercising the same, centralized, authority manage the peace? Why could government not direct the economy and society in ways that would maximize efficiency and prosperity? Because, Diefenbaker argued from the other side of the House, left hand on hip, right hand jabbing the air, Canada was a parliamentary democracy, with individual and collective liberties that the Liberals were trampling underfoot. He stormed in opposition even as the Grits set about building post-war Canada with little concern for anyone who might object to their methods.

The King government, which had been embarrassed by the Gouzenko revelations, worried about the possibility of communist subversion in the public service. The Liberals responded by convening a secret commission comprised of two Supreme Court judges, who investigated allegations of communist infiltration. Fourteen men were arrested and held without benefit of counsel, a clear violation of their civil rights but permitted under the War Measures Act, which was still in force. Other arrests and charges followed. Diefenbaker was a sworn foe of communism, but he told the House, "I do not believe the minds of liberty-loving Canadians, however much they hate communism, have become so apathetic" as to accept the suspension of habeas corpus. It was time, he argued, "for a declaration of liberties to be made by this parliament . . . a bill of rights, under which freedom of religion, of speech, of association . . . freedom from capricious arrest and freedom under the rule of law, should be made part and parcel of the law of the country." It was a theme that he would return to time and again. "It was," said Denis Smith, "a subject that suited his individualism, his sense of tradition, his sympathy for the voiceless, and his rhetorical genius."[8] And he believed it, too.

Along with that belief came less sound ideas, though ideas that were obvious and necessary for an opposition conservative party. Taxes and deficits were both too high, he believed, and the autocratic "What's a million?" C.D. Howe too willing to spend public money in place of relying on private enterprise. But government investments were needed at war's end to prevent recession during demobilization, and Howe was committed to restoring the private economy as swiftly as possible. Diefenbaker's calls for liberty were right and just at a time when the Liberals were far too willing to suspend those liberties in the interests of national security. But his economic policies would have done more harm than good.

John Bracken was finished as leader of the Progressive Conservatives. The cabal of Toronto and Montreal business interests that controlled the party had never been comfortable with a Westerner as leader, and they weren't ready to let him have another run at the prize. Besides, they had a much more attractive candidate, one with a proven record as a winner: Ontario premier George Drew.

Drew was born into a political family: his grandfather sat behind John A. Macdonald in Canada's first Parliament. Born and raised in Guelph, Drew stood out at Upper Canada College—a tall and handsome youth who seemed to attract the word "patrician." Wounded in the First World War, he rose to the rank of lieutenant colonel in peacetime and liked to be called Colonel Drew. He was hot-headed and anti-union, but as leader of the Ontario Conservatives in 1943, he narrowly defeated the Liberals on a program of public spending on health care and education. He governed, successfully, as a fiscally responsible progressive, a pattern that the Ontario Progressive Conservatives would follow for four successful decades. But Drew's eyes were always fixed on Ottawa, and when Bracken announced he was stepping down in 1948, at the same time Mackenzie King resigned as Liberal leader, Drew's name was immediately, if unofficially, in the ring. So was John Diefenbaker's.

His determination bordered on the perverse. Diefenbaker had already run once for the leadership, when it was clear he had little hope of winning. Now he was about to do it again. Drew was heavily favoured to win. The Chief, as his closest supporters were already calling Diefenbaker, had little hope. He recognized the odds but threw his hat in anyway. Why?

Principally, because he had become the leader of the unofficial opposition within the official opposition, and so was bound to run. Diefenbaker was a for-the-little-guy populist within a party anchored in Bay Street and St. James Street; a Westerner in a party that looked on his region as an underdeveloped fiefdom of Central Canada. And he was comfortable running as an underdog, happily tilting against establishment windmills even as his personal sense of destiny convinced him he one day would prevail.

He campaigned across the country, with David Walker, a Toronto lawyer who had become a close friend, managing the national campaign. Diefenbaker knew he was strong in Saskatchewan and Manitoba, and felt optimistic about his chances in British Columbia and Ontario. But Drew's forces owned Quebec, Alberta, and the Maritimes and were strong in Ontario as well. Diefenbaker's message to the party faithful stressed the evils of communism but also the monopolistic practices of big business, which "if not eliminated, will destroy free business enterprise for the many."[9] The October convention at Ottawa's drab Coliseum was a considerably rowdier affair than the staid coronation for Louis St. Laurent that the Liberals had held in the same venue a few weeks before. Again, Diefenbaker's name came in for criticism; the *Ottawa Citizen* wrote an editorial lamenting that he "has felt impelled to deny that he is of German origin. As it happens, Mr. Diefenbaker is of Dutch descent, and a fourth-generation Canadian at that."[10] He wasn't of Dutch descent, though it should hardly have mattered. But the result was foreordained in any case: Drew, on the first ballot, with 827 of 1,242 votes; Diefenbaker trailing badly with 314; also-ran Donald Fleming with 104.

By December, Drew was in the House, representing the riding of Carleton, just west of Ottawa. Eschewing the traditional non-partisanship of an Opposition leader's first speech in Parliament, Drew lit into the Liberals for, as he saw it, violating the rights and liberties of the provinces, and lit into the public service, which to him was a haven for communists. "Make no mistake about it," he told the House, "we are fighting for personal and economic freedom in Canada today. We are in a very real danger of losing that fight to the bureaucrats who accept the basic philosophy of Karl Marx no matter what political name they adopt." Since the Liberal government and the federal public service were increasingly becoming indistinguishable, Drew might as well have been calling Louis St. Laurent a Red.

Drew's accusation was outrageous, and it outraged the Liberal front bench. After the speech, St. Laurent rose to his feet, demanding Drew offer proof of his wild claims. The Conservative leader had none. Unlike U.S. senator Joseph McCarthy—who waved a sheet of paper that he alleged contained the names of communists within the State Department, though he had no such list—Drew had not considered that he could simply lie, could assert evidence without having any. To any reasonable observer, he looked like a fool; his debut in Parliament was an embarrassment.

An election was due in 1949, which St. Laurent called for June 27. Could the Liberals be defeated? It certainly seemed possible. A man with no political lineage who had been plucked from Quebec's corporate and political establishment to serve as King's lieutenant for French Canada, with no natural ties to English Canada, led a party that had been in power since 1935. The Liberals could reasonably be accused of arrogance so great that they no longer recognized the difference between the party and the government. Likewise, the public service in Ottawa had become so accustomed to serving Liberal politicians that it was difficult to discern where one ended and the other began. Most dangerous was an erosion of respect for the importance of individual rights if they conflicted with Ottawa's agenda. And beyond all that, as *Maclean's* observed, "the great intangible is the public's sheer weariness of the Liberal Government. Even some of the Liberals' own backbenchers sometimes feel that they've been in power long enough."[11]

"Time for a change"—accompanied by a progressive, pragmatic fiscal and social agenda that mirrored what he had delivered as premier—could have been Drew's campaign theme. And his platform did offer expanded health care, unemployment insurance, and social security. But all that came after the section that would make it illegal to support communism. "In the name of freedom we do not intend to permit treacherous, anti-Christian agents of that evil tyranny to destroy the freedom for which Canadians paid so great a price," the platform declared.[12] Anti-communist sentiment ran high in the United States, where Secretary of State Dean Acheson had been publicly embarrassed by defending his friend and colleague Alger Hiss against accusations of being a spy for the Soviets. Hiss was a spy, as it turned out, and people worried about how many other moles had infiltrated government, and whether even Acheson and other Democratic leaders could be trusted. But the red-under-every-bed anti-communist fervor was less intense in Canada. Besides, Drew's promise of sweeping tax cuts contradicted his promise of increased spending.

Fighting once again to hold Lake Centre, which the Liberals had tried to gerrymander into a seat they could win, Diefenbaker found the campaign materials from headquarters so useless that he dumped them in the lake. Beyond that came the question of personality. St. Laurent had already begun developing an attractive political persona: Uncle Louis, the kind, compassionate, grandfatherly leader, perhaps a bit staid for such dynamic times, but highly capable and surrounded by younger, energetic men who benefited from his wisdom. Drew came across as aloof, out of touch—patrician.

Though Drew had hoped Maurice Duplessis would come to his aid in Quebec, that was never likely. For one thing, the Progressive Conservative leader was openly biased against the French, condemning the baby bonus as a scheme to promote larger French families. Duplessis might have overlooked such things, if the Conservatives had a realistic hope of defeating the Liberals. But they didn't, and the wily premier had no intention of wasting political capital on a lost cause. Besides, the Liberals loved it when Conservatives courted the Quebec boss. "In 1949 and 1953, the favorite campaign photographs of Liberal newspapers were shots of Drew and Duplessis beaming at each other," Blair Fraser wrote in *Maclean's*. "The cordiality between the Conservatives and the Union Nationale was just warm enough to alienate voters in other provinces, but not enough to win any in Quebec."[13]

For the Tories, election night was a disaster. The Liberals carried 193 ridings, a huge landslide. Drew's Progressive Conservatives were reduced to forty-one seats, a loss of twenty-four. In every province outside Ontario, the party held only one or two or three seats. (The night was also a debacle for the CCF, which lost more than half its seats, falling from twenty-eight to thirteen.)

The Conservatives had become trapped in a politically fatal vortex of their own making. The execution of Louis Riel and the fights over conscription in the two wars had rendered the party unelectable in French Quebec. Liberal immigration policies had filled the Prairies with Eastern Europeans, who were either Catholic or Orthodox, entrenching the Liberal reputation for both religious and ethnic (so long as those ethnicities were European) tolerance. This left the Conservatives with nothing but their Protestant English base, anchored in Toronto, whose residents were still mostly British—almost every mayor of Toronto between 1850 and 1950 belonged to the Orange Lodge—along with rural Ontario and English enclaves in Quebec. It also left the party with a well-deserved reputation for loyalty toward the British Empire and hostility to almost everything else. The party was also seen as sympathetic to the big business interests of Bay Street and St. James Street, though in truth corporate Canada got on fine with the Liberals. And the Conservatives' only strategy for breaking out of this weakening base—for Toronto was becoming less British by the year as immigrants from Italy and Portugal and other parts of Southern and Eastern Europe started to arrive—was to seek common cause with nationalists in Quebec. But this never worked, for as much as those nationalists despised the Liberals, they knew in their hearts that the Tories despised them just as much.

Nonetheless, despite the electoral shellacking he had received, Drew's hold on the leadership was secure, because he was solidly in control of the party's Ontario base. Diefenbaker, again the lone Tory in Saskatchewan, had no prospects of advancement. He was an outsider in a party that had been overwhelmingly rejected. Edna's health, both physical and mental, was precarious. He was at a low ebb that was about to get lower.

IV

However ambivalent the attitude of Mike Pearson toward the querulous, vain, and hesitant Mackenzie King, the prime minister was quite impressed with Pearson's "very quick intelligence and a most pleasant manner."[14] Yes, he chafed at the undersecretary's ambition: Pearson's constant efforts to project Canada on the world stage conflicted with King's isolationist instincts, and the department's insistence of acquiring "palatial" embassy residences in major capitals for Canada's ambassadors offended the prime minister's penny-pinching sensibilities. But King recognized the abilities of Robertson, Wrong, Reid, et al., and in Pearson he recognized something more: the qualities of a fine politician. As far back as October 1946, he confided to his diary that in a conversation about the future of the party with *Winnipeg Free Press* journalist Grant Dexter—such exchanges were common back then—King had speculated that "if Pearson could be brought into public life, he would make the best of any successor to myself," though this "was something only the future can settle."[15] He had mentioned the possibility to Pearson during a carriage ride in Paris that year, though at the time the undersecretary insisted that he wished to remain in the public service. The truth was that Pearson didn't believe he could tolerate sitting at any cabinet table chaired by King.

Although St. Laurent succeeded King as leader of the Liberal Party on August 7, 1948, King clung to the prime ministership until November, and no one pressed the issue. During the interval, St. Laurent confided to King his intention to make Lester Pearson his secretary of state for external affairs. King in his response was at his very best. The prime minister was indignant with Pearson over his peremptory assertion of Canadian foreign policy in the Korean affair, and Pearson had not hidden his disappointment when King flirted with, and then abandoned, a possible free trade agreement with the United States. But King was as convinced about Pearson's political future in 1948 has he had been in 1946. When St. Laurent mooted Pearson for External, King noted in his diary, "I favoured that very strongly," adding, "My own view, though I did not express it, is if Pearson does come in, he will succeed St. Laurent when he gives up the leadership, whether in government or in opposition."[16] King may have been ill and weakening, but he could still read political tea leaves like none other.

If he was going to enter cabinet, Pearson needed to win a seat in a by-election. St. Laurent wondered if the career diplomat had it in him, but King observed, "that is the real test of the man."[17] Pearson had his own concerns, mostly financial. His public service pension would be meagre and a life in politics would be financially precarious. But those concerns were taken care of at a dinner hosted by Walter and Liz Gordon, when Walter promised he would ensure Mike and Maryon were financially secure. One of Mike's closest friends, Gordon was a partner in the accounting firm of Clarkson, Gordon and Company. He set up a trust fund that took care of the Pearsons' financial future. (Such an arrangement today would end any politician's career if it were discovered.)

Pearson liked to portray himself as an innocent who stumbled through his career, being drafted or cajoled into joining the public service, advancing through its ranks through "hard work and long hours,"[18] and making himself available for any task, no matter how daunting. But he was as ambitious as he was capable. If he lacked the intellectual depth of Hume Wrong and Norman Robertson, he possessed the much more marketable skill of being liked by people who had the power to advance his career. He was charming, witty, industrious, trustworthy: qualities that served him well at Oxford and through his years at External. Such skills were readily transferable to the political arena. Also, he was famous in a way no Canadian had been famous before: as a skilled diplomat who had made a vital contribution to the creation of at least two new United Nations agencies, as a negotiator who participated in the talks that helped give birth to Israel, and as a representative of Canada who was respected in Washington, London, and the UN. He had gone about as far as it was possible to go as a public servant. The next logical step was to progress from undersecretary to secretary at External Affairs, from bureaucrat to politician. With the federal public service and the Liberal government practically one and the same, the transition seemed natural.

This was also the time that people began noticing the difficulty they had in reading Mike Pearson. He had developed the affability shell characteristic of many politicians: friendly with all, impenetrable to most. This carapace is a necessary tool for anyone expected to listen to differing points of view with empathy, knowing that their decision will disappoint at least one side. In Pearson's case, the shell appeared to evolve as he transitioned from public service to public office. The prominent public servant Arnold Heeney noted in 1955, "LBP in fine form. . . . He continues to be consistently vigorous and interested and stimulating and cheerful, but over the years, although consistently friendly and satisfactory with me, he is increasingly impersonal—a deep one whose secret self very few if any can know."[19]

Pearson confessed to Gordon that the fifty-something public servant didn't know if he could take the rough and tumble of political life. But Gordon noted in his memoirs, "Everyone seemed to like him; he had hosts of friends and, as far as he knew, no enemies."[20] Gordon told his friend that only he could determine whether his hide was thick enough for political life, but that since he placed such great store in creating a new North Atlantic alliance, he could do it better as minister than as deputy minister. A few days later, Pearson phoned to say that King had arranged for him to run in a by-election in Algoma East, to be held October 28. "I do not believe either of us knew where Algoma East was," Gordon recalled. "Mike said it was somewhere in Northern Ontario."

The vast riding stretched from Manitoulin Island to the CNR transcontinental line and from Sudbury to Sault Ste Marie: thirty-two thousand square kilometres of rocks and lakes and boreal forest far removed from the pastoral towns of Southern Ontario that Lester Pearson grew up in. But it was reliably Liberal: Tom Farquhar had held it with two-to-one margins over hapless Conservative challengers since 1935. He was happy to step aside for the new secretary of state for external affairs, especially with a Senate appointment as compensation. King called a by-election, and Farquhar obligingly escorted the Liberal candidate through the riding, encouraging him to wave at every passer-by as the two cruised along Highway 17, until Pearson waved at a farmer only to have Farquhar advise, "You can stop waving now; we're out of the constituency." To further cement Pearson's fortunes, Louis St. Laurent showed up at a church basement gathering on Manitoulin Island, as English and Orange a locale as you could find. But the Liberal leader had a splendid time, and so did the crowd. Though she hated the idea of her husband becoming a public figure, Maryon joined Mike as they travelled Highway 17 and the side roads of the riding, shaking hands and chatting amiably with constituents. The preacher's son had no difficulty in casual conversations with local folk, though large crowds would prove more of a challenge. In any case, the Conservatives didn't run a candidate, and Pearson cruised to an easy victory, one of eight he would enjoy in that riding.

Although King was still prime minister, St. Laurent chaired Pearson's first cabinet meeting as minister for external affairs. He was late, something rare for him, and St. Laurent was speaking as he entered. The former secretary for external affairs waved his successor to a seat at the bottom of the table. It was an inauspicious start, but things rapidly improved. As foreign affairs minister, Pearson enjoyed something rarely granted to his successors: a dynamic and coherent foreign policy, one he had helped shape. That policy has come down to us today through the Gray Lecture that St. Laurent gave at the University of Toronto when he was secretary of state in January 1947. But that famous address cast Canadian foreign policy within the context of the struggle for national unity: St. Laurent was well aware of how the conscription crises had torn the country apart. As a bureaucrat, and as someone who had been outside Canada more often than in it over the past three decades, Pearson had no such concerns, and his very-similar address, delivered twelve months later, more purely distills the philosophy of the time. As the historian Adam Chapnick observed, "If any speech from the period truly focused on Canada's international role, this was clearly the one."[21]

In remarks that could not have pleased Mackenzie King, Pearson spoke of Canada's "negative, timid policy" toward the League of Nations and collective security in the 1930s, and the constant and continuing fear that London and Washington would fall out, leaving Canada the abandoned child of feuding parents. But whereas the United States had been outside the League, now not only was the U.S. in the UN, but the UN was literally headquartered in the U.S., in New York. Beyond that, the fact that war could now be "annihilative" and that there was "no security in distance" required Canada to work with like-minded nations to prevent it. Finally, "subversive, aggressive communism" yoked to a "Slav empire" represented an existential threat to Canada's freedom and to the freedom of all democracies.

Canada should respond to these challenges, Pearson said, by maintaining a foreign policy that was cooperative with, but independent from, both the U.K. and the U.S., offering "steady and consistent, firm but unprovocative resistance" to communist aggression or to aggression of any kind, while opposing "panicky and provocative measures when things deteriorate," to which the United States was wont to succumb.

Second, while recognizing that the new Cold War had fatally impaired the United Nations' ability to guarantee collective security, he argued that "within the U.N. there is no reason why free states, on a regional basis, should not form a security system, the members of which are willing to accept greater responsibilities for cooperative defence in the interest of greater security."[22] He was describing NATO, one year before Canada signed its charter as a founding member.

This country's role in the world had seldom, if ever, been so carefully considered and cogently expressed. But then the architects of this new foreign policy—St. Laurent and Pearson and Wrong and Robertson and Reid et al.—had been shaping it for years, in London and Washington and Ottawa throughout and after the war, as a newly sovereign Canada triangulated between the waning British and rising American empires, even as cooperation turned to confrontation with Soviet Russia. The principles laid out in Pearson's speech would guide Canadian foreign policy for a generation, as Canada worked behind the scenes to soothe Anglo-American discord, to defuse potential confrontations around the world, and, when back-channel diplomacy was not enough, to stand with the democracies in confronting Communist aggression.

That aggression was accelerating. On March 10, 1948, Foreign Minister Jan Masaryk, the last non-communist member of the Czech government, had been found dead in his pyjamas in the ministry's courtyard, having jumped or been pushed from a window. Post–Cold War investigations concluded he had been murdered, though the authorities at the time insisted the much-loved politician had committed suicide. The last flicker of liberty in Czechoslovakia died with him, as the Soviet Union continued its absorption of Eastern Europe. In June, Stalin blockaded West Berlin, hoping to starve it into submission. President Harry Truman responded with one of the greatest Western achievements of the Cold War: a logistically staggering airlift of supplies into the besieged city. At the height of the operation, American and British planes were reaching Berlin every thirty seconds. But one miscalculation on either side could bring on war.

Ernest Bevin, orphaned at six, a tough bear of a man with almost no formal schooling, had been fighting communists since his days with the Dockworkers Union in the 1920s. Now he was foreign minister in British prime minister Clement Attlee's Labour government, urging his European counterparts to band together for mutual protection from the Soviets. He convinced other European nations to sign the Brussels mutual defence treaty on March 17, 1948, seven days after Masaryk's death. But Bevin, who knew

Europe could not survive a Soviet attack without the Americans, also pushed for an Atlantic alliance. In this, he was echoing a Canadian initiative.

A year earlier, in the summer of 1947, in a speech at the Couchiching Conference and in a memo circulated within External Affairs, Escott Reid had argued for the need for the North Atlantic nations to "band together, under the leadership of the United States, to form 'a new regional security organization' to deter Soviet expansion."[23] A month later, St. Laurent had delivered a similar message at the United Nations. But the Canadian call for a North Atlantic alliance was ignored, until events in Europe pushed the major powers to take it up on their own. By the summer of 1948, talks were underway. Pearson both aided and hindered those talks.

King, in his final months in office, accepted the need for some kind of Atlantic security arrangement, though he approached the matter with none of Pearson's enthusiasm. "N.A. has more to attend to than it can attend to now," he complained to his diary.[24] But even the British and Americans lacked Pearson's grand vision for an organization that would promote economic and cultural as well as military cooperation, to present Europe and North America to the world—especially the developing world—as a prosperous, democratic, united, and robust alternative to communism. In talks in Washington that spring, Pearson argued that the new treaty "should not be exclusively military in character . . . there were economic and even spiritual defences against attack which should not be overlooked."[25] Not only were the Americans and British unimpressed with the idea of robust spiritual defence, the Canadians themselves were divided, with Hume Wrong as ambassador to Washington opposing anything other than a strictly military alliance. The Americans were always one step away from retreating into isolationism, and an alliance as entangled as Pearson envisioned it would send them running, Wrong feared.

Dean Acheson, as secretary of state, resisted Pearson's hopes for a comprehensive alliance, dismissing it as "typical Canadian moralizing." But when Canada warned it might not join the alliance if it were purely military, the Americans agreed to compromise, accepting Article 2, which pledges to promote democratic and economic cooperation. All sides ignored "the Canadian Article," as it was called, from the first day. Nonetheless, Pearson was euphoric at the signing ceremony in Washington on April 4, 1949. Canada had been instrumental in negotiating a new Atlantic security pact, which would become by far the world's most important and powerful military and political alliance of both the twentieth and early twenty-first centuries.

NATO and the Marshall Plan saved Western Europe. An increasingly well-fed population abandoned domestic communist parties, while American security guarantees deterred Soviet Russia. One month after the creation of NATO, Stalin abandoned the Berlin blockade. The prospect of yet another war in Europe, once so close that Truman had asked Congress to authorize the draft, receded.

Pearson was busy on other fronts as well. India had announced its intention to become a republic. But how could it then remain a member of the Commonwealth, with its shared acknowledgment of the British monarch as each member's head of state? At the Commonwealth prime ministers' conference of 1949, the association seemed on the brink of collapse. But Pearson, filling in for St. Laurent, engineered a compromise: all members, whatever their constitutional makeup, would recognize the British monarch as head of the Commonwealth. That compromise endures to this day.

The next year, at the Commonwealth Conference on Foreign Affairs in Colombo, Ceylon (today, Sri Lanka), Pearson and other foreign ministers agreed that wealthier countries should provide direct foreign aid to poorer states to prevent the spread of communism. At first, the idea seemed preposterous. Canada still had, for all intents and purposes, a whites-only immigration policy. Taxpayers would ask why their money was being diverted to programs best handled by missionaries and other charities. But he came around, and brought a skeptical cabinet around, though it took half a dozen meetings. (Pearson later said that negotiating peace in the Middle East was a piece of cake compared to convincing the St. Laurent government's cabinet to commit to foreign aid.) Such aid, he argued, was important in pushing back against communist advances in the region. And Canada would be making friends in the world outside the Great Power blocs. In any case, the richer countries of the North had a duty to aid the development of the emerging post-colonial South. Canada became a founding member of the Colombo Plan, which expanded beyond its Commonwealth roots.

———

In all of this, Canada's foreign affairs minister advanced his own and Canada's reputation abroad. Pearsonian diplomacy—he had become an adjective—involved friendly but persistent negotiations. It involved belonging to a web of international forums while remaining firmly within the Western alliance: America's closest ally, but no one's vassal. Often it involved Canada offering to mediate difficult situations, as a medium-sized country with no colonial past and no agenda other than to advance peace and collective security. But even Pearson could not have prevented war on the Korean peninsula.

At the end of the Second World War, Russia and the United States occupied Korea, which had been under Japanese occupation since 1910, dividing the country between them at the 38th parallel. Neither the new occupiers nor the Koreans themselves could decide on the shape of the new country. Nor were the Americans willing to hand their portion of the peninsula over to the Russians or their Korean clients. The commission that Canada was supposed to have been a part of until King vetoed the idea accomplished nothing. The Americans installed Syngman Rhee as ruler of the new Republic of Korea, with Seoul the capital, in 1948. The Soviets did the same in the north, with Pyongyang the capital and Kim Il-sung the leader. There were border clashes from the beginning. On June 25, 1950, with the tacit approval of the Russians, Kim's army crossed the 38th parallel, quickly overwhelming both the South Korean and American forces.

On the day of the invasion, Pearson and his acting undersecretary, Escott Reid, were at their cottages in the Gatineau Hills. Neither had a telephone, so when Pearson's assistant, Mary Macdonald, learned of the invasion from the CBC on the two o'clock news, she rowed out into the middle of the lake to tell Reid, and then drove to Pearson's cottage. Mary and Mike found a payphone at a general store, where he phoned St. Laurent, who was at his summer home in St. Patrick, Quebec. Caught flat-footed, the Canadians remained so in the days to come. Pearson did not think the Americans would commit to defending South Korea or that the UN would succeed where the League of Nations had failed. But there had been no American troops in Abyssinia, and the Soviet Union was a very different antagonist than Italy. Moreover, the Soviets were boycotting the Security Council, making collective action possible. On June 27, the Americans succeeded in getting the council to pass a resolution authorizing UN member states to take any action necessary "to repel the armed attack and to restore international peace and security to the area." The UN and North Korea were at war—though the polite term was "police action"—and Canada was part of that war.

Mackenzie King did not live to see Canada at arms once again. His health and his heart had been steadily failing. He suffered a massive heart attack on July 20, 1950, and died two days later. The state funeral was at St. Andrew's Cathedral, Ottawa, but he was laid to rest beside his parents in Mount Pleasant Cemetery, Toronto. With an ironic appropriateness beloved of historians, St. Laurent's cabinet, on the train ride back to Ottawa, decided to commit troops to Korea, something the old man would have agreed to only reluctantly, if at all.

The war lasted three years. The Americans and South Koreans were forced into a pocket in the southern tip of the peninsula, but rather than counterattack from there, General Douglas MacArthur brilliantly orchestrated an amphibious assault at Inchon, near Seoul, then recklessly pursued the retreating North Koreans across the border. That brought the Chinese into the fight, which became a stalemate along the 38th parallel. The numbers of civilian losses were horrifying: between seven and eight million in the two Koreas. A quarter of the population of North Korea might have been killed through American bombing, though the figures are uncertain.

Canada fought hard in the war. Twenty-seven thousand men served in the conflict; more than 500 died and 1,200 were wounded. The 25th Infantry Brigade, the heart of the expeditionary force, consisted of three infantry battalions and two armoured squadrons. The Battles of Kapyong, Hill 355, Kowang San, and Hill 187 are part of this nation's military lore, though even Canadians familiar with Passchendaele or the Falaise Gap may not know their names. Canada had ended the Second World War with, and still retained, one of the world's largest navies, which included an aircraft carrier. During the war, Canada assumed much of the responsibility for patrolling the North Atlantic.

The Korean War was a stalemate, the first of several American ventures in Asia that ended in frustration or worse. Dean Acheson, Lester Pearson, and those around them were Atlanticists; they were descended from

Europeans, and many had gone to English universities. Americans and Canadians lived and breathed the culture and politics and struggles of Europe. But they knew next to nothing of the culture and politics and struggles of Eastern Asia, of China and Korea and Vietnam. The Americans would pay a high price for that ignorance.

Pearson may have known the limits of Western power in Asia better than his American counterparts. In what became known as "quiet diplomacy," Canada stood with the U.S. throughout the war, while in private expressing misgivings about UN forces crossing the 38th parallel and urging the Americans to come to terms with Communist China. Acheson rejected these entreaties from his old—by now, really former—friend, and became increasingly irritated at what he considered to be the insufferably sanctimonious attitude of the Canadians. For their part, the Canadians tried to work with the British to restrain the American juggernaut, with its vast power but limited experience. Meanwhile, Canada accelerated its commitment to NATO as tensions increased, flashpoints multiplied, and war seemed as inevitable as it was inconceivable.

V

In 1947, the Diefenbakers moved into a larger house in Prince Albert, a mock Tudor affair in the comfortable enclave of West Hill, overlooking the downtown. Furnishing it offered Edna a diversion from the loneliness she felt when John was away in Ottawa. By 1948, she was well enough to accompany him to the capital. They found an apartment in Centretown, a few blocks south of the Château, which allowed Edna to entertain guests: tea or bridge parties with the ladies, intimate meals with friends, sometimes even a big do. She appears to have gotten over her inferiority complex about being seen in the capital. Friends of the Diefenbakers described her as animated, cheerful, gregarious, a delightful host, fun to be around. She accompanied her husband faithfully on his constituency rounds, boasted to anyone who would listen of the wonderful work he was doing in Ottawa, carried on as the Edna of old. But there must have been tensions behind the scenes. In February 1950, Diefenbaker made inquiries about the famous Battle Creek Sanitarium, founded in Michigan in 1866 by the leaders of the Seventh Day Adventist Church. It appears that he was also visiting Olive Freeman at this time. He had courted her when he was single, but she was too young then and the family moved away. But Mary wrote to John that she had received a note from "Ollie," who was now living in Toronto. "I knew where you would be, last weekend," she wrote her son, "when she told me where she was."[26] Did Edna visit Battle Creek? Was John having an affair? Were the rumours that Edna was seeing other men true? We don't know. We do know that people began to notice that Edna seemed tired at times. Others were surprised by how much she had aged. Her mother Maren told a friend that "Edna's blood is just not right" and that she was giving her daughter eggnog to improve it.[27] Edna said she just needed to get away from Saskatchewan (and Mary) and back to Ottawa for the opening of Parliament.

They had only been in Ottawa three weeks when the couple travelled to Washington, D.C., for a rare outside-of-Canada meeting of the Canadian Bar Association. While they were there, Edna consulted a specialist. She was warned she might have leukemia. Edna seemed relatively strong and happy as they took the train back to Saskatoon. John was scheduled to attend a conference in New Zealand that began November 24. They agreed that after the conference he would briefly visit Australia and that she would meet him in Hawaii for a vacation. Edna was excited by the prospect of such a glamorous adventure. But as John prepared to fly to Honolulu, he received a telegram urging him to return to Canada at once. He arrived in Prince Albert on December 22, where two doctors met him at the station. Edna was gravely ill and needed to be admitted to St. Paul's hospital in Saskatoon for tests.

Diefenbaker was distraught. "I can't go on without her. She is so brave," he told friends.[28] Living without her "is beyond my imagination." Their marriage, like so many, had had its difficulties. But John and Edna Diefenbaker loved each other, and the thought of losing her devastated him.

In December 1950, Alfred Atherton, father of Jack Atherton, the young operator charged with manslaughter in the deaths from the CNR train crash, came to Edna's room. She had been on a train heading west on the day of the crash, and feared that a friend of hers might have been in the wreck. The friend wasn't, but Edna, like many, suspected the Atherton boy was being set up to protect more senior figures. Alfred had asked Diefenbaker to take the case, but he declined, citing his parliamentary duties and his wife's illness. Now the father, desperate to protect his son, was in Edna's hospital room pleading with her to convince her husband. He succeeded. "I think that the company is trying to shift the blame onto that poor young man," Edna told John. Diefenbaker thought so too, but he was not a member of the British Columbia bar, and he did not want to leave his wife. Edna asked him to take the case for her sake. He agreed.

Get-well wishes poured in, from Ottawa as well as from across the Prairies. Paul Martin, the minister of health, was deeply fond of Edna and consulted specialists to see if there was anything more that could be done. Tommy Douglas, now premier of Saskatchewan, called her every day, or as often as the doctors and nurses allowed. John stayed by her side. People visiting her the night before she died found him with a comb and mirror, helping to fix her hair. She died in his arms on the morning of February 7, 1951.

Reporters loved Edna Diefenbaker. One called her "the unelected member of Parliament." There were warm tributes in the Ottawa papers. Saskatoon's First Baptist Church was packed to the rafters at her funeral. Her coffin was buried deep in the family plot of Woodlawn Cemetery in Saskatoon, so that John's could one day rest on top of hers. John grieved deeply. "How will I go on without her?" he wept at the funeral.[29] But he had made a promise, and the Atherton trial would begin soon.

After paying the fifteen-dollar fee, Diefenbaker was admitted to the bar of British Columbia. The preliminary hearing began March 13, a little more than a month after Edna's death. Another lawyer had prepared the case: conducting interviews, attending the inquest, researching railway regulations. Diefenbaker took over in the packed Prince George courtroom. He elicited testimony from railway workers that exonerated Atherton: fadeouts on the phone line were common and may have caused the young man not to hear the crucial instruction about the siding. The call was monitored, and if Atherton had failed to repeat back the proper instructions, the mistake should have been caught by those listening in. But it was a classic Diefenbaker strategy to not only show grounds for reasonable doubt but to point to someone else as the true culprit. In this case, that someone was the Canadian National Railways.

That portion of the line was one of the most dangerous in British Columbia, the evidence showed, and yet the railway had failed to install an automated signal that would have prevented the crash. Almost all the deaths had occurred on cars with cheap wooden sides on the troop train; the other train had steel-sided cars that protected the passengers. For the hundreds of thousands of veterans of the Second World War, the lack of concern for the lives of troops from higher-ups rang a cruel bell.

At the trial in May, the deputy attorney general led for the Crown. "The CNR is not on trial here," protested Colonel Eric Pepler. "There is only one question here, was the accused guilty of criminal negligence, or was he not?"

"There could have been an indictment against CNR for lack of safety measures, but there was not," Diefenbaker shot back. "It was against my client."

As the defence pressed the fact that it was mostly servicemen in wooden cars who were killed in the crash, Pepler again objected: "We are not concerned with the death of soldiers."

"Oh, Colonel, oh!" Diefenbaker exclaimed. He probably won the case at that moment, despite the fact that several witnesses who worked for the railway had been much more forthcoming during the preliminary hearing than they were at trial. Why was that? One lineman confessed on the stand that the company's lawyers had gone over his testimony with him.

"He had been to 'school' since then," Diefenbaker told the jury, "been to CNR 'school' in Jasper, and the CNR brass were helping." By the end of his summation, Pepler was reduced to mumbling protests from his seat.

Diefenbaker asked the jury to send this message: "No small men shall be made goats by the strong or the powerful in this country."[30] There were railwaymen on that jury, and former servicemen. It took them forty minutes to acquit.

John Diefenbaker defended Jack Atherton soon after he had lost the wife he loved. Having twice failed to win the Conservative leadership, his political career seemed to be at a dead end. George Drew was firmly in control of the Conservatives, a party that had become comfortable in perpetual opposition—as content as the Liberals, it seemed, with the decades-old political status quo. He was fifty-five, and there didn't seem anywhere left to go.

But railwaymen, veterans, and workers across the country took a lesson from the Atherton trial. There was one politician in Ottawa who cared about them, one man who had their backs, who went into a courtroom and proved that it was the owners, not the workers, whose arrogance and negligence put lives at risk. John Diefenbaker always came to the defence of the little guy. The little guys wouldn't forget.

SIX

Oil and Gas

(1952–1956)

I

The Israeli paratroopers dropped into the Mitla Pass, a strategic bottleneck in the Negev desert fifty-six kilometres east of the Suez Canal. When darkness fell, French airplanes resupplied the paratroopers and the four columns of the Israel Defense Forces that were crossing the Sinai Desert behind them with everything from Jeeps to cigarettes. The French had picked up the supplies from the British base at Cyprus. Gamal Abdel Nasser, Egypt's president, was watching his five-year-old son blow out the candles on his birthday cake when an aide brought word that Israeli troops were in the Sinai. He left quickly, telling his wife he had to go to a meeting.

Nasser was bewildered. The Israeli invasion made no sense, unless the British or French were behind it. But that made no sense either. Yes, the British were upset over his decision to nationalize the Suez Canal, and the French were frustrated with his support for Algerian rebels. But talks to guarantee unrestricted access to the canal were going well at the United Nations, and how would an Israeli invasion of Egypt influence events in Algeria? Egypt's president had failed to calculate the real motive for the Israeli attack, who truly was behind it, and the endgame they had in mind.

The Suez Crisis of October 1956, which occurred days before an American presidential election and at a time when Russia was moving to brutally suppress a reformist government in Hungary, brought the world dangerously close to nuclear war. Lester Pearson's role in helping defuse that crisis would earn him the Nobel Peace Prize—a fitting capstone to his brilliant career as a diplomat, and yet another step, it seemed, in his inevitable ascent to the office of prime minister. At that moment, no one would have predicted events would take a more tortuous path.

II

Pearson sometimes wondered whether he was a good father to Geoffrey and Patricia. He had spent most of the Second World War either in London or Washington. After the war, he travelled constantly as a diplomat and minister. He missed Geoffrey's graduation from Trinity College School—Mike was at the 1945 San Francisco Conference that established the United Nations—and could only send a letter: "Your mother and I are proud, very proud, of what you have done," he wrote. "Parents—at least most parents—don't talk much—possibly not enough—about these things—and if I were with you I probably wouldn't be a notable exception. But I can at least write what would be more difficult to say, that you have made us both very happy and proud of the part you have played at school, and we both know you will keep up the good work at college and after."[1] On Patsy's twenty-first birthday, he wrote, "It's hard, and a little sad to think tomorrow you'll be 21. Why oh why did you have to grow up so quickly?"[2] The children didn't complain about his many absences. Both adored their father, even if they were sad to see so little of him. But growing up in boarding schools—Bishop Strachan, in Patsy's case—bred a sense of independence. Although Patsy went to Vic like her parents, Geoff broke his father's heart by attending Trinity College, the elitist Anglican enclave at University of Toronto one block west of Mike's beloved Victoria College. Both married very young. Geoffrey had met Landon Mackenzie when they were both at Trinity; in his second year at Oxford, they decided to marry. Mike urged his son to "wait for a time," but the two were wed on December 26, 1951, and were together until Geoffrey's death in 2008. In 1952, exercising his ministerial prerogative, Mike tipped Geoff off in advance that he had passed his foreign service exams. "You can stop worrying—you are on the list and fairly near the top. Congratulations. Good show, as we say at Oxford."[3] Patsy married a medical student, Walter Hannah, in 1950, and took up nursing, despite Maryon's protests.

The average age of people getting married was falling. Post-war affluence and the deep stigma of bastardy pushed couples to wed and to have babies early and often. The 1950s were defined by accelerating affluence, as millions of Canadians joined the new middle class: the husband commuting to a semi-skilled but well-paying job at a factory, or to an office in the city; the wife raising on average 3.7 children in a suburban home with central heating and maybe even a portable air conditioner in the bedroom. Home life had been transformed by technology: the electric refrigerator, the electric stove, the electric washer and dryer. And in the living room, a television. The new medium made its first appearance in Canada at Toronto's Canadian National Exhibition in 1938, but war put a stop to all that. After the war, though, TV took off in the United States, and Canadians living near the border—which was most of them—rigged antennas to capture the signal from Buffalo or Detroit or Seattle. The St. Laurent government decreed in 1949 that the public broadcaster, the Canadian Broadcasting Corporation in English and Radio-Canada in French, would operate television stations across the country. From the beginning, Canadians preferred American fare—*Howdy Doody*, *The Ed Sullivan Show*, *The Honeymooners*. But there was also *Hockey Night in Canada* with Foster Hewitt, and *Wayne and Shuster* and *Juliette*. *La famille Plouffe* in Quebec was a big hit. Some predicted that television would spell the end of movies, but each medium accommodated the other, with Hollywood going big—*The Ten Commandments*—or grittily small—*Blackboard Jungle*. A new, dissident beat started to pulse through pop culture. Beatnik poets rejected the suburban complacency of the 1950s, while white and Black musicians experimented with the fusion of gospel, jazz, country, and rhythm and blues, all of it accelerated by new technologies: the electric guitar and amplifier, the long-playing and 45-rpm record, hi-fidelity stereo.

In 1954, Bill Haley recorded "Rock Around the Clock," and nothing has been the same since.

The St. Laurent government surfed an economy that bounded from strength to strength. Canadian GDP doubled in the 1950s, as factories manufactured ships and airplanes for the Korean War, and then cars and television sets in the years of peace that followed. On February 13, 1947, after more than two thousand mostly fruitless attempts, a deeper-than-normal test in Leduc, Alberta, produced a gusher of oil and new prosperity for the province. Iron-ore production had increased fivefold. The Canadian dollar was even stronger than the American dollar, as raw materials flooded south to feed the United States' industrial maw, and tariffs protected branch-plant manufacturers. Though critics worried that Canadian culture was at risk of being absorbed by American books and radio and TV, and economic sovereignty surrendered to American investors, confidence in Canada had never been more robust. By act of Parliament, Canadian citizenship replaced British citizenship in 1947. After a contentious referendum, Newfoundland and Labrador had entered Confederation in 1949. That same year, the Supreme Court of Canada replaced Britain's Judicial Committee of the Privy Council as the ultimate appellate court for civil as well as criminal cases.

It was an age of miracles. Poliomyelitis had arrived in Canada in 1910, a virus that threatened children and young adults, especially, with paralysis and even death. Many recovered fully, but an estimated eleven thousand Canadians were left paralyzed by the disease between 1949 and 1954. In March 1953, Dr. Jonas Salk announced that he had successfully developed a polio vaccine, and within a few years the virus no longer stalked children, who were now also routinely being vaccinated for diphtheria, tetanus, and whooping cough. Childhood mortality rates were plunging and life expectancy steadily increasing. A man could be expected to live into his sixties, and a woman even longer, though about 55 per cent of men and 25 per cent of women smoked cigarettes, which a growing body of evidence linked to lung cancer.

Beneath it all lurked a fear unlike anything humanity had faced. John Hersey's powerful reporting in 1946 on the aftermath of Hiroshima—the *New Yorker* devoted an entire edition to the piece—brought home to everyone the devastation of the atomic explosion and radioactive fallout. That explosion was a mere foretaste of the apocalyptic hydrogen bomb, first tested by the United States on November 1, 1952, and by the Soviet Union three years later. The Hiroshima bomb wiped out everything and everyone within a 1.5-kilometre radius; a hydrogen bomb's reach was eight to sixteen kilometres. Both countries developed fleets of aircraft to deliver these city-killers, as they were called, to the other's cities and missile sites. Both were at work on developing ballistic missiles and thermonuclear weapons small enough to be carried on them. Both American president Dwight Eisenhower, who succeeded Harry Truman in 1953, and Nikita Khrushchev, who came to power that same year after the death of Josef Stalin, embraced nuclear arsenals, even as both realized that neither country could survive a nuclear war. Schoolchildren were taught to "duck and cover" at the first flash of a nuclear explosion, and the more ambitious and industrious adults constructed bomb shelters in their backyards. But everyone lived with the certain knowledge that a global thermonuclear exchange—a dry, technical term for the ultimate horror—would kill hundreds of millions, with a post-apocalyptic wasteland greeting the survivors.

It was the task of world leaders to prevent such a holocaust; in Canada, the job principally belonged to Louis St. Laurent's foreign minister, Lester B. Pearson, one of the world's best-known Canadians. Pearson had quietly, but unsuccessfully, campaigned to become secretary general of the United Nations in 1952, the same year he presided over the General Assembly, but the Russians once again said nyet; he was asked to become the first secretary general of the new North Atlantic Treaty Organization, but turned it down. There was an election coming, St. Laurent was turning seventy, and everyone knew that Pearson was a potential successor. There were rumours he would be shuffled out of External to give him experience in domestic policy. There were also rumours he wasn't much interested in domestic policy. In any event, he stayed where he was.

A cloud from Washington cast a lingering shadow, though. In August 1951, Elizabeth Bentley, who had defected from a Soviet spy ring, gave testimony before a secret congressional committee that implicated Pearson as a Soviet sympathizer or worse. According to Bentley, in the early 1940s, when Pearson was in Washington, he had passed on valuable information to Hazen Sise, an alleged communist who was working for Canada's

National Film Board in D.C. Sise, in turn, passed the "hush-hush" information to Bentley and others; she then transmitted the information to her Soviet handler. The FBI promptly opened a file on Pearson, and that file remained open until he retired from public life. Worse, for Pearson, word of Bentley's testimony leaked to the press. There were stories that fall in the *Washington Star*, the *Toronto Star*, and elsewhere. More than a decade later, FBI director J. Edgar Hoover would warn Attorney General Bobby Kennedy of "important security evidence" regarding the new Canadian prime minister.

It was all stuff and nonsense, of course. In the late 1940s, Pearson vehemently denounced the Soviet Union within cabinet, urging closer military cooperation with the United States. His 1948 speech on foreign policy contained not a whiff of appeasement. While some journalists and diplomats urged a realist approach to dealing with the Soviet empire, for Pearson the contest was ideological and implacable. The leader who contributed to the creation of NATO and spoke of the "spiritual . . . nature of the struggle against revolutionary communism" was working a pretty convincing cover if indeed he was a Soviet mole.[4] But conspiracy theorists, then and now, neither needed nor desired evidence to buttress their theories. Cold warriors in Canada were convinced the Liberals in particular were soft on communism at best and fellow travellers at worst. Even today, if you Google "Lester Pearson communist spy," you will find dark theories linking O.D. Skelton, Norman Robertson, Pearson, Pierre Trudeau, and others in speculative conspiracies.

Pearson's gossipy nature was probably to blame. Throughout his career, journalists marvelled at his indiscretions. He was hardly alone. A politician, a reporter, each with a drink in hand, the lowered voice, "between you and me . . . "—thus are front-page stories made.

Pearson had known Hazen Sise since the 1930s. The lanky young architect went to Europe to work in Le Corbusier's Paris office before joining Canadian physician Norman Bethune to serve the doomed Republican cause in the Spanish Civil War, where he drove an ambulance. Returning to Canada, he took a job at the National Film Board in Ottawa, before being transferred to Washington. Pearson found Sise, like all the passionate leftists of the 1930s, too ideologically intense for his taste, but that would not have stopped him from talking with him, the Canadian colony in Washington being even smaller in the 1940s than it is today. During the war, he had negotiated an entente with Fred Rose, a Communist Party leader and future MP, to secure the cooperation of Canadian communists for the war, and their release from internment. And Pearson had defended diplomat Herbert Norman, who was subjected to investigations by both Canadian and American security services in 1951. Neither side found anything incriminating, but the taint would endure and would later embroil Pearson in a far grimmer controversy involving Norman. Perhaps Pearson couldn't resist passing on a tidbit that Sise repeated, until the information made its way into Soviet hands. It wouldn't have been anything of real importance; Pearson knew better. And perhaps he hadn't said anything at all.

Two years later, a new controversy erupted when Pearson refused to allow Igor Gouzenko to testify before Senator Joe McCarthy's witch-hunting committee, which, in seeking to root out communists in D.C. and elsewhere, was routinely destroying the lives of public servants and Hollywood personalities. Gouzenko had already provided all the useful information that he could, Pearson reasoned. The former Russian spy had a book coming out and was seeking publicity. By testifying, he might damage the reputations of innocent victims. Some Americans had been suspicious of Pearson ever since Elizabeth Bentley's testimony. His refusal to cooperate with McCarthy's committee poisoned his reputation among better-dead-than-red types. Colonel Robert S. McCormick, publisher of the *Chicago Tribune*, characterized Pearson, with typical understatement, as "the most dangerous man in the English-speaking world."[5] In the midst of the furor, late in November 1953, the Progressive Conservative Party's critic for external affairs rose in the House of Commons in defence of the minister across the way. The American attack on the secretary of state for external affairs was an attack on Canada's sovereignty, he maintained. Pearson was so grateful for the support that he sent Diefenbaker a note of appreciation. Pearson considered Diefenbaker an able and responsible critic. In that period, at least, each viewed the other with respect.

None of these shadowy allegations in any way tarnished Pearson's reputation with Canadians in the leadup to the 1953 election. That election may have been the most pro forma in Canadian history. Despite the lacklustre performance of the Conservatives under George Drew, the former Ontario premier remained entrenched as leader, bolstered by business interests in Toronto and Montreal. Dalton Camp, a rising young star in the advertising industry, and in Progressive Conservative circles in the Maritimes, came on board briefly, but was off the campaign before election day. "The Progressive Conservative Party was in a state of ruin," Camp wrote years later. The party ran behind both the Liberals and the CCF in the West, and the Liberals commanded more than two thirds of the vote in Quebec. It was "hopelessly outmanned, outmanoeuvered and outclassed," its leadership "made up of amiable and elderly mediocrities."[6] The centrepiece of the Conservative campaign platform was a promised five-hundred-million-dollar tax cut. The Liberals pounced: George Drew wanted to help out his business friends by cutting funding for schools and hospitals and pensions and wharf repairs. On election day, August 10, the Tories were once again decimated: thirty-three of their fifty-one seats were in Ontario. In British Columbia they took three seats; in every other province, only one or two. Algoma, of course, returned Lester B. Pearson, secretary of state for external affairs, to Parliament as part of the fifth consecutive Liberal government. Everyone in Ottawa wondered whether he would lead the Liberal Party in the next election.

III

Diefenbaker barely survived the federal election of 1953. George Drew's Bay Street business-friendly agenda had so little appeal to Prairie farmers that Diefenbaker insisted that he have control over all campaign materials for Saskatchewan. The Progressive Conservative campaign in the province was a campaign to save John Diefenbaker's seat, nothing more and nothing less. His old nemesis Jimmy Gardiner, still the Liberal party boss in the province, had so gerrymandered Lake Centre during redistribution that the riding was now virtually unwinnable for a Conservative. Diefenbaker's friends convinced him that his best hope lay in once again seeking the nomination in Prince Albert, where the Liberal incumbent, Francis Helme, had decided not to run again. It took some convincing. He had already lost twice in that riding, and "third time's a charm" is just a saying. But Diefenbaker was far better known now, and he wouldn't be contesting the seat against an incumbent prime minister, as he had in 1926 with King. In April 1953, he finally made the switch, assisted by a smoothly prepared nomination campaign that even manufactured the illusion of all-party support. Still, victory was far from certain in Mackenzie King's old riding, which had gone Liberal or CCF—Edward LeRoy Bowerman had defeated Mackenzie King in the riding in 1945, forcing him yet again to find a friendly seat in a by-election—in every contest since 1925. Diefenbaker campaigned flat-out—when other MPs travelled to London to witness the coronation of the young Queen Elizabeth, he stayed home, working the new riding, visiting every town and village and crossroad as well as Saskatchewan's third largest city and his adopted hometown. He was lucky. The Liberals and the CCF split the progressive vote, allowing Diefenbaker to come up the middle with 44 per cent support. But it was a tough fight; Diefenbaker was, yet again, the only Progressive Conservative MP in Saskatchewan.

His political life was a contradiction: as one of the best-known Conservative MPs in the country, he was in constant demand for speeches and interviews, which he enjoyed. But he was increasingly less interested in the grunt work of scrutinizing legislation in committee, leaving that to more junior colleagues. Though George Drew treated him with wary respect—he knew Diefenbaker could and would wield the knife if he thought Drew's hold on the party was weakening—the two were anything but close. Diefenbaker represented the populist, little-guy wing of a party that remained firmly in the hands of the business class. If Drew ever won an election, Diefenbaker would no doubt be offered a senior cabinet portfolio, most likely Justice or External Affairs. But a Drew government was unlikely, and Diefenbaker was approaching sixty. There was simply no path to the prime ministership for him. So he fretted and complained and gave speeches and talked about giving it all up. But his heart wasn't in that, either. Besides, Olive would never have stood for it.

After Edna's death, John travelled frequently to Toronto to meet with Olive Freeman Palmer, who was widowed and an official in the province's education ministry. There had been tough times for Olive: her husband Harry Palmer, a cellist with the Toronto Symphony, died in 1937, four years after they were married and three years after their daughter Carolyn was born. A single mother, Olive fell back on teaching, which she did well. In Owen Sound, in 1944, Olive snuck into the back of a hall to watch John

Diefenbaker give a speech. He noticed her, and later recalled that he couldn't remember a thing he said for the rest of his talk. Whatever did or did not happen during Edna's final years, the two began dating shortly after her death. They kept the courtship secret, but once John won Prince Albert, securing his political future—"I'm using House of Commons stationery again!" he wrote her excitedly, the day after the election[7]—they married. It was a quiet ceremony at a Baptist church in Toronto in December 1953, and the couple were honeymooning in Mexico when the news became public.

Olive was fifty when she and John began courting. For her, his arrival must have been manna from heaven: decades after her first husband died, she had found a man she had been attracted to since she was a teenager, someone who brought to the relationship increased financial stability and a small measure of fame. But in truth, John was the lucky one. Edna's death had frightened him. His mother was ailing and he faced the future alone, with his amiable if ineffectual brother Elmer as perhaps his only close friend. Olive anchored that future and he, in turn, treated her with greater respect and deference than he had Edna. She was better read than he was, for one thing, feeding him lines from Pericles and Homer for his suddenly erudite speeches in the House. Olive spoke French, which John tried but failed to even half-grasp. She was a confident woman who had raised her child in the Depression. John might even have been a bit intimidated by Olive, who clearly had his measure and who didn't mind in the slightest fitting her needs in around Mary's. When Olive and John's mother first met, the old woman had a large photo of Edna—whom she had treated abysmally— beside her bed, and her first words to Olive were: "This is John's first wife. Whatever you do, you'll never be a patch on her."[8] But it was like water off a duck's back for someone as confident and centred as Olive.

Clement Brown, who was a parliamentary correspondent for *Le Droit* in the 1950s, believed that Diefenbaker could not live alone, that he needed to have a strong woman in his life: first his mother, then Edna, then Olive.[9] Marjory LeBreton, who worked in Diefenbaker's office when he was Opposition leader—she went on to become a prominent Conservative organizer, senator, and minister in Stephen Harper's cabinet—believed that Diefenbaker "got on better with and was more trusting around women than he was around men."[10] In any case, Olive well understood her role: to take over from Mary—and, more ambiguously, Edna—as the leader in promoting and defending Team John. Many of Diefenbaker's older friends were saddened by the fact that he ceased to mention Edna or even acknowledge her existence in later years. That criticism may have been unfair. Alvan Gamble, a friend of Diefenbaker's in the 1940s and '50s, said that Diefenbaker confided to him that he and Olive had agreed that "neither of them would carry a ghost into their marriage," and that is why Diefenbaker rarely spoke of Edna. "It is completely untrue that he forgot about her."[11]

John's letters to Olive in these years are filled with the excitement and joy of romance. "Why do I write so frequently after seeing you?" he wrote her early in their courtship. "My official explanation is that I want you to have a letter awaiting you on Monday morning—one guess would give you the real reason!"[12] "I am in a rush today, but must get a note to my Ollie."[13] "My darling, Well, I was happily surprised to receive your letter this morning on arrival. It was almost equal to you being here for it breathed a warm message. You're a wonderful girl, Ollie, to write such a letter."[14] During and after his years as prime minister, many friends and associates were harshly critical of Olive Diefenbaker, believing that she reinforced her husband's growing sense of persecution and paranoia. That may be true. But it is also true that the couple were deeply devoted to each other throughout their lives together.

John Diefenbaker was both rootless and rooted. Politically, he remained in the wilderness, secure in his new riding—he would come to be known as the Man from Prince Albert—while uncertain about his political future. But he was happily married and so more settled in his private life than he had been in years. If he and Olive both agreed, he might eventually have retired from Parliament, setting up a quiet but lucrative law practice in Toronto (though his law work had become so slipshod and distracted that his partners in Prince Albert were leaving the firm or thinking of it). A seventh decade spent in a substantial brick home in Forest Hill or the Annex, with John in the office for a few hours each day, the couple entertaining friends or simply enjoying quiet evenings together, would appeal to both, provided John could reconcile such a life with his frustrated ambition. Or he might stay in Parliament, a respected but irrelevant opposition MP who had long ago missed his chance but who was still good for a quote. There were worse ways to end a career in politics. And as 1953 gave way to 1954 and then 1955, there was no reason to believe Diefenbaker had any other future.

IV

Fighting the Second World War had left Britain so impoverished that food rationing after the war was more severe than during it. (Bread rationing, for example, only began in 1946.) The new Labour government's centrally planned economy didn't help, and the difficulties of European reconstruction caused many of the shortages, but the burdens of sustaining an empire after the money had run out also contributed. That empire was crumbling. India and Pakistan won independence in 1947—in the chaos of partition, a million died and fifteen million were displaced. The British withdrew from Palestine in 1948; Sudan achieved independence in 1956. All this the British government was willing to tolerate, but Anthony Eden, who finally succeeded Winston Churchill as prime minister in 1955, was not prepared to surrender British influence in Egypt, without which it might lose control over the Suez Canal and access to the oil on which the country and its navy depended, along with what was left of its influence in the Middle East. And yet events conspired against the British. The Egyptian military overthrew King Farouk in 1952, Gamal Abdel Nasser became president in 1954, and Nasser announced plans to nationalize the Suez Canal on July 26, 1956, the nightmare scenario. In Eden's mind, the only way to end that nightmare was to dispose of Nassar and regain control over Egypt and the canal. "What's all this nonsense about isolating Nasser or 'neutralising' him as you call it," an agitated Eden protested, when shown plans for containing the Egyptian president. "I want him murdered, can't you understand?"[15]

France had suffered the humiliation of defeat and occupation by the Germans, and the shame of Vichy France. A restored but weakened France lost Indochina to Ho Chi Minh in 1954, and the imperial power was now embroiled in a vicious fight with the Algerian Front de Libération Nationale (National Liberation Front; FLN) to prevent Algeria, with its large population of French settlers, from winning independence. That Nasser openly supported the FLN against the French drove successive Fourth Republic governments to distraction. They, too, wanted him gone and they, too, depended on the canal—a nineteenth-century French engineering marvel and source of national pride—for oil. In the wake of the Second World War, oil had replaced coal as the fuel of choice for Western economies. Steam engines had given way to diesel even as oil and gas furnaces replaced coal-fired ovens and millions of cars guzzled gas. Two thirds of Europe's oil came from ships that transited the canal. If Suez was closed, the Continent would be starved of the one commodity that had emerged in the wake of the war as more vital than any other.

But direct intervention by colonial powers in what was then called the Third World had become unfashionable; the United States—though it held sway in the Caribbean and Central America, controlled islands across the Pacific, and had only granted the Philippines independence in 1946—did not view itself as an imperial power and did not approve of British or French pretensions. Furthermore, the Soviet Union was also making a play for Nasser's loyalties, providing him with arms, with funding for the gigantic Aswan power dam on the Nile, and with pilots to ensure safe passage of ships through the canal. What were Britain and France to do? Their answer to that question constitutes one of the greatest geopolitical blunders of modern times.

On October 22, 1956, Israeli prime minister David Ben-Gurion met secretly in the Paris suburb of Sèvres with French foreign minister Maurice Bourgès-Maunoury, British foreign secretary Selwyn Lloyd, and other senior officials. Over the next two days, they hashed out what all sides considered a viable, even clever, plan to overthrow Nasser and retake the canal. Step One: Israel would invade Egypt in the Sinai. Ben-Gurion felt his nation had good cause: raids from Gaza threatened Israeli lives and property, and an Arab blockade of the Gulf of Aqaba prevented secure access for shipments to Africa and Asia from the Israeli port of Eilat. Step Two: Britain and France would urge the Egyptian army to fall back to an area sixteen kilometres west of the canal and the Israelis to keep sixteen kilometres east of it. When Egypt refused—why would it fall back from its own sovereign territory?—British and French troops would occupy the canal zone and seize control, which they would justify as a police action to keep the two warring sides apart. This would somehow lead to the fall of Nasser and restore European control of the canal.

Israel attacked on October 29, with covert French assistance. But while the Israel Defense Forces performed impressively, the British bungled on every front. They couldn't get their forces into position in time. They underestimated the rage with which other Arab states, some of them British allies, greeted the affair. Worst of all, they hadn't told the Americans what they were up to. When Eisenhower learned of the Anglo-French ultimatum on October 30—from press reports!—the language in the Oval Office resembled what you'd hear in a barracks after leave has been cancelled. St. Laurent and Pearson were every bit as angry. Britain had misled them as well. The United Kingdom's two closest allies felt personally betrayed. The next day, Britain and France launched a bombing campaign against Egypt.

The situation was incredibly dangerous. First of all, the United States was days from the November 6 presidential election, which risked distracting Eisenhower's attention. Second, the invasion took place in the middle of another crisis, in Hungary. On October 26, Hungarian soldiers had torn the red stars off their uniforms and joined thousands of protesters in demanding an end to the Soviet occupation. A new prime minister, Imre Nagy, promised democratic reforms, which threatened the Soviet empire's hold on Eastern Europe. Third, Khrushchev was exploiting the situation in the Middle East—and distracting attention from Hungary—by threatening military action, which could force the United States and NATO to come to the defence of Britain and France. "You know, we may be dealing with the opening gambit of an ultimatum," Eisenhower told his advisers, after hearing of Khrushchev's threat. "We have to be positive and clear in our every word, every step. And if those fellows [the Soviets] start something, we may have to hit 'em—and, if necessary, with everything in the bucket."[16] The world was sliding toward nuclear war.

Eisenhower's reaction was unequivocal. The United States opposed the Israeli invasion. It opposed the intervention of the United Kingdom and France. While no friend of Nasser, the U.S. would not condone his violent removal. Hostilities must end. Meanwhile, British intervention in Egypt was turning into a debacle. Nasser responded to the Anglo-French bombing by sinking forty ships in the canal, rendering it useless. And the British still hadn't managed to seize control of that now-useless canal.

Something had to be done to get the Israelis out of the Sinai, the British and French out of Egypt, and the Russians out of the calculation. And there was an added complication for Canada: Britain's actions threatened to split the Commonwealth apart and ruin the tripartite cooperation among the U.K., the U.S., and Canada that had always been the country's diplomatic linchpin.

On November 1, Pearson flew to New York, where the United Nations was in chaos. There were rumours that Secretary General Dag Hammarskjöld was threatening to resign. On the Security Council, the United States was voting with the Soviet Union on resolutions that France and Britain were vetoing. But there was an idea in the air. Eden, thinking it would take weeks for the relevant parties to get their act together, had suggested the United Nations sponsor a "peace mission" to end the conflict in Egypt. Pearson seized on the idea. Word circulated on the floor of the General Assembly that Pearson of Canada was going to propose that troops be sent under UN supervision to police the canal.

November 2 was the critical day. Hungary announced it had withdrawn from the Warsaw Pact and appealed for international aid. Anglo-French bombing of Egypt continued. The UN debated an American motion calling for an immediate ceasefire and withdrawal. Day turned to night, and then to morning. Canadian diplomats worked the floor of the General Assembly and the adjoining lobbies, rallying support for a police force from non-aligned nations. Pearson told the General Assembly a ceasefire would be simply a return to the status quo unless there was a police force to supervise it. He shuttled back and forth between the Americans and the British, seeking a peace agreement between the two of them as much as one in the Middle East. "No one was better placed than the moderate, mediatory Canadian to propose solutions that might be accepted across great divides," wrote Antony Anderson in his account of those days.[17]

On November 3, Eisenhower reviewed Pearson's proposal and suggested modifications. Pearson readily agreed to them. Henry Cabot Lodge, the U.S. ambassador at the UN, told the General Assembly that the United States supported the Canadian proposal. On November 5, the General Assembly adopted that proposal. For a while, the forward momentum of the Sèvres conspiracy prevented a ceasefire. The Israelis triumphed in battle, French and British troops landed in Egypt. But events were evolving in favour of peace; Hammarskjöld worked tirelessly and skilfully to put meat on the bones of Pearson's resolution. The Americans warned the Brits that unless hostilities ended, the United States would block British efforts to prop up the pound. A panicked Harold Macmillan, chancellor of the Exchequer and once a strong supporter of the Suez affair, warned Eden that in a matter of weeks Britain wouldn't have enough hard cash to pay for food and energy imports. Britain would literally starve. Eden, bitter and defeated, called the French prime minister to say that the jig was up. A ceasefire and a UN police force were the only way out. In the days that followed, Eisenhower was re-elected, Nasser accepted the UN force, and the Soviets crushed Hungary's bid for freedom as the world looked away.

A Canadian general led the new United Nations Emergency Force, though Nasser vetoed the use of Canadian troops because they wore the Red Ensign, which included the Union Jack, on their uniforms. Pearson was disappointed that the final terms and conditions of the UN peacekeeping agreement did not include a genuine multilateral effort to secure a Middle East peace, which he had advocated. Without that effort, he warned, war would eventually return. He was proven right eleven years later. But Hammarskjöld was simply trying to get the best terms that all sides could live with. If Pearson was disappointed that his peacekeeping proposal had not led to permanent peace, consolation came a year later on the morning of October 14, 1957, with news that, for helping to defuse the Suez Crisis, he had been awarded the Nobel Prize for Peace.

Pearson had earned that prize. His years of tireless effort, unrelenting support for the United Nations, and skilful diplomacy had won him respect in Cairo and Tel Aviv, London and Paris, Washington and New Delhi. Lester Pearson had devoted his professional life to building the capital that he spent over a few crucial days in November 1956. He did not save the world—if anyone could make that claim, it was probably Eisenhower, who navigated those treacherous days with firmness and skill despite being in the final hours of a presidential election campaign—but he helped secure the peace. He deserved the Nobel Prize. Unfortunately for Pearson, it arrived at a time when everything else had fallen to pieces.

V

The older we get, the more we become what we are already, but not in a good way. That was certainly true of Clarence Decatur Howe in 1956. Though American born and raised, Howe is one of the most important, and least understood, figures in Canadian history. More than anyone else, he built the infrastructure of modern Canada: taking it out of the Depression, making it a vital ally to Britain and the United States in the Second World War, equipping his adopted country to thrive in the peace that followed.

His record of accomplishment was extraordinary. As minister of transport under Mackenzie King in the 1930s, he reorganized the port system, stripping it of patronage and pork; put Canada's bankrupt railways on a solid financial footing; and launched a national passenger airline, Trans-Canada Air Lines, which he treated with something approaching personal affection.

In the Second World War, as minister of munitions and supply, Howe retooled Canada's economic infrastructure, providing the resources to train pilots from across the Commonwealth—Roosevelt called Canada the "aerodrome of democracy"—manufacturing guns and shells and tanks to meet Britain's wartime needs, and eventually making Canada a major supplier of all manner of military equipment to both the Americans and the Brits, while also equipping the Canadian army, navy, and air force. After the war, as minister of reconstruction under King and then St. Laurent, he shifted the economy to peacetime prosperity while making Canada a key player in the development of nuclear energy, and then equipped the country to fight another war in Korea. After Korea, as minister of trade, he completed the shift in the economy from east–west with Great Britain to north–south with the United States, while helping convince the Eisenhower administration that if it didn't build the St. Lawrence Seaway in partnership with Canada, Canada could and would build the engineering colossus itself. (Alarmed at the thought of losing control of such a vital piece of continental infrastructure, Dwight Eisenhower pushed past political obstruction, and the two countries agreed on joint development in 1954.)

Howe was known as the Minister of Everything. But, in fact, he was always the Minister of One Thing: one big project at a time, one obsession that drove him forward: transportation infrastructure, war materiel, post-war prosperity, and finally, his last great project, his own national dream: a natural gas pipeline, stretching from Alberta across the Prairies and the daunting shield lands of Northern Ontario to bring energy to the industrial core. The pipeline would mark the end of a lifetime of service to Canada.

But when he took on the pipeline project, Howe was approaching seventy, and his heart was giving him trouble. St. Laurent was past his prime, drifting into periods of lethargy and increasingly disconnected from his own government. (A tour of Europe and the Middle East in 1954 might have contributed. Such trips were arduous in the days before jet-powered passenger flight, and St. Laurent returned exhausted.) Many of the old guard who had served with King and St. Laurent—Brooke Claxton at Defence; Douglas Abbott at Finance; Lionel Chevrier at Transport—were gone or going. The younger cohort, such as Pearson at External, Jack Pickersgill at Citizenship and Immigration, and Paul Martin at Health and Welfare—Pearson's former student was now a cabinet minister, with great talent and great ambition—saw Howe as almost an embarrassment: an autocrat who was contemptuous of both Parliament and them. He had somehow managed to convince King and St. Laurent that he should be able to retain the emergency powers he had been granted in wartime, which the opposition rightly decried as undemocratic. Some of his own colleagues thought he was far too friendly with the Americans, welcoming so much foreign direct investment that he had imperilled Canada's economic sovereignty. And they chafed at the cost and risk of the pipeline project, which was ironic, given that its purpose was to preserve Canadian energy independence.

The business community was also skeptical. Natural gas producers in Alberta and consumers in Ontario wanted to secure a much easier north–south flow, with Alberta exporting into, and Ontario importing from, the U.S. market. Arrangements in Ontario to purchase Texas natural gas were so far advanced that Howe had to deploy a ludicrous ruse to force a pause: he refused to grant a licence for a pipeline across the Niagara River on the grounds that the river was a navigable waterway. (Critics rightly observed that the only vessel that navigated the Niagara River was the *Maid of the Mist*, what with the falls and all.) Howe knocked heads and shook hands and pushed together a consortium, Trans-Canada Pipelines Limited, to build the pipeline. But there were two problems: the pipeline would need

American investment, and no one was prepared to pay the cost of laying pipe across Northern Ontario.

The real problem was that Howe's powers were waning. Cabinet shocked him in 1954 by rejecting his proposal for a federal government bond guarantee to finance the project. Parliament shocked him in 1955 by stripping him of his emergency powers. But Howe, indomitable, found financing in the United States and, in the spring of 1956, convinced cabinet to provide Trans-Canada with an eighty-million-dollar loan. There was only one problem: to meet its obligations, Trans-Canada had to begin construction that summer, which meant Parliament would need to quickly authorize the loan. But the opposition was dead set against the pipeline and voted to block it. The government's solution was to impose closure: limiting debate on the legislation and forcing votes to meet the deadline. Today, imposing time limits on debate is unusual but not unprecedented; in the 1950s, it was practically unheard-of. In any case, imposing time limits after long debate was one thing. Imposing them on the day the legislation was introduced was an outrage—"a shameless prostitution of the closure rule," in the words of an indignant Eugene Forsey, already one of the country's leading authorities on parliamentary procedure.[18] Both the Conservatives and the CCF resolved to do everything in their power to frustrate passage of the bill.

Howe had always possessed two great flaws, said Donald Fleming, who had faced him in opposition for more than a decade. The first was a contempt for Parliament, or for anyone or anything that thwarted his will. "Who's to stop us?" he famously taunted opposition MPs in 1951. The second was a prodigious temper, which could send him into rages, in public as well as in private, that terrified those around him. "At seventy years of age, far from mellowing he had become more intolerant of obstacles to his will and volcanically short-tempered," Fleming observed.[19] And now he had to lead the campaign to push the pipeline bill through the House of Commons, despite implacable opposition from both the Conservatives and the CCF.

Drew, Fleming, and Davie Fulton led the fight for the Tories, coordinating closely with the CCF's Stanley Knowles, a gaunt, bookish United Church minister from Winnipeg who was devoted to the social gospel and parliamentary procedure. For the next five weeks, they made life a living hell for Howe and for the Speaker, Louis-René Beaudoin, who was a master himself of Commons procedures, but who was vain and weak. Knowles and his newfound allies in the Conservative caucus spun out endless points of procedure, prolonging debate even after the Speaker had ruled. A brief example, from May 14:

MR. SPEAKER: Mr. Harris moved, seconded by Mr. Pickersgill: That we do now proceed to the orders of the day.

MR. KNOWLES: May I ask a question? Would Your Honour indicate what the effect of that motion would be? What would it do to the motion made by the government whip and also to the motions on the order paper between this point and the orders of the day?

MR. SPEAKER: The motion is that we now proceed with the orders of the day. It supersedes the present motion which is under consideration, and if it is defeated we carry on with the routine proceedings on the order paper. If it is agreed to we immediately proceed to orders of the day. To me it is as simple as that. Those who are in favour of the motion will please say yea.

SOME HON. MEMBERS: Yea.

MR. SPEAKER: Those who are opposed will please say nay.

SOME HON. MEMBERS: Nay.

MR. SPEAKER: I declare the motion carried.

MR. FULTON: Will we now have questions on the orders of the day?

MR. SPEAKER: No.

MR. FULTON: No questions?

MR. SPEAKER: The motion having been carried, we now proceed to orders of the day.

MR. FULTON: Before the order is read may I ask a question of the Minister of Citizenship and Immigration?

MR. SINCLAIR: No, you cannot.

MR. FULTON: As I apprehend the situation—

MR. SPEAKER: Order. I am on my feet and the hon. member has asked if he can ask a question of the Minister of Citizenship and Immigration—

MR. FULTON: On the orders of the day.

MR. SPEAKER: Yes, but we are not on orders of the day. We are proceeding to orders of the day by virtue of the motion that has just been carried and therefore the question time does not take place today. . . .[20]

And on and on, day after day. The fight was not over whether the pipe-line was a good idea or a bad idea. The fight was over the right of Parliament to debate and decide. As Stanley Knowles put it, the government's promise to Trans-Canada that construction would start on time had rendered Parliament irrelevant: "This free and independent parliament of a sovereign nation is bound by a commitment that the government of this country has made to a private company."[21]

Diefenbaker was not in the front lines of the fight in Parliament. He delivered a powerful radio address in March, in which he invoked Parliament's effort to strip Howe of his emergency powers. "That battle we won," he declared. "But let me tell you that the fight we put on then will appear a mere skirmish beside the battle he will wage when the bill regarding the Trans-Canada Pipelines comes before Parliament."[22] He did intervene once, on May 17, in a speech that covered all the bases: the arrogance of C.D. Howe, the silence of the prime minister, American own-ership of the pipeline, the need for close scrutiny of the bill in committee. And on the day Fleming marched defiantly out of the House, to rousing cheers from the opposition after Beaudoin ejected him for defying the Speaker, Diefenbaker shouted out, "Farewell John Hampton!" comparing the member for Eglinton to the dissident British MP whose defiance of King Charles helped launch the English civil war. (Tory MP Ellen Fairclough conveniently had a Red Ensign at hand, which she draped over Fleming's chair.)

But Diefenbaker had doubts about the opposition's campaign. He was reluctant to join forces with the CCF, which was powerful in Saskatchewan, his political base. He believed Howe's pipeline would bring prosperity to Prairie producers, just as—in his pre-political years as an engineer and businessman—Howe's innovations in storing and shipping grain had benefited Prairie farms. "My feelings were always tinctured with great admiration for the man," Diefenbaker revealed years later.[23] Besides, the Prince Albert MP was by nature a loner, unwilling to be part of any team, even a team of his fellow MPs seeking to embarrass the government. He was right about the value of the pipeline, which continues to ship gas from the Prairies into Central Canada to this day. But while he spoke about Liberal arrogance over invoking closure in speeches outside the House, he let others lead the charge in Parliament. He may not have understood then, though he certainly did later, that the pipeline affair had turned the public against the Liberal dynasty, and had turned many in the Parliamentary Press Gallery against it as well.

The drama peaked on June 1, one day before the House was due to vote on third reading. The day before, Beaudoin had ruled favourably on an opposition motion, which appeared to doom any possibility of a final vote. Now he rose to inform the House that his previous ruling had been in error, and moved a motion from the chair—a highly irregular procedure, and probably illegitimate—to invalidate the previous evening's proceedings. Opposition members advanced on the Speaker's chair in rage.

"What took place in the dark?"

"Why did you change overnight?"

"Are you afraid?"

M.J. Coldwell, the CCF leader, advanced on the chair, shaking his fist. Beaudoin tottered, unsteady on his feet.

"Hitlerism!"

"This is Black Friday, boys."[24]

One group of MPs began singing "Onward Christian Soldiers"; another, "There'll Always Be a Pipeline" (to the tune of "There'll Always Be an England"). One pugilistic Liberal MP had to be held by his coattails.

But the motion passed, and the bill passed the House and the Senate, receiving Royal Assent June 6, one day before the Trans-Canada deadline.

Throughout the weeks of tumult, St. Laurent spoke only once, though that one defence of the pipeline and of Howe was detailed, precise, and effective. More of such leadership might have helped. But MPs, the press, and anyone in the public who cared to notice could see that the PM was a spent force, older than his seventy-four years, no longer really in the game. He should have stepped down before the debate, and he certainly should have stepped down after it, to give the party time to renew itself before an election that, according to parliamentary procedure, didn't need to be called until 1958.

St. Laurent and Howe had both agreed after the 1953 election that they would retire in a year or so, for the sake of party renewal. But now both had decided to stay on. The pipeline fight had hardened attitudes on both sides.

And the prime minister remained popular, so popular that many Liberals feared the pipeline debate could cost them the election unless they sheltered behind public affection for Uncle Louis. It may or may not be true that Howe told his colleagues that St. Laurent would front the next election "even if we have to run him stuffed."[25] If so, they misread the public mood. For the first time in decades, Canadians had been transfixed by a debate in Parliament. And when they looked at the long-governing Liberals, they did not like what they saw.

Parliament straggled to a close in August. Many Liberal MPs, including Howe, returned to their ridings convinced that the pipeline debate was a teapot-tempest the public would soon forget. Conservatives couldn't wait for the House to resume. Whatever the polls might say, they believed the government was vulnerable, the prime minister disengaged, the younger members of the front bench almost as dismayed by the senior leadership as the opposition were. The next year would not be an ordinary year. Change was in the wind.

But the Conservatives had a problem, one they had not expected. George Drew was not at all well.

VI

Filibustering has one great drawback: there are more government MPs than opposition MPs. That was particularly true after the election of 1953, which sent 169 Liberals to Ottawa, but only 51 Progressive Conservatives, 23 members of the Canadian Commonwealth Federation, and 15 Social Crediters. Moreover, the Socreds, with 11 of their seats located in Alberta, backed the government on the pipeline. A filibuster can include endless objections, points of procedure, and speeches that go on for hours. During the pipeline debate, the House often sat until long after midnight, only to resume in the morning. The Liberals could rotate their MPs, giving them time to rest and recover. But the Tories and the CCF were forced to keep much of their caucus in the House much of the time, or risk having debate collapse through lack of quorum. Most of the opposition MPs were middle-aged or older, and not in the best of shape. PC MP Howard Green collapsed the evening of the day Fleming was expelled. Four days later, another Tory MP, Jim Macdonnell, went to the hospital and stayed there for two weeks. The physical and emotional toll was terrible on both sides of the aisle: on June 6, in the peak of the furore, Liberal MP Lorne MacDougall had a fatal heart attack while in Centre Block. His wife was in the gallery when he was stricken.

Speaker René Beaudoin suffered, in some ways, the cruellest fate. "The cultured, refined, always courtly MP for Vaudreuil"[26] and author of a massive revision of Beauchesne's *Parliamentary Rules*, had been spoken of as possible Quebec premier or even prime minister. But during the pipeline debate he faced the ultimate humiliation for any Speaker: a motion of censure from the opposition. George Drew accused him of destroying the speakership. Rumours abounded that on the night before June 1, when Beaudoin had reversed his previous ruling, thus saving the pipeline schedule, Liberal cabinet ministers had visited the Speaker. Someone claimed to have seen Jack Pickersgill's car in the driveway. Though Beaudoin survived the vote of censure, he was a marked man. Loathed by the Conservatives and shunned even by his own party, he gave up his seat in Parliament two years later, divorced his wife, and married his mistress, twenty-four years his junior. He abandoned the law, his second marriage fell apart, and he drifted from job to job, at one point working as a bartender in Tempe, Arizona. "Once the toast of prime ministers and presidents, Beaudoin died of a heart attack in the back of a taxi with all of $3 in his pocket," Mark Maloney of the *Toronto Star* wrote years later. "He was 57."[27]

As leader of the official opposition, George Drew led much of the attack on the pipeline bill. He was on his feet constantly, making speech after speech, issuing objection after objection. Attacking the Speaker took a toll on him as well as on Beaudoin. He had suffered a serious bout of meningitis the year before, but appeared to have fully recovered. He hadn't. In August 1956, a viral infection sent him to the hospital. Weeks later, he was still unwell. The doctors and his wife Fiorenza both feared for his life. Grattan O'Leary, the eloquent and proudly conservative editorialist at the *Ottawa Journal* (he covered the Hill from Laurier to Trudeau) met with Drew's physician, along with Léon Balcer, president of the party's National Association, and MP Jim Macdonnell, who himself had been hospitalized during the pipeline debate.

"Either he retires or you gentlemen will soon be attending his funeral," Dr. Ray Farquharson warned. A second specialist concurred. O'Leary and others prepared a letter of resignation and took it to Drew. His wife pleaded with him to sign. He did, reluctantly, but recanted hours later, phoning O'Leary, who remembered the call this way:

"I'm withdrawing the letter," Drew announced.
"You can't do it, George." I gave it to him from the shoulder— what Fiorenza hadn't dared tell him. "The doctor says you'll be dead in six months if you don't get out."
There was a long silence. "All right," George said.[28]

The news arrived like a late-summer storm. Yes, Drew had lost two elections, but so had Robert Borden before becoming prime minister. The former Ontario premier had ably led the Conservatives in the pipeline debate, setting the government back on its heels. Though the Liberals were confident the furor would soon be forgotten, many Conservatives believed their time had finally come. And now, when they were at last on the upswing, at least in their own estimation, the leader had been forced to resign due to ill health. Did God have it in for the Progressive Conservative Party?

O'Leary, who was as much a part of the Conservative leadership as anyone at head office, wanted Sidney Smith to take over. One of Canada's most distinguished professors of law and, since 1945, president of the University of Toronto, Smith had been part of the Port Hopeful crowd, along with Donald Fleming and Roland Michener, who had advocated for a more progressive agenda for the party. Smith turned down the offer, and "who could blame him?" O'Leary wrote years later. "What attraction was there of an out-of-office party with fifty members?"[29] With Smith out, Donald Fleming went in. The son of a teacher, like Diefenbaker, the Toronto lawyer was a devout, teetotalling Presbyterian with a ferocious capacity for work and for getting into fights. His father said the boy was born with his fists clenched and had been that way ever since. He was also bilingual and could count on strong support from Quebec delegates. Much of the party establishment rallied around him.

Davie Fulton also decided to throw in his hat. He had the pedigree: two of his ancestors had been premier of British Columbia, and his father had been attorney general. He had been educated at Oxford. Fulton was forty-two when he sought the leadership: young, brilliant, aloof, he drew the reverence of some and the scorn of others. He was also bilingual and had performed admirably in the pipeline debate. Fulton was running, as Fleming had run in 1948, to position himself for a later leadership race.

And then there was Diefenbaker. Everybody knew he wanted it, even more now than in 1942 or 1948. But there was one problem: he was a bit of a retread. He was no better liked than before within the party—some still hadn't forgiven him for breaking with the leadership by supporting the baby bonus, back when King was PM. "There was some doubt whether Diefenbaker was really a Conservative," O'Leary remembered later. "He was a bit too much of a Western radical for the Eastern establishment of the party."[30] To some, in his seemingly infinite capacity to remember and never forgive any slight, real or perceived, he seemed almost unbalanced. "Many others regarded Diefenbaker as too unstable to be the national leader," wrote Donald Fleming in his memoirs. "Some questioned whether his health would be equal to the strains of office."[31] He was starting to show signs of hearing loss, a potentially fatal impediment to a politician's future. Fleming ran for the leadership because he knew Diefenbaker had no support in Quebec; his relentless crusade for human rights had not gone down well in a province more concerned with cultural cohesion than individual liberty. Diefenbaker had openly opposed Maurice Duplessis's Padlock Law, by which the government could deprive anyone promoting communism—or, for that matter, anyone who annoyed Duplessis—of their property rights. He opposed as well the Union Nationale's persecution of the Jehovah's Witnesses.

But Ontario was the key, and from the beginning it was clear the delegates were for Diefenbaker. Leslie Frost, the all-powerful premier, liked to say he governed from the barber's chair in Lindsay, the small city east of Lake Simcoe that he represented. Old Man Ontario, as he was affectionately known, put his formidable machine at Diefenbaker's disposal. Allister Grosart, who had handled advertising for George Drew's 1953 campaign, came on board. To Fleming's dismay, many of the party establishment he had counted on for support abandoned him, even as caucus swung solidly behind the Chief. "It became obvious that even those who were not ready to support Diefenbaker were reluctant to show their colours openly against him," Fleming later remembered, either because they were convinced Diefenbaker would win or "on fear of his reputed vindictiveness. I doubt if they gained anything from their abstention."[32]

There was more to it than that. Robert Stanfield had broken decades of Liberal rule to become Progressive Conservative premier in Nova Scotia. He was for Dief. Hugh John Flemming had done the same in New Brunswick (both had been helped by Dalton Camp) and was also onside. Another supporter was Duff Roblin, the new Progressive Conservative leader in Manitoba who in two years' time would become its premier. The rise of conservative parties at the provincial level was itself a sign the tide was beginning to turn. And the charismatic if unsteady leadership of John Diefenbaker might even carry the Conservatives to victory in Ottawa.

But the real reason Diefenbaker dominated the 1956 leadership race was simply that he was the people's choice. Though the member for Prince Albert was seen by party insiders as insufficiently loyal, the rank and file regarded those insiders as a group of inbred incompetents who had managed to lose five consecutive federal elections. If he abandoned the party line, it was because that line embraced the interests of big business over the working man. When George Drew first entered hospital in August, most of the senior ranks of the party, including many in caucus, were skeptical of Diefenbaker as leader. By October they had come around, simply because they had no choice. "My people are for John," one MP explained. "If I were to oppose him I'd probably lose the nomination and I'd certainly lose the election."[33] It didn't hurt that, while Diefenbaker had never been all that loyal to the party hierarchy, he had always been a popular draw at local Conservative association or constituency meetings, and had collected a back-pocketful of IOUs along the way. For once, ordinary members of caucus, rather than just the power brokers, had a say. And they chose Diefenbaker.

He limited himself to a single cross-country train tour, with carefully prepared reception committees at every stop. A new medium, television, had entered the political mix: this would be Canada's first televised leadership convention, and it demanded choreographed enthusiasm. The camera liked

Diefenbaker. Though, at sixty-one, he was no longer the dashing young criminal attorney, his baritonal oratory and sly, knowing grin came over well on television.

During the campaign, he masterfully defused a political bomb. In the wake of the Suez Crisis, the St. Laurent government asked Parliament to approve funding for the Canadian contingent assigned to Suez. Many Canadians—especially Conservatives—were angry that Canada had not stood with Britain in its hour of need. Others were angry that Canada had not stood with France. To have abandoned both founding nations and made common cause with the Yankees seemed outrageous. Those who supported the new state of Israel also felt betrayed. But millions of others were proud of Canada's role in helping to defuse the crisis.

The debate on November 26 quickly grew heated. Conservative MP Howard Green excoriated St. Laurent and Pearson for being a "chore boy" to the United States as it sought to replace Britain as the dominant power in the Middle East. St. Laurent and Pearson both reacted furiously, with Pearson accusing the Conservatives of being "a colonial chore boy running around shouting 'ready, aye, ready.'"[34]

For once, Diefenbaker defused rather than heightened tensions in the House. Speaking more in sorrow than in anger, he chastised St. Laurent for criticizing Britain and France, reminding him that those two nations had "stood for freedom for generations." He placed much of the blame on Russia and on Nasser, and proposed a new Quebec Conference, to reconcile Britain and France with the U.S and restore the Western alliance. The idea was fanciful, but that didn't matter. The press considered the speech a tour de force.

The Conservatives met in Ottawa's still-dreary Coliseum on December 10, with the vote slated for December 14. Along with choosing a leader, delegates approved resolutions to introduce a public health insurance plan, adopt a new flag, improve benefits for veterans, and bolster Old Age Security, an agenda the Liberal Party would also have been comfortable with. The biggest controversy surrounded Diefenbaker's decision not to have a nominator from Quebec. Instead, he chose New Brunswick premier Hugh John Flemming to nominate him, with British Columbia MP George Pearkes as his seconder—an Atlantic and Pacific duo, *a mari usque ad mare*. Pierre Sévigny,

Diefenbaker's organizer in Quebec, was incensed, as was party president Léon Balcer, who took the contretemps to the press. But Diefenbaker wouldn't back down. He hated any thought of special consideration for Quebec, and didn't want his candidacy defined by Central Canadian interests. It was all splendid fodder for columnists, but it didn't influence the final count in the slightest: Diefenbaker won on the first ballot, with 774 votes, 60 per cent of votes cast. Fleming came in at number two, with 31 per cent, and Davie Fulton received 9 per cent. Some Quebec delegates walked out in protest—more fodder!—but most of the attention focused on Diefenbaker's acceptance speech after Fleming and Fulton rushed to Diefenbaker, raised his arms, and moved that the result be declared unanimous. The new leader was at his best, telling the delegates and the nation, "I will make mistakes, but I hope it will be said of me . . . he wasn't always right, sometimes he was on the wrong side, but never on the side of wrong."[35] Whatever that meant, it sounded magnificent.

He had failed so many times—failed to win a seat federally or provincially, failed as leader in Saskatchewan. When he finally did win a seat in Parliament, he failed to win the leadership, then failed again. Even now, his newfound support was a matter of convenience; some were already fingering their knives. But he was leader of Her Majesty's Loyal Opposition, at last. He would fight an election within months. And he, if no one else, was certain he would win. His Prairie prediction to his mother would come true.

On the day before the vote, as Dalton Camp tells it, the adman found himself in a room of the Château Laurier with Frost, Flemming, some party bagmen, and others accustomed to being in control, employing "the blunt, easy speech of men among their peers." They felt bad for Donald Fleming, but were sure his time would come. They all agreed that though Diefenbaker "would be difficult, if not impossible, as a leader, and a failure, after one election he would retire and the party could then find a younger, abler man."[36] The Grits were bound to win the next election, no matter who was leader. Gallup had them at 50 per cent and the Tories at 30.

Conservatives had been thinking that way for decades. For the boys in the backrooms, nothing had changed.

SEVEN

The World Turned Upside Down

(1957–1958)

I

For the Liberals, things seemed close to perfect. Not only was the party popular in the polls, but St. Laurent's favourability rating hovered near 75 per cent. It appeared that the public had forgotten about the pipeline debate, just as C.D. Howe and others had predicted—that, as one letter writer to the *Ottawa Journal* lamented, "Canadians are incapable of moral indignation."[1] Instead, the governing party was bathed in the glow of Preserving World Peace, thanks to Mike Pearson's intervention in the Suez Crisis. The Conservatives had been forced to replace their leader, and had chosen, remarkably, the volatile and erratic John Diefenbaker. The country was due for an election, and as far as the Liberals were concerned, the sooner the better, while the Tories were still recovering from the leadership campaign. Always the gentleman, St. Laurent informed the opposition leaders in February that he intended to visit the governor general in April for a June poll. Finance Minister Walter Harris, worried about rising inflation, introduced a very cautious budget on March 15 that included a minor decrease in taxes, a small boost to the baby bonus, and a six-dollar-a-month increase in Old Age Security. Not an election budget by any means, but one wasn't needed. The platform would simply be, trust Uncle Louis one last time. Canada had achieved a remarkable level of political "stasis": the Liberals entrenched in Ottawa, the Progressive Conservatives in Ontario, the Union Nationale in Quebec, Social Credit in British Columbia and Alberta, and the CCF in Saskatchewan. With Canadians enjoying previously unimaginable levels of affluence, it seemed 'twould be ever thus.

But there were warning signs that St. Laurent and his advisers should have noticed but didn't. For one thing, opinions on Pearson's performance in the Suez Crisis were far from unanimous. Many supporters of Britain thought Canada had let the side down. Most of them were Conservatives, but there were Liberals and undecideds as well. As well, the Liberals didn't have Brooke Claxton to lean on. When he stepped down as defence minister in 1954, Claxton was no longer available in the equally important role of chief electoral tactician. His meticulous, detailed, leave-nothing-to-chance approach had helped the Liberals secure victories in the elections of 1945, 1949, and 1953. Now he was gone, and there was no one of equal talent available to replace him. There were worrying economic signs as well. Unemployment was increasing, trade numbers were down, wheat sales were slumping, and industrial growth was weak, even as inflation surpassed 4 per cent in April.

It was a time of increasing ferment. African Americans fought for civil rights in the South, organizing demonstrations and demanding admission to schools and universities. Politicians and other supporters of Jim Crow responded with arrest warrants and blockades. Disgust with authority arrived on movie screens via *Paths of Glory*, a dark film about military incompetence in the First World War from the brilliant young director Stanley Kubrick, while the Beat Generation produced its finest work of subversion: Jack Kerouac's *On the Road*, a raucous, rebellious tale of travel. Nineteen fifty-seven was the year the Russians put Sputnik, the world's first satellite, into orbit, shaking confidence in American technological prowess. James Dean pouted, Marilyn Monroe flirted, Elvis Presley shook his hips, Doris Day tried to pretend none of it was happening. The Liberal leader was seventy-five.

Dissent roiled beneath Canada's placid surface as well. Intellectuals in Quebec chafed at the thuggish ways of Maurice Duplessis's Union

Nationale. Economic nationalists worried about the growing share of Canadian businesses owned by American corporations. Women formed an increasingly large minority of the workforce, but their pay didn't come close to matching their male equivalents. The Nova Scotia Association for the Advancement of Coloured People advocated for the rights of Black Nova Scotians in the wake of the arrest and conviction of Viola Desmond, who was evicted from the Roseland Theatre in New Glasgow in 1946, after she insisted on sitting on the main floor where whites sat rather than in the balcony with other Blacks. Métis in Manitoba established the Winnipeg Friendship Centre in 1959, to provide advocacy and services. Changes to the Indian Act in 1951 had removed the prohibition on First Nations holding potlatches and wearing traditional dress. Elvis played Vancouver's Empire Stadium on August 31, 1957, causing several thousand teenagers to go temporarily insane. Hugh MacLennan's *The Watch That Ends the Night*, seen as a great advance in Canadian fiction, won the Governor General's Award in 1959.

An ugly story darkened the winter of 1957. In Washington, the Internal Security Subcommittee, the same congressional body that had slandered Pearson and Hazen Sise, once again threw up the name of Herbert Norman, the Canadian diplomat who had already been investigated and cleared six years earlier. Norman was extraordinarily gifted. As ambassador to Japan, he had become fluent in Japanese, assisting Douglas MacArthur when the American general became proconsul of the defeated empire. "He's the most valuable man we have," MacArthur told Pearson. "We want to thank you for letting him help us.[2] When Republicans first alleged that Norman might be a closet communist, both the FBI and the RCMP gave him a thorough vetting. The truth, which Norman never tried to conceal, was that he had attended communist study groups at Cambridge and Harvard, but had never joined the party or betrayed his country or the confidence of his government. After both agencies cleared him, Pearson, as foreign affairs minister, sent Norman to New Zealand as high commissioner, perhaps to place him outside the range of the Americans' radar. Early in 1956, he was posted to Egypt, where he walked straight into the Suez Crisis. Pearson valued Norman's efforts to help convince Nasser to accept a Canadian-led international peacekeeping force. But that brought him back to the Americans' attention, and the subcommittee didn't hesitate to release the earlier allegations to the press. Pearson, furious, sent a diplomatic cable to Secretary of State John Foster Dulles, protesting "in the strongest terms" the "irresponsible allegations" of the committee. Diefenbaker was equally incensed, calling on Pearson to issue "the strongest possible protest . . . against this attack, which is detrimental not only to the Canadian diplomat but to Canadian international relations."[3] Norman asked Pearson to thank the leader of the official opposition for his support in the House. "This I am very happy to do," Pearson wrote to Diefenbaker.[4]

On April 4, 1957, in Cairo, Herbert Norman wrote several notes—one for his wife, several to close friends, and one to his employer—then climbed up to the roof of the Wadi el Nil building and jumped off. The suicide rocked Canada. "Wave of Anger Sweeps Ottawa Over Norman's Suicide in Cairo," the *Globe and Mail* headline blared, in end-of-the-world font. For Pearson, "my feelings never reached a lower point in my public career."[5] Diefenbaker and other opposition leaders were incensed that a congressional committee's unwarranted slander had contributed to a diplomat's death. What was the government's response? Pearson wrote an even harsher note than he had sent to the Americans on April 10, after they appeared to ignore the first, warning that if the United States government could not guarantee the confidentiality of information supplied by the Canadian government, Canada would reconsider sharing intelligence with the United States. Diefenbaker caught the implication instantly. Did that mean the rumour that Norman was a communist had first been furnished by the RCMP? The answer appeared to be yes. Pearson, caught out, acknowledged that Norman had flirted with communism as a university student, but that it never interfered with his trustworthiness as a public servant. In that case, Diefenbaker responded in the House, the minister "has either spoken too much or too little. He cannot hide in that way from his responsibility."[6] The debate trailed off unpleasantly, on the final sitting day of the twenty-second Parliament. Diefenbaker learned two things. Lester B. Pearson was not always completely candid. And he could be rattled.

II

In February 1952, Vincent Massey had become the first of Canada's governors general to be born in the country—a fitting capstone to his career, since he was more British and more aristocratic than any British aristocrat. (Lord Salisbury had once said of him, "Vincent's a fine chap, but he does make one feel like a bit of a savage."[7]) After London and other prestigious postings, St. Laurent had asked him to chair the Royal Commission on National Development in the Arts, Letters and Sciences, which everyone called the Massey Commission. Its implied mandate was to find a way to prevent the total Americanization of Canadian culture. Massey's proposed solution amounted to major government subsidies to nurture Canadian high culture through federal funding for universities, the creation of a national library, and, most important, a new national council to support the arts. The Massey Commission might have missed its target. High culture was arguably more robust than popular culture in Canada in the 1950s. When the locomotive works wound down in Stratford, Ontario, after the war, with the town facing a grim future of decline, local businessman Tom Patterson decided to defy that fate by launching a Shakespeare festival. Armed with nothing more than this improbable idea, he somehow convinced the acclaimed English theatre director Tyrone Guthrie to come to Stratford to perform Shakespeare under a tent. Guthrie, in turn, recruited actors Alec Guinness and Irene Worth. The Stratford Festival—whose inaugural season was rescued from bankruptcy in part through a donation from Massey—debuted in 1953. It was such a success that the permanent Festival Theatre, with its unique thrust stage, opened in June 1957. But the Stratford Festival wasn't operating in a vacuum. There were professional theatre companies in Montreal (Théâtre du Nouveau Monde) and Toronto (the Crest Theatre). Most major cities had a professional symphony orchestra, and Winnipeg and Toronto both hosted ballet companies. The Royal Conservatory of Music churned out so many first-rate musicians and singers that the Canadian Opera Company, Canada's first, would launch its inaugural season in Toronto in 1958. But on the pop culture side, aspiring singers and actors such as Paul Anka and William Shatner sought their fortune in the United States. Most of the homegrown fare on the CBC was awful. But Vincent Massey could hardly have been expected to urge the federal government to come to the aid of pop culture.

One of Louis St. Laurent's last accomplishments as prime minister was to establish the Canada Council for the Arts in the winter of 1957. He was initially skeptical of Massey's recommendation—"funding ballet dancers?" he snorted—believing that the arts were in provincial jurisdiction.[8] But after years of lobbying, not least by Pearson and by Massey himself, and after a hefty windfall from the estates of two wealthy industrialists landed in the government's coffers, he gave way.

So there was a most cordial relationship between Louis St. Laurent and Vincent Massey when the prime minister visited the governor general at Government House on April 13, 1957, to ask that Parliament be dissolved and writs issued for a general election. Both men were in their seventies. Both had devoted their lives to the service of their country. And both believed more service lay ahead.

The Liberal election platform was virtually policy-free, consisting instead of a recitation of all the growth and prosperity the Liberals had delivered to Canadians: "314,000 new jobs since 1953!"[9] The Liberals would run on their record, banking on popular affection for St. Laurent, while waiting for the unstable new Tory leader to implode. This was very much in keeping with what the Liberal Party had become in the era of Jack Pickersgill.

The son of an Ontarian who moved to Manitoba to become a farmer, Pickersgill had started his brilliant career at External Affairs—after the seemingly inevitable path of taking a degree at Oxford and teaching history— before moving into the prime minister's office, where he eventually became such a close adviser to Mackenzie King that "I cleared it with Jack" was as good as the PM's signature. He was so indispensable to Louis St. Laurent that, even after Pickersgill became clerk of the Privy Council—effectively the head of the public service and the deputy minister to the prime minister— both men agreed his talents were being wasted. A brilliant judge of political horse flesh and gifted with a wicked sense of humour, Pickersgill's only flaw was his evident-to-all conviction that his intellectual and political skills were unequalled. (Diefenbaker liked to say of Pickersgill that he was the only man he knew who could strut sitting down.) Since Pickersgill's behind-the-scenes manoeuvring had been crucial to arranging Newfoundland's entry into Confederation in 1949, Premier Joey Smallwood arranged for his election in the remote riding of Bonavista—Twillingate, as exotically named as its new MP, soon to become minister of citizenship and immigration.

Pickersgill was part of a powerful cabinet that represented regional interests—such as Agriculture Minister Jimmy Gardiner in Saskatchewan; up-and-coming Robert Winters, who represented the Maritimes; and Jimmy Sinclair—whose daughter Margaret would become Pierre Trudeau's wife and Justin's mother—in B.C. Business looked to Howe and to Finance Minister Walter Harris to have its interests protected, while Paul Martin, a socially progressive Windsorite, spoke for francophones outside Quebec and for the left wing of the party. The men around that table, chaired by St. Laurent with increasing detachment, worked seamlessly with a bureaucracy that considered its relationship with the party to be both intimate and permeable. They gave Canada good, safe, solid, almost anonymous government. As the political scientist Paul Fox put it in 1955, "The Liberal government aims at operating noiselessly, like a respectable mammoth business operation which fears nothing more than making people aware that it is there. The shadows flit silently along the wall, as in Plato's cave, and the citizen is never sufficiently disturbed to turn his head."[10] What these men failed to understand was that their faceless corporate governance, headed by an amiable—they thought beloved—old man, was vulnerable to a political evangelist supported by modern marketing techniques and to the remorseless gaze of the television camera.

Because Canada was so slow to adopt television, the 1957 election was the first one properly broadcast on TV. In the United States, TV had been increasingly dominating political coverage since Dwight Eisenhower faced off against Adlai Stevenson in the 1952 presidential election. Canada was late to the game because the federal government couldn't decide whether to the adopt the European model—where networks were funded by governments, with a mandate to promote culture and national pride—or the American approach of private broadcasting and popular fare. The CBC only entered the field once it became clear that Canadians were taking matters into their own hands by putting up antennas and catching programming from the nearest U.S. city. Once the Corp established stations in the major cities, the new medium caught on like wildfire. There were an estimated 146,000 television sets in Canada in 1952; in 1956, there were 2.3 million.

The camera was cruel to Louis St. Laurent. It made him look even older than his seventy-five years. He made things worse by refusing to wear makeup or read from a teleprompter, relying on notes instead. That forces you to lower your head, which looks terrible on television. He avoided televised appearances as much as possible, which limited the damage but also the exposure.

At the national level, leadership was lackadaisical, with little coordination in messaging and communications. Powerful cabinet ministers, who were responsible for the national campaign in their regions, seemed complacent and disengaged. They had run so many successful election campaigns that they seem to have dismissed the possibility of failure. St. Laurent began his campaign in Winnipeg with a stump speech that, according to one local official, "read like an auditor's report, replete with numerous statistics, and was delivered in a similar manner."[11] The Western tour that followed was dominated by hecklers, an annoyance that the old master was now too old and frail to swat away. Instead, the speeches just became dryer and duller, and his encounters with both hecklers and reporters increasingly testy. Astonishingly, campaign organizers decided to send the hot-tempered C.D. Howe out on a Western tour—where, sure enough, he repeatedly lost his temper, telling one hostile questioner in the presence of reporters, "Look here, my good man, why don't you just go away and vote for the party you support? In fact, why don't you just go away?"[12] As the tour rolled through Quebec and the Maritimes, and St. Laurent's appearances became even less focused, his attitude became even more disengaged. Then, in Ontario, disaster struck. On June 7, with only days left in the campaign, party organizers brought St. Laurent and the Ontario candidates together on the stage at Maple Leaf Gardens for a "Peace, Prosperity, and Security" rally. But it sounded as though more people heckled than cheered. (It always does, even when supporters outnumber opponents.) At one critical moment, a lad of fifteen rushed up on the stage and tore up a Liberal poster in front of the dumbfounded prime minister. Security officials tried to hustle the teenager offstage, but he tripped and fell down the stairs, hitting his head on the concrete. The crowd watched in silence as the young protester was carried away for treatment. As it turned out, there was no serious injury, except to the Liberals' electoral prospects.

But if the campaign appeared to be in trouble on the ground, polling data assured party leaders that the public remained largely onside. Liberal headquarters detected a tightening of the race, and in the final days of the campaign, a poll from the Canadian Institute of Public Opinion had the Liberals at 43.5 per cent, down three points from the beginning of the campaign, and the PCs at 33.5 per cent, up four points. That was still enough for a comfortable majority government, and Gallup's last poll had the Grits at 48 and the Tories at 34. There was no reason to be concerned. Or so it seemed.

III

John Diefenbaker had always been terribly disorganized, as his law partners (and no doubt the law firm's secretaries) could bitterly attest, and always distrustful. Fortunately, with an election mere months away, the new leader was able to make the obvious decision to leave the shadow cabinet in place, which had the added benefit of avoiding bruised feelings in caucus. But he did need to put together a campaign team and a platform, and he didn't trust the people in the leader's office who had worked for George Drew, probably with good reason. On this occasion, at least, this led to him to make some smart decisions.

First, he listened to Gordon Churchill, a Winnipeg MP who chafed at the PCs' obsession with winning seats in Quebec, even though the party's even greater obsession with loyalty to the British Empire made it anathema among francophones. Chasing after Quebec votes was a waste of time and money, Churchill had written in a memo after the 1953 election. In that campaign, 45 per cent of Tory spending had been devoted to Quebec, without result. Going forward, he argued, the party should focus on where gains were realistically possible. The memo leaked, of course, leading to accusations of Tory intolerance toward French Canada. But Churchill repeated the advice to Diefenbaker shortly before the leadership convention, and Diefenbaker took it. Funds were apportioned tactically across the country, with special emphasis on ridings in Atlantic Canada, Ontario, and the West where gains were most likely to be made, though Quebec got its fair share as well. The party's best hopes in Quebec rested in convincing the aging but still all-powerful premier, Maurice Duplessis, to lend his Union Nationale party machinery to the cause. Duplessis was tempted (he hated Liberals) but cautious (he thought the Tories had little chance of winning). So he compromised, lending support to fifteen PC candidates in the province who he thought had a shot. This assistance would prove crucial.

Diefenbaker's second smart decision was to bring Allister Grosart and Dalton Camp on board. Although Canada had no equivalent to New York's Madison Avenue—which had emerged as the centre of modern American advertising and marketing, led by a handful of creative geniuses—several firms in Toronto sought to ride the same wave. Post-war affluence had empowered consumers who could comfortably afford a suburban house, a car, a refrigerator. But *which* refrigerator? Advertisers married insights from the new science of psychology to the technologies of print, radio, and especially television to convince consumers of the virtues of whatever brand they were selling. These same techniques were infiltrating politics, turning politicians into brands and policies into pitches. For the first time in the country's history, one of the political parties in a federal election would be marketed like soap. Grosart, a public relations executive, had used modern advertising techniques to put Leslie Frost into office as Ontario premier. Camp had done the same for Flemming in New Brunswick and Stanfield in Nova Scotia. They would craft a slick campaign centred on the party leader and a simple yet powerful message: "Time for a Change." All of this was worlds away from the complacent, oblivious Liberal approach.

Unlike the Liberals, the Conservative campaign made heavy use of television. Luckily for them, in contrast to St. Laurent, "Diefenbaker was a natural on television," wrote historian John Courtney in his analysis of the 1957 and 1958 campaigns.[13] The quivering-jowl outrage over Liberal arrogance and indifference and the evangelical call for a national redemption transcended meeting halls and auditoriums and intrigued millions of people watching the news clips at home.

After several stumbles and shuffles, Grosart was put in overall charge of the campaign; Camp, in charge of advertising. At one point, the young advertising executive didn't think he would be on the campaign, and didn't think he wanted to be. Diefenbaker had dressed Camp down in the parliamentary restaurant because of an event months before, when Camp had seated Olive at a table for the spouses rather than at the head table with Diefenbaker. The temper tantrum confirmed what Camp had heard and suspected: that Diefenbaker was too temperamental and vindictive to lead. Also, he didn't like or trust Allister Grosart, and submitted a letter of resignation once it became clear Grosart, not Churchill, would be in charge of the election campaign. Diefenbaker would have none of it. At the press gallery dinner in March, he grabbed Camp's head in the crook of his arm—surely knowing that the members of the press gallery would notice—and told him he hadn't read the resignation letter.

"I want you with me, do you understand? I want you with me, and that's all there is to it."[14] So Camp was back on board.

Camp made one early, quick, and wise decision: to bury the Progressive Conservative party brand, which was toxic, and replace it with Brand Diefenbaker. Election campaigns had always placed a heavy emphasis on the party leader, but this one would take that to an extreme never seen before. The campaign slogan was "It's Time for a Diefenbaker Government"; the oxymoronic "Progressive Conservative" label was almost nowhere to be seen.

Grosart, Camp, and other strategists knew the party had to reach beyond its base to people who didn't usually vote, or who usually voted Liberal but might be persuaded to change. Diefenbaker was perfectly cast for the part: a crusading Prairie lawyer with no ties to the Bay Street crowd, an outsider estranged from the Old Guard of his own party, a one-man party who might appeal to voters who had never voted Conservative: immigrant voters, suburban voters, voters that the Liberals took for granted.

One pivotal moment came early in the campaign, at Toronto's Massey Hall. The speech was inspired by Merrill and June Menzies, a young married couple who were both economists and who had sent Diefenbaker a dense, forty-three-page analysis of what they considered Canada's national priorities. Diefenbaker was so impressed by the document he hired Merrill as a policy adviser. We can only assume June's ongoing contribution came through advice to her husband.

Menzies had started out a Liberal, but became disenchanted with the party's unambitious, managerial approach, and with its heavy emphasis on the financial and manufacturing sectors in Ontario and Quebec. Too much of the Canadian economy, he thought, depended on American investment, and the Liberals were far too willing to let American firms ship raw product from Canada's mines and forests for processing in the U.S., where the better-paying jobs were to be found. A nascent economic nationalism was emerging within and outside both the Liberal and Conservative parties, which Menzies sought to tap. Meanwhile, the Maritimes were in decline and distress, the West felt neglected, and the North beckoned, rich in resources that could be harnessed in the national interest. In 1955, *The Old Chieftain*, the second of Donald Creighton's magisterial two-volume biography of John A. Macdonald, had become a best-seller, reviving the founding father in the imaginations of Canadians, including his vision of uniting Canada from coast to coast through the transcontinental railroad and through his National Policy of industry-protecting tariffs. It was time for a new national policy, Menzies believed. Diefenbaker had said as much in Parliament, though they were just words. Menzies gave substance to those words, which Diefenbaker unveiled at Massey Hall on April 25, at the beginning of the campaign. It is a speech that should be studied by every Canadian conservative today.

First and foremost, Menzies and Diefenbaker believed conservatism should not mean sacrificing social supports on the altar of tax cuts. Back at the convention, the new leader had convinced the party to abandon its opposition to the baby bonus, a program that had been sending cheques to mothers for more than a decade. At Massey Hall, he condemned the Liberal budget's modest increase in social security—he liked to refer to the finance minister mockingly as "Six Bucks" Harris, in honour of the modest increase in pensions in the last budget—and promised to improve social supports for older Canadians and for veterans.

He promised as well to adopt an aggressive immigration policy: "Canada needs increased population if her development is to keep pace with her vast resources." He vowed to reverse the "centralization complex" of the St. Laurent government and restore a more respectful balance between the federal and provincial governments. He also pledged to make the Senate a more effective institution, a Conservative trope that would be oft promised but never delivered.

Inspired by Menzies, Diefenbaker castigated a complacent Liberal administration that was willing to sell off the nation's assets and that had forgotten how to dream. He proposed "a national policy of development in the northern areas which may be called the New Frontier Policy. . . . The North, with all its vast resources of hidden wealth, the wonder and the challenge of the North must become our national consciousness."

And then there were the parts of the speech that were simply John Diefenbaker, that only he could deliver, with that quavering but powerful baritone, those fierce eyes, the head shaking side to side, the outrage at the Liberals' despoiling of Parliament —"that great institution treated with shocking contempt, sorely wounded, robbed of its rights, its independence gone"—his dream of a Canada united in common purpose rather than divided by region and language. Building cadence through parallel construction that subtly invoked both Lincoln's Gettysburg Address and Churchill's wartime speeches, Diefenbaker called Canadians to a higher purpose: "The policy of this party is based on its abiding faith in freedom; in the maintenance of our institutions which are the buttress of that freedom; in the sovereign independence of Canada; in our dedication that the State shall be the Servant and not the Master of the people." No Conservative had spoken like that in living memory. This was Macdonald's heir.

Others saw the turning point coming a month later, when Diefenbaker spoke in Vancouver, on May 24. The Western metropolis was booming, like so much of the rest of the country. Most immigrants were British or American, but Little Italy was expanding, along with Chinatown, despite the best efforts of municipal, provincial, and federal governments to keep Asians out of the country. Canada had taken in more than thirty-seven thousand Hungarians fleeing the Soviet crackdown in 1956, with about 20 per cent of them settling in British Columbia, which saw its Hungarian population double in 1957. The Social Credit government of W.A.C. "Wacky" Bennett encouraged the growth of forestry. Schools were bulging with the children of the baby boom; the first open-air shopping malls skirted the fringes of the suburbs. The city had long been hostile to Conservatives, but when Diefenbaker arrived at the Georgia Street auditorium, the hall was packed with three thousand people, and another two thousand listened outside through loudspeakers. Diefenbaker arrived in style, in a thirty-car motorcade fronted by a Dixieland band playing "When the Saints Go Marching In." "Across this country Canadians as a whole agree that something is happening," Diefenbaker prophesied, and the press began to wonder whether maybe he was right.[15]

For a brief moment, Dalton Camp fell in love with John Diefenbaker. Camp was overseeing the Maritime campaign and accompanied the Chief on his first swing through the region, where the Grits had taken twenty of twenty-six seats in the last election. Camp had never watched Diefenbaker on the campaign stump before; few had, outside Prince Albert, before this campaign. What he saw amazed him. There, in a darkened hall in Amherst, on the Fundy shore, the Chief gathered all the worries and fears of everyone in the room and made them his own: the decline of industry and agriculture, the doomed coal-mining industry, the young going down the road. "In Diefenbaker's passion is incorporated all the grievances of his audience," Camp wrote later. "He absorbs their indignation and, at the end, after they have laughed with him, cheered him, felt their nerve-ends respond to his voice, they find that he has repossessed their hopes, and they believe in him as they have not believed in anyone in a long, long time, if even then."[16] He marvelled as well at Diefenbaker on the street, grasping the hands of those he met, looking into their eyes, listening intently to whatever was on their mind, whether it was the old man rocking on a park bench or a young waitress holding a pot of coffee. Edna had taught him well, and Olive was a firm support, but there was more to it than that, more than even Camp understood. This was a man who had overcome his diffidence and shyness to dominate a courtroom. He had sat in jail cells and listened while a broken woman sobbed a life story of neglect and abuse. He had heard things few politicians had heard from people few politicians had ever met, let alone listened to. People—little people, many called them—caught this in him, understood it, embraced it.

He campaigned in a whirlwind: two national tours by plane and train and bus, multiple events each day, plunging into crowds, waving from the train, whipping people into a frenzy at rallies. His pace was so intense, the *Globe and Mail* warned in an editorial headlined "This Pace Can Kill" that he needed to slow down and protect his health. But the *Globe* misunderstood the man: Diefenbaker fed on campaigns, fed on the enthusiasm of crowds, fed on the worship of the Chief by those who felt they'd been forgotten by the urban Central Canada's elites. Diefenbaker forged a bond with those voters in 1957. Through five elections, he never abandoned them and they never abandoned him.

Still, few, apart from Diefenbaker, expected victory. The Conservatives had won only 51 seats in 1953, compared to 169 for the Liberals. No party could close such a gap. Neither had Diefenbaker's whirlwind campaign, for all its energy and slew of policies, provoked more than a modest reaction among voters, according to the polls. *Maclean's* magazine went to the printers just before election day with an editorial that assumed yet another Liberal government: "We have given that government an almost unexampled vote of confidence, considering the length of its term in office," the editors wrote. "It could easily be forgiven for accepting this as a mandate to resume the kindly tyranny it has exercised over parliament and the people for more than twenty years."[17]

Maclean's got it wrong. "Dewey Defeats Truman" wrong. The pollsters got it wrong, too. The Liberals and even the Conservatives got it wrong. On June 10, 1957, John George Diefenbaker and Louis Stephen St. Laurent—the latter in Quebec City, the former in Prince Albert—watched as their worlds turned upside down.

It started in the new province of Newfoundland, where the Tories took two seats—they'd been shut out in 1953. Having been practically shut out of the Maritimes in 1953 as well, they now had nineteen seats to the Liberals' seven. Two swings through the region by the leader, Tory premiers in both New Brunswick and Nova Scotia, and the exertions of Dalton Camp had worked wonders.

Though the Liberals still owned Quebec, with sixty-two seats, the Progressive Conservative seat count increased from four to nine, thanks to the selective efforts of Maurice Duplessis.

Ontario was decisive. The Tories had taken thirty-three seats in 1953, compared to fifty for the Grits. But with the help of Leslie Frost's well-oiled machine, the Diefenbaker Party had captured sixty-one seats, reducing the Liberal count to twenty-one. But even more important than the number of new seats in Ontario was where they were located.

York County, surrounding Toronto, had increased its representation from three to seven seats in the 1949 redistribution. Growth there was explosive: the ridings of York Centre, York-Humber, and York-Scarborough had grown on average by 46 per cent between the 1953 and 1957 elections. The voters of York County were part of what was emerging as the most important electorate in the country: the Ontario suburban middle class. Farm boys who had gone off to war but then moved to suburbs where the good jobs were when they returned. New arrivals from Europe, displaced by war or fleeing chronic poverty, who had quickly found well-paying work and houses they could afford on the edge of cities. People fleeing the cramped downtowns for a house with a big backyard for the kids and a garage for the car. The Tories had taken three of the region's seats in 1953; in 1957, they took all seven. Suburban Ontario had switched from red to blue.

The Western results were equally important. Liberal dominance in the West had been eroding for years, to the benefit of Social Credit on the right and the Canadian Commonwealth Federation on the left. But in 1957, the Progressive Conservatives finally broke through. In Manitoba, they captured eight seats; they had won only three in 1953. The Liberals fell from seven to one, while the CCF climbed from three to five.

Diefenbaker had been the only Tory MP to win in Saskatchewan in election after election. Now he had the company of two other MPs, with the Liberals slipping from five to three, and the CCF at ten.

The Social Credit Party dominated in Alberta, as before, with thirteen seats. But the Conservatives climbed from two to three, while the Liberals fell from four to one. In B.C., the Liberals went from eight seats to two and the Conservatives rose from three to seven. The Liberals had lost the West. They would never get it back.

Diefenbaker, sitting with Olive and Elmer and Allister Grosart, listened to the early returns on the radio in his Prince Albert home. Throughout the campaign, Olive had stood by her husband's side: silent, smiling, loyal. She was his rock, his solace at the end of a long day, his confidant and companion and quiet adviser. Publicly, she was the personification of the loyal and dutiful wife. She was privately so as well, though her judgment of those she considered insufficiently loyal could be swift and harsh. Elmer was there as brother and friend and acolyte, always faithful in good times and bad. But this night was better than good. As the results rolled in from Atlantic Canada, Quebec, and Ontario, and it became increasingly likely that Diefenbaker might become prime minister, the mood shifted from hopeful to exultant. The entourage left the house and headed for campaign committee rooms in the Lincoln Hotel, to celebrate with supporters. But Diefenbaker soon had to leave. There was no television station in Prince Albert, and he needed to get to a microphone. He had already agreed to fly to Regina, to broadcast a statement from the CBC station there. By the time he reached the studio, it seemed certain he had won. But Diefenbaker offered a sober address nonetheless. With a crude riding map of Saskatchewan behind him, the presumptive prime minister–designate told Canadians, "This is a moment of deep dedication rather than of elation."

While not declaring outright victory, he promised that if the results did confirm a Conservative government, "I shall honour the trust given to the Conservative Party and myself. I shall keep the faith. I shall maintain spiritual things without which political parties no less than individuals cannot discharge a full and complete life." He cited Matthew 20:27: "He who would be chiefest among you shall be servant of all."[18]

When his plane landed back in Prince Albert at midnight, as many as three thousand cheering supporters were waiting for him at the airport. Diefenbaker and the crowd celebrated together that night. The next day, he and Elmer, Manitoba leader Duff Roblin, some friends, and three reporters went fishing at Lac la Ronge. He didn't catch the most fish or the biggest. As he showed off his meagre catch, somebody remarked, "Not much of a fish you caught there, eh?"

"No," Diefenbaker replied with a grin. "I caught the big one yesterday."

IV

Mike Pearson held Algoma East, though other cabinet ministers weren't so lucky. Nine went down, including Finance Minister Walter "Six Bucks" Harris and, remarkably, C.D. Howe, who lost Port Arthur to a young CCF candidate, Doug Fisher, a high school history teacher. (Fisher would hold the seat for the next three elections, before becoming a columnist for the *Toronto Sun* and, eventually, dean of the Parliamentary Press Gallery.) When Howe realized he was beaten, "he swore for five minutes, in a style that would have commended him to his lumberjack constituents," according to his biographers, then went to the local television station to concede, where he came across Doug Fisher's mother, who had always voted for Howe until duty required that she support her offspring. When she met the defeated Liberal titan, Mrs. Fisher became distressed. "Oh Mr. Howe," she mourned. "What will you do now?"[19]

That Pearson prevailed in Algoma East despite a strong challenge from a local mayor testified to the loyalty of the voters toward their MP, because he was seldom there during the campaign. He was the busiest Liberal on the trail, travelling to sixty ridings to show the flag, either because the riding didn't make it onto St. Laurent's leisurely schedule or because, in the case of Victoria, St. Laurent had been there and organizers needed someone with more energy and confidence to come in and repair the damage. Those sixty candidates owed Mike Pearson a favour, and they now knew he would be cashing the cheque.

St. Laurent could have met the House and tried to govern with the support of the CCF and Independent MPs. The Liberals had, after all, won the popular vote, 40.5 per cent to 38.5 per cent. Mackenzie King would have tried to brazen it out. But St. Laurent never gave the idea a moment's thought. For one thing, he was a far more honourable man than King. For another, he was seventy-five and had lost almost half his cabinet, and there was no reason to believe CCF leader M.J. Coldwell would be willing to prop up the Liberals after twenty-two years in government. His face drained, St. Laurent made a disjointed statement to the CBC from the Château Frontenac on election night, consulted with his cabinet, and on June 18 travelled to Government House to tender his resignation to the governor general. He then retired to his summer house in St. Patrick, Quebec, on the lower St. Lawrence River's southern shore near Rivière-du-Loup, where the rich and powerful had been summering since the Gilded Age.

On September 2, Labour Day, Pearson received an urgent phone call from St. Laurent's son Renault. Mike and Lionel Chevrier must come immediately. Chevrier, a Franco-Ontarian, had represented Cornwall in the House and sat in St. Laurent's cabinet before stepping down to become president of the new St. Lawrence Seaway Authority. In 1957, St. Laurent brought him back into Parliament in a secure Montreal riding, designating him heir-apparent as the party's Quebec lieutenant. But the election changed all that. Two days after the phone call, Pearson and Chevrier were being driven from the Quebec City train station to St. Laurent's home, while Renault and his brother-in-law spoke of how depressed St. Laurent had become. When they arrived, Pearson found St. Laurent "in shocking condition, dejected, and looking much older." He wanted to resign, but felt he owed it to the party to stay. Quitting now would look like running away. He had already told the press that he would meet with caucus in the fall. Such was the sad, but not uncommon, end for many in public life. The addiction of politics, like Sauron's ring, sucks the life out of them, but still they cannot let go. Pearson and Chevrier gently assured St. Laurent that no one would blame him for laying down the leader's mantle, that announcing his intention to resign but to stay on until a new leader was chosen was the best and most honourable course. Mike worked past midnight on a statement that St. Laurent could issue to that effect.

The next day, when Pearson showed the statement to the old leader, "he stared uneasily at the draft, at times reading, at times merely brooding," Pearson later recalled. But eventually, "he looked up and said it was just right." Pearson and Chevrier and family members then went to work on convincing St. Laurent that he should not travel to Ottawa and hold a press conference, but should merely issue the statement through his office. Eventually, St. Laurent agreed to this as well. "I have never had a more difficult, indeed more distressing two hours, or taken part in a more painful task," Pearson recalled in his memoirs. "I do not think I have ever felt more sorry for anyone; but I know I would have felt even worse had he decided to try to carry on. To resign was sad, to continue would have been tragic."[20]

The new leader would be chosen at a convention in January, and Pearson's name was top of the list. "I was caught up in a turmoil of contradictory emotions," he later reminisced. He had never wanted or sought to be prime minister, he insisted. His move from undersecretary to secretary of external affairs was more an in-house promotion than the launch of a political career. He had little experience in politics, was worried about his lack of familiarity with Quebec and his poor command of French, and was hoping to reduce his hours at the office, not increase them. Still, he felt he had no choice. Any member of a political party who was being called upon by other members of that party to lead it "had no right to reject the invitation of his friends to allow his name to go before the convention," he later wrote. "Whatever his personal feelings, his public obligation was overriding."[21]

This is mostly hokum. Pearson wanted to be prime minister. Douglas Abbott, the former finance minister, believed that once Pearson realized the Russians would never let him become UN secretary general, he set his sights on 24 Sussex Drive. Abbott was probably the only one who could have beaten Pearson in a leadership contest, but his accession to the Supreme Court in 1954 removed him from contention. His successor, Walter Harris, also believed that Pearson was angling for the leadership, a prize Harris coveted. But losing his seat in the 1957 election took Harris out of contention as well.

Lester Pearson was raised the son of a small-town Ontario Methodist minister, and socialized at St. John's, Oxford. Both cultures disdained open displays of ambition. One did not seek a prize; one waited modestly to have it bestowed. Annie Pearson's son would never elbow his way into the Liberal leadership; he would have to be reluctantly persuaded. Or so it must seem.

There were many willing to do the persuading. C.D. Howe, still a powerful voice within the party, considered Pearson to be one of the few remaining in caucus who was qualified for the leadership. Everyone knew that St. Laurent, though officially neutral, wanted Pearson as his successor. Jimmy Sinclair, the Liberal B.C. boss, hoped for and predicted a Pearson win. Jack Pickersgill, though a friend of Walter Harris, told Harris that he would be supporting Pearson. The former foreign minister had virtually unanimous support among the senior ranks of the party. And the press.

The Parliamentary Press Gallery of the 1950s was a boys' club. There had never been more than one woman member since the first one— Genevieve Lipsett-Skinner, of the *Vancouver Sun*—arrived in the 1920s. Reporters on the Hill smoked and drank, and some of them caroused with women who were not their wives. Most of them identified with a political party, though they had become less slavish in their devotion than in the past. The *Toronto Star*, the *Ottawa Citizen*, the *Montreal Star*, the *Winnipeg Free Press*, and the *Vancouver Sun* were Liberal; the *Globe and Mail*, the *Toronto Telegram*, the *Ottawa Journal*, the *Montreal Gazette*, and the *Winnipeg Tribune* were Conservative. The French-language press was generally nationalist, and many younger journalists would later identify with Quebec separatism. In 1958, three men dominated English-language political journalism in Canada: Bruce Hutchison of the *Victoria Daily Times*, Grant Dexter of the *Winnipeg Free Press*, and Blair Fraser of *Maclean's*. Dexter was one of many who had trained under and were disciples of John Dafoe, the legendary editor of the *Free Press*, one of Canada's most influential newspapers. The leading figures in the gallery in these days typically had similar backgrounds: farm boys or sons of the working class, with little formal education but keen minds and a prodigious work ethic. Most of them arrived at Parliament Hill as young men in their twenties or even their teens, and stayed connected to it for decades. Most were large-L Liberals without shame; they sought to convince voters of the party's wisdom and sought also to influence its policies and strategy. And they were devoted to Mike Pearson. "I loved the guy," Hutchison told John English.[22] Grant Dexter considered it his mission "to help Mike shine."[23] Dexter's devotion was particularly close: according to Hill veteran and author Robert Lewis, in the last months before the Second World War, Pearson leaked information to Dexter that Dexter passed on to Dafoe, that Dafoe then used—without ever revealing the source—to promote stronger opposition to Hitler in the editorials of the *Free Press*.

But these men were not uncritical. They condemned the use of closure during the pipeline debate. They believed that St. Laurent's time was long past, that the Liberals needed a new leader, and that the leader should be Mike. "We are going to have a fairly long period of critical years," George Ferguson, editor of the *Montreal Star* and another pupil of Dafoe's, wrote Pearson in 1956, "and the plain fact is that, without you, the Cabinet's policies will drift from bad to worse."[24] Grattan O'Leary may have considered himself a de facto leader within the Conservative Party, which he was, but most political journalists wanted to see the Liberals in power and Lester B. Pearson as prime minister, and considered it their mission to help bring about that happy state of affairs.

In any event, the conclusion was already foregone. The day after St. Laurent announced his retirement, newspapers were declaring Pearson heavily favoured to win the leadership. Paul Martin had made no secret of his ambition to lead the party, but the Liberals traditionally rotated between a Quebec Catholic and an English Protestant, so Martin's timing was wrong. Besides, his eagerness for the job was just a touch unseemly. And it was lost on no one that sixty-two of the Liberals' 105 seats were in Quebec. The party had been badly beaten in Ontario and the West. The route back to power clearly lay in appealing to Protestant English voters west of the Ottawa River. Martin, a French Catholic, was demographically the wrong man for the job.

The only problem was that no one knew what Mike Pearson stood for. He had spent his entire career in the foreign service, but Canadian voters cast their ballots on domestic issues: taxes and job security, health care and roads and pensions. Where was he on these issues? No one was sure, including Pearson himself, but it hardly mattered. On October 14, the Norwegian Nobel Committee announced that it had bestowed the Peace Prize on Lester B. Pearson "for his crucial contribution to the deployment of a United Nations Emergency Force in the wake of the Suez Crisis." What party in its right mind would reject as leader someone who had just won the Nobel Peace Prize?

Liberals gathered in conclave on January 16, 1958, at Ottawa's Aberdeen Pavilion—better known as the "cow palace" or "cattle castle" for its principal function of hosting agricultural displays during the Central Canada Exhibition. Despite Martin's feisty campaign, the outcome was never in doubt: 1,074 votes for Lester B. Pearson, 305 for Paul Martin, 1 for the Reverend Harold Lloyd Henderson. (Henderson claimed he did not vote for himself.) But the outcome of the convention mattered less than its tone. Delegates were angry about the defeat seven months ago and anxious to reverse that defeat. Pearson channelled that anger and impatience. He promised that as leader of the official opposition he would force an election, "and soon."[25] Hutchison and Dexter met with Pearson during the convention, to warn against such a course. Pearson dismissed them impatiently. "It's no use, Grant. I've made up my mind," he told Dexter. "We're going to force an election. That's final."[26]

There was only one problem with Pearson's impatient strategy. The Tories were doing well in the polls, and for a reason. John Diefenbaker was giving Canada good government.

V

Upon returning from his brief fishing trip after election night, Diefenbaker discovered that Louis St. Laurent, with untypical ill grace, had declined to make the government airplane available, forcing the Conservative leader, Olive, and other members of his party to return to Ottawa on commercial flights. When Trans-Canada Air Lines lost one of his suitcases, Dief had a temper tantrum in the airport, which the *Globe and Mail*'s Clark Davey witnessed and reported on, earning him a dressing-down from the incoming prime minister. St. Laurent wanted to wait until after the military vote was counted before acknowledging defeat. That vote produced no substantial change; Diefenbaker was sworn in as prime minister on June 21, by the same Vincent Massey who had amiably consented to Louis St. Laurent's request that Parliament be dissolved two months prior. Everything John George Diefenbaker had dreamed of as a boy had come true—improbably true, given his tortured path to Parliament, the dismal track record of his chosen party, and his alienation from that party's establishment. But he and Mary had never lost faith. After it was clear he had won the election, John visited Mary, who was in hospital in Saskatoon. In his memoirs he reported, "My mother said to me, 'You've been given the opportunity to do something for your country. Do not forget the poor and afflicted. Do the best you can for as long as you can.' And that was the last time that she, with her Highland ancestry and her refusal to exult, ever said anything about the fact that I had become Prime Minister of my country."[27] Was there a sense of hurt, there, a longing for at least a little exultation?

But there was no time to contemplate such things. Diefenbaker was due to leave for a Commonwealth Conference in London in two days. He was no doubt grateful for the briefing he received from Pearson, the outgoing secretary of state for external affairs, the day before the swearing in, though the two men must surely have been thinking that they might soon be confronting each other as party leaders. Diefenbaker told Pearson that, at least for the moment, he would serve as his own foreign minister, a reversion to the era of Mackenzie King and his predecessors. Pearson advised that this would be possible for the short term, but that a minister would need to be found eventually. As it turned out, the cabinet was only half appointed when

Diefenbaker left for London; the complete ministry would not be in place until September.

Diefenbaker's visit to London was a special moment for him and an unusual one for Britain and the Commonwealth, both of which had gotten used to Canada only ever having Liberal governments. He met his idol, Winston Churchill—now a very old man who, according to Diefenbaker's friend William Macadam, after dinner produced a bottle of cognac that he said had been given to him by de Gaulle. When Diefenbaker said he did not drink, Churchill, alarmed, asked, "What, are you a prohibitionist?" "No," Diefenbaker replied, "I just don't care to drink." Churchill harrumphed, "In that case, you only hurt yourself."[28] He also met with the young Queen Elizabeth, who impressed him greatly. But the Commonwealth Conference held a political purpose as well: lessening Canada's increasing dependence on, and integration with, the American economy.

During the election campaign, Diefenbaker had warned of the ever-greater reliance on American investment that many feared was turning Canada into a vassal state. This was a view shared by many Liberal supporters as well. Walter Gordon had declined an offer to join the St. Laurent government because Gordon, who was becoming increasingly concerned about the American domination of the Canadian economy, did not believe he could sit at the same cabinet table with C.D. Howe. Instead, at Finance Minister Walter Harris's invitation, he headed up the Royal Commission on Canada's Economic Prospects. The commission's report noted that 60 per cent of Canada's merchandise exports went to the United States, double the figure of two decades before. The share of imports from the U.S. had increased to 73 per cent from 63 per cent. American companies were investing heavily in the resource and manufacturing sectors. "Many Canadians are worried about such a large measure of economic decision-making being in the hands of non-residents," the report stated. "There is little evidence to suggest that foreign-controlled Canadian companies are being operated in a way which is at variance with the best interest of Canada, but it is not axiomatic that this will always be the case."[29] The commission recommended that foreign companies operating in Canada should have Canadians in senior positions and Canadians should own a substantial minority share of the company. But the report was dead on arrival. "C.D. Howe was furious,"

Gordon later wrote. He interpreted the report as a direct criticism of his policies, "and to some extent that was true." Nonetheless, both Gordon for the Liberals and Merrill Menzies for the Conservatives were tapping into growing unease among Canadians about American control over the economy. Yes, times and wages were good, but Canada's birthright was being shipped by rail to American smelters and refineries, even as the manufacturing sector was being turned into what would later be called "(Canada), Inc."

Diefenbaker's solution to American domination was diversification: Canada should increase its trade with Commonwealth nations and, in particular, with Great Britain. At the conference, he convinced the other leaders to agree, reluctantly, to a Commonwealth trade and commerce conference the following year, and when he returned to Canada, he grandly announced that his government's goal was to divert 15 per cent of what Canada imported from the United States to imports from Britain. He seemed to have made the number up in his head. Such a thing was quite impossible, as staff in the Prime Minister's Office and at Finance quickly informed him. Imports from the U.K. would have to more than double to meet that goal, and there wasn't that much Canada wanted to buy from Britain. In any case, the scheme flew in the face of the British government's desire to negotiate a free trade agreement with the newly formed European Economic Community, a customs union involving France, West Germany, Italy, and the Benelux countries. Britain would be gradually weakening its preferential trade ties with the Commonwealth, not strengthening them. Harold Macmillan, the smoothest and slipperiest of prime ministers, decided to let the Canadians down while letting them save face and also making a point to the Europeans that Britain had other options. Later that year, his government proposed a full-on free trade agreement with Canada. Tariffs had been gradually coming down around the world under the General Agreement on Tariffs and Trade, established after the war, but Canada had always protected its manufacturing; agreeing to free trade with Britain would hurt Canadian businesses, at least in the short term, along with the electoral prospects of the new Conservative government. Diefenbaker turned the idea down flat. His first international foray had not gone particularly well.

When he returned from the Commonwealth Conference, the new prime minister discovered he needed to make an immediate decision on whether to integrate even more closely with the United States. Since the end of the war, the Canadian and American governments had been jointly preparing for the defence of North America in the event of a nuclear war by constructing three early-warning radar lines on Canadian soil. But the Americans were pushing for an integrated continental air defence agency under joint—but really American—control. Though the St. Laurent government reluctantly agreed, it put off any formal announcement until after the 1957 election, lest the loss of Canadian sovereignty become an election issue.

Now, as General Charles Foulkes, chief of the defence staff, explained, the Americans were urgently asking Canada to make the new air defence command public and operational. Diefenbaker agreed and signed into being the North American Air Defense Command (NORAD). In future years, the prime minister would come to wish he had taken more care in defining the terms of reference for NORAD, but he made the right decision nevertheless. Headquartered in Colorado, commanded by an American, with a Canadian deputy commander, NORAD has helped keep the peace from then till now.

The new cabinet was earnest, committed, and uncertain. None of its ministers had served in government, including the prime minister. The new PM was pleasantly surprised to discover that most of the senior ranks of the public service—including Robert Bryce, clerk of the Privy Council, who was an anchor for the new administration—were anything but Liberal obstructionists. Many public servants agreed that a change of governing parties was needed and were eager to cooperate. The government had a full agenda, but there was little anyone could move on until the opening of Parliament, slated for October 14. Diefenbaker would happily have moved the date forward, but the previous government had invited Queen Elizabeth to open Parliament, which etched the date in stone. John invited Elmer to stay with him at 24 Sussex Drive. "It is a fairy castle," Elmer wrote Mary, "surrounded by beautiful grounds and overlooking the beautiful Ottawa River. . . . There is a large staff of servants who wait on you hand and knee—so that is something different for me."[30] John wrote to Mary that all of Ottawa High Society was trying to get a seat in a gallery for the throne speech. "Everybody wants to get in but few will succeed in doing so. . . . There will be a tremendous number of disappointed people who spend their lives trying to climb the social ladder."[31] Now he was on the very top rung of that ladder.

No monarch had ever opened Canada's Parliament, and the beautiful young queen and her dashing husband Philip were wildly popular. As MPs joined senators in the upper house, Elizabeth announced her ministers would ask Parliament to fund a new dam for the South Saskatchewan River, institute paid vacations for workers under federal jurisdiction, and provide improved pensions for the elderly, veterans, and the disabled, along with price supports for farmers.

The young queen ended the address by invoking the words of the first Elizabeth, in her final address to Parliament: "'Though God hath raised me High, yet this I count the Glory of my Crown, that I have Reigned with your Loves.' Now here in the new world I say to you that it is my wish that in the years before me I may so reign in Canada and be so remembered." For Diefenbaker, only one thing marred this near-perfect day: this was also the day the Norwegian Nobel committee announced Lester B. Pearson had won the Peace Prize.

The next day, Diefenbaker accompanied Elizabeth and Philip to the United States, where she embarked on a four-day state visit. The Americans were enamoured of the royal couple, who appeared to enjoy watching American football as the Maryland Terrapins defeated the North Carolina Tar Heels 21–7. They visited, at the Queen's request, a local supermarket, something still foreign and exotic to most Brits. Diefenbaker and Eisenhower, in their first meeting as prime minister and president, discovered they liked each other. They were the sons of Western farmers who had grown up poor and who loved to fish. (In 1958, Eisenhower came to Ottawa. After the president had addressed Parliament, Ike and John took their fishing gear and tried their luck on Harrington Lake.) "President Eisenhower and I were from our first meeting on an Ike-John basis, and . . . were as close as the nearest telephone," Diefenbaker remembered later in his memoirs. On this first visit, the two leaders affirmed their mutual commitment to NATO and joint defence of the continent, including the new air defence command.

On November 25, Diefenbaker and the provincial premiers met in Ottawa for two days of talks in which Diefenbaker promised to fund public hospital insurance care. The St. Laurent government had passed legislation establishing the program, but it was weighted with so many conditions that many premiers predicted it would be years before the program was implemented, if ever. The Diefenbaker government promised to remove all the conditions, thus laying the groundwork for medicare. The government also transferred tax points to the provinces, establishing a principle that would resonate for decades to come: Liberal governments tend to centralize power in what they consider the national interest. Conservative governments tend to decentralize in the name of respecting provincial rights.

But mostly, Diefenbaker was on the move. The most important move was a trip to Paris for the first meeting of NATO heads of government since the organization had been formed in 1949. The Russian launch of Sputnik had signalled that NATO could no longer assume superiority in nuclear weapons. During the Paris talks, Diefenbaker fell in with Harold Macmillan's proposed two-track approach: unwavering solidarity in confronting the Soviet military threat, including the possibility of stockpiling intermediate-range ballistic missiles in Europe, coupled with proposed negotiations to ease tensions. The Canadian delegation took charge of the wording of the final communiqué, which emerged after several revisions "in worthy and forgettable prose."[32] Then it was on to New York for a speech at the United Nations, to Quebec City and to Saskatoon—"We went to the fairgrounds with a *police* escort!" he wrote Mary. "What do you know about that!"[33]— to Dartmouth and McGill for honorary degrees, to every fall fair and party assembly and get-together he could squeeze in, while also insisting cabinet meet three times a week. At sixty-two, he was fit and energized, a human dynamo in love with his job. The legislative agenda was ambitious: along with public hospital care, the government raised pensions to fifty-five dollars a month—take *that*, "Six Bucks" Harris—with additional supports for veterans and the disabled. There were price supports and cash advances to farmers, a constituency that Liberals had come to neglect. Infrastructure was a priority, with cabinet signing off on the much-promised, never delivered South Saskatchewan River Dam. There were two new royal commissions: one on energy and the other on transportation. The government ended an iniquitous practice of paying married women a lower unemployment insurance rate than men; a winter seasonal works program was established to combat rising unemployment; one hundred thousand Canadians were taken off the tax rolls and the corporate tax rate was reduced for small businesses; new legislation was enacted providing for the humane slaughter of animals. No Canadian Parliament had ever authorized so many initiatives in so little time.

By Christmas, most of the promises of the throne speech had been fulfilled. The three opposition parties were broke and dispirited. The government was popular—comfortably into majority territory in the polls—and so was Dief the Chief, with large and enthusiastic crowds greeting him everywhere he went, and he went everywhere. Cabinet ministers and party strategists were hankering for another election, to capitalize on Conservative popularity. But with the government only a few months old, and legislation sailing through the House and Senate unobstructed, what possible excuse could there be for calling one? In a masterstroke of bad timing, Lester B. Pearson, leader of Her Majesty's Loyal Opposition, provided it.

VI

Mike Pearson had always been less interested in domestic policy and in partisan politics than in foreign affairs. Even in his years in cabinet, his focus had been outside the country. Now he led a Liberal Party that didn't have a lot of money, didn't have an agenda, was unused to opposition, and faced a Conservative government soaring in the polls. Worse, the party was divided, between pragmatists who wanted to avoid an election the Liberals might well lose, and militants who wanted the Conservatives—who they saw as fundamentally illegitimate as a governing party—removed from office as quickly as possible.

When Parliament returned January 20, 1958, the first order of business was a vote of interim supply, in which the House authorizes the government to continue spending money for a set period. Because it's a money bill, the vote on interim supply is a vote of confidence in the government. Pearson had two apparent options: He could simply do nothing and let the supply bill pass, on the grounds that he had only just taken up the leadership and needed time to organize the party and draw up a platform. But that would contradict his loaded-for-bear vow at the leadership convention the week-end before to bring the government down at the first opportunity. Or he could move a motion of non-confidence and risk an election if the CCF and Social Credit voted with the Liberals. Neither scenario was attractive, which is why Pearson seized on a third option presented to him by Jack Pickersgill: Pearson should urge the government to resign, on the grounds of manifest incompetence, and advise the governor general to appoint a Liberal ministry in its place. The other opposition parties would never be able to support such a poison pill. If the Conservatives wanted a winter election, which both politicians and voters disliked, they would have to pull the plug on their own.

Normally, when a new official opposition leader debuts in Parliament, the leader and the prime minister exchange polite and amusing best wishes, with the PM typically saying something like "I hope that my honourable friend enjoys many years as leader of the official opposition." But on this day, after the ritual exchange of pleasantries—in which Pearson assured Diefenbaker, "I shall also try my very best to emulate my right hon. friend the Prime Minister in at least one respect as Leader of the Opposition; namely, to stay in this position for as short a time as he was successful in doing"—the new Liberal leader took to his feet and launched a stern attack on the government. Given "the dismal and depressing decline of the Canadian economy since last summer and the paralysis of the government in the face of growing problems," the government should "make way in this parliament for a government pledged to implement Liberal policies," Pearson proposed. And he generously added, "I would be prepared, if called upon, to form such a government to tackle immediately the formidable problem of ending the Tory pause and getting this country back on the Liberal highway of progress from which we have been temporarily diverted."[34]

The House was stunned. Pearson's own caucus hadn't known this was coming. "Mike, it's sad to see you come to this," Donald Fleming inter-jected. Diefenbaker was exultant. Laughing, he turned to Howard Green. "This is it," he declared. And then he rose to his feet.

For more than two hours, punctuated by a dinner break, Diefenbaker laid into Pearson. The proposed amendment "is the resignation from responsibility of a great party" he told the House. "It is a program designed in a spirit of resignation while at the same time pretending to the Canadian people that it is designed to be courageous," an amendment "saturated with fear of what the electorate will do to it."[35] And then he pulled out a bundle of papers that had been given to him by Patrick Nicholson, a correspondent for the Thomson chain of papers and a personal friend. The document was a memorandum to cabinet from March of the previous year, prepared by Mitchell Sharp, a senior official in the trade and commerce department, warning of an approaching downturn. The economy was softening, demand falling, trade decreasing, and unemployment rising, the document stated. So the St. Laurent government had been clearly warned that a recession was on the horizon, but rather than seek to counter the slowdown through stimulative spending and tax cuts, then-finance minister Walter Harris had presented a stay-the-course budget and the Liberals had promised continued good times in the campaign, blaming the Tories for the downturn once they were out of power.

"They hid the facts; they concealed the record; they did not let the Canadian people know what was taking place," Diefenbaker stormed. "We were on the slide, really on the slide, when they left power on June 21, and now, for political purposes, having concealed this document, they have the effrontery to pretend to the Canadian people that we are responsible."

The prime minister should never have seen that memorandum. The cabinet discussions of a government are not revealed to the successor government, to preserve freedom of discussion within cabinet. But having gotten his hands on the document, there was no way on earth Diefenbaker wasn't going to use it, and Pearson had given him the perfect opportunity.

"Dief scored point after point on Pearson and the Liberals to the thundering applause of his supporters," Fleming later wrote. "Pearson looked at first merry, then serious, then uncomfortable, then disturbed, and finally sick. His followers knew all too well that he was destroyed."[36] The next day in the House, CCF MP Colin Cameron chastised Diefenbaker for unnecessary cruelty. "When I saw him bring whole batteries of rhetoric, whole arsenals of guided missiles of vitriol and invective in order to shoot one forlorn, sitting duck—a sitting duck, indeed, already crippled with a self-inflicted wound," he told the House, "I wondered if the Prime Minister really believes in the humane slaughter of animals."[37] Pearson's own verdict: "The Prime Minister tore me to shreds."[38]

In that one speech, Pearson made three cardinal errors. First, he gave Diefenbaker the perfect excuse to call an election. The new Liberal leader was declaring that the government was illegitimate and should resign at the very moment when Diefenbaker was casting about for a reason to go to the polls. Second, he reminded voters of the Liberal Party's deep arrogance and sense of entitlement. Finally, and fatally, Pearson put Diefenbaker back in the role he most cherished: opposition underdog fighting the Machine. The Man from Prince Albert would be able to campaign not only on his government's brief but impressive record in health care, pensions, and other reforms but as the people's champion against vested interests.

Diefenbaker let the Liberals twist for a few days before visiting Vincent Massey to ask for dissolution. The man who had been Pearson's sponsor, mentor, and guide would now issue the writs of election that would lead to his former protege's humiliation. For everyone knew, almost from the moment that Parliament was dissolved, that Diefenbaker was headed for another win. And not just any win. He had become, for the moment at least, a sensation.

The post-war world had entered a period of almost maniacal hero-worship of cultural icons. It began, perhaps, with the bobby soxers: young women who screamed and swooned over Frank Sinatra. Elvis Presley earned an even more devoted following, and the Beatles, a boy band out of Liverpool that would transform popular music, would become, in the words of John Lennon, "more popular than Jesus." In the election of 1958, John Diefenbaker surfed a similar wave. Or, as John Duffy put it in his analysis of the election, "Running Lester Pearson against John Diefenbaker in 1958 was like booking Pat Boone versus Elvis—a dull crooner opposite a rock star."[39] At party gatherings, ecstatic supporters literally reached out to touch the hem of his garment. For decades, voters had been accustomed to the placid meanderings of aged Liberal leaders. Diefenbaker offered them an inspirational alternative: finger jabbing, jowls quivering, eyes blazing, head shaking, he asked them to "Follow John"—the campaign's simple but inspired slogan—and his vision for "One Canada," which could mean either greater national unity, equal consideration for all regions, a major push to develop the Arctic, or whatever you wanted it to mean.

Or maybe it was something much older: John the Evangelist, preaching of revival, of a path to salvation for a country seized with its own untapped potential, unsure of its destiny, worried over its encroaching southern neighbour, frightened at being wedged between two nuclear superpowers. For Diefenbaker, salvation lay in exploiting Canada's resources, opening up its north, and summoning the people—not the institutions, not the interests, not the elites, the *people*—to greatness. "Join with me," he pleaded. "Join with me to catch the Vision of men and women who rise to things that ordinarily hold you to the soil. Join with me to bring about the achievement of that Canada, One Canada, the achievement of Canada's destiny."[40] For a moment, it was possible to believe that the country was not just a collection of squabbling regions constantly under threat of breaking apart or being absorbed by the United States, but a young and confident nation, bounded not by two oceans but by three, with a united purpose and a limitless future.

Like all great public orators, Diefenbaker was inspired by his audiences as much as they were by him. "An audience has its effect on you," he confessed years later, in a rare moment of openness with an interviewer. "It moves you. The exhilaration of the ups and downs, while exacting a tremendous physical reaction, is exhilarating beyond words."[41]

But there was more to the campaign than Diefenbaker's populist, charismatic appeal. In the 1957 election, Ontario premier Leslie Frost had put the province's well-oiled political machine at the service of the federal party; that machine was available again. And now Maurice Duplessis decided to truly enter the game. At the federal–provincial conference on health care, Diefenbaker had made it clear that he preferred a more respectful federalism—in which Ottawa funded the provinces but let them tailor social programs to local needs—to the Liberals' autocratic approach of requiring provinces to meet federal standards. Duplessis appreciated the greater provincial autonomy resulting from Diefenbaker's approach. While the old Quebec lion had only been prepared to offer limited support in key ridings last time out, this time the Union Nationale went all in, sweeping aside the hapless federal PC operation in the province and putting the full UN machine to work on behalf of grateful Tory candidates.

Diefenbaker campaigned more vigorously even than the year before. He had more energy because the crowds had more energy, and he fed from the energy of the crowds. Pierre Sévigny—so movie-star handsome that he had screen-tested with MGM before the war, in which he lost a leg at the Battle of the Rhine—was also a writer and strategist and candidate in the riding of Longueuil. He recalled a Winnipeg rally at which five thousand people listened in rapture while Diefenbaker rhapsodized about "One Canada where people will live in harmony, One Canada where everything will be great." "When he had finished his speech," Sévigny wrote, "as he was walking to the door, I saw people kneel and kiss his coat. Not one, but many. People were in tears. People were delirious. And this happened many a time after."[42]

Against such hysteria, Pearson never had a chance. The Liberal election platform—tax cuts to stimulate demand, unemployment insurance for people who lost their job for health reasons, a national minimum wage— was lost in the exultant Tory campaign. Pearson, who would never be comfortable on the stump, offered a pale and flaccid alternative to the Diefenbaker magic. "I was by no means a natural vote-seeker," Pearson acknowledged in his memoirs, "and I disliked intensely some elements of campaigning." The campaign was inexperienced, disorganized, and short of funds. In Kingston, one passerby told him, "Mr. Pearson, you are a very nice man, but go home. You're wasting your time."[43]

The passerby was right. As the results rolled in, Pearson and his advisers sat slack-jawed at the numbers being posted by the CBC. At first, there was hope. Joey Smallwood, who ruled Newfoundland and Labrador with an iron glove, worked furiously, and successfully, to stay the Tory tide in his province: the Liberals held seven seats to the Conservatives' three.

But Robert Stanfield's organization delivered a Tory sweep in Nova Scotia. Prince Edward Island was also a sweep, and the Progressive Conservatives took seven of ten seats in New Brunswick. Dalton Camp, who once again organized the campaign in the Maritimes, had once again come through.

But for the Liberals, it was in Quebec that the wheels came off. Fifty seats for the Progressive Conservatives and only twenty-five for the Liberals. The Tories hadn't done that well in French Canada since the Riel Rebellion. Duplessis's machine was not the only reason: Quebecers often vote federally in waves, and when it became clear that the Conservatives were sweeping the rest of the country, they joined the sweep. Next door, in Ontario, things were even worse for the Grits: PCs: sixty-seven; Liberals: fourteen; CCF: three. The Conservatives had always been stronger in Ontario than in other parts of the country. This time they owned the joint.

But the lasting, permanent damage was in the West. In the previous campaign, the Conservatives had finally broken through in a region that, for decades, had been closed to them. On March 30, 1958, they took permanent control. The Progressive Conservatives won every seat in Manitoba and Alberta, sixteen of seventeen seats in Saskatchewan, and eighteen of twenty-two seats in British Columbia. The Liberals were shut out. Social Credit was shut out. Both CCF leader M.J. Coldwell and Social Credit leader Solon Low lost their seats.

For decades, Westerners had looked with resentment at the vested interests—the banks, the railway companies, the fat-cat politicians—who served their own needs while ignoring the needs of Western businesses, Prairie farmers, all the descendants of those Eastern Europeans who had filled the Prairies and who for decades had voted Liberal in gratitude. More recently, they had turned either to the social democrats or the increasingly mainstream Social Credit Party, which better understood their concerns. Now, in 1958, they overwhelmingly embraced a man who was one of them, who had grown up among them, who understood their grievances and their needs, who had already acted to support farmers and small businesses. They followed John.

The election of 1958 reshaped the political geography of the country. While the Liberals would return to dominance east of the Ottawa River, they would never fully recover in the West. In most elections from then till now, the Liberals would hold some or most of Quebec and conservatives of one ilk or another would dominate the Prairies, while urban Ontario and B.C.'s Lower Mainland would decide the result. But that was for the future. On election night 1958, John Diefenbaker's Progressive Conservatives won the greatest electoral landslide in Canadian history: 54 per cent of the vote; 78 per cent of the seats. (Brian Mulroney would do better in the seat count in 1984, but not in the popular vote or seat percentage.) The Liberals took the worst shellacking they'd ever received: 34 per cent of the vote, 48 of 265 seats.

Pearson watched the results in the Château Laurier, after a dinner of oyster stew. "The oysters were wonderful," he later reported, but "the television show was about the worst I ever saw."[44] When he gamely acknowledged defeat on television, people noted that the carnation in his lapel had wilted.

That night on the CBC's television network, Diefenbaker promised, "We will keep your faith, honour our pledges, and give you, to the best of our ability, good government for the benefit of the greatest number of Canadians."[45] Then he and Olive, who was bravely disguising serious back pain, joined the raucous celebration in Prince Albert, where the band played "When Johnny Comes Marching Home."

This was his hour, his time. John Diefenbaker had not only achieved his lifelong dream of becoming prime minister, he had also won the largest electoral victory in the history of the country. His political capital was enormous. Now what would he do with it?

EIGHT

The Chief

(1958–1961)

I

He rose each morning at 5:30, padded downstairs, poured himself a glass of milk, and then dove into whatever file seemed most intractable. At 8 a.m., after a brisk morning walk, he arrived at the suite of offices in East Block reserved for the prime minister and his staff. A typical day would consist of a dozen appointed meetings and a dozen more informal calls. His staff of twenty-six was about the same number that Louis St. Laurent had relied upon. He ate his lunch—typically a thermos of soup, a plate of cold meat, cheese, an apple, and a bottle of milk—at his desk.

He kept to—and enjoyed—a punishing schedule. Vacations were rare, perhaps two or three weeks a year, typically fishing trips in Saskatchewan or the Caribbean. One of those Caribbean visits was painfully memorable. In February 1965, Liberal MP John Turner and his wife Geills were arriving at a beach in the Caribbean when Turner noticed an older man struggling against the undertow. Turner, who was an Olympic-class athlete in university, leapt into the water and rescued the drowning man. It was Diefenbaker.

A future prime minister had saved the life of a former prime minister. "I never mentioned it," said Turner.¹ But word got out.

Diefenbaker, like all prime ministers who have come after him, was deeply fond of Harrington Lake, the newly created retreat for prime ministers in Gatineau Park, which offered fine fishing and a refuge from the political turmoil of the capital. And though he rarely took holidays, Diefenbaker loved to travel. On October 28, a few months after his landslide victory, John and Olive, along with brother Elmer, foreign affairs liaison Basil Robinson, and a few others, began a 'round-the-world jaunt even more ambitious than St. Laurent's excursion in 1955. While that trip had exhausted the Liberal prime minister, Diefenbaker found it exhilarating. As it happened, the trip coincided with an emerging crisis within the Western alliance. Charles de Gaulle, recently returned as president, had written Eisenhower and Macmillan demanding that France be given equal place with the United States and Great Britain within the alliance. Macmillan was worried that, if rebuffed, de Gaulle would take France out of NATO, while also vetoing British efforts to obtain a free trade agreement with the European Common Market. After consultations with Macmillan in London, Diefenbaker met the imperious French president in Paris. Diefenbaker, at six feet in height, was one of the few world leaders who could almost look the six-foot-five de Gaulle in the eye. The two sat at a small table, less than a metre apart, engaging in a lively exchange in which Diefenbaker warned that any leadership of NATO that excluded the smaller powers would lead to the breakup of the alliance. France was merely seeking to have its voice heard, de Gaulle responded. There was no consensus, but both leaders appeared to enjoy the cut-and-thrust of the exchange. Then it was on to Bonn, where Diefenbaker commiserated with the aged West German chancellor Konrad Adenauer over French impertinence, and to Italy, where he joked with Pope John XXIII. "How does it feel to be Pope, anyhow?" Diefenbaker, the Baptist, asked the pontiff. Laughing, the Pope replied, "Well here I am near the end of the road and on top of the heap."²

For the Asian leg of the tour, Diefenbaker hoped to take the temperature of Commonwealth nations while seeing for himself how Canadian aid money was being spent under the Colombo Plan. In Pakistan, he learned that the government was largely indifferent to the Commonwealth, though

Canadian assistance in a dam project was appreciated. In India, Diefenbaker revealed to Prime Minister Jawaharlal Nehru that Canada was increasingly inclined toward recognizing the Communist regime in Beijing, though Diefenbaker was concerned about how the Americans might react. One highlight of the trip was a hunt for Bengal tigers. Diefenbaker had only hunted fowl, but he happily took to a boat with rifle and pith helmet while workers beat the bushes in an effort to flush out a beast or two. It was probably for the best all around that none appeared. Ceylon's (Sri Lanka's) prime minister had little time for the Commonwealth but much respect for Communist Moscow and Peking (Beijing). The hospitality of Malayan (Malaysian) prime minister Tunku Abdul Rahman was much warmer toward the now visibly tiring prime minister, which revived his spirits.

After stops in Singapore and Indonesia—by now the stock of ceremonial gifts of Inuit carvings and maple syrup was running dangerously low—it was on to Australia for meetings with Prime Minister Robert Menzies, who was both loquacious and strong willed. As is sometimes the case when people meet others much like themselves, the two did not get on. Diefenbaker was due for several days of relaxation in New Zealand, but word that his mother had become ill sent him hurrying home shortly before Christmas. Overall, the trip was a great success; officials at External were impressed with how quickly the prime minister mastered his files and how he charmed most of those he engaged with.

But as the electoral triumph of 1958 gave way to the hard realities of governing in 1959, criticism burbled, though mostly still below the surface. The prime minister was indecisive, unpredictable, prone to changing his mind and then changing it back again. Cabinet meetings ground on interminably as Diefenbaker sought consensus, not from any desire to preserve cabinet unity but from his reluctance to take a political risk. Cabinet colleagues and senior civil servants grumbled to each other about the dithering. The prime minister had no long-term agenda other than to prepare for the next election. He was happy to take credit for everything in government that went right, but swift to blame subordinates, including ministers, if things went wrong. He increasingly came to believe that the civil service sought to undermine his government—especially the Pearsonalities, as he called them, in External Affairs—when in truth most deputy ministers and others in the senior ranks wanted the government to succeed. He obsessed over personalities and partisan politics, complaining about disloyal "termites" in the Tory caucus while giving too little thought to policy. And he micromanaged to a dangerous degree.

Internal discontent, spoken sotto voce in 1958 and '59, became a full-throated outcry as the term dragged on. And it became the verdict of history. "The office of prime minister he had coveted for years seemed in some essential ways beyond his ability to master," concluded Diefenbaker's ablest biographer, Denis Smith. ". . . He was suspicious of colleagues, unfamiliar with the play of political compromise, inexperienced in sharing tasks and authority." Ultimately, "the weaknesses of the ministry were those of the prime minister himself."[3] More succinctly, and cruelly, Peter C. Newman concluded, "He gave the people a leadership cult, without leadership."[4]

Yet to pronounce John Diefenbaker a failure as prime minister is to let the foibles of the man obscure the accomplishments of his governments. By obsessing over his personal insecurities, his disorganization, his dithering, his displays of pique, posterity has failed to notice his governments' impressive and enduring achievements. While the missteps and the dustups were of their time, the raft of legislative and other accomplishments contributed substantially to the society we live in today. We are the inheritors of Diefenbaker's legacy, and we undervalue that legacy when we focus on the tantrums rather than on the record.

II

The baby boom peaked in 1959 at 3.9 children per woman, with most families living in rapidly expanding suburbs. Inner cities still bifurcated between established, comfortable neighbourhoods and teeming slums that violated every building code. Municipal and provincial governments responded with slum clearance projects, often replacing smelly and chaotic but interconnected communities with sterile subsidized housing developments sitting next to the latest cross-town freeway. The damage to the downtowns from 1950s urban planning is with us still.

There was no recognizable social safety net. Old age pensions couldn't keep an elderly widow out of poverty. Recent immigrants who couldn't find jobs had little to fall back on. Seasonal workers in rural areas found work in the fields at harvest time, in the bush in the winter, and made do in between. People with good jobs had company health care plans, but fully one third of the population lacked proper coverage. Should government offer means-tested support for those who couldn't afford private plans, which was Alberta's approach, or move toward universal coverage, as Saskatchewan was doing? Did people who had used up their unemployment insurance still deserve government support? Should the churches continue to play a major role in health care, education, and poor relief, or should the state take over? And who was responsible—Ottawa, the provincial legislature, or city hall? Neighbours debated these issues with neighbours; politicians with politicians. In the case of religion and the state, the debate in Quebec was growing strained.

On March 17, 1955, fans had rioted outside the Coliseum after the Montreal Canadiens' beloved Maurice Richard was suspended for the rest of the season because he struck a linesman during a particularly ugly on-ice brawl. Twelve police officers and twenty-five civilians were injured, and fifty stores looted or vandalized. The Richard Riot served as a warning: French Quebecers were increasingly fed up with the Anglo elites who owned all the businesses and controlled all the sports teams and propped up their rotten-to-the-core provincial government. They were tired of the priests who educated their children and ran their hospitals and threatened eternal damnation if they had the slightest bit of fun. But there was light on the horizon, promising an end to la *Grande Noirceur* (Great Darkness), the dawn of a not-so-quiet revolution.

Though the hysterics of McCarthyism had abated, a new strawman emerged. Orde Morton joined External Affairs after obtaining degrees at University of Manitoba and Oxford. Promotion was swift, until one day he was asked to meet with a security official. We heard about the men you were friends with when you were in Rio de Janeiro, the official told him. We know of your friendship with the Swedish diplomat. "I think he used the word 'tendencies,'" Morton remembers. "The whole thing was over in twenty minutes."[5] His career in the public service was over as well.

Committing a homosexual act was serious felony in Canada and the United States; conviction for "gross indecency" carried a prison sentence.

With the permission of the St. Laurent government and the acquiescence of the Diefenbaker government, the RCMP and military police began to hunt for and root out homosexuals in External Affairs and the armed forces. Better to expose them and fire them than to let them carry on as a hidden security risk, the thinking went. In fact, it was a witch hunt, one that R.B. Bryce, the cabinet secretary, viewed uneasily, urging the RCMP to limit its investigations to public servants whose homosexuality might pose a security threat. But no government in the 1950s or '60s did anything meaningful to deter the RCMP. Thousands of dedicated public servants and military personnel had their careers and lives upended through police persecution. Meanwhile, preachers and prudes warned against letting "queers" near children. Homosexuals lived in constant, quiet fear of exposure.

III

The Conservative caucuses and cabinets of 1957 and 1958 were the most diverse in Canada's history until then, and remain unmatched in the precedents they set. With his German background on his father's side, Diefenbaker became Canada's first prime minister of neither British, Irish, nor French extraction. His name, which had been a source of ridicule in the past, now testified to the diversity within the Conservative caucus.

In 1957, Diefenbaker had made Ellen Fairclough Canada's first woman cabinet minister, but in the mostly symbolic role of secretary of state. In 1958, he promoted her to the difficult portfolio of Citizenship and Immigration. Cabinet also had its first Ukrainian minister, Michael Starr (born Michael Starchewsky), who with a grade-ten education had worked his way up to success in business and politics, having previously served as mayor of Oshawa. He became minister of labour. Diefenbaker made James Gladstone, of the Blackfoot Confederacy, the first Indigenous member of the Senate. Caucus also included Douglas Jung, a lawyer and war hero who was the first MP of Chinese descent.

The Diefenbaker cabinet was anchored by Donald Fleming at Finance, Davie Fulton at Justice, Gordon Churchill at Trade and Commerce, and George Pearkes—winner of the Victoria Cross in the First World War; temporary commander of the Canada Corps in the Second—at Defence. And then there was "Gorgeous George" Hees at Transport. His patrician family had sent the strikingly handsome student to private schools, Royal Military College, University of Toronto, and Cambridge, where he excelled more at athletics than scholarship. In 1938, as a star linebacker for the Toronto Argonauts, he helped bring the Grey Cup to Toronto. He fought courageously in the war before being invalided home. Infuriated with the Liberal government's handling of troop requirements, he ran for the Progressive Conservatives and lost in 1945, but arrived in the House five years later. "He was a big man in every way," Peter C. Newman recalled after his death in 1996, "his smile the radiance of a searchlight, his large frame planted on the ground with a permanent backward lean, as if he were holding the world on a leash."[6] Though Hees considered running for the leadership in 1956, he switched to becoming an ardent Diefenbakerite once it was clear that the Man from Prince Albert could not be stopped. As transport minister, Hees oversaw the opening of the St. Lawrence Seaway and broke ground or cut ribbons for a slew of new international airports across the land. But, though better-briefed on his files than his critics suspected, Hees broke no new policy ground as cabinet minister. Unlike Ellen Fairclough.

She was tall, wiry, and tough as Hamilton, the steeltown she called home her whole life. Her parents took in boarders to make ends meet, and there was no money for an academic education, so Fairclough became a stenographer, then a bookkeeper, and took correspondence courses to qualify as an accountant, which was almost unheard of for a woman at the time. She was devoted to church and family, but also to the Progressive Conservative Party, sitting on Hamilton city council before entering Parliament in a 1950 by-election. Her husband Gordon supported her ambition from the day they first met as teenagers. When Governor General Vincent Massey asked Ellen's advice for an event he was thinking of holding for the wives of MPs, Gordon interjected, "Be careful, sir, that's me you're talking about." Massey threw back his head and laughed.[7]

Fairclough was only the sixth woman to sit in the House of Commons, though there were two women in caucus—the only women in the House— when Diefenbaker formed his first cabinet. He had committed publicly to appointing Canada's first woman cabinet minister, and Fairclough was senior, but he was reluctant because she was a George Drew loyalist and had supported Davie Fulton for leader in 1956. "I have to form a cabinet, and it looks as if I shall have to form it largely of my enemies," Diefenbaker told Fairclough, who insisted she was not his enemy and would be completely loyal.[8] Whether he assigned her to Citizenship and Immigration as a reward or a punishment is debatable. Immigration ministers are bombarded incessantly with requests for exemptions or special treatment from immigrants and members of Parliament acting on their behalf. They also have the difficult task of deciding how many new arrivals to let in; during the Diefenbaker years, with rising unemployment, there was considerable pressure to restrict unskilled immigrants from entering the country. And then there was the colour bar.

Since Confederation, the unstated purpose of the federal government's immigration policy had been to keep Canada white. A succession of acts gave cabinet the power to bar any peoples from entering the country "owing to their peculiar customs, habits, modes of life and methods of holding property and because of their probable inability to become readily assimilated."[9] At various times, and for various reasons, orders-in-council banned anyone from Asia, people who were Black, Jews, Doukhobors and Mennonites, and others deemed undesirable. Apart from explicit exclusions, head taxes and other financial requirements blocked potential immigrants from poorer countries. In the late 1800s, workers were brought in from China for the dirty and dangerous work of constructing the continental railway, but then the door slammed shut. In 1911, Wilfrid Laurier's cabinet approved, but did not implement, an executive order banning "any immigrants belonging to the Negro race, which race is deemed unsuitable to the climate and requirement of Canada."[10] Immigration officials were rewarded for finding reasons to exclude African Americans fleeing Jim Crow. A "gentleman's agreement" with Japan curtailed emigration from that country. A "continuous journey" regulation sought to ban immigrants from Southern Asia by saying that travellers to Canada would not qualify as immigrants if the ship that delivered them stopped at another port during the journey. When the *Komagata Maru* brought four hundred South Asian nationals to Vancouver in 1914, it was turned away. The Chinese Immigration Act of 1923 explicitly forbade Chinese immigration and remained in place until the King government repealed the act in 1947. However, Mackenzie King made it clear in a speech to the House that "the people of Canada do not wish, as a result of mass immigration, to make a fundamental alteration in the character of our population. Large-scale immigration from the orient would change the fundamental composition of the Canadian population."[11] By 1956, overt exclusions were off the books, but a rigid quota system ensured that the overwhelming majority of immigrants were from the "old Commonwealth" of the United Kingdom, Australia, and New Zealand, along with the United States, Ireland, France, and, at the bottom, other countries in Europe.

Throughout his life, John Diefenbaker had suffered discrimination because of his German background. As a boy in Saskatchewan, he grew up among immigrants from Central Europe who had also faced discrimination from Canadians of British origin. By the time he became prime minister, newly decolonized Commonwealth governments were pressuring Canada to lift what were in effect race-based restrictions. And the civil rights movement in the United States uncomfortably highlighted Canada's own whites-preferred approach to immigration. It was time to remove the colour bar. As someone who, while in opposition, had campaigned relentlessly against discrimination in employment, Fairclough was able and willing to impose reform.

Things began badly. When, at Fairclough's recommendation, cabinet eliminated a backlog of applicants from Italy by disqualifying most family members from entry, the uproar from the Italian community, the Ontario government, and the Liberal opposition forced a quick reversal, with Fairclough taking the blame. But the imbroglio provided grounds for her to launch a thorough review of immigration policies and practices. Much of the opposition came from within the department itself. Her own deputy minister, the stiff and formal Colonel Laval Fortier, fought her at every turn. Cabinet was indifferent to immigration reform, especially after having been burned on the Italian fiasco. In 1960, her colleagues turned down her proposal for a royal commission on immigration. (That may have been just was well, for such a commission could have taken years to report.) But Fairclough persevered. She procured a new and more agreeable deputy minister, George Davidson, who shared her desire for reform and who understood how the immigration agenda fit within the broader priorities of the government.

"Essentially we were attempting to make education, training, and skills the primary criteria for immigration, rather than family relationships and country of origin," she wrote in her memoirs.[12] It helped that Canadian churches were arguing for an end to racial discrimination, as were an increasing number of newspaper editorial boards.

On October 18, 1961, Fairclough came to cabinet with a set of proposed new regulations that would end all discrimination against applicants based on race, skin colour, or country of origin. Cabinet watered down the wording slightly but left the substance of the reforms intact. Explaining the new regulations in the House of Commons, Fairclough declared, "Any suitably qualified person from any part of the world can be considered for immigration to Canada entirely on his own merits without regard to his race, colour, national origin or the country from which he comes." Henceforth, she promised, Canada would select its immigrants "without discrimination of any kind."[13] Historians would later judge that, with Fairclough's new regulations, "Canada took a major step towards a totally non-discriminatory immigration system."[14] Today, Canada brings in more people, from more places, than almost any other developed country in the world as a percentage of population. Open immigration free of discrimination, the bedrock of modern multiculturalism, began with Fairclough's reforms.

As citizenship and immigration minister, Fairclough also had responsibility for Indigenous affairs—which, remarkably, was not considered worthy of its own ministry. Thus, she oversaw another of the government's major achievements, enfranchising First Nations. In this case she was enacting a reform that her prime minister considered a high priority.

For some Indigenous people in Canada in the 1950s, life was improving; for others, it was getting much worse. Indigenous veterans of the Second World War returned to Canada unwilling to meekly return to second-class (if that) status. First Nations pressed demands that would sound familiar seven decades later: the need to improve conditions on reserves, the need to settle land claims, the need to respect treaties. Federal and provincial governments had started to cooperate in providing services on reserves that, at least in theory, were separate from but equal to services provided elsewhere in the province, though they were not equal at all. A joint parliamentary committee concluded in 1948 that treaty rights needed to be respected and

Indians (as they were then called) granted full citizenship, within the context of integration with, rather than assimilation into, the settler society. Nonetheless, thousands of First Nations children continued to be taken from their families and communities and sent to residential schools, where some died and many more suffered emotional, physical, and even sexual abuse. In remote communities in Labrador and the North, federal officials had concluded the best way to provide services to the Inuit was to rip them from their ancestral communities and force them to relocate, often hundreds of kilometres away. The trauma of these dislocations would last for generations. And federal politicians remained wary of granting First Nations full citizenship status, including the right to vote. "Without the vote, First Nations people could easily be dismissed as politically irrelevant," the Royal Commission on Aboriginal Peoples would later conclude.[15] Political partisans were suspicious of enfranchising a community whose voting tendencies they could not reliably predict.

To John Diefenbaker, this had always been wrong. He had grown up around Métis and First Nations people in Saskatchewan. He had represented them in court. And while his embrace of One Canada, in which all were equal and none were special, ignored the unique claims of both French and Indigenous people within the federation, it at least was willing to confer equality to all, Indigenous or settler, British or French or German or Chinese. On his watch, First Nations would have the same right to vote as everyone else. "I felt it was so unjust that they didn't have the vote," he recalled later in life. "I brought it about as soon as I could after becoming prime minister."[16]

In the majority government's first Speech from the Throne, the administration promised to put forward "amendments to the Citizenship Act and the Indian Act to eliminate certain discriminatory provisions in these statutes."[17] The government then introduced changes to the Indian Act and the Elections Act that enfranchised all status Indians in federal elections. Much of the resistance to granting voting rights to First Nations came from Indigenous Canadians themselves. They had been deceived and betrayed so often by so many governments that they feared being given the right to vote was a trick to deprive them of existing rights. "What we British Columbia Indians want to know, Sir, is will we become extinct Indians or tribes or bands by voting in the federal elections," Percy Paull wrote to Diefenbaker.[18]

Writing in reply, the prime minister assured Paull, "The legislation in question confers an additional right or benefit: it takes nothing away. If an Indian wants to vote in the federal elections—and it is my hope that all Indians will do so—he does not have to surrender any rights whatsoever."[19]

With passage of a revised Canada Election Act in 1960, all registered Indians in Canada acquired the right to vote in federal elections. We should make neither too much of this nor too little. The right to vote did not confer political power on First Nations, who were too few in number, and too thinly spread across the land, to greatly influence the outcome of elections. We also need to remember that, in granting the franchise, the Diefenbaker government was covering its political flank. As with immigration reform, the federal government was insulating itself against accusations of racism at a time when racial unrest in the United States and the struggles of decolonization in the developing world dominated the news. Nor did conferring voting rights on First Nations end the noxious practice of scooping up Indigenous children from their parents and then shipping them to residential schools or placing them in foster care. The trauma from these evils endures to this day.

And yet, getting the vote mattered for First Nations. It marked an important transition from the state of paternalistic dependence that they had been subjected to since before Confederation to a new standard of independence. That was still a very long way from recognition that First Nations were "citizens plus": fully equal to all other Canadians in their civil liberties, but endowed also with special rights and claims as the descendants of the original inhabitants of lands that had been taken from them, of treaties that had not been upheld, of land claims ignored.

Winning the vote was only a step. But it was an important step nonetheless.

IV

Maryon Pearson offered the most succinct verdict on election night, 1958. "We've lost everything," she lamented. "We even won our own seat."[20]

Had Pearson gone down to defeat in Algoma East, then the path would have been clear. He would resign, the first Liberal leader since Edward

Blake in the 1880s who had failed to become prime minister, and leave it to another—Paul Martin, perhaps—to rebuild the party. That rebuilding could take a decade. The Progressive Conservatives under Diefenbaker bestrode the House like a colossus. It would surely take two elections, at least, to unseat them. Pearson would be sixty-one in April. Maryon wanted him home.

But he decided to stay on and do the rebuilding himself. His sense of duty demanded it. "We would love to get out of it all, but how can I now?" he wrote an American friend. "So I will carry on, as long as the party wants me, and in four years I'm pretty certain that they will have had enough in Canada of this Baptist evangelist and his vision!"[21] If we are to believe Lester Pearson's self-narrative—that he had drifted into academia, stumbled into the foreign service more or less by accident, received repeated promotions without seeking them, been talked into elected office almost against his will, assumed the Liberal leadership without wanting or asking for it—then this was the first big career decision he'd ever made, a decision to buck the odds and stay and fight rather than drift into retirement.

The party's position wasn't as weak as it seemed. Yes, it had been reduced to forty-nine seats, but this was the Liberal Party of Canada, the so-called natural governing party. And if the surviving MPs in the House were holdovers from the St. Laurent years, they included deeply talented holdovers. Pearson could count on the enormously experienced Jack Pickersgill, Paul Martin, and Lionel Chevrier to manage the day-to-day business of opposing the government while he set about rebuilding the party. A naïf in matters of both domestic politics and policy, he leaned on Allan MacEachen, an economics professor and proud Cape Bretoner—he was fluent in Gaelic—who in 1958 lost the riding of Inverness—Richmond that he'd held in the two previous elections, and who came on board as a policy adviser. MacEachen was joined by Maurice Lamontagne, who had been defeated in Quebec East and who advised Pearson on Quebec issues. Mary Macdonald was another essential member of the team. Pearson's executive assistant had long been his eyes and ears in Algoma East; now she also advised him on who was saying what about whom and, in her own understated way, what she thought about it all. The title executive assistant didn't begin cover the depth of her contribution.

He also had a clear sense of where he wanted to take the party: to the left. This dismayed some of his supporters, especially those in the West, especially those in the Western press, such as Bruce Hutchison and Grant Dexter, who feared a drift, if not into socialism, then at least into statism. Hutchison worried that in response to Diefenbaker's charismatic populism, the Liberal Party "will swing sharply to the Left, in the direction of more welfare, more Danegeld, more Keynes, and more of everything I don't like."[22] He was right. Pearson's instincts were progressive—he believed that the Liberal Party could not allow itself to remain, as it had under King and St. Laurent, committed to minimal interference in the market, closer integration with the American economy, and continental defence, while occasionally coming up with a pension boost here or relief for the unemployed there. Hutchison was worried that Pearson would be swayed by people like Walter Gordon. He was right about that too.

Gordon had already come to the Pearsons' aid by setting up the Algoma Fishing and Conservation Club, whose donors took care of the financial need that came with Pearson moving from the public service to Parliament. He had put up three thousand dollars of his own money to finance Pearson's leadership bid and ended up acting as unofficial campaign manager. Now he was eager to help rebuild the party, preferably in his own image.

He started, at Pearson's invitation, by convincing the St. Laurent-era and even King-era old boys in the Liberal Party national office to retire, replacing them with younger and more able men. The party was two hundred thousand dollars in debt (more than two million dollars in today's funds) and the bank was knocking at the door, so Gordon criss-crossed the country pressing the sort of people who could write cheques that mattered to write them.

That earned him influence, and Gordon didn't waste it. In a series of speeches and in policy memos to Pearson, he outlined where he thought the Liberal Party should go: on the economy, modest tariffs mixed with both rules and incentives to slow, and if possible reverse, the encroachment by American industry; on the welfare state, as it was already being called, more of it, with supports for seniors, for the poor, and for middle-class families under increasing pressure to make ends meet. On defence, a gradual retreat from NORAD, with Canada refusing to accept nuclear-armed aircraft and interceptor missiles, confining its role to helping detect and warn of inbound threats. He believed that any policy proposal should be put to two tests: "Will the proposed policy result in more jobs and less unemployment? Will the proposed policy result in a further loss of Canadian independence, or the reverse?"[23]

Charming, especially when in the presence of his wife Elizabeth, vigorous, profoundly competent, and generous with his money, Gordon exercised a deep influence on Pearson in these years, or seemed to. He told Pearson that he was willing to consider the position of finance minister—which would involve a major financial sacrifice—but only if the Liberal leader agreed with his program. Pearson did, or at least said he did. "Mike called to say he had read the attached draft and the copies of the other three speeches I had sent him. He said he agreed *completely* with my ideas," Gordon wrote in a note to himself. "He repeated this two or three times saying this is exactly how he feels on these various issues."[24] Gordon appeared not to read anything into Pearson's suggestion that, since they were both on the same page, there was no need for Walter to come up to Ottawa to talk things over.

By 1960, Pearson had surrounded himself with an able and dedicated group of advisers, some on the payroll and some working informally for a leader they loved and admired and very much wished to make prime minister. Key among them was Tom Kent. The English-born journalist—he had been an editorial writer for *The Guardian* and *The Economist*—came to Canada in 1954 as editor of the *Winnipeg Free Press*. In 1958, he went to Ottawa as an adviser to the new Liberal leader. Grant Dexter and others hoped Kent would instill some laissez-faire common sense into Pearson. Instead, Kent's world view migrated toward progressivism, and before long he was pushing an agenda so activist that it reminded his detractors of the Regina Manifesto, the foundation document for the CCF. But Kent was saying what Pearson wanted to hear. Another key player was Keith Davey, a broadcast account executive who led a cabal of young Liberals determined to wrest control of Toronto, which had been a Tory bastion for decades, away from the Progressive Conservatives. Davey—who knew, or quickly got to know, everyone who mattered—so impressed Gordon that he made him national director of the party, which was one of Gordon's smartest moves. The Rainmaker, as Davey came to be called, would work political miracles for both Pearson and Pierre Trudeau.

The team was in place, the ideas were percolating, but how to make it all gel? The Kingston Conference was the answer, and it was Pearson's own idea. He wanted the Liberal Party to reconnect with the intelligentsia of the universities, and a thinkers' conference of prominent intellectuals was the way to do it. Mitchell Sharp, the senior bureaucrat who had authored the memo warning of an oncoming recession that Diefenbaker had used to such devastating effect in the House on the eve of the 1958 election, had left the public service over disagreements with his minister, Gordon Churchill. Pearson asked him to organize the gathering at Queen's University in the fall of 1960. Those attending included a young lawyer, John Turner, who presented a paper on reforming the justice system, and Jean Marchand, a labour leader from Quebec. Frank Underhill, one of the founders of the CCF, was there, along with Tom Kent, who pushed forward several of the ideas under debate. Many of the proposals that came out of the Kingston Conference for government assistance in health care, pensions, and old age security had been in the 1958 platform. But now the media were listening. So were the critics, such as Dexter and Hutchison, who were appalled by the leftward drift of the party. Most important, perhaps, the Kingston Conference helped break the Liberal Party from its King and St. Laurent legacy, while also galvanizing many of the young activists who would become key players in the years to come. The party followed up the Kingston initiative with a winter 1961 policy conference— the first to be held in public—that codified many of the key planks in what would become the Liberal platform.

"In many ways, those were the most productive and satisfying years of my political life," Pearson later recalled of his time as Opposition leader.[25] He had taken a party with a long record in government but with two consecutive lost elections, cut away the deadwood, brought in a new and highly capable team of advisers, and established the policy principles that would guide the party, as it turned out, for the next thirty years. And he must have appreciated just how much he was admired, respected, even loved by those who were willing to dedicate themselves to his service. "Everyone likes you, holds you in the highest respect and is fundamentally loyal to you," Walter Gordon wrote him in 1959. "You have immense prestige and your power within the party is more or less unlimited."[26] That so many people felt that way about someone who had led his party to a humiliating defeat says much about Pearson's character and how it drew others to him.

V

There was another reason Diefenbaker moved to extend the franchise to First Nations in 1960 and supported ending discrimination in immigration. Failing to do either would have contradicted the principles of the new Bill of Rights.

The "rights of every Englishman" evolved over centuries, from Anglo-Saxon times to Magna Carta to the Glorious Revolution. But while Americans appended a bill of rights to their constitution, rights within the Westminster system that Canada inherited existed mostly through the texts of certain acts and through centuries of jurisprudence. They could be, and sometimes were, suspended during civil emergencies, such as the Second World War, and remained partially suspended in Canada even after the war had ended. The round-ups and prosecutions that followed Igor Gouzenko's defection violated habeas corpus, the right not to be arbitrarily detained, but Ottawa got away with it because of those emergency powers. In any case, ancient prejudices coexisted with ancient liberties; throughout his life Diefenbaker had witnessed ethnic and religious discrimination: employers who wouldn't hire Catholics, landlords who didn't rent to Jews, ads that read "Irish need not apply." It had long offended him. It offended him in the wake of a failed attempt in 1945 to deport Canadians of Japanese origin through an order-in-council. "To deport Canadian citizens was the very antithesis of the principles of democracy, one of the first of which is that minorities are entitled to protection," he told Parliament.[27] (That protest at least partly offset his support for the internment in the first place.) It offended him in 1946, when he first proposed a bill of rights in response to the arbitrary detention of communists. He believed that a bill of rights should have accompanied the legislation in 1947 that made Canadians citizens of Canada and not British subjects. He advocated for such a bill in 1948, when a parliamentary committee took the matter up for study. The committee achieved nothing, but Diefenbaker persevered, introducing a bill of rights as a private member's bill year after year. His efforts, though heartfelt, were also politically convenient, for he was railing against the rights abuses of the Liberal government. But once he won government, the duty was on him to act. And he did.

Diefenbaker himself introduced Bill C-60 in Parliament on September 5, 1958. In some ways, the bill was overdue. The idea that human rights should be embedded in more than precedents and assumptions was gaining ground. The Canadian diplomat John Humphrey, from his post at the United Nations, played an important role in drafting the UN's Universal Declaration of Human Rights, adopted in 1948. Closer to home, Tommy Douglas's CCF government had enacted the Saskatchewan Bill of Rights in 1947, which guaranteed that "every person and every class of persons shall enjoy the right to freedom of conscience, opinion and belief, and freedom of religious association, teaching, practice and worship," along with freedom of expression, freedom of assembly, freedom from arbitrary arrest and detention, freedom from discrimination in employment, and the right to vote.[28]

But there was also resistance. Canada was the only country to initially abstain from supporting the UN Declaration, by order of then-undersecretary of state Lester Pearson, on the grounds that some of its provisions were within provincial jurisdiction. Embarrassed when it found itself isolated, Canada hastily abandoned that stand and declared its support.

Diefenbaker's bill also came in for criticism. Traditionalists argued that the ancient liberties embedded in the unwritten constitution and centuries of judicial precedent did not need buttressing by some American-style rights code. Reformers found the bill too weak. For one thing, it applied only to the federal government; provincial governments might establish different, even conflicting, rights in their areas of jurisdiction, creating a rights hodge-podge across the country. For another, the bill contained an opt-out clause that said Parliament could pass an act that violated the terms of the Bill of Rights so long as it declared openly that it was doing so. Fundamentally, the argument against the bill was that it was just that—a bill, which would become a statute, neither more nor less powerful than any other statute. The constitutional lawyer Bora Laskin wrote a devastating critique arguing that the bill "suggests very forcibly . . . that in Canada civil liberties have no exclusive constitutional value but may exist or be treated separately and differently in the various provinces no less than on the federal level."[29]

Laskin and others wanted to see the contents of the bill entrenched in the Constitution. But that would require provincial agreement, and Diefenbaker had no stomach for such protracted negotiations. "Let's clean our own doorstep first," he told critics.[30] Another approach might have seen Ottawa ask Westminster for a unilateral revision of the British North America Act. But that would have enraged the provinces.

In any case, entrenching a bill of rights in the Constitution was farther than Diefenbaker wanted to go. His aim was to strip the executive of the authority to limit the rights of individuals without the consent of Parliament. And if Parliament itself moved to violate human rights? Well, at least it would have to take note it was doing so in defiance of the bill.

After almost two years of debate, Diefenbaker reintroduced the Bill of Rights on July 1, Dominion Day, 1960. The new act, he said, represented "the essence of the conscience of the people of Canada." Speaking as everyman, the prime minister maintained the bill "will remove from any government the right to deny me the right to belong to an unpopular minority. It will deny any government, no matter how powerful in the future, the right to deny recourse to the courts." He hoped that provincial governments would emulate the federal bill, bringing uniformity to the rights of Canadians across the land. But more than anything, he believed the Bill of Rights gave every citizen the right to declare: "I am a Canadian, a free Canadian, free to speak without fear, free to worship God in my own way, free to stand for what I think right, free to oppose what I believe wrong, free to choose those who shall govern my country. This heritage of freedom I pledge to uphold for myself and all mankind."[31]

Pearson, in response, proposed amendments to improve the bill's effectiveness, while lamenting the lack of sufficient consultation. But the government was determined to have its bill, and the opposition parties had no wish to go on the record opposing it. Having received unanimous support at second and third reading, the Bill of Rights was proclaimed into law on August 10.

The immediate impact was underwhelming. The Supreme Court took little note of the new bill, treating it as a piece of legislation that had no particular impact on other legislation that contradicted its principles. The Canadian Supreme Court had only been the country's final court of appeal since 1949, when appeals to the judicial committee of the Privy Council were discontinued. It remained a cautious, conservative tribunal that largely concerned itself with determining whether Parliament and the provincial legislatures were operating within the spheres of their jurisdiction. Otherwise, the Court deferred to the supremacy of Parliament. The American concept of judicial review—in which courts decided whether a given piece of legislation was constitutional, often with specific reference to that country's Bill of Rights—was mostly alien to this land. Since Parliament was supreme, Diefenbaker's Bill of Rights could not invalidate any other piece of legislation, provided that legislation was in accord with the British North America Act. The bill was, for all intents and purposes, moot. And then came *R. v. Drybones*.

On April 8, 1967, Joseph Drybones was found drunk in the lobby of the Old Stope Hotel in Yellowknife. Drybones was a status Indian and guilty under the Indian Act of being intoxicated while off reserve. He was fined ten dollars plus court costs. But the penalties for being found intoxicated off reserve under the Indian Act were more severe than for any non-Indian who was found drunk in the lobby of the Old Stope Hotel. Besides, there were no reserves in the Northwest Territories and so any Indian could be found in violation of the act, even if they were drinking in their own home. Drybones appealed, and in 1970 the Supreme Court ruled the section of the Indian Act relating to intoxication off reserve violated the Bill of Rights in that it discriminated on the basis of race, rendering that section of the Indian Act invalid. "An individual is denied equality before the law if it is made an offence punishable at law, on account of his race, for him to do something which his fellow Canadians are free to do," wrote Justice Roland Ritchie, for the majority. Drybones was acquitted.

Suddenly, it looked as though the Bill of Rights might have real teeth, that all existing legislation would have to conform with its principles, and that Canadian judges were prepared to scrutinize the actions of Parliament through a rights-based lens. *Drybones* "appears to have given new life to the Bill of Rights, which until this time had remained dormant at the behest of our judiciary," wrote Paul Cavalluzzo in his 1970 analysis of the decision.[32]

But it was not to be. Four years later, Ritchie reversed himself in a decision that severely fractured the Court. Writing for a plurality of four judges,

John Diefenbaker and his uncle Edward Diefenbaker in a wagon, 1907. As a boy, John froze his legs when stranded in a winter storm. Luckily, he recovered. (University of Saskatchewan, University Archives & Special Collections)

Pearson at flying school, 1917. An instructor decided that "Lester" was too prissy and called him "Mike." It stuck. (Library and Archives Canada)

Lieutenant John Diefenbaker in uniform, First World War. Neither Diefenbaker nor Pearson saw combat for mysterious reasons. (University of Saskatchewan, University Archives & Special Collections)

Oxford University vs. Switzerland, c. 1922. Mike Pearson is in white on the right. The Swiss were trounced. (Library and Archives Canada)

Diefenbaker in legal robes, 1924. The young lawyer hung out his shingle in Wakaw, Saskatchewan, whose residents, his research suggested, were "particularly litigious." (University of Saskatchewan, University Archives & Special Collections)

"J'accuse." Opposition MP John Diefenbaker makes life miserable for a Liberal cabinet minister in the House of Commons. (University of Saskatchewan, University Archives & Special Collections)

Radio-Canada reporter René Lévesque interviews External Affairs Minister Lester Pearson outside the Canadian embassy in Moscow, October 1955. (Library and Archives Canada)

Pearson at the United Nations in the midst of the Suez Crisis, November 1956. (Library and Archives Canada)

Maryon with Mike Pearson as he shows off his Nobel Peace Prize in Stockholm, 1957. (Duncan Cameron, photographer)

Diefenbaker chatting with a farmer during the 1957 election campaign. These were his people. (University of Saskatchewan, University Archives & Special Collections)

John Diefenbaker, now prime minister, with his mother Mary in 1958. She had always believed in his destiny. Beside them, Olive and Elmer. (Diefenbaker Archives, University of Saskatchewan)

President John F. Kennedy with Diefenbaker, 1961. They would become mortal political enemies. (University of Saskatchewan, University Archives & Special Collections)

The Pearson Pennant. Thankfully, a parliamentary committee ultimately chose a simpler and more elegant design. (Public domain)

In 1967, Pierre Trudeau talks with John Turner, while Jean Chrétien looks on and Prime Minister Lester Pearson has a good laugh. All four served as prime minister. (Library and Archives Canada)

John Diefenbaker in 1970, beside a statue of his idol, John A. Macdonald. (University of Saskatchewan, University Archives & Special Collections)

In 1969, Lester Pearson and John Diefenbaker could laugh about it all. The duel was over. (*Toronto Star*)

with a fifth concurring, he declared that the Indian Act did not discriminate against Jeannette Corbiere Lavell. As that act decreed, Lavell had lost her status when she married a non-Indian, even though an Indian man could keep his status if he married a non-Indian woman. The Court's tortured reasoning involved the difference between criminal and non-criminal cases, the status of legislation prior to the implementation of the Bill of Rights, and the overriding responsibility of the federal government to carry out its constitutional responsibilities, including its responsibilities to Indians, whatever any other piece of legislation might say. But the truth of the matter lay with Bora Laskin, now a member of the Court, who, having criticized the Bill of Rights as inadequate, came to its defence. "If, as in *Drybones*, discrimination by reason of race makes certain statutory provisions inoperative," he wrote in his dissent, "the same result must follow as to statutory provisions which exhibit discrimination by reason of sex."[33] That the Court was unwilling to accept this plain truth meant simply that it had embraced the Bill of Rights in *Drybones* only to flee from the implications of that embrace in *Lavell*.

Both *Drybones* and *Lavell* took place in the midst of historic debates that dominated Canadian political life in the 1970s. Should the Canadian constitution be removed from Westminster and patriated to Canada, complete with its own Bill of Rights? On that, provinces disagreed among themselves and with Ottawa. Canada had also gone through its only peacetime suspension of civil liberties, with the imposition of the War Measures Act in response to the kidnapping of British consul James Cross and the kidnapping and murder of Quebec cabinet minister Pierre Laporte in 1970 by members of the Front de Libération du Québec, the FLQ. It would be another decade—one that included the arrival of a separatist government in Quebec and a No vote in a referendum on sovereignty—for the English premiers to agree to patriation along with a Charter of Rights and Freedoms, qualified by a notwithstanding clause imported from the Bill of Rights—all of this over the howling objection of Quebec premier René Lévesque.

At the time of *Drybones* and *Lavell*, "the Court wasn't ready for the Charter," observed former Supreme Court justice Rosalie Abella.[34] Its conservative judges, steeped in decades of deference to Parliament, weren't prepared to interpret parliamentary statutes through a rights-based lens. By the time the Charter went into effect, a very different Court was ready to take on that challenge.

But Diefenbaker's Bill of Rights was crucial to the evolution of the Charter, Justice Abella believes. "It defined in print, for the first time, that there are human rights," and that courts had to take those rights into consideration when determining where justice might lie.[35]

Thomas Axworthy, who served as principal secretary to Pierre Trudeau, believes that the Charter of Rights and Freedoms "would never have happened if Diefenbaker had not lit the way with his life-long dedication to human rights." While Trudeau is justly celebrated as the originator of the Charter, Axworthy wrote in 2002, "few recognize that the Charter builds on the foundations of the 1960 Bill of Rights, Diefenbaker's proudest achievement."[36]

VI

Because he had no clearly developed agenda for governing, Diefenbaker fell back on leading a cabinet that governed through consensus. By convention, cabinet does not vote. Its members discuss the order of business and either agree to accept, agree to reject, or agree to defer. Once cabinet has reached agreement, its members are expected to defend that agreement, whatever their personal views. In contemporary practice, cabinet more often than not rubber stamps the agenda of the prime minister. But in Diefenbaker's time, cabinet ministers still exercised considerable autonomy, and because he had few priorities of his own, Diefenbaker was content to let ministers run their departments. Much of Diefenbaker's legacy rests on their achievements. The legacy of Davie Fulton fits that bill.

Brilliant, uptight, dedicated, Fulton never won Diefenbaker's confidence and trust because the British Columbia MP had run against the Chief in the 1956 leadership race. Nonetheless, Diefenbaker wisely made Fulton justice minister, and he performed brilliantly in the role, surrounding himself with a group of highly talented advisers that included his assistant deputy minister, Guy Favreau. Prison reform was his greatest contribution. Up until the Diefenbaker government, federal prisons were brutal warehouses, with inmates offered little time out of their cells and little or nothing in the way of counselling and rehabilitation. In frustration, prisoners at Kingston Penitentiary rioted in 1952, setting fire to the building. In the first major legislative reforms since the nineteenth century, the Diefenbaker government created the National Parole Board, which established a uniform set of conditions for granting parole, along with other policies aimed at making prisons places of rehabilitation as well as incarceration. The Penitentiaries Act of 1961 introduced other measures, which led to a massive upgrading of prisons across the country, including the construction of ten new ones. These humane and landmark reforms were Fulton's doing, though it was no coincidence that the prime minister was a former defence attorney.

Canada took a major step toward ending capital punishment in the country on Fulton and Diefenbaker's watch. When he came to office, the number of executions each year had been slowly declining. There were thirteen executions in 1949, St. Laurent's first full year as prime minister. In his final full year, there were eight. During the Diefenbaker governments, there were never more than two or three in any year. Cabinet had to approve each one, and sentiment to end the practice was growing, though more in elite circles than among the general public. Fulton divided the crime of murder into two categories: first-degree murder was a planned and deliberate act that could warrant the death penalty. The killing of a police officer or prison guard was also considered a capital offence. An unplanned killing was murder in the second degree. That distinction remains in Canadian law to this day. In any case, capital punishment had reached the end of the hanging rope. The last two executions in Canada occurred in 1962. Ronald Turpin had killed a police officer while fleeing a robbery. Arthur Lucas had been convicted of murdering a police informant and his common-law wife. Both men were hanged two minutes after midnight in Toronto's Don Jail on December 11, 1962.

Fulton was also a key player in negotiating the Columbia River Treaty. Talks to cooperatively develop the river, which flowed through British Columbia and Washington State, had been dragging along since the 1940s. The B.C. minister helped bring the negotiations to a conclusion, and in January 1961, Diefenbaker and Eisenhower signed the treaty to share in the development and electrical generation of the river, though deteriorating relations with Eisenhower's successor, disagreements with British Columbia premier W.A.C. Bennett, and Diefenbaker's own obstinacy delayed work on the project for another three years. The Columbia River Treaty was a textbook case of the Diefenbaker government launching an initiative that the Pearson government concluded. Both governments share credit for its success.

Finally, Fulton proposed a formula for patriating and amending the Constitution that became integral to constitutional reform. The fact that Canada's constitution resided in Westminster and was not an act of Canada's Parliament remained one of the last vestiges of the country's former colonial status. But no government had been able to devise a way to patriate and amend the Constitution to which provincial governments, especially Quebec, would assent. At a 1960 federal–provincial conference, Fulton proposed an amending formula in which amendments affecting all provinces would require the unanimous consent of the provinces; amendments affecting one or more provinces would require those provinces' consent; amendments that did not concern provincial powers would require the consent of two thirds of the provinces comprising 50 per cent of the nation's population. Fulton's formula would be taken up by Guy Favreau when he became justice minister, and the Fulton–Favreau formula would constitute the basis of the amending formula of the patriated Constitution.

A constitutional amending formula. Prison reform. Criminal law reform. The Columbia River Treaty. Fulton's accomplishments as justice minister were formidable. But Diefenbaker showed his gratitude by demoting him to Public Works. Fulton made little secret of his desire to succeed Diefenbaker as leader of the Conservative Party, an intolerable act of disloyalty as far as the Chief was concerned. Fulton left the government and returned to British Columbia in 1963 in a failed effort to revive the British Columbia Conservative Party. After he was made a judge in 1973, alcohol increasingly became an issue. In 1981, a second drunk-driving conviction landed him in jail for fourteen days, forcing him to quit the bench. Alcoholics Anonymous helped him turn things around, but Fulton would forever carry the reputation of a political leader whose potential had been wasted, not least because he never earned the trust of his prime minister.

Donald Fleming had also run against Diefenbaker in 1956; he too was never fully trusted by the Chief. Fleming fought constantly with Diefenbaker and with cabinet members to rein in spending, a fight he often lost. But on his watch, the debt-to-GDP ratio continuously declined. At his recommendation, Diefenbaker established a royal commission to reform the taxation system that eventually resulted in the capital gains tax. And it was the Diefenbaker government, under the guidance of its finance minister, that entrenched the federal fiscal framework that remains in place to this day.

Diefenbaker's predecessor, Louis St. Laurent, was determined to solve the fiscal imbalance created by the Second World War and the emerging welfare state. The provinces had effectively surrendered their taxing power as a wartime measure, with Ottawa transferring revenue back to the provincial governments to fund roads, education, and other priorities under provincial jurisdiction. After the war, Quebec had wrested back control over its finances, but the tax rental agreements remained in place for other provinces, which suited the poorer ones just fine. Ontario, however, chafed at the situation, and other provinces had their own concerns. Meanwhile, as the boomer kids clogged the schools and their parents searched for greater security in financing their own health care and future pensions, voters demanded both more spending and more coherence from all levels of government. St. Laurent patiently negotiated with the provinces, finally producing a grand and historic compromise: Ottawa would deliver block grants to provinces whose weaker tax base made them unable to deliver social services at a level comparable to wealthier provinces. Equalization was born, perhaps St. Laurent's greatest achievement as prime minister, and a testament to the commitment of better-off Canadians to lift up the disadvantaged. Equalization is "a principle that should be cherished," wrote the journalist and historian Mary Janigan. "It is a gift from the generation that came from the Second World War to make a better world."[37]

But the formula was imperfect. The poorer Maritime provinces didn't believe their grants would make it possible for them to provide schools, hospitals, and social assistance at a level even close to that provided in Ontario, even as their young increasingly decided to go down the road in search of jobs and a better life. Premier Leslie Frost was incensed at the cost Ontario taxpayers were expected to bear to improve the quality of life outside the province. Dissatisfaction with the Liberal equalization program contributed to Frost's strong support for the Conservatives in the 1957 election. Diefenbaker and Fleming got the message. Soon after winning power, the federal government transferred three percentage points of tax from Ottawa to the provinces, increasing the fiscal capacity of Ontario and other "have" provinces. At the same time, Ottawa bolstered transfers to have-not provinces, principally Quebec and Atlantic Canada. In 1961, Fleming completed the transfer of a substantial portion of the federal taxing power back to the provinces, with equalization firmly entrenched to help the have-nots. The rebalancing placed equalization on a sounder footing, making it so integral to the federal system that it was incorporated into the Constitution. An issue of constant federal–provincial tension was finally off the table, though complaints about a fiscal imbalance between the federal and provincial governments continue to bedevil the federation to this day.

The tax-point transfer weakened Ottawa's fiscal clout within the federation. "All your power's gone now," Saskatchewan premier Tommy Douglas told a finance official, almost as a lament,[38] though Ottawa in years to come would find new ways to wield its influence, especially when Liberals were doing the wielding.

Some of the Diefenbaker government's most important accomplishments were in areas that attracted little attention in urban Central Canada, such as agriculture. Post-war innovations in machinery, fertilization, and crop management had turned the Prairie dustbowl into a breadbasket. Farmers now produced too much wheat rather than too little, for the American Prairies were also producing bumper yields, and American policies in the 1950s closed the door to many Canadian agricultural exports. Agriculture Minister Alvin Hamilton, Dief's political protégé from Saskatchewan, wore an easy grin and had a tendency to shoot from the lip, but he had a keen mind, and the farmer's son had the interests of farmers at heart. On his watch, the Diefenbaker government consolidated and expanded a patchwork scheme of supports—the budget of the agriculture department nearly tripled—while taking marginal land out of production and returning it to pasture or woodlots. Most important, in 1961 the government negotiated a hundred-milliondollar wheat sale to Communist China, along with a revolving line of credit to help the regime meet its payments. Cabinet resisted—the Americans were hotly opposed to the sale—and Hamilton was ready to resign, but Diefenbaker weighed in and secured agreement. "Diefenbaker really should get credit for making the political decision," Hamilton said later.[39]

The Americans had every reason to be chagrined. By negotiating wheat sales with China, along with helping its government finance the purchase, Canada had not only established a major new market for Canadian food products—while helping to alleviate a self-induced famine that killed tens of millions—but the Diefenbaker government was also tacitly acknowledging the reality of the regime in Beijing. Diefenbaker had mused to foreign leaders that he was inclined toward Canadian recognition of Communist China, despite American opposition. The wheat sale reflected that inclination. A decade later, Pierre Trudeau's government would formally recognize the existence of the world's most populous nation.

Hamilton also oversaw the Roads to Resources road-building program, which laid down four thousand kilometres of roads in the northern reaches of the Western provinces and into the Yukon and Northwest Territories, including the first stretch of the Dempster Highway north from Dawson City to a new town, Inuvik, established as a new administrative centre for the Western Arctic. (A subsequent Conservative government, Stephen Harper's, broke ground on the final stretch of the highway, from Inuvik to Tuktoyaktuk, in 2014.) The roads helped open up the Far North to oil, gas, and mineral exploration. The Diefenbaker government also brought universal public education to the Inuit, though they continued to live in deep poverty. The Conservatives financed much of the new Trans-Canada Highway. The major portions of road that were either non-existent or not up to "Trans-Canada standard" included an east-to-west highway across Newfoundland, large stretches of Northern Ontario, and the Rogers Pass in B.C.—all the hard parts, in other words. By the end of the Diefenbaker era, most of the road was in place. And as we've seen, the Conservatives were responsible for the South Saskatchewan River dam project, a major work of infrastructure often promised by Liberal governments but never delivered. Two dams, completed in 1967, brought electrical power, flood control, and drinking water to the region, and its announcement delighted Premier Tommy Douglas. The 225-kilometre Diefenbaker Lake was aptly named after the prime minister, though he was less than delighted that the Pearson government named one of the dams after his old nemesis, Jimmy Gardiner.

Tommy Douglas had plenty of reasons to find common cause with John Diefenbaker, apart from the premier's admiration for Edna back in the day.

The two men were Saskatchewan Prairie populists who had lived through hard times. As premier, Douglas had introduced free health care in hospitals. The Diefenbaker government stripped the obstacles out of the St. Laurent government's version of the plan and made the program national. Without that change, Tommy Douglas believed, Canada "would not have had hospital insurance for many years."[40] With universal hospital insurance now in place, Douglas then announced plans to create a universal public medical care program for Saskatchewan. Should the federal government follow suit? Diefenbaker had no mandate from the voters for such an ambitious and expensive endeavour. But he was willing to point his government in that direction. In 1961, he created the Royal Commission on Health Services to recommend measures that would "ensure that the best possible health care is available to all Canadians," a mandate that clearly favoured some form of public insurance.[41] And he further stacked the deck with his choice of the commission's chair: Emmett Hall. The two had gone to law school together; it was Hall who, after breakfasting with the judge, warned Diefenbaker to lighten up on his too-dark-to-see defence in the Chernyski case back in 1919. Hall had endured the Prairie depression, leaving him committed to government action to alleviate poverty and reduce inequality. On becoming prime minister, Diefenbaker had elevated Hall to chief justice of the Saskatchewan Court of Queen's Bench, then to chief justice of Saskatchewan, and then to the Supreme Court. But Hall could fulfill his duties as a judge while still chairing a commission. And anyone who did not know that Hall would come down in favour of universal public health care did not know Hall, Douglas, or Diefenbaker, and their shared Saskatchewan history.

Regional development assistance in the Maritimes, the Prairies, and the North; expanded public health care; a new fiscal framework with the provinces; enhanced pensions; reform of the prison system; the end of race-based immigration; voting rights for First Nations; the Bill of Rights; the Columbia River Treaty; silo-emptying wheat sales to China; the Trans-Canada Highway; the South Saskatchewan Dam, Roads to Resources, and other major infrastructure programs. From the summer of 1957 to the end of 1961, the Diefenbaker government moved decisively on a broad range of major files. And there was one other great achievement—in this case, in foreign affairs.

VII

On June 18, 1990, Nelson Mandela stood before the combined houses of Parliament to thank the people of Canada. He had been free for only four months, after spending twenty-seven years in prison for his leading role in opposing apartheid in South Africa. But apartheid was finally crumbling, as President F.W. de Klerk and his former prisoner had begun the protracted dance that would lead to free elections four years later and to Mandela becoming South Africa's first Black president. Prime Minister Brian Mulroney didn't try to hide his pride as Mandela thanked Canada for its leadership in rallying the world to condemn the suppression of Black South Africans. Joe Clark, who, as Mulroney's secretary of state for external affairs, had also pushed to isolate South Africa despite resistance from Ronald Reagan in the United States and Margaret Thatcher in Britain, was every bit as proud. Three decades before, as young conservative activists, Mulroney and Clark had been inspired by the leadership of John Diefenbaker, who made Canada the first member of the "old Commonwealth"—read "white Commonwealth"—to confront the evil of apartheid.

Commonwealth leaders had agreed to meet in London in the first week of May 1960. Top of mind, though it was not even officially on the agenda, was the issue of South Africa, which was about to hold a referendum on becoming a republic. Everyone expected the white population, who alone were allowed to vote, to vote Yes. Black South Africans had no say in their future. With Elizabeth no longer South Africa's queen, the new republic would have to apply for readmission to the Commonwealth. The white, developed nations were inclined to say yes to a country that had been a valuable ally in two world wars. But the newly independent African and Asian members were understandably determined to say no. The conflict threatened to tear the Commonwealth apart.

Whenever an intractable issue presented itself, Diefenbaker preferred to delay deciding, hoping that the passage of time would reveal a path forward. This was especially true of the South Africa question because his own government was split on the issue, with the secretary of state for external affairs and his secretary of cabinet on opposing sides. Diefenbaker's foreign minister was Howard Green, whom the prime minister appointed after Sidney

Smith—who left his position as president of the University of Toronto to take on the task—died suddenly of a heart attack. Green was not a natural fit for External. He had never travelled to Washington and was so devout that he neither smoked nor drank nor worked on Sundays. But Green was loyal, capable—as public works minister, he cleaned out the patronage and pork that had festered for decades in that department under the Liberals— and shared Diefenbaker's conviction that the best way to counterbalance growing American influence was to strengthen ties with Britain. In this case, that meant supporting the Union of South Africa's readmission to the Commonwealth, which Harold Macmillan and Australian prime minister Robert Menzies both favoured. On the other side of the argument, Privy Council clerk Robert Bryce was certain that letting South Africa rejoin would give aid and comfort to apartheid, while estranging newly independent Commonwealth states such as Ghana and Nigeria and splitting the Commonwealth in two. Cabinet was, as usual, divided on the issue.

Diefenbaker was divided himself. The suppression of Black South Africans offended his sense of justice; it offended also the principles of his Bill of Rights. He was four-square opposed to apartheid, in public and private. But white South Africa was almost as closely tied to Britain as Canada itself and was a mature and developed state. How could it be expelled from the Empire, or whatever was left of it? Canada's prime minister decided to keep a low profile at the conference, listening more than talking, while quietly prodding the South Africans to find some way to include Black representation, however token, in its parliament. But the Afrikaners wouldn't budge, and the Commonwealth members ultimately agreed to put off any decision until after South Africa held its referendum, a very Diefenbaker-like solution.

Delay only amplified the problem. Macmillan and Menzies sought some form of compromise in which India, as leader of the non-white members, and the African states might agree to the temporary readmission of South Africa while a commission of some sort sought to establish to what extent, if at all, the Commonwealth should interfere in the internal affairs of its members. Had he been prime minister, Lester Pearson would no doubt have been part of those delicate negotiations, perhaps even a leader of them. But Diefenbaker wanted nothing to do with such talks, for they would have pushed him over to one side of the argument: keeping South Africa in. He preferred to remain neutral, watching the eddies and currents of the debate. "His consistent aim was to preserve his freedom of manoeuvre and decision," wrote Basil Robinson, Diefenbaker's liaison to External Affairs—in effect, his foreign policy adviser. "This proved to be a wise tactic, though it involved a lot of zig-zagging along the way."[42]

Commonwealth leaders convened again in London in March 1961. The previous October, 52 per cent of white South African voters, a bare majority, had supported making South Africa a republic. Canadian public opinion overwhelmingly opposed apartheid, especially after the Sharpeville massacre of March 1960, when police opened fire on a crowd of Black protesters, killing 69 and wounding 180. The Canadian Labour Congress urged Diefenbaker to lead a movement to expel South Africa from the Commonwealth; most newspaper editorials agreed. But Diefenbaker didn't want to lead anything. He continued to search for a compromise that would authorize South Africa to stay inside the Commonwealth but allow him to maintain his opposition to apartheid. The legislation establishing the republic was not yet in place. Perhaps the Afrikaners would show flexibility by permitting some token Black representation in Parliament. Perhaps the whole thing could be put off until after the republic had been formally proclaimed. His prevarications won him no friends. While impatient developing nations wondered why Canada would not take a stand, Macmillan castigated the unfaithful Canadians. "John Diefenbaker is going to be troublesome about S Africa," he wrote privately. "He is taking a 'holier than thou' attitude, wh[ich] may cause us infinite trouble. For if the 'whites' take an anti-S Africa line, how can we expect the Brown and Blacks to be more tolerant."[43]

When the March summit convened, it became increasingly clear that the African and Asian leaders would brook no further delay. It also became clear to Diefenbaker, after conversations with South African prime minister Hendrik Verwoerd, that there would be no give on the South Africans' part. Verwoerd is considered one of the architects of apartheid, and from that perspective he was right to resist permitting even token political representation by Black South Africans. Imagine if Nelson Mandela had been elected even to a non-voting role in the National Assembly in Cape Town in 1962, rather than sentenced to life in prison. The pressure from within to weaken and ultimately dismantle apartheid would have proved irresistible. Verwoerd refused every offer of compromise.

Noting Diefenbaker's preference for further delay, Macmillan thought that Canada could perhaps be kept onside with the other white dominions in favour of somehow keeping South Africa inside the Commonwealth. He was wrong. At a crucial moment, Indian prime minister Jawaharlal Nehru spoke forcefully in favour of refusing South Africa's readmission to the Commonwealth. Diefenbaker spoke next. He praised South Africa's deep ties to the Empire and to the Commonwealth, and continued to argue in favour of delaying any final decision. However, he stressed that "to accept South Africa's present request would be construed as approval of, or at least acquiescence in, South Africa's racial policy."[44] Macmillan and Menzies knew that this meant Canada had broken with them and sided with the developing states. So did Verwoerd. South Africa withdrew its application for readmission, blaming the "Canadian-African-Asian bloc."[45]

Macmillan and Menzies were incensed at what they considered Diefenbaker's betrayal. "Without him, we could have got through," the British prime minister believed, while Menzies spoke of Diefenbaker leading "the attack on South Africa." Based on that anger, historian Kevin Spooner concludes, "While it would be overstating the case that South Africa's departure was the result of the prime minister's actions, Diefenbaker's involvement did influence the outcome."[46] Basil Robinson, in his memoirs, echoed that view. And Diefenbaker's resolve, however belated, inspired a generation of young conservatives, including Brian Mulroney and Joe Clark, to fight against apartheid in particular and human rights abuses in general. It would not be going too far to say that Diefenbaker's stand on apartheid established a Conservative tradition in foreign policy anchored in a staunch defence of democratic values and human rights that were reflected in the foreign policies of Brian Mulroney and Stephen Harper.

Let the last word go to Nelson Mandela. In his 1990 address to Parliament, he thanked Brian Mulroney, who had "continued along the path charted by Prime Minister Diefenbaker, who acted against apartheid because he knew that no person of conscience could stand aside as a crime against humanity was being committed."[47]

NINE

Cries and Alarums

(1959–1961)

I

Had the Diefenbaker era ended in 1961, it would have been viewed as a considerable success. Immigration reform, voting rights for First Nations, the Bill of Rights, the wheat sale to China, the stand against apartheid, regional development and infrastructure programs, reforms to the justice system, the introduction of universal hospital care, and other successes would have stood as a solid legislative agenda. The crises and controversies to come would not have occurred, or would have been left to his successor. But it was not to be. Major controversies dogged the final years of the Diefenbaker era, tarnishing its legacy. What went wrong? Olive might have had something to do with it.

Fiercely protective of her husband, she became increasingly critical of anyone whose support was less than unqualified—"she would publicly rip you up and down if she thought that you were taking any credit for anything she thought belonged to John," Alvin Hamilton recalled—which led to an increase in the coterie of sycophants surrounding the prime minister, and a decrease in those whose advice might be critical.[1] But if Olive stoked

Diefenbaker's mistrust and sense of grievance, that sense of grievance did not need much stoking: it dominated Diefenbaker's personality, in power and out. On the whole, he was gregarious and friendly as prime minister; he and Olive were far more likely to invite MPs and public servants to 24 Sussex Drive, the prime ministerial residence, than St. Laurent had been. People found him witty, though the wit could be cutting. But Diefenbaker never got over the fact that he was an outsider in his own party, that many of his most senior cabinet ministers had been rivals for the leadership or had supported his rivals. He was not, by nature, trusting. Eventually that lack of trust was returned.

Merrill Menzies believed that when Diefenbaker acted on his own instincts he was rarely mistaken. But he could be misled by bad advice from those around him. (Menzies himself departed the Prime Minister's Office in 1960, dismayed by the diminishing reform impulse of the administration.)

He was both controlling and indecisive. Nothing of significance moved forward without his imprimatur, which might be expected of any prime minister. But that imprimatur was hard to obtain. He sought consensus within cabinet for whatever needed to be done. But the more intractable the issues were, the harder it was to reach consensus. Rather than impose his will, he would convene cabinet three or more times a week, often without notice, forcing ministers to cancel meetings and abandon plans. Hours of discussion might lead to a decision or, more likely, to the PM appointing several ministers to study the issue and report back. Important files could remain inactive for months, with ministers and public servants growing increasingly frustrated. Sometimes they shared those frustrations with the press—strictly off the record, of course.

He was also as notoriously disorganized as prime minister as he had been as a lawyer. He never succeeded in putting together a staff that could prioritize files, keep him on schedule, and offer sound and candid advice. His small retinue of devoted secretaries—headed much of the time by the loyal and capable Marjory "Bunny" Pound—kept the wheels from falling off, but more than once vital documents went missing, agendas disintegrated, major decisions went undecided. Things got so slapdash that one day the Order Paper for the House of Commons was blank, meaning there was nothing for members to debate, to the deep embarrassment of House leader Gordon Churchill. Diefenbaker blamed all and sundry, but the fault was his for failing to establish a coherent legislative agenda.

Well, not entirely his. Diefenbaker had to fight against the vested Central Canadian interests that dominated the political parties, including his own. The Prairie populist never had the confidence of the Conservative establishment. They had sought to block his rise and acquiesced only grudgingly to his leadership victory in 1956, confident they could soon replace him with someone else. They were as surprised as anyone by his spectacular success in the 1957 and 1958 elections. The big bosses on Bay Street knew that Diefenbaker was no friend of theirs.

His instincts were those of a defence attorney, the David seeking a chink in the armour of the prosecuting Goliath. Those skills proved to be a formidable asset in opposition, but they were useless or even harmful in government. He never seemed able to grasp that *he* was now Goliath, with all the resources of the federal government at his disposal. More than any prime minister before or since, he was an opposition politician even when in office.

If Diefenbaker had won the leadership in 1942 or 1948, he might have had enough flexibility to adapt to political reality while also shaping the party into something that better reflected his own values. Instead, he inherited the very machine he had raged against, able to change neither the machine nor himself.

Diefenbaker was a regional politician, but a prime minister must transcend region. MPs from the West were fiercely loyal: if not for Diefenbaker, they wouldn't have had their seats. He was also enormously popular in the small towns and on the farms of rural Ontario, and could spin his populist charm into parts of the Maritimes that had traditionally been loyal to the Grits. Toronto, though, was suspicious: the home of fat cats and party bosses, of Annex dinner parties and Rosedale soirees where his kind were not welcome. And the Quebec wing of the party was never loyal to Diefenbaker, owing as much to the Union Nationale for their seats as to the Progressive Conservatives. Diefenbaker, in turn, had no interest in, or understanding of, Quebec. This ignorance was not grounded in animus. In fact, his government was responsible for an important advance in francophone rights in the federal government. The Conservatives made the House of Commons truly bilingual.

Until the Diefenbaker government, the House had functioned, for all intents and purposes, as an English-speaking club. Though the Constitution decreed that Parliament should operate in both official languages, MPs who spoke in French found that they quickly emptied out the chamber. This issue was no longer one of technology: Belgium had had simultaneous interpretation in its federal Parliament since the 1930s, and the new United Nations in New York was offering simultaneous interpretation in a plethora of languages. In Canada, the Junior Chamber of Commerce operated and rented out a simultaneous-interpretation service. But the King and St. Laurent governments considered the cost prohibitive. Lester Pearson, as secretary of state for external affairs, advised against offering simultaneous interpretation in the House, on the grounds that it would discourage MPs from learning both official languages. The argument was specious: only about 15 of 265 MPs were fully bilingual, which meant most francophone MPs rarely spoke. One Quebec MP gave his maiden speech three years after arriving in the House. The Quebec press was pushing for simultaneous interpretation and Diefenbaker agreed. Shortly after the 1958 victory, he introduced a resolution declaring that the House should acquire the equipment and personnel to provide simultaneous interpretation in both official languages. Pearson, realizing this was not a debate he should be on the wrong side of, agreed. The resolution passed unanimously, and on January 15, 1959, the House of Commons became a truly bilingual environment. There is no evidence that the arrival of simultaneous interpretation deterred—or for that matter encouraged—the efforts of MPs to become bilingual.

The prime minister was responsible for another inspired innovation: in choosing a French Canadian to replace the retiring Vincent Massey as governor general, he established the principle of French and English rotation in the viceregal role. And Diefenbaker chose not just any French Canadian: he chose Georges Vanier, who had served with Pearson in London, had distinguished himself in war and in diplomacy. Vanier and his wife Pauline combined a patrician bearing with a personal warmth that made them beloved of all Canadians. He remains the most revered governor general in Canada's history.

But Diefenbaker's attitude toward Quebec in general, and toward his Quebec caucus in particular, was baffling and self-defeating. In his first cabinet, only two ministers were from Quebec, and one of them was English. Their ranks expanded after the landslide victory of 1958, but some of the ablest Conservative MPs from that province remained on the back benches while he promoted instead characters such as Henri Courtemanche, a Quebec lawyer and Diefenbaker's secretary of state who was booted up to the Senate shortly before allegations became public that he had been receiving kickbacks in the early 1950s. His minister of mines, Paul Comtois, was so hapless that the Chief took the opportunity of a vacancy to appoint him lieutenant governor of Quebec. (Comtois would die, tragically, attempting to rescue the sacraments from the chapel when the lieutenant governor's mansion burned in 1966.)

At root, Diefenbaker never accepted the compact under which Canada had operated through decades of Liberal rule. That compact acknowledged the reality that French Canada was a place with its own language and culture and customs and privileges, which its provincial government was pledged to protect and the federal government to respect, while the English—read British—dominated the rest of Canada, along with big business in Quebec itself. Diefenbaker resented that compact and fought against it. At his best, his approach revealed a nascent multiculturalism. Canada is not "a melting pot in which the individuality of each element is destroyed in order to produce a new and totally different element," he said in 1961. "It is rather a garden into which have been transplanted the hardiest and brightest flowers from many lands, each retaining in its new environment the best of the qualities for which it was loved and prized in its native land."[2] That appreciation of multiculturalism was evident in his choice of cabinet ministers, in his race-blind approach to immigration, in extending the franchise to First Nations, in his Bill of Rights. But it also reflected a plain ignorance of Quebec.

Diefenbaker should have appointed Léon Balcer—or someone else who was equally capable and more loyal—as Quebec lieutenant, and then listened to him and taken his advice on who to promote and demote, how to handle Quebec City, which issues to advance and which to avoid. But he never did, and so squandered the opportunity to deepen Tory ties in the province. He might have failed anyway—from his day to ours, Conservative efforts to court nationalists-but-not-separatists in Quebec have proven mostly unsuccessful and never deep-rooted. But Diefenbaker never even tried.

As an ardent Diefenbaker supporter, a young Brian Mulroney watched in dismay as Léon Balcer and the rest of the Quebec delegation walked out of the Conservative convention in 1956. Five years later, while at Laval University's law school, he helped organize a conference entitled "The Canadian Experiment: Success or Failure?" Mulroney wrote to Diefenbaker warning of a growing grassroots movement in support of separation. "The basis of separation is that nearly every French Canadian is made to feel a second-class citizen in his day-to-day dealing with business and government. French Canadians are also concerned with their language, their culture and their religion, hence the vital importance to them of bilingualism among English as well as French Canadians, and complete control of education and of provincial rights in general."³ He proposed that bilingualism be extended throughout the federal government and that funding be provided for bilingual education; he advocated, too, for the adoption of "O Canada" as the national anthem (it was still "God Save the Queen") and of a new Canadian flag. But Diefenbaker ignored the recommendations, which would later be taken up by a government of a different political persuasion.

Most important, perhaps, Diefenbaker failed to understand the seismic shifts underway in Canadian society as the boomers entered their teens. Both Diefenbaker and Pearson were in their seventh decade as the fifties gave way to the sixties. But while Pearson would prove able to adapt, Diefenbaker could not. Every year, without really realizing it, he became further estranged from the times in which he lived. For those times they were a-changin'.

II

On June 23, 1960, the U.S. Food and Drug Administration approved the most important medical breakthrough of the twentieth century after penicillin: the birth control pill. Driven by the unrelenting advocacy of Margaret Sanger, who had been campaigning for women's reproductive rights for decades, and financed by her friend Katharine Dexter McCormick, heir to the International Harvester fortune, the first brand-name product, Enovid, could produce unpleasant side effects and in rare cases induce heart failure. But millions of women were willing to chance it. Within five years, one out of every four married women under forty-five in the United States had used a product so transformative, and so controversial, that everyone simply called it "the pill." It took nine years before Canada legalized oral birth control—the complaint that everything comes to Canada ten years after it arrives in the United States was exaggerated but not unfounded. The pill revolutionized sexuality and the rights of women, who could now engage in sex freely with little fear of becoming pregnant, and who could decide for themselves how many babies they would have. As soon as they enjoyed that power, they exercised it. The baby boom was over. Modern feminism—"women's liberation," many called it, or "women's lib," usually said derisively—was on the march.

The early sixties marked the dawn of social revolutions, musical revolutions, technological revolutions, and, in Quebec, the first stirrings of the Quiet Revolution. Throughout the 1950s, Maurice Duplessis had dominated life in French Canada, channeling its people's innate nationalism through the political and religious conservatism of the Union Nationale and the Roman Catholic Church. But there were growing voices of dissent—the newspaper *Le Devoir* and journal *Cité Libre*, and a small group of intellectuals, including Pierre Trudeau, and labour leaders, including Jean Marchand. Duplessis's death in 1959, followed by that of his successor, Paul Sauvé, unleashed a pent-up energy suppressed for decades. The signs had been there—a 1949 strike by asbestos workers against their Anglo-American bosses, the Richard riot in 1955—but now they were made manifest in the June 1960 provincial election. The Liberal Party and its leader, Jean Lesage, used the anodyne slogan *"C'est le temps que ça change"* ("It's Time for a Change"). More potent was the phrase coined by André Laurendeau in *Le Devoir*: *maîtres chez nous*, "masters in our own house." It was time to shake off the shackles of the Church, to seize control of the means of production from the American and English-Canadian overlords, to project and protect the political and cultural autonomy of Quebec. Where would it end? How even would it be defined? No one yet knew—including Trudeau, Marchand, and former journalist and now cabinet minister René Lévesque as they talked and argued around the table at the home of their friend Gérard Pelletier late into the night.

The Cold War was going badly for the Americans. Compounding the humiliation of Sputnik and the failure of the Americans to get something, anything, into space, on May 1, 1960, a U-2 spy plane disappeared over Soviet airspace. Convinced the Russians could never shoot down the sophisticated aircraft, the Americans made up some flummery about a weather plane veering off course. But the Russians *had* shot it down, and produced both the wreckage of the plane and its captured pilot, Gary Powers. After an ailing, aged Dwight Eisenhower reluctantly confessed the truth, Nikita Khrushchev stormed out of a long-planned arms-control meeting. Fidel Castro's Cuba was firmly in the Soviet camp, the Chinese under Mao were attempting to industrialize—though the Great Leap Forward caused the death of millions by starvation—and, to keep Communist North Vietnam at bay, Eisenhower felt he had to send military advisers to aid the regime in South Vietnam.

On November 6, 1960, the young and charismatic Massachusetts senator John Fitzgerald Kennedy narrowly defeated Eisenhower's vice-president, Richard Nixon, to become the thirty-fifth president of the United States. The veterans of the Second World War were gradually taking the reins of power from their elders. "Let the word go forth from this time and place, to friend and foe alike, that the torch has been passed to a new generation of Americans—born in this century, tempered by war, disciplined by a hard and bitter peace," Kennedy declared at his inaugural address. ". . . Let every nation know, whether it wishes us well or ill, that we shall pay any price, bear any burden, meet any hardship, support any friend, oppose any foe, in order to assure the survival and the success of liberty." Stirring. And dangerous.

III

Under British and American guidance, Canada had become an aircraft-manufacturing powerhouse during the Second World War, churning out sixteen thousand bombers, fighters, and other aircraft. The British manufacturer Hawker Siddeley, seeking to take advantage of that expertise, purchased Victory Aircraft from the Canadian government in 1945, establishing A.V. Roe Canada. The company set out to create an interceptor fighter for the Royal Canadian Air Force (RCAF). But development of the CF-100 Canuck was plagued with failure and cost overruns. C.D. Howe, who (of course) was pulling the strings, arranged for Crawford Gordon, one of his best men at the Department of Defence Production, to take over the company. Gordon had been recruited as one of Howe's "dollar-a-year" men during the Second World War, and was so brilliant, and so young, that he was dubbed "the Boy Wonder." He was still only thirty-six when he moved from the top spot at Defence Procurement to the presidency of A.V. Roe. He was a driven man, a hard drinker and heavy smoker who thrived on success but couldn't handle failure.

Gordon became devoted to Avro and its potential as a world leader in military aviation. But while Canadians took great pride in their made-in-Canada interceptor, government officials blanched at the costs. "I must say," Howe wrote Claxton in 1952, "I am frightened for the first time in my defence production experience." Those costs were about to climb sky-high, as Avro began work in 1953 on its next-generation fighter, the supersonic CF-105, the Avro Arrow.

The Arrow was gorgeous, with a sleek, swept-back delta wing design; powerful—able to fly at twice the speed of sound thanks to its Canadian-made Orenda Iroquois turbojet engines; and advanced, with state-of-the-art avionics, including an early version of an on-board computer. But the plane became obsolete literally on the day the first prototype was rolled out for public view, October 4, 1957, for that was the day the Soviet Union launched Sputnik. According to Howe's biographers, the previous spring, "the Cabinet's Defence Committee bowed to the obvious: the Arrow could be cancelled—after the next election."[4] When the Liberals lost that election, cancelling the Arrow become John Diefenbaker's responsibility.

The Arrow suffered from several fatal flaws. First off, it was too expensive. By the time the prototype rolled out, the estimated cost of $1.5 million to $2 million a plane had escalated to $8 million. "We have started on a program of development that gives me the shudders," Howe told the House of Commons in 1955.[5] He was opposed to the Arrow from the get-go. Only the obstinate determination of the RCAF to have its own supersonic jet fighter kept the project going.

Second, the plane was entering a crowded market. Its biggest competitor was Convair's F-106 Delta Dart, which the Americans had in development. The British were also working on a supersonic interceptor fighter of their own. Why would the great powers acquire a Canadian fighter over their own product? And with the Korean War over, the government was cutting back on defence spending, slashing RCAF squadrons from twenty to nine. The domestic market wouldn't be able to justify the cost of the plane.

But most important, by the time the Arrow was ready to go into production, in 1958, surface-to-air missile (SAM) technology had advanced to the point that a good SAM system posed a greater threat to bombers than interceptor fighters, or so its supporters claimed. Both the U.S. and the Soviet Union were racing to perfect their nuclear-equipped intercontinental ballistic missile technology. Fleets of slow-moving bombers would become less and less relevant in strategic calculations, reducing the importance of the supersonic interceptor fighter. The Americans went ahead with the F-106; many other interceptor fighter programs were shelved.

Cost, competition, and obsolescence convinced first the Liberal and then the Conservative cabinet that the Arrow program should be terminated. But it would be a hard decision. A.V. Roe had become Canada's third-largest private-sector employer. The core of its operation consisted of its airframe and engine companies located on a sprawling testing and production facility beside Malton (now Pearson) Airport, on the northern edge of Toronto. Canadians took great and justified pride in the research and engineering capacity of the country's aviation industry, which could compete with the best in the world. Cancelling the Arrow would lead to thousands of layoffs and put the very future of Canada's aviation sector at risk. And the economy was struggling. Shutting down the biggest airplane production facility in the country would increase unemployment.

As well as deciding on the Arrow, the new Conservative government had to decide on the future of the Mark VI version of the CF-100 Canuck fighter. Jet-aircraft technology had advanced so swiftly in the 1950s that the subsonic warplane was obsolete. But when the government informed A.V. Roe of its intention to cancel the production order for the CF-100 in 1957, executives replied that cancellation of the contract would result in thousands of layoffs—fifteen thousand to be exact, if Arrow were cancelled, too. And those layoffs would mostly take place in ridings held by Conservatives, including Transport Minister George Hees. A minority government that could be thrown back into an election in months could ill afford such a risk. Cabinet reconsidered.

George Pearkes, the defence minister, cooked up a workable compromise. The government would buy, and essentially give away to NATO allies, twenty of the older Mark V version of the CF-100. The Arrow would continue development for one more year, including the construction of thirty-seven pre-production aircraft. Job losses would be limited to 1,450 workers, some through attrition. The can would be kicked at least a little way down the road.

A year later, now with a large majority government, cabinet faced the same problem with the Arrow. In the meantime, test flights had met with remarkable success—and efforts to convince the Americans or British to place an order, with remarkable failure. Instead, Washington came back with a counterproposal: Canada should beef up its radar defence system and accept the new Bomarc surface-to-air missiles, probably with nuclear-tipped warheads, all of which the Americans would help pay for. Pearkes brought the proposal to cabinet in August 1958. For a month, ministers agonized, before coming up with a lame compromise: Avro should abandon work on the plane's fire control and missile systems—adequate substitutes could be purchased from the Americans—but continue work for six more months on the aircraft itself and its Iroquois engine. The hope was that, in those six months, Avro would find a buyer for the aircraft or, well, something would turn up. Pearkes warned cabinet that every year the government kept the Arrow alive added four hundred million dollars— more than four billion present-day dollars—to the defence budget, increasing both taxes and debt. The Canadians and Americans were already preparing for the upgrading of radar instillations and the transfer of two Bomarc missile batteries to Ontario and Quebec. Crawford Gordon had no new proposals. All he had was attitude. According to one version of events, at a meeting between Diefenbaker and Gordon on September 17, 1958, "an intoxicated Gordon was rude and belligerent while puffing cigarette smoke in Diefenbaker's face, who was a non-drinker and non-smoker. Gordon ended up being thrown out of the Prime Minister's office for his behaviour."[6]

Essentially, Gordon was playing chicken with cabinet: the company had blackmailed the government into continuing production of the CF-100 and development of the Arrow a year before; Gordon was gambling he could force the Conservatives to let production begin, after which the company would make as many planes as the RCAF would buy.

But by February 1959, Diefenbaker had made up his mind. "Look, this is going to cost a billion dollars," he explained to Grattan O'Leary. "We have no market for them, we can't sell them. So why spend a billion dollars on a plane we have no use for?"[7]

Diefenbaker informed the House of the government's decision on February 20. That same day, A.V. Roe closed down all operations and fired its employees, using a loudspeaker to deliver the news. The fifteen thousand layoffs shocked both the prime minister and Ontario premier Leslie Frost, who heard the news at the same time as everyone else. Frost was furious, and blamed Diefenbaker for the layoffs. Lester Pearson, in the House, accused the government of "fumbling, confusion and delay" in the matter.[8] But he did not criticize the decision itself; as a cabinet minister in the St. Laurent government, he surely knew that the Liberals had reached the same decision almost two years before. Newspaper editorials and opposition politicians condemned the Conservatives not so much for cancelling the Arrow as for failing to preserve the technical and engineering base of Canada's aviation industry by finding an alternative project. Diefenbaker responded, "If the Avro Company will come forward and give me a practical suggestion to keep the facilities of Avro Aircraft intact, it will receive the most serious and immediate consideration."[9] But there was no practical alternative. The Americans had already resolved that all their military aircraft would be designed and built in the United States. The British and French were also unlikely to choose a Canadian product over one of their own. There was simply no market for the plane. Diefenbaker had made the right decision. He should have made it sooner.

But the Arrow myth was born almost the minute after the real Arrow died. Why were the prototypes destroyed? Why were the tools and design materials burned? To keep proprietary information from falling into Russian hands, was the reason given, but it seemed inadequate. More satisfying was the notion that John Diefenbaker, furious at being criticized and at Gordon's impudence, had the surviving Arrows destroyed in a fit of pique. And he destroyed an entire industrial sector as well, critics raged. The Arrow's designers, engineers, and workers migrated south to the United States, where many of them would find work in the NASA space program. The Arrow spawned a slew of books and conspiracy theories, and a 1997 CBC docudrama starring Dan Aykroyd as Crawford Gordon. (Christopher Plummer as George Hees was delightful, but Robert Haley's Diefenbaker bore no resemblance.) To this day the legend of the Arrow fuels anger and regret: a beautiful plane, a world-beater, was senselessly scrapped by a cabal of small-minded Tories, taking the pride of the Canadian aviation industry with it.

None of it—including the CBC movie—is true. C.D. Howe, for one, told anybody who asked that the Conservatives had made the right decision. But the Arrow myth damaged Diefenbaker's legacy. Though it may strike some as ironic, it became axiomatic among Canadian progressives that the federal government should have found a way to preserve the aviation side of its arms-exporting industry.

The Arrow was damaging in other ways. Wounded by the criticism from the press and public, estranged from his former ally Leslie Frost, the prime minister worried that the Tories' Toronto bastion was now at risk. Diefenbaker became more cautious. He didn't want another Avro Arrow debacle before the next election. That growing caution and indecision in the wake of the Arrow's cancellation probably damaged the government more than the Arrow's cancellation itself. "The resultant agonies . . . just frightened him to death," William Hamilton, the postmaster general, later recalled. "He began to be more and more cautious until finally we came down, in the latter stages, the last year or so, to only making the decisions that one was forced to make, rather than making the decisions that one should make. The government began to suffer from paralysis—and it was due to the Arrow."[10]

There was another victim. Fired from A.V. Roe, unable to stick at anything else, living on borrowed money, probably sunk in depression, Crawford Gordon died in New York of liver failure brought on by alcoholism on January 26, 1967. He was fifty-two.

The Arrow controversy coincided with a very different dispute involving not high-tech workers in aviation but lumbermen, historically seen as among the lowest of the low among Canadian workers. The lumber industry was vital to Newfoundland's fragile, dependent economy, and in Grand Falls, the Anglo-Newfoundland Development Company operated as a government unto itself. It also owned most of the buildings in the town, and most of the local residents worked in the mill. But while pay was good for the millworkers, the loggers in the woods lived in execrable conditions and worked sixty-hour weeks for far less pay than their counterparts on the mainland. No wonder they flocked to the International Woodworkers of America (IWA) in droves when the union arrived in 1958. The company rejected a conciliation report that recommended a modest wage increase, a fifty-four-hour work week, and improved conditions in the camps. The IWA struck. The company used the RCMP—the national force had a contract to serve as Newfoundland's provincial force—to escort strikebreakers through the picket lines. Nonetheless, the strikers were winning, as logging inventories at the Grand Falls mill fell to dangerous levels. That's when Premier Joey Smallwood declared holy war on the union, taking to the airwaves on February 12 to denounce the IWA for spreading "their black poison of class hatred and bitter, bigoted prejudice" and declaring "it is not a strike they have started; it is a civil war."[11] His government pushed through the docile legislature a bill creating a new union, which the government recognized as the only legitimate union representing loggers in the province. On March 10, striking loggers fought an ugly battle with the RCMP and members of the Royal Newfoundland Constabulary that left one member of the constabulary dead. The attorney general appealed to Ottawa for reinforcements for the RCMP. Commissioner L.H. Nicholson and Justice Minister Davie Fulton believed the government's contract with Newfoundland required that officers be dispatched, but Diefenbaker over-rode both of them. He had no intention of letting the national force be used as strikebreakers. Nicholson resigned in protest, and the enmity between Smallwood and Diefenbaker deepened. But the premier prevailed. The death of the police officer united public opinion against the IWA, and the loggers reluctantly joined the government's house union. If it was any consolation, the terms of the agreement they approved mirrored what the loggers had been asking for. But the bitter dispute and the resignation of the RCMP commissioner did nothing to improve the Diefenbaker government's reputation for sound management.

IV

Almost from the day he won his sweeping majority-government victory, Diefenbaker's relationship with the press started to go downhill. Up until then, the Chief had always enjoyed cordial relations with the five dozen or so journalists in the Parliamentary Press Gallery. As an opposition front-bencher, he was a quote machine who could always be counted on for an off-the-record explanation of what was really going on behind the curtain, usually at someone else's expense. He knew that journalists could shape his public narrative, and he cultivated their support. The day after election night in 1957, he went fishing with two aides and three reporters, only to later turn on one of them, Clark Davey, when he reported on Diefenbaker's airport hissy fit. Diefenbaker expected loyalty from journalists, something most were not willing to give. This he simply could not understand.

It was certainly true that the most important bylines of the era were biased toward the Liberal Party in general and Lester Pearson in particular. But they were now shut out of access, though Foreign Minister Howard Green trusted his friend Bruce Hutchison "well enough to speak with an indiscretion that would have horrified Diefenbaker," Hutchison later recalled.[12] Grant Dexter, who had replaced Dafoe as editor-in-chief of the *Free Press*, returned to Ottawa in 1954. But his health deteriorated and he died of a heart attack in 1961. Blair Fraser remained a powerful force on the Hill, but he was tainted in the eyes of some by his friendship with Pearson.

New centres of both opposition and support emerged within the fourth estate. The Diefenbaker government decreased the importance and increased the independence of the CBC, by handing its regulatory responsibility over to the arms-length Board of Broadcast Governors—it would become the Canadian Radio-television and Telecommunications Commission (CRTC) in 1968—which in turn led to the private, independent television stations that eventually formed the Canadian Television Network. (Something else to add to the Diefenbaker record: the creation of the modern television system, consisting of public and private broadcasters regulated by an arm's-length agency.) John Bassett, proprietor of the *Toronto Telegram* and CFTO, Toronto's powerful private TV station, ran twice to become a Progressive

Conservative MP, losing both times. The *Telegram* was pro-Tory, pro-Diefenbaker, and pro-monarchy, not always in that order. The *Globe and Mail*, if more critical, was also fundamentally sympathetic. But coverage in the *Toronto Star* and *Maclean's* ranged from skeptical to hostile, and the commentary of CBC correspondents sometimes bordered on vitriolic. It didn't help that the government failed to recognize that a bitter three-month strike by Radio-Canada producers was galvanizing a generation of nationalist, even separatist, journalists in Quebec, including correspondent René Lévesque.

And then there was Peter C. Newman, who burst onto the cloistered, incestuous world of the press gallery like a force of nature—a brilliantly talented journalist, initially filling in for Blair Fraser and quickly emerging as the most influential correspondent in Ottawa. Newman's portrayal of Diefenbaker in *Maclean's* would become the leading narrative of the prime minister and his governments. That the narrative was flawed, inaccurate, and the product of the author's own insecurities hardly mattered. Newman defined the Diefenbaker legacy for generations.

The Neumanns, a prosperous Jewish family, had fled Czechoslovakia in 1938, hours before the Nazis arrived. Eventually they reached Canada and Peta Neuman found himself alone and miserable at Upper Canada College, where he more than mastered English and the mores of the sons of the business elite, becoming Peter C. Newman. His father's sudden death and the first of what would end up as four marriages prompted him to drop out of university and take a job at the *Financial Post*. By 1957, at 27, he was a father; was already secretly engaged to the woman who would become his second wife—the equally brilliant and talented Christina McCall—had written a highly successful book on Canada's business elite; and was ready to take on the Hill.

The press gallery was housed in an overstuffed attic packed with desks and papers and not-yet-empty bottles, a "combination of fire trap, speakeasy and rumour mill," as Newman put it, populated by "stenographers instead of investigators." "Prisoners of their slovenly habits," he wrote in his memoirs, "they felt invulnerable and unconcerned about the accelerating seismic changes in the country" and were dedicated only "to not being struck off the guest list for the prime minister's annual garden parties."[13] No doubt they loved him too. But Newman cultivated sources like nobody's business and wrote like a dream. He fell in love with Diefenbaker's vision of One Canada moving forward with purpose and limitless potential, but quickly became disaffected, portraying Diefenbaker as a preening and dithering prime minister possessed of "an almost morbid inability to make up his mind," who had "never administered anything more complicated than a walk-up law office," and who was hopelessly in over his head.[14]

Newman's account was distorted—he would fall in and out of love with every prime minister and Liberal leader from Diefenbaker to Michael Ignatieff—but his wisdom became conventional. The Diefenbaker government's accomplishments in immigration, health care, provincial relations, and the justice system; its role in the struggle against apartheid; its advances in protecting the rights of women, workers, and Indigenous people would be ignored or discounted. Instead, he was written off as a dithering windbag and his government's achievements ignored.

V

John Diefenbaker became prime minister just as Canada descended into a moderate recession that clung to the economy until early 1958. Unemployment, which had reached a rock-bottom low of 2.4 per cent in 1951, climbed steadily to 7 per cent that year, and stayed above 6 per cent until 1962, when it began a prolonged descent that would benefit the Pearson governments. As is usual with Canada, the cause lay outside the country's borders: natural resource exports defined the economy, and when global demand diminished, sales suffered. A second recession arrived in 1960 and lasted for a full year before growth resumed. When the economy contracts, government revenues contract, producing deficits and debt. The arrival of the post-war social safety net, while softening the impact of unemployment on the unemployed and protecting the economy from too much of a dip in demand, forced up government spending and further increased deficits and debt. Diefenbaker, who considered unemployment the worst imaginable social ill, sought to combat it through tax cuts, infrastructure spending, winter work programs, and other stimulants, deficits be damned. Though the Chief knew little and cared less about economic theory, the best available economic advice agreed with him.

Keynesian economic theory, which was "in full flower in the postwar period," as Donald Fleming put it, held that in times of economic contraction, governments should stimulate the economy through some combination of tax cuts and spending, and then pay down the resulting deficit through tax hikes and spending cuts once growth resumed. But "I never adopted Keynesian thinking altogether," Fleming wrote in his memoirs, though he "detected strong traces of Keynesian thinking among economic advisers in the Department of Finance."[15] Fleming correctly noted that the political, not the economic, cycle often dictated fiscal policy, with governments imposing whatever harsh medicine was required in the early years of their mandate and easing off the brake as the next election approached.

Fleming sought to keep the budget balanced, an exercise at which he consistently failed. He blamed Diefenbaker and the rest of cabinet. The prime minister's populist instincts favoured keeping people on the job. His cabinet ministers, like so many before and since, favoured fiscal restraint for every department but their own. Every winter and spring, budget deliberations would drag on and on, through meeting after meeting after meeting, in a process Fleming described as "almost degrading," adding, "For this, Diefenbaker must, of course, bear the principal responsibility."[16] Once a budget had been agreed to, the Chief and his ministers invariably set about undermining it, authorizing this expenditure and that new program over the protests of the finance minister, who later confessed, "Why I did not resign and walk out I still wonder."[17]

In the first government and in the early years of the second government, Fleming had an ally in James Elliott Coyne, governor of the Bank of Canada. Patrician, aloof, parsimonious, austere, and utterly devoid of tact, Coyne was the sort of man who would leave a party and go upstairs to read if he found the conversation dull. He was also brilliant, having risen through the ranks of the bank, though the Rhodes Scholar and lawyer had no formal education in economics. He replaced Graham Towers as the bank's second governor in 1955, to the surprise of many, who thought Louis Rasminsky, Towers's executive assistant and executive director of the International Bank for Reconstruction and Development, would be named. In his memoirs, Fleming recalled, "Ken Taylor, Deputy Minister of Finance, told me St. Laurent had concluded Quebec would not accept a Jew as governor.

From another source I was told that St. Laurent thought the chartered banks would not accept a Jew as governor."[18] It is a sad fact that anti-Semitism remained entrenched in Canada in the 1950s and beyond.

The St. Laurent government asked the bank to take on a task it had not previously performed: managing monetary policy. (Before that, the bank had focused on helping the federal government combat unemployment during the Depression and implement wage and price controls during the war.) In the 1950s, the bank's economists were still mastering the craft of controlling the money supply and adjusting interest rates to promote growth while limiting inflation.

The bank's first responsibility, Coyne believed, was to keep inflation in check, and the way to do that was to raise or lower interest rates and to take other measures as needed to control the supply of money and regulate supply and demand. When Diefenbaker and Fleming were in opposition, they loudly opposed the bank's tight-money policies, which restricted growth along with inflation. "The little man—the farmer, the fisherman and the small businessman—is being crushed by the Liberal government's tight money policy," Diefenbaker proclaimed during the 1957 election, promising "tight money will disappear under a Conservative administration."[19] Fortunately for the new government, the bank eased interest rates in its early months, for which the Conservatives were happy to take credit. However, when interest rates increased in 1958 and 1959, Fleming was at pains to establish that the setting of those rates was exclusively the jurisdiction of the central bank and its governor. Several members of cabinet who advocated expansionary policies urged Fleming to replace Coyne, but Fleming insisted the governor needed to remain in place until his term expired on December 31, 1961. Fleming might also have secretly welcomed the restraining hand that Coyne's restrictive policies placed on unfunded growth.

In many ways, Fleming and Coyne sought to implement what would become conventional economic wisdom in the 1990s and beyond: the bank should focus on keeping inflation low and the finance minister should keep the budget balanced, except in emergencies, the combination of which would promote sustained economic growth. But that hard-fought wisdom would arrive only after years of stagflation and rising debt. The men who held the levers of power in the Western nations in the late 1950s and early 1960s had endured the misery of the Great Depression, with its record levels of unemployment. They had witnessed the ability of Big Government to do Big Things, from winning the war to building post-war infrastructure. For them, Job One was limiting unemployment and promoting growth. Any debt or inflation that resulted could be managed. Coyne stood outside the economic orthodoxy of the time.

By 1960, with the weak recovery of 1958 and 1959 giving way to another recession, and with the prime rate approaching 6 per cent—well above the American level—voices inside and outside the government were baying for Coyne's head. Commercial bank presidents complained that the central bank's restrictive policies were making it difficult to lend money. No fewer than twenty-nine economists from Canadian universities sent a letter to Fleming demanding that Coyne be replaced. "As economists," they wrote, "surely we are justified in expecting that the Bank of Canada should act as a stabilizing force in the economy and not as one whose actions tend to exacerbate our economic and financial difficulties."[20]

The reality, in hindsight, was more complex. In the late 1940s and early 1950s, Canada and the United States stood virtually alone as developed economies untouched by the ravages of the Second World War. But by the late 1950s, with Europe and Japan recovering, Canada faced increased competition in global markets, resulting in excess economic capacity. Some belt-tightening was inevitable. But Coyne's relentless focus on containing inflation—buttressed by the internal analyses of bank economists that wrongly predicted unemployment would soon come down—lay outside the accepted economic consensus of the time and was bound to provoke resistance. And by 1960, he had lost Donald Fleming as an ally. The finance minister, alarmed by an unemployment rate that had reached 7.5 per cent, had decided on stimulus. The federal government's expansionary fiscal policy and the bank's restrictive monetary policy were now at odds.

The governor was probably unaware of how isolated he had become. Coyne "was an unregenerate Grit," Diefenbaker was convinced, "and Liberal Party strategists used him for their own ends."[21] Fleming had grown increasingly weary of a governor who wilfully ignored the wishes of the duly elected government and its finance minister. The bank's governor had not a

friend in cabinet and few, if any, on Bay Street or in the economics departments of universities. To compound matters, Coyne decided the best way to
get his side of the argument across was through a series of speeches. The
famously reticent banker embarked on a road show, which became more
colourful with every appearance.

From his very first address, to the Ontario division of the Investment
Dealers of Canada on December 14, 1959, Coyne sounded a warning: that
the gap between the demand for capital to finance government works and
private investments and the domestic capital available was being financed
by an influx of foreign capital, which in the long run would prove unsustain-
able. "It seems clear that no economy as advanced as ours should allow itself
to be moulded into a pattern of employment which is dependent on capital
expenditures financed by foreign borrowing on such a scale," he maintained.[22] It was and is within the purview of a Bank of Canada governor to
warn of structural imbalances within the Canadian economy. But the
speeches became increasingly critical of the fiscal and economic development
policies of governments at every level. "We have for at least five years been
living beyond our means on a grand scale," he said in Winnipeg. The country was importing more goods than it exported and covering the margin by
borrowing from abroad. Governments were investing in infrastructure,
businesses in plants, and individuals in houses beyond the capital capacity
of the country, with foreign capital brought in to finance the gap. Coyne, as
ardent an economic nationalist as Walter Gordon, believed that Canada was
literally selling its economic sovereignty. And in comparison to the United
States, he noted, "a larger proportion of our capital spending has gone into
the development of facilities for our greater comfort and enjoyment, rather
than into an increase in productive facilities. . . . We are incurring foreign
debt to pay for both a level of capital spending and a standard of comfort
which are higher than would be justified by our own earning capacity."[23]
The balance of payments deficit was more than erroneous; it was sinful.

His solution was simple: governments at all levels must reduce spending;
imports must not exceed exports in value; spending in all sectors must be
financed by earnings rather than debt. Coyne was under no illusion about
the social cost of these policies: "fewer houses and perhaps lower-cost
houses . . . smaller consequential expenses on streets, sewers . . . fewer

miles of new high-cost highways . . . less in the way of natural resource development . . . less hydro-electric development . . . less spending on public buildings and other public facilities." Under Coyne's prescription, Canada would be poorer, but it would be living within its means.

In Hamilton, he warned of two pernicious trends: borrowing from foreign (read American) sources by provincial and municipal governments, and "direct foreign investment in business enterprises in this country." He dismissed as "absurd" objections that eliminating foreign borrowing and foreign investment would increase unemployment. And he warned, "If we do not effectively change the trends of the past we shall drift into an irreversible form of integration with a very much larger and more powerful neighbour. I do not believe this is what Canadians want."[24]

In all, Coyne gave fourteen speeches, the last in March 1961. Fleming told the House of Commons that the governor had every right to speak his mind, though his remarks did not reflect government policy. But the governor's speeches were deeply embarrassing, and Fleming eventually asked him to stop, which he did. By then, James Coyne's days were numbered.

As Donald Fleming prepared for his 1961 spring budget, there was much he could take pride in as finance minister. He and Coyne together had consolidated the wartime debt on terms that ended up being more favourable for the federal government and for taxpayers than for bondholders. Despite relatively weak economic growth, he had kept deficits modest and the debt-to-GDP ratio going down. He had negotiated a new and durable fiscal framework with the provinces and entrenched equalization as a core principle and federal responsibility. But the Bank of Canada governor was giving him grief.

Coyne's relentless focus on inflation conflicted with Fleming and Diefenbaker's priority of reducing unemployment. And Coyne's speechifying about Canada's loss of economic sovereignty and need for austerity conflicted with both federal and provincial fiscal priorities, forcing Fleming to rush to New York to reassure foreign investors that Canada welcomed their money. Ontario premier Leslie Frost was especially incensed with a governor whose policies, if implemented, would cripple Ontario's manufacturing and resource sectors. The commercial banks had lost all faith in him. His warning that Canada was "on a path to ruin" unless it raised tariffs and restricted foreign investment was nothing less than a partisan attack on the Conservatives' fiscal policies—which were, in any case, outside his purview. By February 1961, even members of the bank's board of directors were expressing concern over the governor's obstinacy.

The easy solution would have been to let it be known that the governor of the Bank of Canada's term would not be extended when it ended on December 31, 1961. Instead, Fleming decided to fire Coyne that spring. The ostensible reason was that the bank's board of directors had doubled Coyne's pension to twenty-five thousand dollars a year, a most handsome sum, without consulting with or even informing the finance minister and without making the change public. Fleming in his memoirs goes on for several pages about how "appalled" he was to learn of this gold-plated pension. But the board had made the decision the year before, and Coyne had taken no part in the discussions. The governors, most of them Conservative appointees, had increased the pension to compensate any future governor appointed from outside the bank who might be terminated. Though Coyne would be a beneficiary of that decision, it wasn't taken with his interests in mind.

There were other reasons that Fleming laid out when he met with Coyne on May 30 to tell him that cabinet had instructed the minister to ask for the governor's resignation: the embarrassing speeches; a restrictive monetary policy that conflicted with the government's expansionary fiscal policy. He might also have mentioned the low esteem in which Coyne was held by the banking and business community, by most economists, and by provincial governments across the land. And he could not and would not promise Coyne that he would receive the enhanced pension.

Coyne made no move to offer his resignation, and cabinet had no power to force it. The board of directors were to meet on June 12. Fleming, Diefenbaker, and cabinet placed their hopes on the board requesting the governor's resignation. The board did indeed request it, but Coyne decided to defy the board as well as the government. Instead of resigning, he went public, issuing a statement in which he said the government had asked him to resign over his enhanced pension. "This slander on my integrity I cannot ignore or accept," he declared, adding, "I cannot and will not resign quietly under such circumstances."[25] The war between the governor and the government was now front-page news.

On June 14, Fleming told the House of Commons, "During Mr. Coyne's period in office there has been a steady and deplorable deterioration in the relations of the Bank of Canada with the public. The governor, by a course of ill-considered action and a series of public declarations of policy on public issues quite outside the realm of central banking, and by his rigid and doctrinaire expression of views, often and openly incompatible with government policy, has embroiled the bank in continuous controversy with strong political overtones." [26] Such a statement about the governor of the Bank of Canada by a minister of finance was as sensational then as it would be now. Fleming went on to say the bank's policies of combatting inflation with high interest rates conflicted with the Conservative government's efforts to combat unemployment. Coyne refused to work with the government as part of a team dedicated to economic growth and had defied the request of the bank's board of governors that he resign. He raised the pension issue. "It is the government, not the governor, which has been continuously defending the integrity of the Bank of Canada," he told the House. And he said legislation would soon be forthcoming "to meet the needs of the situation."

On June 20, as well as presenting his budget, Fleming introduced a one-sentence piece of legislation, stating, "The office of the Governor of the Bank of Canada shall be deemed to have become vacant immediately upon the coming into force of this act." The government, not wishing to give Coyne a public forum to make his case, refused opposition demands that the bill be studied in committee; instead, the Tories used their majority to push through passage on July 7. This turned out to be a politically suicidal mistake. Public opinion heavily sided with Coyne, according to a Gallup poll. The autocratic governor had been transformed into a wronged man, a principled public servant taking on the vested interests. Coyne could now add to the bill of indictment that he was being muzzled by the government. And the Conservatives had forgotten about the Senate and underestimated the growing political guile of the leader of the Opposition. In the House of Commons on January 20, 1958, John Diefenbaker had made mincemeat of Mike Pearson, leading to the greatest majority government in Canadian history. Three years later, a much more experienced Liberal leader was ready to return the favour.

VI

Following the calamitous defeat of 1958, Pearson had consulted with Senator Charles "Chubby" Power, who had been Mackenzie King's chief tactician during the last period of Liberal opposition in the Bennett years. Powers had advised Pearson to pick his spots—to focus opposition on key issues on which the Liberals could inflict the most damage. On some issues, Pearson convinced his caucus to vote with rather than against the government, with the Liberals sometimes criticizing this or that approach but never obstructing. They supported, for example, the government's efforts to complete the Trans-Canada Highway. The Liberals also commended the Tories for successfully overcoming opposition by the Quebec government to direct federal support for universities in that province. (The other provinces were already happily taking the money.) They voted with the government in extending the franchise to members of First Nations, and supported as well Diefenbaker's Bill of Rights.

But when they opposed, they did so with vigour. The Avro Arrow affair offered the Grits a tremendous boost. Though they knew the government was right to cancel the plane, they exploited A.V. Roe's sudden and brutal decision to simply shut down production, throwing thousands of workers onto the street. The Tories had long been dominant in Toronto, but the Avro Arrow affair would help make them as unpopular there as the Liberals had become in the West.

The Liberals' situation in Toronto would have been improving even without the Avro imbroglio. In the 1940s and 1950s, large numbers of Poles, Ukrainians, Hungarians, Portuguese, and others fleeing the ravages or repressions of Europe flooded into Canada, many of them settling in Toronto. Italians were especially numerous, with twenty to thirty thousand landing in Canada each year. These new arrivals quickly discovered that the Liberal Party was seen as welcoming immigrants while many Conservatives resented anyone who wasn't pro-British. They voted accordingly. As the demography of Toronto and its suburbs transformed in the 1950s, its voting patterns transformed as well. In 1955, Nathan Phillips became Toronto's first Jewish mayor, ending the city's unbroken string of Protestants. In 1958, Italy surpassed Britain as a source of immigrants, many of whom settled in Toronto. Even without the fallout from the Arrow, Toronto's political landscape was shifting.

The economy was also fertile soil. The duty of any opposition party is to warn Canadians that things are going to hell in a handbasket, and that the government of the day is to blame. The Grits were aided in this endeavour by the fact that times were not as good as they had been. That this was largely for reasons outside the ability of the Canadian government to influence made no difference at all. From time immemorial, opposition parties have castigated the government of the day for weaknesses in the economy that Ottawa could do little to redress. The Liberals made hay over both rising unemployment and a growing number of strikes, from ferry operators in B.C. to the loggers in Newfoundland.

The Liberals had a particular advantage in opposition: they knew more about governing than the government. Pearson had been foreign affairs minister for almost a decade before becoming leader of the official opposition. Jack Pickersgill had served as clerk of the Privy Council and minister of citizenship and immigration. Lionel Chevrier had been transport minister, while Paul Martin had spent years in the Health and Welfare portfolio. And Diefenbaker was probably right that the public service contained figures, some of them senior, more loyal to the opposition than to the government, and willing to pass on this or that bit of information, from time to time, that might prove useful. On good days, the Liberals were able to successfully portray the front bench of the Diefenbaker government as disorganized and incompetent. As the fifties gave way to the sixties, there were more and more good days.

Aided and advised by Pickersgill, Pearson largely abstained from the cut-and-thrust of parliamentary debate, counting on his small but able caucus to do the dirty work for him. This earned him criticism for being weak in opposition, but he and his front bench calculated that the best route to returning the Liberals to government was to portray Pearson as a prime-minister-in-waiting. And now, as Conservatives twisted in agony over the Coyne affair, he could see a path to power.

In general, the Liberals agreed with the Conservatives—or at least with one faction of the Conservative cabinet—that interest rates were too high and that the main focus should be on easing unemployment. But no Opposition leader was going to let an open, public dispute between the government of the day and the central-bank governor of the day over the country's economic direction go by unnoticed. The Liberals goaded the Conservatives over Coyne's incendiary speeches, asking if the governor was espousing government policy, forcing Fleming to repeatedly declare that the governor wrote his own speeches, and that they did not reflect the minister's views.

Now the government was trying to fire the governor. How best to attack? Pearson and his front bench focused on the right of any accused person to offer a defence. By ramming the legislation to fire Coyne through the House without hearings, the government was depriving the governor of an opportunity to explain himself. Very well: if Coyne could not speak to MPs, he would speak to senators, who were still mostly Liberal. Pearson asked the Liberal Senate caucus to convene hearings on the bill.

The temperature was manageable but the humidity intense on July 10, 1961, as hearings commenced. The Senate Banking and Commerce committee room had no air conditioning, and most of the men smoked, making oxygen rare and precious. For seventeen hours, over three days, Coyne defended himself, egged on by sympathetic Liberal senators and a largely sympathetic press. The Conservative senators appeared uninformed and ineffective. Fleming did not appear, although he maintained in his memoirs the decision was Diefenbaker's, not his. The governor had the floor and the committee entirely to himself. When he finished, the governor strode the short distance from Centre Block to the Bank Building, where four hundred employees were waiting to present him with a medal of appreciation "for his courage and integrity in defending the position of the Governor of the Bank of Canada, June and July, 1961." The next morning, the committee voted nineteen to seven in favour of the motion: "Your Committee recommends that this Bill should not be further proceeded with, and the Committee finds that the Governor of the Bank of Canada did not misconduct himself in office." That afternoon the Senate adopted the motion and went on summer break. Later that day, Coyne resigned.

There were plenty of losers in the affair. Coyne was the only governor of the Bank of Canada to be forced out of his job. His policy of fighting inflation through higher interest rates even if it led to a temporary increase in unemployment would ultimately be vindicated, as the stagflation of the 1970s forced central banks around the world to adopt similar policies. But at the time his views were radical and unpopular, alienating the commercial banks, the academic community, and cabinet. He compounded his isolation by delivering a series a speeches entirely outside the purview of a bank governor, advocating nationalist and protectionist policies that alarmed foreign investors. The Diefenbaker government had every right not to replace him at the end of his term.

Instead, Diefenbaker and irate cabinet ministers pushed Donald Fleming to oust the governor prematurely. Fleming, another big loser in the affair, lacked the strength either to defend the governor, whose tight-money preferences he shared, or to demand his dismissal over his partisan speechifying. When he did decide to act, he used what appears to have been the trumped-up excuse of outrage over a pension increase that Coyne had nothing to do with. As finance minister, he was crippled.

But the biggest loser was Diefenbaker. The government had been behind in the polls since 1960, but governments often are at mid-term. The prime minister had been castigated for cancelling the Avro Arrow, but it was the right decision, if badly handled. The government had plenty to be proud of on the domestic front, and the prime minister had earned high praise for opposing apartheid in South Africa. But Diefenbaker viewed policy as politics, and when the policies of the bank interfered with his impulse to keep workers off the dole, he pushed to have Coyne fired, and then failed spectacularly, leaving the government with a reputation for both tyranny and incompetence. The Coyne affair brought Diefenbaker down.

There were winners as well. One, strangely, was the Bank of Canada. Fleming desperately needed to restore both the bank's credibility and his own. He asked Louis Rasminsky, who probably should have been governor instead of Coyne in the first place, to take the role. But Rasminsky had a condition. The government of the day and the bank would jointly set monetary policy. Once it was set, the bank must be free from government interference. If a finance minister disagreed with the actions and policies of a governor, the minister must say so in a public letter, at which point the governor would resign. Fleming agreed, and those terms, later codified in law, have governed the relationship between the government and the bank ever since. Perversely, the smooth functioning of the relationship between the Bank of Canada and the federal government that exists today could be counted an accomplishment of the Diefenbaker government. But the cost!

The other winner was Mike Pearson. He oversaw a well-run leader's office that promoted both the Liberal agenda and the party's leader. His small team of MPs punched far above their weight. In the Coyne affair, Pearson promoted a successful strategy of defending the integrity of the governor without having to defend the governor's policies, while using the Liberal majority in the Senate to frustrate the government's aims and maximize its pain.

In 1958, the idea of winning enough seats back from the Conservatives for the Liberals to form government had seemed preposterous. Less than four years later, it didn't seem preposterous anymore.

TEN

Things Fall Apart

(1961–1963)

I

John Diefenbaker had hoped Vice President Richard Nixon would win the 1960 presidential election. Though more hawkish than Dwight Eisenhower, Nixon was a known quantity: a pragmatic political professional whom Diefenbaker felt he could work with. In John Kennedy, on the other hand, "he perceived a difficult challenge," wrote Basil Robinson, Diefenbaker's foreign policy adviser, "a man whose personal and political attributes—youth, wealth, connections and charisma—contained much that was alien or even threatening."[1] The Canadian prime minister greeted the American senator's victory with concern that would turn to alarm, then anger, and finally rage. For John Fitzgerald Kennedy, thirty-fourth President of the United States, played a larger role than Liberal leader Lester B. Pearson in bringing the Diefenbaker government down.

Kennedy was the first president born in the twentieth century. The senior ranks of his administration were dominated by young men. Most of them were fit, handsome, cultured, educated at Harvard or Yale, and quite certain they were right and everyone else was wrong. They did not consult; they informed. To disagree with them was to be wrong or stupid or worse. This intellectual certainty would produce disastrous results in Indochina, it would hamper the administration's ability to work with Congress, it would impair relations with allies and opponents alike. And it swiftly led Kennedy to decide Diefenbaker was his least favourite head of government.

Shortly after the inauguration, the Chief flew down to Washington for a face-to-face that he thought went well. Diefenbaker found Kennedy friendly, well-briefed, and willing to work cooperatively with Canada on continental defence and on economic issues. The prime minister told the House of Commons he found the first meeting "a revealing and exhilarating experience."[2] But Kennedy came away with a very different impression. Diefenbaker struck him as insincere, untrustworthy, dull. "I don't want to see that boring son-of-a-bitch again," he told his brother Robert, the attorney general.

The two men simply grated on each other. During the Washington visit, Kennedy pointed to a mounted sailfish he had caught during his honeymoon. Diefenbaker replied that while in Jamaica he had caught a 140-pound (63.5 kilogram) marlin. "You didn't catch it," Kennedy scoffed. "Yes, I did," Diefenbaker retorted; it took three hours and ten minutes to reel it in. Kennedy seemed unconvinced.[3] That fish story would come to symbolize the entire relationship.

The day of Diefenbaker's visit to Washington was one of personal sorrow. Mary Diefenbaker had been in decline for years, confined to a hospital bed in Saskatoon, and suffering repeated bouts of dementia. Nonetheless, John phoned his mother almost every day and wrote to her every few days. There is one note from May 1957 in which the newly-appointed prime minister appears to be responding to her rebuke for not calling him: "I'm sorry that I can't get to phone you when I have a break. But the fact is that I can't do so and therefore have to take the means of writing you."[4] Whenever he returned to the riding or was in Saskatchewan for whatever reason, he visited. He also paid the cost of her hospital care and had Elmer secure a television set for her. But the doctor in charge of her care had recently warned that the end could come soon, and John agreed there should be no heroic measures. He received word during his visit to Washington that Mary had suffered a major heart attack. She died that day, aged eighty-eight.

John's friend Emmett Hall was among the four hundred people who joined the family for her funeral at Saskatoon's First Baptist Church. Four days later, John urged Elmer to come visit him in Ottawa. They had lost William years ago; William's brother Edward had passed in 1960. It was just John and Elmer and Ollie now. He was sixty-five.

Kennedy had agreed to pay a state visit to Ottawa in May. By the time of the visit, the international situation had darkened. In April, the Kennedy administration had sanctioned a landing by Cuban expatriates in the Bay of Pigs, aimed at overthrowing the Castro regime. The mission failed disastrously, confirming Diefenbaker's suspicion that the president's inexperience and belligerence would worsen Cold War tensions. It's possible that Dwight Eisenhower might have planted those suspicions. The two older leaders had gotten on well; one of Eisenhower's last acts as president had been to invite Diefenbaker to Washington to sign the Columbia River Treaty. Eisenhower considered Kennedy an irresponsible hawk who was willing to accelerate the arms race. "In private he expressed his anger and disgust at Kennedy's harping on a 'missile gap,' and other exaggerated remarks," wrote Eisenhower biographer Stephen Ambrose.[5] Harping about American weakness by both Democrats and Republicans angered Eisenhower, who in his farewell address to the nation warned against "the acquisition of unwarranted influence, whether sought or unsought, by the military-industrial complex." Did Eisenhower warn Diefenbaker to be on guard against Kennedy's militaristic impulses? There is no record, but the Canadian prime minister shared Ike's deep concern.

Tensions were also growing between Canada and the United States over Prime Minister Harold Macmillan's efforts to bring the United Kingdom into the European Economic Community (EEC), which was flourishing under French and German leadership. The only viable solution to lagging British growth was to become part of the EEC. When Macmillan met with Kennedy in Washington, the president encouraged greater integration, believing it would strengthen European unity and collective defence. But Diefenbaker shared the alarm of High Commissioner George Drew and newspaper magnate Lord Beaverbrook, who had been born Max Aiken, who hailed from New Brunswick, and whose conservative, working-class tabloid the *Daily Express* at one time had the largest circulation of any newspaper in the world. Beaverbrook and Drew and Diefenbaker were convinced that closer ties with Europe would undermine Britain's Commonwealth connection. Diefenbaker was also worried about the impact of such ties on preferential access for Canadian goods into the British market. As we've seen, Diefenbaker's economic nationalism took the form of lessening dependence on the American market by encouraging trade within the Commonwealth. His government had sponsored a Commonwealth trade conference in Ottawa in 1958. Nothing much came of it, but Diefenbaker took pride in his efforts to strengthen those ties. Now the Brits seemed willing to abandon the Commonwealth, and Kennedy was egging them on.

From the moment Air Force One touched down at Uplands RCAF base on May 16, 1961, things went awry. Kennedy had a tendency to mispronounce Diefenbaker's name, calling him Diefenbawker, a significant slight to a man who was inordinately sensitive about his name. The president also scored no points when he declared that he had been nervous about attempting to speak French while in Canada, but that after hearing the prime minister's French, he felt reassured. A simple tree-planting ceremony at Rideau Hall would have long-lasting repercussions. While shovelling the ceremonial dirt, Kennedy wrenched his notoriously bad back, which required him to wear a brace that he had managed to do without for several years.

The president was probably in considerable pain when he and Diefenbaker met in the prime minister's office the next day, where the marlin was prominently mounted, something the prime minister did not hesitate to point out. The atmosphere was cordial enough, but the agenda was disconcerting from the Canadian perspective. The Americans had a series of asks, and the Canadians had all the wrong answers. Kennedy wanted Canada to join the Organization of American States (OAS), but Diefenbaker preferred to keep Canada out of that regional association, on the grounds that disagreeing with the U.S. inside the OAS would cause tensions, while agreeing would make Canada look like a lackey. Kennedy wanted Canada to increase foreign aid to bolster the soft-power front in the Cold War. Our deficit is already too high, Diefenbaker responded. The Americans were unhappy that Canada continued to have diplomatic relations with Cuba and were very unhappy about Canadian wheat sales to China. Diefenbaker would not retreat on either front. Kennedy wanted Canada to become more involved in efforts to stabilize Indochina; Diefenbaker correctly worried that the region was a potential quagmire.

But the issue that mattered most was The Swap. Having scrapped the Arrow, Canada needed an interceptor fighter, preferably one that would help to keep its aviation industry afloat. The Americans had come up with an ingenious proposal: They would sell Canada sixty F-101 Voodoo interceptor fighters to complement the Bomarc interceptor missile installations at North Bay, Ontario, and Macaza, Quebec. Canadair in Montreal would manufacture two hundred F-104 Starfighter aircraft for use by Canadian forces in NATO. The RCAF would take over operating the Pinetree Line of radar installations from the United States Air Force. The solution was elegant and cost-efficient, except for one thing. The Bomarc missiles and the missiles on the F-101 would be equipped with nuclear warheads, without which they would have little hope of taking out Russian bomber squadrons. The F-104 missiles would be armed with tactical nuclear weapons designed to eliminate Soviet forces invading Europe.

Nuclear strategy was evolving rapidly in the early 1960s. Until then, both the Americans and the Soviets assumed that war between them would involve one side launching a massive, bomber-based assault that would seek to cripple the other side's capacity to retaliate. Canada's role in NORAD was to help the Americans shoot down as many Russian bombers as possible, though all sides understood that in any attack, enough bombers would get through to launch a devastating nuclear strike.

But tactics were changing. Both sides were already deploying intercontinental ballistic missiles, or ICBMs, which would soon replace bombers as the principal method for delivering a nuclear attack. They could strike much more quickly and could not be shot down. And beyond tactics was the matter of optics. Diefenbaker told Kennedy that he had a problem with public opinion, which was swinging against the idea of Canadian forces deploying nuclear weapons. Why, he probably couldn't even bring his own cabinet to accept nukes. The prime minister assured the president that he personally favoured equipping Canadian NORAD forces with the weapons; he just needed time to bring public opinion around. Kennedy, puzzled and annoyed, pushed repeatedly for a Canadian commitment, but Diefenbaker would not give one. The meeting soured their relationship. Kennedy expected America's allies to support the United States as it confronted the threat of Soviet domination. But the Canadian prime minister had a very different perspective. "Mr. Kennedy may have been a god to himself and all Americans," Pierre Sévigny remembered years later, "but he was just another young politician to John Diefenbaker, and John Diefenbaker made it amply clear to John F. Kennedy that he was willing to deal with him on equal terms, but on no other basis."[6]

Kennedy had already antagonized the Canadians when he delivered a speech to Parliament the day before. Posterity remembers the address for its eloquent description of the relationship between the countries. "Geography has made us neighbours. History has made us friends. Economics has made us partners. And necessity has made us allies. Those whom nature hath so joined together, let no man put asunder." Diefenbaker and his aides remember it for something else: Kennedy publicly called upon Canada to join the Organization of American States, whose members "would be heartened and strengthened by any increase in your Hemispheric role," even though Diefenbaker had rejected the proposal in preliminary talks that day.[7] The prime minister was not amused.

Kennedy had failed to convince the Canadians to accept nuclear weapons for NORAD and NATO, or to join the OAS, or to increase foreign aid, or to take a greater role in combatting communist infiltration in Southeast Asia. And he had hurt his back. For his part, Diefenbaker resented the pressure from the American side. He was furious over the inordinate amount of time Kennedy spent chatting with Pearson at a dinner hosted by the Americans at the ambassador's residence. (The long conversations between Kennedy and Pearson even raised American eyebrows.) And Diefenbaker was both angered and intrigued by a briefing note that Walt Rostow, one of Kennedy's advisers, had inadvertently left behind. Titled "What We Want from the Ottawa Trip," the memorandum advised the president to "push them towards a decision to join the OAS . . . push them towards a larger contribution on the India [aid] consortium and foreign aid generally . . ." and so on.[8] Diplomatic protocol required Canada to promptly return the document to the Americans, but Diefenbaker decided to keep it. The persistent repetition of the word "push" in the memo galled him. Back in Washington, Kennedy described Diefenbaker as "boring" and "insincere" and "shallow" and "erratic." "He was simply pissed off with him," Ted Sorensen, Kennedy's speechwriter, told Canadian journalist Knowlton Nash years later. "He was aggravated. Diefenbaker got under his skin."[9]

Nonetheless, The Swap went ahead: the Bomarc missiles arrived in 1961, with nothing on the end of them, while the CF-101s waited for nuclear-tipped missiles, without which the fighter was practically useless. Meanwhile, at a summit in Vienna in June, Khrushchev "beat the hell out of me," Kennedy acknowledged ruefully, having relied on charm rather than doing his homework to counter the blustery but experienced Soviet leader. Soon after the summit ended, the East German government, with Russia's support, began building a wall along the partition between East and West Berlin, to halt the exodus of a thousand people a day that threatened the very survival of the Communist regime. In late August, the Soviets abandoned a moratorium on above-ground nuclear testing. On September 1, a grave but determined Diefenbaker gave a speech to the Canadian Bar Association affirming Canada's resolve to help protect the citizens of West Berlin and West Germany. Even Pearson felt the speech "struck the right note."[10] The situation had become so grave that Diefenbaker consulted with the leader of the Opposition over his plans to increase conventional defence commitments in Europe. The Kennedy administration should have welcomed those commitments. Instead, pressure increased for a decision on accepting nuclear-tipped missiles. But Diefenbaker had become paralyzed over the issue for a simple, stark reason: his defence minister and his external affairs ministers were at loggerheads.

The previous September, Diefenbaker had appointed Defence Minister George Pearkes lieutenant governor of British Columbia. The First World War veteran and winner of the Victoria Cross had navigated the cancelling of the Arrow, but everyone, including Pearkes, agreed that equipping the Canadian Armed Forces for the nuclear age should be someone else's job. Diefenbaker went with Doug Harkness, whom Fleming described as "tough, abrasive and courageous." He had served heroically in the war, winning the George Medal during the Sicilian campaign. Harkness was the sort of man who kept his moustache and his speech clipped, who often wore a regimental tie, who knew what was right and who was wrong, and didn't mind telling you. Diefenbaker initially appointed him agriculture minister, but by

1960 the minister had angered so many interests that Dief worried about losing the farm vote. He moved Harkness to Defence: "I thought he would adopt an attitude towards the senior Defence officers similar to the one he had toward farmers," he later wrote. "I was mistaken."[11]

Harkness accepted, uncritically, the advice of his deputy minister and air force chiefs that Canada's security and its NATO commitments dictated tactical nuclear weapons for defence in Canada and offence in Europe. By the fall of 1961, the Kennedy administration was pushing the government hard to accept the weapons, and Harkness was pushing every bit as hard himself. But Howard Green pushed back.

The external affairs secretary was listening to the advice of Pearson's friend Norman Robertson, on his second tour of duty as undersecretary, and to his disarmament adviser, General E.L.M. "Tommy" Burns, who questioned the wisdom of tactical nuclear weapons in general and Canada's use of them in particular. For one thing, as soon as the Russians became aware that RCAF bases in Europe had aircraft with tactical nuclear missiles, those bases would be targeted for missile attack. For another, the cost in lives of battles fought by armies using tactical nukes would be appalling. And military logic dictated that any battle fought with tactical nuclear weapons would quickly escalate into a strategic exchange.

Strategic calculations were also being transformed. In February 1960, the United States had successfully tested the submarine-launched Polaris missile. There would soon be dozens of virtually undetectable nuclear missile submarines on both sides, lurking in the ocean depths, ensuring that neither side could ever hope to cripple the other through a massive first strike. At the least, the other side would be able to launch a devastating submarine-based counterstrike. Nuclear war now guaranteed MAD: Mutually Assured Destruction.

All of this convinced Green that accepting nuclear-tipped missiles would be useless and dangerous. It would also erode, even eliminate, Canadian sovereignty, for in the end the Americans would decide whether to launch nuclear weapons on Canadian soil or on Canadian aircraft overseas. For Green, like Harkness, black was black and white was white and grey was cowardice. In 1957, during the crafting of the first cabinet, someone suggested putting Howard Green in Justice. Diefenbaker shook his head. "Not

Howard. He'd hang every prisoner in the country."[12] Having concluded that tactical nuclear weapons were futile and dangerous, Green set about converting Canada into a leader in encouraging disarmament efforts. He adamantly opposed Harkness, the generals, and American pressure to accept the weapons.

Cabinet's position reflected the country's. In the 1950s, the population accepted, more or less uncritically, that Canada should support the United States in containing Soviet aggression and protecting the continent from nuclear attack. But as tensions mounted over Berlin and elsewhere, more and more voices warned that humanity was rushing toward annihilation. In Canada, the anti-nuclear and feminist group Voice of Women, formed in 1960, had quickly gained influence and reach. The prime minister found himself caught in a schism within his own government and within the country over what role Canada should play in a cold war that at any hour might turn hot. As always, when confronted with a difficult choice, Diefenbaker sought to delay. His model and idol was John A. Macdonald—"Old Tomorrow" they had called the first prime minister, because of his penchant for putting things off. But with each month Diefenbaker delayed, Kennedy grew more impatient and more determined to force a Canadian yes.

II

Bruce Hutchison, the economist John Deutsch, and other old-school liberals had reason to despair over the influence that Tom Kent and Walter Gordon exerted on Mike Pearson. While the Liberal leader was temperamentally inclined toward foreign affairs—Gordon worried with good reason that Pearson would abandon the leadership if the right offer to head an organization dedicated to global security came along—the Methodist minister's son instinctively graduated toward the social gospel dressed up in modern garb by people like Kent, Pearson's policy adviser.

The British expat and many similarly inclined intellectuals sought to transform liberalism, which in its classic form celebrated the freedom and responsibility of each individual in contrast to the stultifying class structures embraced by traditional conservatism. But classical liberalism, the liberalism of C.D. Howe and Bruce Hutchison, ignored the reality of cyclical poverty, in which a young child was perfectly free to be raised in squalor, to receive only the most rudimentary education, to depend on charity for health care, to sleep in a slum or in a shack with dirt floors and no running water. The liberalism of economist John Kenneth Galbraith—son of an Elgin Country farmer; wage and price czar in the Roosevelt administration during the war; and author of *The Affluent Society*, which influenced thinking in the Kennedy administration—maintained that individual freedom and responsibility only had meaning if children started life with something like an even chance: with good quality public education, access to inoculations and fluoridated water and other elements of public health care, and a home with heating and running water. Tom Kent's liberalism would rely on the state to provide these services to parents who couldn't afford them, while allowing capitalism to control the overall economy. Pearson agreed with Galbraith and Kent.

Modern liberalism, however, was not the only alternative on offer. Although both Social Credit and the CCF had been devastated in the 1958 election, both were regrouping. Tommy Douglas, the premier of Saskatchewan and father of medicare, returned to Ottawa to lead the New Democratic Party (NDP), which was the old CCF reinvigorated with support from the Canadian Labour Congress. Robert Thompson, an Alberta chiropractor, had defeated Réal Caouette for the leadership of the Social Credit Party in 1961. But that party was deeply divided between its English Protestant Western wing—there were Social Credit governments in British Columbia and Alberta—and its French Catholic wing, where Caouette remained dominant.

Facing a massive Conservative majority government, and the new NDP, Pearson appreciated the need to modernize both the policies and the electoral machinery of the Liberal Party. Things were well in hand on the policy front, thanks to the Kingston Conference, the subsequent policy conference that converted the Kingston principles into party policy, and the policy committee that Pearson had set up to develop an election manifesto. But as Dalton Camp and Allister Grosart had revealed, polls and advertising had taken over election campaigning. Smart political operatives had memorized *The Making of the President*, Theodore H. White's chronicle of the 1960 election and the new power of Madison Avenue to shape election campaigns.

The Liberals went straight to the source, by covertly hiring Lou Harris, Kennedy's pollster, to advise on public perceptions of the Liberal leader. Keith Davey would meet Harris at the Ottawa airport, and the two of them plus Walter Gordon would surreptitiously visit Stornoway, the residence of the Leader of the Official Opposition, where Pearson would greet them by asking, "Okay, how bad am I this month?" The answer was: pretty bad. While the Liberals had moved ahead of the Progressive Conservatives in the polls, John Diefenbaker remained much more popular and trustworthy in the minds of Canadians than Lester B. Pearson, whom they viewed as remote and condescending. The team did the best they could with what they had, urging Pearson without success to ditch the bow ties for neck ties and working with speechwriters to soften his lisp. But the Liberal leader would always have trouble connecting with voters.

III

As 1961 gave way to 1962 and to the federal election that everyone knew was coming, John Diefenbaker had two decisions to make: when to call the vote, and what to run on.

Gone was the vague vision of One Canada. The Tories had a record, some of it unenviable. Yes, there was much to be proud of. But the decision to cancel the Arrow had rendered the party unpopular in its former electoral bastion of Toronto. Unemployment and interest rates had both been high, and growth was only now starting to pick up. Worst of all, the Coyne affair had left the government looking arrogant and incompetent, and left it trailing in the polls. Nonetheless, after much to-ing and fro-ing, and after allowing Donald Fleming to submit one last budget, Diefenbaker asked Georges Vanier to dissolve Parliament on April 19 for an election on June 18.

The Conservatives ran on their record, as any incumbent majority government must. Their manifesto, "Getting Things Done for Canada and Canadians," contained no grand plans and promises. Instead, it recited the record of the past five years: pension increases, price supports for farmers, grain sales to China, the Bill of Rights, public hospital care, the almost-completed Trans-Canada Highway, Roads to Resources, lower income and corporate taxes, fiscal rebalancing with the provinces, increased financial support for universities, penal and criminal-law reform, unemployment insurance that no longer discriminated against women, an immigration policy that no longer discriminated against non-Europeans, voting rights for First Nations, an impartial agency to regulate telecommunications.

The Diefenbaker government had increased supports for veterans and those with disabilities. There were major public works launched in areas previously neglected by the Liberals, such as the South Saskatchewan Dam project, a new bridge to link New Brunswick to Maine, and the launching of the Winnipeg floodway project. New environmental measures included loans to municipalities for sewage treatment plants and funding for soil and water conservation. Finally, in addition to fighting apartheid, Canada on Diefenbaker's watch made important contributions to global affairs by increasing support for foreign aid, even if it wasn't enough to suit Jack Kennedy. Alvin Hamilton, as well as increasing supports for farmers and selling wheat to China, had advocated the creation of a world food bank to which nations could contribute their agricultural surpluses and provide financial support. The Americans seized on the idea, which led to the creation of the UN's World Food Programme, the largest agency dedicated to combatting hunger around the globe.

There were the prominent firsts: the first woman cabinet minister, the first francophone governor general, the first Indigenous senator. And finally, the Diefenbaker government had decided to celebrate Canada's approaching centennial by holding a grand world exposition in Montreal.

"Government must assume a full measure of responsibility for those social requirements which, by their very nature, cannot be assumed by business and the business community," Diefenbaker declared in the document's preamble. "This has been the basis of Government policy in the last four years."[13]

Any government in the progressive post-war era with such a record could credibly have asked for a strong second mandate. But there was the Avro Arrow. And the Coyne affair. Even worse, Diefenbaker had been branded in the public mind as a preening and dithering leader, for which he had only himself to blame.

He could perhaps have campaigned on the record of his team of ministers. But that was not in his nature. Instead, the campaign centred on

Diefenbaker himself. As for the other parties, he lumped the Liberals in with the new NDP of Tommy Douglas in a campaign whose motto was "free enterprise versus socialism." This was an improbable theme given the generally progressive nature of the prime minister and his government. In the end, he spent much of the election attacking Pearson, the press, the backroom boys, Bay Street, and socialism.

The Liberal platform, in sharp contrast, focused heavily on election promises: "the progressive, practical and responsible way in which a new government can serve the public interest," as Pearson stated in the introduction.[14] Much of it was quite bold: publicly funded health care for children and seniors, with others making monthly contributions in exchange for care; a new national pension plan to supplement existing supports; government grants and loans for university students; grants to municipalities for slum clearance; regional economic support for Atlantic Canada. Parts of the manifesto appeared contradictory: lower corporate taxes but a balanced budget. And it included a striking new proposal to address Quebec's growing restiveness: any province could reject a proposed national plan while still receiving federal compensation, so long as the province crafted a similar plan of its own.

In retrospect, the two platforms complemented each other. The Conservatives had, during a time of recession and unemployment, emphasized social and economic supports until growth could be restored. By 1962, growth was back, vindicating the Conservative approach: Canada in that year recorded 8 per cent growth in GDP, the highest of any major developed country. Unemployment was dropping and inflation was low and steady. Now the Liberals were proposing to expand entitlements, many of them first introduced by the Tories. The Diefenbaker government had assisted municipalities with infrastructure; the Liberals would go farther, with plans for slum clearance. The Conservatives had implemented public hospital care; the Liberals would expand public health care to include visits to a doctor. The Conservatives had eliminated race-based immigration; the Liberals would improve and expand the program. The Conservatives had returned taxing authority to the provinces while entrenching equalization; the Liberals would allow provinces to opt out of programs, with compensation. Pearson was proposing to expand and improve on the Diefenbaker agenda while introducing new policies of his own, just as Diefenbaker had expanded and improved upon the St. Laurent agenda while introducing new policies of his own. Liberals and Conservatives in Canada; Democrats and Republicans in the United States; Labour and Conservatives in Britain: the social and economic policy consensus in the 1950s and '60s ran deep.

But elections are about much more than platforms: they are usually influenced by "events, dear boy, events," as Harold Macmillan memorably put it. And the election of 1962 was powerfully influenced by events that occurred during the campaign, most of them damaging to the Conservatives.

Diefenbaker had to contend with a press gallery that had gone from practically worshipping him in 1958 to practically despising him in 1962. The *Globe and Mail* was still on board, thanks to a reconciliation between publisher Oakley Dalgleish and Dief negotiated by Leslie Frost. And other conservative-minded newspapers such as John Bassett's *Toronto Telegram* stayed loyal. But much of the media was out for blood, having become convinced that Diefenbaker was both hapless and hostile toward them. They were right about the last part, at least.

President Kennedy waded in by inviting forty-nine winners of Nobel Prizes to dinner at the White House. One of the laureates was Lester B. Pearson, winner of the 1957 Peace Prize and the only guest who was not living in the United States at the time. Not only that, but Kennedy met privately with Pearson for twenty minutes before the event—the two chatted amiably about world events while Kennedy dressed for dinner—and named him in the opening paragraph of his remarks: "Mr. Lester Pearson informed me that a Canadian newspaperman said yesterday that this is the president's 'Easter egghead roll on the White House lawn.' I want to deny that!" (He also memorably paid tribute to his guests by saying, "I think this is the most extraordinary collection of talent, of human knowledge, that has ever been gathered together at the White House, with the possible exception of when Thomas Jefferson dined alone.")[15] For a Canadian Opposition leader in the midst of a national election, such treatment by the president of the United States was pure gold. Diefenbaker was livid.

But then he was livid most of the time when it came to relations with the Kennedy White House. The president and his advisers continued to push relentlessly for Canada to accept tactical nuclear weapons for the new

Bomarc missiles and Voodoo jets. The Americans had been trying to block the Canadian sale of wheat to Beijing by withholding equipment needed to load the vessels. (They eventually relented.) And they continued to encourage Harold Macmillan to pursue closer ties with the European Economic Community, even as Canada led the charge within the Commonwealth to prevent that integration. When, a few days after the dinner for the Nobel laureates, Macmillan dropped in on Ottawa after visiting Kennedy in the U.S., the British prime minister was treated to a rant by the Canadian prime minister about American meddling in Commonwealth affairs.

But much worse lay in store for Livingston Merchant when the departing American ambassador paid his respects to Diefenbaker shortly after the Macmillan visit. Face flushed, jowls quivering, and voice quavering in rage, Diefenbaker accused Kennedy of trying to swing the June 18 election in favour of Pearson. He brought out the Rostow memo from the meeting a year before, waved it in Merchant's face, and threatened to make public the American efforts to strong-arm Canada into accepting missiles and joining the OAS. The prime minister was practically senseless with rage, an astonished Merchant told Kennedy on the phone afterwards. Kennedy's rage was equally intense. He called Diefenbaker a "prick," a "fucker," and a "shit," and warned of "cutting his balls off."[16] But there was nothing the Americans could do about the memo. In the end, the Chief put it back in the vault. But whatever was left of positive relations between the president and the prime minister lay dead on the floor.

Diefenbaker faced a crisis even worse than the precipitous decline in relations with the United States. Just as the campaign was getting underway, Canada fell victim to a sudden and unexpected run on the dollar. The reasons for that run stretched back to the 1944 meeting at Bretton Woods, when all participating countries had agreed to fix the exchange rate of their currencies against the American dollar. To the chagrin of the International Monetary Fund (IMF), Canada unpegged its currency in 1950, the only country to do so, on the grounds that the volatile nature of natural-resource exports made a fixed exchange rate hard to defend. By the early 1960s, the Canadian dollar had floated above the U.S. dollar, which made Canadian exports less competitive. Fleming announced in his June 1961 budget that the federal government would seek the orderly devaluation of the dollar, which is what had happened. But the Coyne affair, the general impression that the Canadian government had been weakened by that crisis, and possibly the election campaign itself brought speculators into the market determined to profit from forcing the Canadian dollar down. Bank and Finance officials warned that Canada's foreign reserves were being rapidly depleted, and that the dollar needed to be pegged again. Fleming agreed and so did Diefenbaker, though he soon changed his mind. But by then it was too late. With the IMF's concurrence, Fleming announced that the Canadian dollar would henceforth trade at 92.5 cents. The Liberals had a field day.

The Canadian dollar had just lost almost eight cents in value, they wrongly maintained. Everything will get more expensive. Hard Tory times had gotten even harder. Diefendollars appeared in editorial cartoons and on the street, festooned with an image of the jowly Conservative leader and with the denomination "92½ cents." The PCs fought back with facts: a lower dollar would encourage exports and create jobs; tourism would benefit; food prices wouldn't increase because most food was home-grown. It hardly mattered.

Diefendollars. Devastating.

Four years earlier, most Liberals had wondered how many election cycles it would take before Diefenbaker's massive Progressive Conservative majority could be whittled down to size. The answer suddenly appeared to be: only one. Governments defeat themselves, of course, and the Tories were doing a fine job of it. But the Liberal campaign had assets of its own: a progressive, coherent program for government and sophisticated marketing techniques imported from south of the border. Four years earlier, Allister Grosart and Dalton Camp had revealed what a sharp political advertising campaign could do to swing the vote. In 1962, it was the Liberals who had the edge, courtesy of Lou Harris and the marketing and advertising whizzes assembled by Keith Davey. They had chosen an advertising firm, MacLaren, that successfully flogged everything from Macleans toothpaste to General Motors cars and trucks. "Grits were attracted to all the things that were shaping consumer society: television, science, psychology and, yes, advertising," wrote Susan Delacourt in her analysis of that campaign.[17] MacLaren convinced the Liberal brain trust that the party should adopt the radical new policy of concentrating its energies on marginal ridings held by the other side and curtailing spending on safe ridings or ones hopelessly out of reach. MacLaren test-marketed campaign slogans, ultimately recommending "Take a Stand for Tomorrow," which meant absolutely nothing but sounded fine. Keith Davey was compiling data on voter attitudes to Diefenbaker and Pearson—they liked Dief most in folksy scenes while Pearson looked best in more formal settings. The campaign decided to spend almost half of its one-million-dollar budget on television advertising, cutting back on news-paper ads and abandoning billboards completely.

The Liberal campaign was slick, sophisticated, cutting edge. There was only one problem: Lester Pearson was none of those things. The team did what it could, and Pearson himself logged fifty thousand kilometres, criss-crossing the country by air, train, and car without rest. But Brand Pearson was less appealing to many voters than Brand Diefenbaker, even if Brand Liberal was more popular than Brand PC. In their efforts to import Camelot, the masterminds of the dark arts of marketing and advertising could not alter one stark truth: Lester B. Pearson was no John F. Kennedy.

And in yet another demonstration of the maxim that campaigns matter, the Liberals were blindsided in Quebec. Their hopes for government rested on obliterating the Tories in that province, while also making substantial gains in Ontario. And they had good reason to hope: the Tories had depended for their Quebec sweep in 1958 on organizational support from Maurice Duplessis and his Union Nationale. But Duplessis was dead, the Union Nationale was in opposition, and Liberal Jean Lesage had embarked on revolutionary reforms. What the Grits didn't get was that, outside Montreal, many Quebecers resented those reforms, resented the attacks on the Church and on the old ways, resented the urban sophisticates who were transforming their province. Réal Caouette, the used-car salesman who had almost defeated Robert Thompson for the Social Credit leadership, galva-nized conservative resentment to Liberal reform in the province in a way that neither the Grits nor the Tories had anticipated.

As the returns came in on election night, Mike and Maryon watched the television from rooms at the Château Laurier. They and many other Liberals had convinced themselves that a minority Liberal government was likely. Dalton Camp was equally convinced. But it was not to be. The Liberals practically swept Newfoundland and Nova Scotia, the Tories held Prince

Edward Island, and the two parties split the difference in New Brunswick. The Liberals improved substantially in Ontario, wresting Toronto from the Conservatives and taking forty-three seats to the PC's thirty-five. But Tommy Douglas's NDP was back on the board in Canada's most populous province, with six seats. The NDP also dominated in British Columbia, with ten seats to six for the Tories and four for the Grits. But while the Conservatives still dominated the Prairies, the election was decided in Quebec. The Conservatives fell to only fourteen seats, while the Liberals reclaimed Montreal and environs, taking thirty-five seats. But Social Credit was not far behind, with twenty-six seats in *les régions*. Outside Quebec, the party took only four seats. Caouette had transformed the Socreds into the Créditistes: a party of rural French conservative social protest, a phenomenon that would repeat itself in different political guises for decades to come.

On paper, John Diefenbaker could take considerable consolation from the result. Despite the monetary crises of the past year, which peaked during the campaign itself, the Progressive Conservatives had narrowly won the popular vote. The party had representation in every region of the country. Though the PCs had been reduced to a minority, they should have no trouble governing for two or three years by carefully cultivating the support of Social Credit.

The reality was far more grim. The Tories had lost eighty-nine seats. Metropolitan Toronto, once a Conservative bastion, was now a Liberal bastion. Toronto Centre flipped from blue to red. Peel, to the west of Toronto, where fast-growing Mississauga was located, had been Conservative since 1900. It went Liberal in 1962 and stayed Liberal for many elections to come. The Grits were also strong in Montreal and Ottawa and Vancouver. The PCs in English Canada, like Social Credit in Quebec, had become the party of the rural and small-town ridings, the old Canada, the Canada of the past.

Worse, after five years in government, John Diefenbaker had lost whatever ability he once had to learn lessons, temper expectations, court support from across the aisle, rebuild. John Baird, who served in the cabinets of former Ontario Premier Mike Harris and Prime Minister Stephen Harper, believes that politicians proceed through three stages: first they ask for advice because they need it, second they ask for advice because they want to be seen as consultative, and third, "they don't ask for advice at all because they believe they know everything."[18] John Diefenbaker entered his third government firmly in Stage Three.

In truth, he should have been thinking about stepping down. A change of leadership in 1962 might well have revived the fortunes of the Progressive Conservative Party. Instead, he nursed his resentments, as much toward those inside the party as outside it, and plotted revenge. This was the worst possible attitude. The death watch for John Diefenbaker's third government set in on its first day.

IV

When a federal or provincial election produces a hung Parliament, all sides take stock. Will the party with the most seats be able to govern with the support of the smaller parties? Could the second-place finisher form a more stable government? Does the incumbent prime minister or premier wish to test their support in the House? Political operatives meet with their counterparts. Someone books a suite of rooms in a hotel. Reporters sniff around. None of that happened after June 18. There wasn't time.

As Donald Fleming recalled it, on the morning after the election, while he was still in his pyjamas at his home in Toronto, Bank of Canada governor Louis Rasminsky called to say the finance minister must come back to Ottawa immediately. The markets had parsed the results of election night and did not like what they saw. Any governing party would require 133 votes to carry the House on a confidence vote. The Conservatives had been reduced to 116 seats. The Speaker of the House typically came from the governing party, which would reduce them to 115 seats. The Tories would need 18 votes from across the aisle to pass the Speech from the Throne, the budget, or any other measure of confidence. Tommy Douglas's NDP had taken 19 seats, but that would leave only one vote to spare, and in any case, John Diefenbaker's government had the word "conservative" in its name. How could it possibly govern with the support of the socialists? (Though John Diefenbaker's and Tommy Douglas's world views were more closely aligned than many thought.) Social Credit, on the other hand, was a conservative party and had garnered 30 seats, enough to provide a comfortable majority if the two parties could work out a deal. But unlike the Social

Credit governments in Alberta and British Columbia, Réal Caouette's Créditistes, who now dominated Robert Thompson's Social Credit caucus, were still true believers in C.H. Douglas's funny money theories, which advocated governments issuing credits to citizens to make up the difference between the costs of production and compensation of workers, or something like that. Were the Conservatives about to get in bed with that bunch? Beyond that, speculators had probably calculated that an unstable minority Conservative government would not be able to defend the recently pegged dollar, and there was money to be made in shorting the currency. After all, hadn't they already gone through a currency crisis during the election campaign, and hadn't Agriculture Minister Alvin Hamilton speculated in public that the dollar was probably pegged too high? For whatever reason or combination of reasons, investors were selling Canadian dollars, massively. Unless the federal government could restore confidence, the foreign exchange reserves would be exhausted in a matter of days. Fleming was on the next flight to Ottawa.

There could be no talk of a cabinet shuffle—even though five ministers had been defeated the night before—or a throne speech. The overriding priority of the government had to be protecting the currency. The foreign exchange reserves had been depleted by the previous run on the dollar; the pressure now was even more intense. Fleming and Rasminsky, with Diefenbaker's concurrence, were determined to hold the line at 92.5 cents, come hell or high water. But that would require a massive infusion of funds. The two men set to work.

The IMF was prepared to help. It had urged Canada to repeg the dollar, and would be willing to help defend it, with conditions. Canada had come to Britain's aid during a run on the pound the year before, and could expect aid in return. Fleming reached out to the leaders of the major Canadian and American investment houses; all offered strong support. Most important, Washington was willing to intervene. There was good reason for Washington and London to come to Canada's rescue. The country's standing in the international community had been battered by a string of deficits and even more by the Coyne affair. But it remained one of the most prosperous in the world, its economy rooted in plentiful natural resources and a flourishing manufacturing sector. During economic crises, political leaders always insist that the economy is fundamentally sound. In Canada's case, this was true.

But the government would have to show that it took the crisis seriously. Obviously, Diefenbaker had no intention of seeking a coalition with Social Credit. The minority government would depend on the support of one or more opposition parties on any confidence vote, as minority governments had in the past. But that still left the question of deficits, which might well go higher rather than lower as the Tories sought to garner the votes of opposition parties. To win the support of the IMF and the investment community, the government would need to cut spending. At first, the prime minister and cabinet resisted the cuts, which were bound to be unpopular. Cabinet met eight times between June 20 and June 24. True to form, Diefenbaker appointed a committee to study the issue. But this was one occasion on which indecision was simply not an option. Fleming would certainly resign if he didn't get his way—it was clear he was leaving Finance anyway, but the signal to the markets of a resignation by the finance minister in protest would have been devastating. At one point, Rasminsky and Gordon Churchill got into a shouting match over Churchill's opposition to the cuts. (Fleming said Rasminsky delivered "one of the severest dressing downs I ever heard one man deliver to another."[19]) On June 24, cabinet approved a series of emergency measures that included a temporary surcharge on imports, a reduction in the exemptions from customs duties, and a commitment to make replenishing the Exchange Fund the highest fiscal priority. In exchange, Canada received $300 million in funding from the IMF, $650 million from the U.S. Federal Reserve and Export-Import Bank, and $100 million from Great Britain. That Canada's allies were willing to commit more than a billion dollars in total (more than $10 billion today) to protect the currency was a show of confidence in the Canadian economy that no speculator could ignore. The pressure on the dollar quickly eased and the loans were soon repaid.

Diefenbaker had kept Pearson informed about the measures, which the prime minister announced on television in a special address. Ironically, just as the Coyne affair had ultimately brought increased stability to the Bank of Canada, so too pegging and then defending the dollar in 1962 bolstered the economy for years to come. But Diefenbaker's government would not profit from that stability. Within a week of being reduced to a minority government, the Tories had barely survived a financial crisis. The days of the twenty-fifth Parliament were numbered before it even met. And there was worse to come.

Because of the currency crisis, and because it was his nature to dither, Diefenbaker waited seven full weeks to name his new cabinet. In the midst of that dithering, on July 21 as he stepped off the veranda, his foot went into a gopher hole and he snapped his ankle. Cabinet met to conduct routine business around the bed of the prime minister. For weeks, Diefenbaker nursed his ankle and his grievances. And also his sorrow. Bill Brunt had been a friend and adviser to Diefenbaker since the early 1940s, and one of the few people who could talk to him frankly without repercussions. The Chief had elevated his friend to the Senate in 1957, and wanted him to become Senate speaker. But Blunt was killed in a car crash on July 7, 1962. Diefenbaker was deeply saddened by the loss, and deprived of another voice that could offer him the straight goods.

Neil Crawford, who worked in the Prime Minister's Office from 1961 to 1963, found that the formerly pleasant atmosphere in the PMO deteriorated after the 1962 election, and that Diefenbaker was often ill-tempered with the staff. After one dressing down, Bunny Pound told Crawford, "Look at it this way: when he is mad at you that means someone else is being spared."[20] Alvin Hamilton, who was on the receiving end of more than one Diefenbaker tantrum over the years, believed there was method in the apparent madness. Designed to break the will of its recipient so as to extract information, a Diefenbaker tantrum also "scared the devil out of the lazy and the arrogant."[21]

Obviously, major changes were needed, starting with Fleming, who had been through the wars. Diefenbaker was surprisingly candid. "Don, you and I are in the doghouse," Dief told Fleming. "I think you should be relieved of the portfolio of Finance. You get the blame for everything and it's hurting your future chances."[22] He proposed moving Fleming to Justice, and Fleming agreed. That meant finding a place for Davie Fulton, who was increasingly frank in his criticism of the prime minister. Diefenbaker proposed National Revenue, but Fulton refused the demotion. They settled on Public Works. Ellen Fairclough was moved out of Immigration and put in charge of the Post Office. In her memoirs, she chose not to treat the switch like the demotion it was. But it is very difficult not to notice that Diefenbaker demoted two of the ablest ministers in his government.

Wallace McCutcheon of the Argus Corporation was appointed to the Senate and to the cabinet as minister without portfolio, in a bid to placate Bay Street, while George Nowlan moved from National Revenue to Finance, despite his suspect loyalty.

Inexplicably, Diefenbaker left Howard Green in External Affairs and Doug Harkness in Defence. Green was implacably opposed to permitting tactical nuclear weapons on Canadian missiles and planes; Harkness was implacably determined to honour what he believed was Canada's commitment to the Americans. Diefenbaker should have replaced one of them, depending on how he planned to proceed on the issue. Since he still hadn't decided how to proceed, the obvious solution was to replace both of them with more malleable ministers. Instead, he let sleeping dogs lie. They wouldn't sleep for long.

V

On October 14, 1962, an American U-2 spy plane flying over Cuba took pictures of what analysts quickly concluded were missile sites designed for nuclear weapons. The Americans had been bested by the Soviets and the Cubans again and again: Sputnik, Gary Powers, the Bay of Pigs, the Berlin Wall. Now Nikita Khrushchev and Fidel Castro were conspiring to position medium- and intermediate-range ballistic missiles that could strike Washington and other American cities in a matter of minutes. John F. Kennedy decided that, at all costs, this could not stand.

A committee of senior officials presented him with three options: seek a diplomatic solution, attack the missile sites, or blockade the island. Previous efforts to negotiate with Khrushchev had failed; attacking Cuba could provoke a Russian counterattack in Berlin. On October 16, Kennedy opted to impose a naval *cordon sanitaire* around Cuba; no Soviet ship would be allowed through. The administration chose the term "quarantine" rather than "blockade," for a blockade is an act of war. Would the Russians accept the distinction?

On October 22, at 5:15 p.m., former U.S. ambassador Livingston Merchant, who had been chosen as Kennedy's emissary, met with Diefenbaker to apprise him of the situation—two hours before Kennedy was scheduled to address his nation and the world on television. Diefenbaker was incensed, and with good reason. He already knew there was a major crisis involving missiles in Cuba; Norman Robertson and Robert Bryce had been tipped off by senior U.S. officials, and they in turn had briefed him. That the American president was informing the Canadian prime minister, through an emissary, two hours before he addressed the public was unconscionable. The missiles in Cuba would be able to strike Toronto and Montreal as well as Washington and New York. As Canada was a partner in NORAD, its prime minister should have been consulted rather than informed, and he should certainly have been told well in advance of any televised address. Diefenbaker would have been even more insulted had he known that Kennedy, while sending an emissary to Ottawa, had informed Harold Macmillan directly by phone.

Diefenbaker told Merchant he would make a statement the next day. But when Pearson phoned him to ask whether he would respond to the president's address, the Chief changed his mind and went to the House of Commons. Searching for something meaningful to say, he grabbed some notes prepared by Norman Robertson. But Robertson had intended those notes for a future private conversation between Diefenbaker and Kennedy. Instead, the prime minister rose in the House at 8 p.m. and read them into the public record. The president's speech, he said, was "sombre and challenging." The Soviets had always said their actions in Cuba were defensive. Now the Americans were saying that offensive weapons were being deployed. Diefenbaker urged that the matter be taken to the United Nations, and suggested as well that a team of inspectors from non-aligned nations visit the island and inspect the sites to determine their true nature. "The only sure way that the world can secure the facts would be through an independent inspection," he told the House.[23] The Americans reacted "with surprise and annoyance" in Washington at what seemed to be a lack of confidence in their evidence and in their judgment of the most effective course of action, Basil Robinson later wrote.[24] Was the prime minister questioning the president's word? When American officials offered to show the photographic evidence to French president Charles de Gaulle, he waved them away. The president's word was good enough for him. But apparently it wasn't good enough for John Diefenbaker.

Canada's response should not have surprised the Americans. Expressions of concern, appeals for calm, and a search for a UN-brokered compromise had been the Canadian approach during past crises, and would be for decades to come. But Kennedy was no more charitable to Diefenbaker than Diefenbaker had been to him. Did the prime minister of Canada not believe the word of the American president? Was this how friends behaved?

Later that evening, Doug Harkness asked to meet with Diefenbaker urgently. The United States had gone to Defense Condition (Defcon) 3. At that level, military bases are placed on alert and air force units can launch operations with fifteen minutes of notice. The Americans were asking the Canadians to bring their forces up to the same level. Diefenbaker refused. He would consult cabinet in the morning and then decide. The prime minister didn't want to further inflame a global crisis by mimicking American spear-shaking. Appalled, Harkness and senior commanding officers decided to bring the military up to full readiness anyway, but to do so quietly. Air and army bases went on full alert. The ships that weren't already at sea, cooperating with the American navy in monitoring Soviet activity, were fuelled and armed and made ready to sail at a moment's notice. But at cabinet the next morning, Howard Green argued for a go-slow approach, and Diefenbaker agreed. During an ill-tempered phone conversation with Kennedy on the afternoon of the 23rd, Diefenbaker demanded to know, "When were we consulted?" "You weren't," Kennedy snapped back—the Chief refused Kennedy's repeated requests to place Canada's forces on full alert.[25] On the 24th, the Americans placed the Strategic Air Command and some naval units at Defcon 2, the last stage short of war. Harkness once again urged Diefenbaker to mobilize the Canadian military. Diefenbaker reluctantly agreed to a state of military readiness that, through insubordination, already existed.

By the 25th, differences between Washington and Ottawa had narrowed. Diefenbaker clarified in public that his appeal for a UN intervention had been intended to buttress, not undermine, the American position, and that

Canadian forces stood at alert with their American counterparts. By now, the world was on the brink of nuclear war. Soviet ships approached the American quarantine line. Then all but one stopped short. Kennedy let that one through because it was a tanker with no offensive weapons. Kennedy and Khrushchev exchanged angry, defensive, accusatory messages. Soviet submarines lurked near the quarantine line. Bobby Kennedy thought an attack could come at any hour. In 1959, the Canadian government had authorized construction of a massive, four-storey bunker and fallout shelter in Carp, thirty kilometres west of Ottawa, that could withstand a nuclear blast and house key elements of the federal government in the event of nuclear war. When the *Toronto Telegram* broke the story on the installation's top-secret existence—reporter George Brimmell found it odd that the construction site of what was billed as a simple communications bunker had seventy-eight toilets sitting outside—the newspaper derisively dubbed it the Diefenbunker. Now the prime minister wondered aloud whether cabinet would be able to reach the emergency shelter in time.

Then Khrushchev blinked. He agreed to remove the missiles. Secretly, the Americans agreed to remove some obsolete missiles in Turkey in exchange. The world breathed again.

But relations between the Kennedy administration and the Diefenbaker government had reached what appeared to be rock bottom. Bobby Kennedy was especially angry. At the height of the crisis, he reportedly declared, "In an emergency, Canada will give you all aid short of help."[26] The president had been on the phone with British prime minister Macmillan every day, sometimes twice a day. Kennedy looked to the elder British statesman for advice and support, and received both. But after that one angry phone call on the 23rd, Kennedy never spoke to Diefenbaker again.

VI

Throughout the summer of 1962, the Americans had maintained relentless pressure on the Diefenbaker government to accept tactical nuclear weapons for the Bomarcs and fighters in Canada and for the Canadian NATO contingent in Europe. Friends of the administration would take reporters and businessmen for lunch or dinner or drinks. They would fly influencers to

NORAD headquarters at Cheyenne Mountain. They helped swing editorial and public opinion in favour of Canada accepting its defence commitments and its NORAD and NATO responsibilities. Within cabinet, they could count on the relentless advocacy of Defence Minister Doug Harkness.

But the nuclear disarmament movement in Canada was powerful and growing, and it reflected other growing discontents. Those born during the Depression—part of what came to be known as the Silent Generation—were now in their twenties and thirties. They were invested in career and home and children. And much of what they saw in the world frightened them. Parents demanded a world in which their children weren't at constant risk of extermination through radiation. The initial Pugwash Conference in that Nova Scotia community in 1957 had catalyzed the scientific and intellectual campaign against nuclear weapons. Peace activists protested growing American involvement in Indochina. University students objected to the stultifying intellectual and social conformity they encountered on campus. The sixties had arrived. In Canada, these protests coalesced in 1962 around a campaign to keep the Bomb out of Canada, to keep Canada outside the nuclear-armed club, and to focus on disarmament efforts instead. They found voice in External Affairs Minister Howard Green, the tall, soft-spoken but implacable minister who had become a leading advocate for disarmament talks at the United Nations in New York. On November 6, 1962, he earned high praise for convincing the General Assembly to pass a non-binding resolution calling for a partial moratorium on nuclear testing, shortly after the resolution of the Cuban Missile Crisis.

Diefenbaker, as always, sought to bridge the divide through indecision. He demanded more time to study the issue. The weapons must be under "joint control"—they could not be launched without the approval of the Canadian prime minister as well as the American president. But what would joint control look like? Perhaps some critical component of the weapon— the "missing part"—could be stored on the American side of the border and then be rushed into place in the event of an emergency. Absolutely not, the Americans replied. The emergency, and the war, could be over before the weapons were usable. In December, Diefenbaker inserted himself into a meeting between Kennedy and Macmillan in Nassau, Bahamas, at which the U.S. and the U.K. agreed to replace the Skybolt missile, which was being developed to be launched from a bomber, with the submarine-based Polaris missile to anchor Britain's nuclear deterrent. Diefenbaker got it into his head that this somehow changed the entire strategic equation, justifying yet more study of whether Canada needed nuclear-tipped weapons. This analysis baffled the Americans, but it didn't matter. By now their minds were made up. The Cuban Missile Crisis had convinced them of two things: Canada must take up its nuclear responsibilities, and John Diefenbaker must go.

Controversy transformed into crisis on January 3, 1963, when American general Lauris Norstad, having just stepped down as Supreme Allied Commander of NATO in Europe, visited Ottawa on his farewell tour. At a press conference organized by the Canadian air force, Southam News correspondent Charles Lynch bluntly asked Norstad whether he thought Canada was living up to its NATO commitments in Europe. Yes, Norstad replied, NATO squadrons in Europe would be equipped with nuclear-tipped missiles, "and Canada committed some of its force to meet this NATO-established requirement." Reporters jumped all over the answer, which Norstad confirmed, asserting, "We are depending on Canada to produce some of the tactical atomic strike forces."[27]

Diefenbaker was apoplectic. He was convinced Kennedy had sent Norstad to Ottawa to undermine his government. Alvin Hamilton agreed, declaring, "Kennedy sent Norstad to do this hatchet-job on us."[28] Charles Ritchie, now Canadian ambassador to the United States, also agreed. "The Norstad thing did not happen in a vacuum," he wrote in his diary.[29] Whether by accident or design, the general's ultimatum-by-assumption had brought the issue to a head, just as Mike Pearson was getting ready to deliver a speech.

Pearson had supported the acquisition of the Bomarc missiles in 1959, but within a year he had changed his mind. Canada, he told the House of Commons, should not be a member of the nuclear club in any way, shape, or form. "Canada should categorically reject the proposition that her NATO forces should be equipped with nuclear forces of any kind," he stated.[30] At its 1961 policy conference, the Liberal Party had declared itself opposed to placing nuclear weapons on Canadian soil. But now the Liberal leader was thinking of changing his mind again. His defence critic, Toronto MP Paul Hellyer, pressed him on the issue after Hellyer visited Canada's demoralized forces in Europe. Jack Pickersgill was urging him to take a clear, unambiguous position and stick to it, in contrast to Diefenbaker. Public opinion in the wake of the Cuban Missile Crisis had swung around in favour of nukes. Pearson went to New York for a conference, consulted with UN secretary general U Thant, and worked on an address that he delivered Saturday, January 12 to the York—Scarborough Liberal Association.

To refuse nuclear weapons on moral grounds even as Canada sheltered under the American nuclear umbrella and supplied the uranium used in those weapons was hypocritical, he declared. Canada must live up to its obligations as a founding member of NATO. "War is the evil, the immorality," he said. "By concentrating our emotions on a particular kind of weapon we are in danger of obscuring the real issue, which is disarmament and outlawing war as an instrument of national policy." The question was simple: "How can Canada make her most effective contribution to collective security in order to avoid war?" The answer was clear: Canada "should end at once its evasion of responsibility and put itself in a position to discharge the commitments it has already accepted." If Canada made those commitments and then failed to honour them, then "we deceive ourselves, we let our armed forces down, and betray our allies."[31] Pearson had reversed his own stand and his party's stand by coming down clearly in favour of accepting nuclear-armed weapons on Canadian soil and in Europe. In doing so, he had placed himself on the side of public opinion while making Diefenbaker look vacillating and weak. Several years later, recalling the speech during an interview for a CBC documentary, he explained, "It was at least a decision and I think was the right decision on a vital question of defence." The fact that the government was split on the issue and the Liberal Party was now on the side of public opinion "helped to confirm me in my own mind that not only was the decision right, it was . . . wise." And he gave an impish Pearsonian grin.[32]

In the wake of the Cuban Missile Crisis, certain cabinet ministers had begun meeting to discuss forcing Diefenbaker's resignation. Some of those meetings were more or less formal, as part of talks with the Social Credit Party about obtaining its support in the House. Robert Thompson never confirmed that he demanded Diefenbaker's resignation in exchange for that support, but some ministers and their advisers considered the condition implicit. The rebellion gathered steam in alcohol-fuelled gatherings, which sometimes got underway at noon. George Hees was prominent among the rebels, as was Wallace McCutcheon, the Bay Street businessman who had been brought into cabinet to give it some business smarts, but who was now convinced Diefenbaker must go. Associate Defence Minister Pierre Sévigny was another conspirator, as were Finance Minister George Nowlan and Harkness. Diefenbaker was increasingly telling cabinet ministers and staff that he was ready to quit. Part of the cabinet at least was willing to help him out.

Pearson's Damascene conversion in favour of nuclear arms forced Diefenbaker to clarify his position. He tried to, in a speech to Parliament on January 25. But that rambling address left everyone, including members of his own cabinet, confused. The gist of it seemed to be that Canada and the United States were negotiating on the acquisition of nuclear weapons for the Bomarcs and the fighters. But the Nassau accord had upended strategic calculations, and in any case, technology was evolving so quickly that weapons agreed to one day could be obsolete the next. His government intended to wait until NATO meetings in May to reach a decision.

The press gallery concluded the prime minister was ruling out the acquisition of nuclear weapons. Harkness called a press conference to upbraid them, pointing to passages in the speech that contradicted such a conclusion. But all that was swept aside by a memorandum from the State Department, issued Wednesday, January 30, that flatly contradicted Diefenbaker's assertions. "The Canadian government has not yet proposed any arrangement sufficiently practical to contribute effectively to North American defence," it stated. The Nassau agreements "raise no question of the appropriateness of nuclear weapons for Canadian forces." Finally, "the provision of nuclear weapons to Canadian forces would not involve an expansion of independent nuclear capability" because the weapons would remain under American control.[33]

The memorandum was a direct intervention in the Canadian debate over nuclear weapons by the Kennedy administration. Arguably, that intervention was justified, since the United States' nuclear defence had been compromised by the Diefenbaker government's inactions. But such blatant interference in Canadian domestic affairs, and such a direct criticism of the government of the day—the memorandum insinuated that Diefenbaker had lied to the

House—had never occurred before and has never occurred since. In fury, Diefenbaker ordered U.S. ambassador Charles Ritchie to return to Ottawa for consultations. An open breach had formed in Canada–U.S. relations.

The press gallery knew that cabinet was divided over the nuclear weapons issue, and that ministers were scheming to replace the leader, but journalists had no idea the government was on the brink of disintegration. They found out the following Saturday, at the press gallery dinner, an annual gathering in Ottawa at which journalists and politicians dine together in fancy dress, making fun of each other in speeches and skits. Diefenbaker stormed out of the gathering in a rage after gallery members serenaded him with a song to the tune of "Jesus Loves Me." The hymn parodied Allister Grosart, Diefenbaker's chief political adviser—"People love me this I know / For Al Grosart tells me so"; the political ambitions of George Hees; and the disloyalty of Doug Harkness, while also spreading a cruel and untrue rumour that Diefenbaker was showing symptoms of Parkinson's disease: "There were rumours from George Hees / I had Harkness's disease. . . ."[34]

Charles Lynch believed that it was at the press gallery dinner that the Chief realized the extent of the plot to oust him. Diefenbaker speculated in his memoirs that goading from reporters, amplified by alcohol, tipped the balance among the discontented. Peter C. Newman thought George Hees was the ringleader. Whatever the combination of factors, cabinet met in emergency session the next morning, Sunday, February 3.

Diefenbaker wanted to dissolve Parliament and fight an election over the American memorandum. Harkness angrily declared Diefenbaker had lost the confidence of cabinet. Diefenbaker jumped to his feet and demanded that everyone who was loyal stand with him. But many of the ministers didn't know whether they were standing in solidarity with Diefenbaker or with the wacky notion of dissolving Parliament over a note from State, and so stayed seated. Diefenbaker announced that he would resign and nominated Donald Fleming to be his successor, then left the room. Hamilton and Green left with him, hurling accusations of "Traitor!" back at their colleagues. Fleming got the meeting back under control. Although he would have accepted the post of caretaker prime minister had cabinet united behind the idea, no such unity was to be found. Besides, his son had been seriously injured in a car accident the day before, and Fleming was not planning to run in the next election. A subdued cabinet convinced the prime minister and his loyalists to return. Harkness announced his resignation, shaking hands with the men around the table. (Fairclough was absent.) "I resigned on a matter of principle," he told a reporter the next day. "The point was finally reached when I considered that my honour and integrity required that I take this step."[35] The government was dying.

There was one last hope for the Tories. Neither Social Credit nor the NDP were anxious for a campaign call barely seven months after the last election. Perhaps the Tories and the Socreds could strike a deal. Thompson was willing to make one, provided the Conservatives would promise a budget, a clear statement on defence, and a governing agenda. He might or might not also have expected Diefenbaker's resignation. The conspirators thought he did, and they came up with a plan. Diefenbaker would agree to resign and become chief justice of the Supreme Court. (The position had been made vacant the previous Saturday with the death of Patrick Kerwin.) George Nowlan would become a caretaker prime minister, governing with the support of Social Credit, until a convention chose a new leader for the Progressive Conservative Party. Diefenbaker was mooting his own scenario of resigning in favour of Donald Fleming, or so Fleming remembered it. But all this speculation was idle: Diefenbaker fully intended to remain as leader and he had no intention of going cap in hand to Bob Thompson. Further, he seemed re-energized by the fight to save his leadership and to tilt against the windmill of American interference in Canadian affairs. Realizing there could be no accommodation, Thompson joined the Liberals in two motions of non-confidence. On February 5, the government fell.

Hees and his allies still hoped to bring Diefenbaker down at a meeting of cabinet. But they had left it too late. The Chief and his supporters arranged for a meeting of the full caucus—which had been left out of the plotters' calculation—to precede the cabinet meeting. Diefenbaker delivered a magnificent performance that had MPs howling their support and that reduced Hees to tears. The dissident ministers were forced by MPs and senators to declare their support and shake the leader's hands. But unity was only temporary. The next morning, Hees and Sévigny visited Diefenbaker at 24 Sussex Drive. Both tendered their resignation, further confirming the very public split within cabinet. Sévigny later regretted his decision, admitting, "Mr. Diefenbaker did not deserve the treatment that I gave him and which others gave him at the time."[36]

On February 6, Diefenbaker visited Government House and once again asked Georges Vanier to issue writs of election. There could only be one outcome.

ELEVEN

Mike

(1963–1965)

I

Lament for a Nation, written in the wake of the 1963 Canadian election, was born from more than George Grant's resentment over how Mike Pearson had treated Mary Greey during the war. Though the tract was profoundly conservative, generations of the left have embraced Grant's diatribe, which is read—and misunderstood—to this day. Grant's polemic served as an elegy for his imagined English-Canadian nation, a nation of farms and villages and towns, rooted in agriculture and small shops, bound in identity and values to Britain, and doomed to extinction by the march of consumerism, big business, and American hegemony. (He fully acknowledged that French-speaking Canada represented a separate and unique nation within the English-speaking continent.) That Canada had long been more urban than rural, and that a third of its population was neither British nor French in descent, he largely ignored.

Grant understood Diefenbaker's weaknesses. He portrayed the prime minister as a Prairie populist who only dimly understood what he was trying to preserve, and who was often his own worst enemy. But "his actions during the Defence Crisis make it clear that his nationalism was a deeply held principle for which he would fight with great courage, and would sacrifice political advantage," Grant wrote. "Nothing in Diefenbaker's ministry was as noble as the leaving of it."[1] His defeat at the hands of the Kennedy administration, nominally abetted by the Liberal Party and Lester B. Pearson, represented for Grant nothing less than "the disappearance of Canada."[2]

This mythical disappearing Canada that the rumpled McMaster University professor of religion lamented was, of course, one governed by an Anglo-Canadian elite in which his family figured prominently. The British tradition he honoured was rooted in class privilege. But James Laxer and other emerging intellectuals on the New Left embraced Grant's rejection of corporate imperialism and ignored the rest, including his defence of Diefenbaker.

In any case, few now look upon the election of 1963 as either tragic or triumphant, just as few lament the loss of the British, Tory, Protestant nationalism that Grant championed. Nonetheless, the professor was right, in a way. Populist, rural conservatism tied to the British imperial tradition fell into permanent eclipse with Diefenbaker's defeat. (When conservative populism re-emerged in the Reform Party of the 1980s and '90s, it would seek inspiration from south of the border rather than from across the sea.) And to a degree never witnessed before or since, the election was fought as much between a prime minister and a president as between a Conservative and a Liberal.

It was, after all, the Kennedy administration that had sent a retiring NATO general to Ottawa to remind Canada of its promised nuclear commitments, transforming a simmering controversy into an open crisis. It was the Kennedy administration that, through the State Department, issued the memorandum directly contradicting Diefenbaker's statements in the House of Commons, leading to the resignation of three cabinet ministers and the fall of the government. It was Kennedy's pollster, Lou Harris, who was advising the Liberal campaign. "It's me against the Americans, fighting for the little guy," Diefenbaker declared at the outset,[3] and in many ways it was: Camelot and its Laurentian acolytes on one side; Diefenbaker and the common man on the other. There were no other issues to speak of, as far as the Chief was concerned. "His targets were the Americans, the elite, the media, the big-city sophisticates and the Bay Street power brokers," Knowlton Nash wrote in his analysis of the campaign. The odds against Diefenbaker were long, with the Grits ahead in the polls by fifteen points. A Liberal majority appeared certain. But Dalton Camp, now campaign manager, watched Diefenbaker transform before his eyes. The dark pouches disappeared; the energy was back. "The campaign gave him adrenalin. He needed that."[4]

Dief whistle-stopped across the country, greeting crowds at the train station, shaking hands as he walked down the main street, popping into the barbershop or the Chinese restaurant, working up a lather as he railed against the Yanks and the Bay Street fat cats arrayed against him. He could still bring his most devoted disciples to tears of adoration.

Mike Pearson could do none of that. His handlers had coached him into sounding less academic—he became rather good at issuing short, sharp declarations, accompanied by a decisive nod of the head—and bow ties had finally given way to neckties. But Pearson was no better at connecting with voters in 1963 than he had been in 1962 or 1958. He hated campaigning and it showed. He refused to stick to a simple, endlessly repeated message track, which meant his core campaign message failed to penetrate. People noticed the lisp. "Pearson was not a jugular politician like Diefenbaker," Harris acknowledged afterward. "Now, Diefenbaker had that sense. He was a terrific politician."[5]

As the campaign progressed—or more properly, dragged on—Diefenbaker sought to personify the entire nation, asserting its dignity and sovereignty in the face of bullying American scorn. "We are a power, not a pauper," he declared at one stop. "I want Canada to be in control of Canadian soil." And at his histrionic peak: "A Canadian I was born; a Canadian I will die."[6] (John A. Macdonald had famously maintained, during the 1891 debate on free trade, "A British subject I was born; a British subject I will die.")

Diefenbaker seized on a February 18 *Newsweek* cover story entitled "Canada's Diefenbaker: Decline and Fall." The photograph was outrageously uncomplimentary, the story inside even worse. *Newsweek* was well known to be sympathetic to the Kennedy administration. Dalton Camp had the story copied and sent to every riding association in the country. (You wanted proof that the Americans were interfering in the election? Here it is!) The Chief also threatened to release the Rostow memo again—he had already signalled its existence to the press—and peddled a letter purporting to be from the American ambassador offering Pearson whatever aid and assistance he could provide. The letter was so clearly fraudulent that no responsible news organization would touch it. The Tory shenanigans probably didn't hurt or help the campaign, but they signalled that, in this election, there was nothing Dief wouldn't do to tarnish Pearson's image and tie him to Kennedy.

Against this, Mike Pearson could offer only policy. At least, unlike the Progressive Conservatives, he had some. And since a Liberal victory appeared certain, no matter how wrought up the Conservative leader might become, policy mattered. Those policies included a new national program of universal public health care and a new Canadian flag "which cannot be mistaken for the emblem of any other country." It included a new commission on relations between English and French Canada that would "make a reality of the idea of equal partnership as the only basis on which Confederation can work fairly and effectively," federally subsidized housing, loans for university students, improved pensions, and, of course, the commitment to "obtain defensive nuclear weapons."[7] The Conservative platform, in contrast, repeated the previous year's recitation of accomplishments, with no plans for what would come next. Everyone knew what would come next: a Liberal government. The only question was whether it would be a majority or minority.

For the Liberals, the scariest moment in the campaign featured a rather hilarious near miss. On the evening of March 28, shortly before a campaign event in Edmonton, the phone rang at the Legion Hall where Pearson was due to speak. The janitor answered. It was the White House, calling for Mr. Pearson on an urgent matter. With the Liberal leader already on the platform, the chairman of the meeting whispered the news into his ear. Pearson was appalled. If Diefenbaker ever got wind that the White House had been phoning him to offer advice. . . . Nonetheless, he followed the janitor to the basement and took the call, which was from Max Freedman of the *Winnipeg Free Press*, who was passing along a message from Kennedy that the president was happy to offer any assistance Mr. Pearson might need. "For God's sake, tell the president to keep his mouth shut," Pearson replied angrily.[8] The janitor promised not to tell a soul, and kept that promise. "This was a narrow escape," Pearson recalled in his memoirs.[9]

There were missteps. One was a colouring book caricaturing the Conservatives that didn't interest children and that many parents—and Pearson himself—considered a cheap shot. Another was the truth squad. Judy LaMarsh, an able and sharp-tongued lawyer from Niagara Falls, had arrived in the House as a Liberal MP in a 1960 by-election. The campaign team put her in charge of the squad, tasked with following Diefenbaker around and correcting the record. Diefenbaker turned the tables by introducing and then mocking the truthers, who soon gave up. And a rally in Vancouver went disastrously wrong. Conservative ringers worked their way into the event, shouting and jeering and firing from peashooters at the stage. As the peas bounced off Mike's head, Maryon wept openly behind him. By the end of the campaign, Pearson was exhausted and practically bedridden with a high fever and laryngitis.

Election night 1963 was a mirror of election night 1962, with one crucial difference. Once again, Mike and Maryon watched the results from a suite in the Château Laurier. Once again, the Liberals swept Newfoundland. The two parties split the difference in the Maritimes. The Liberals were even stronger in Quebec than the year before, with forty-seven seats, but the Créditistes held their base, taking twenty seats, and the Tories clung to a rump of eight. Pearson's promise to accept nuclear weapons had not gone down well in a province that traditionally remained aloof from foreign entanglements. Ontario was a rout: fifty-one Liberals to twenty-seven Conservatives, and six for the new NDP. But everything west of Ontario went badly for the Grits. The Prairies had become a desert for them: two seats in Manitoba, one in Alberta, none in Saskatchewan. And while they beat the Tories seven seats to four in B.C., the New Democrats took nine. The Liberals had won government, but they were short of a majority. Mike would have to govern with the consent of Social Credit or, more likely, the NDP.

Diefenbaker spent election night in Prince Albert. He mused to reporters that the results resembled 1925, when the Liberals had placed second in the seat count but Mackenzie King resolved to meet the House regardless. Was he pulling people's legs? Even close confidants like Alvin Hamilton and Gordon Churchill were urging him to acknowledge the Liberal win. Four days after the election, Social Credit eliminated any ambiguity by delivering a letter to Governor General Vanier saying that it intended to support a Liberal administration. Diefenbaker acknowledged defeat and began the arrangements for the transfer of power. On April 22, one day before his sixty-sixth birthday, Lester Bowles Pearson was sworn in as Canada's fourteenth prime minister. Mike was now in charge.

II

On April 1, during the last week of the election campaign, two bombs exploded in Montreal, one at a federal tax building, the other at the railway station. A third, on CNR tracks, was discovered and disarmed shortly before a train carrying John Diefenbaker passed over it. "Is this Ireland?" he exclaimed, when told.[10] Three weeks later, another bomb detonated at the Canadian Forces Recruiting Centre in Montreal, killing the night security guard, Wilfrid O'Neil.

From the very beginning of the Quiet Revolution, some activists had rejected any reforms short of complete independence for Quebec. Since 1960, the Rassemblement pour l'Indépendance Nationale (the Rally for National Independence) had been trying to win Quebecers to the cause. Others wanted to go farther, faster. In 1963, Raymond Villeneuve and Gabriel Hudon left the youth wing of the party and joined with Georges Schoeters, a Belgian who had fought in the resistance during the war, to form the Front de Libération du Québec (FLQ). In theory, the FLQ sought the liberation of Quebec from English, capitalist dominance by way of popular resistance. In practice, it was a terrorist cell seeking to destabilize society through violence.

III

In the last two weeks of the election campaign, as prospects for a Liberal majority government began to slip away, Keith Davey had come up with the idea of Pearson promising that a Liberal majority government would embark on "sixty days of decision": a swift, action-filled antidote to the Conservative drift of the past two years. Davey and others had originally suggested one hundred days, but Pearson said that was too reminiscent of the period between Napoleon returning from Elba and the Battle of Waterloo. He made it sixty days instead. This obstinacy of the leader could be infuriating. Who cared about Elba and Waterloo? But unlike Diefenbaker, who had so much trouble deciding anything, Pearson leaned toward quick decisions, even if the decision was wrong. He was wrong about sixty days. Now that the Liberals were in power, albeit with a minority rather than a majority mandate, they had forty fewer days than they would have had otherwise to keep their election promise. And they had to keep that promise while building a cabinet, that intricate dance of balancing talent against regional, economic, and sectarian interests, one of an incoming prime minister's most difficult challenges. Then Parliament had to be summoned, which meant crafting a throne speech laying out the government's agenda. And then legislation enacting the sixty-days commitments needed to be introduced. But would the legislation be ready in time?

Pearson did not lack for talent when crafting his cabinet. Apart from Walter Gordon, whose experience in the business world made him conspicuously qualified to helm Finance, there were the three lieutenants who had led the opposition to Diefenbaker in the House, and who helped bring the government down. Paul Martin, despite the bitter loss to Pearson in 1957, had proven himself as loyal as he was able, so he succeeded Pearson as the secretary of state for external affairs. The Machiavellian Jack Pickersgill, who like Pearson had been a senior public servant as well as cabinet minister, asked to be made House leader, along with secretary of state. Pearson, surprised that Pickersgill didn't want a more senior portfolio, obliged him. Lionel Chevrier asked for and received Justice. But there were many other able MPs who liked and respected Mike Pearson and who wanted to serve beside him. Pearson sent Mitchell Sharp, who was now the member for Eglinton, back to Trade and Commerce as minister. Paul Hellyer, who had strong views about the need to modernize the armed forces and who had helped convince Pearson to permit nuclear weapons on Canadian soil, became minister of defence. Judy LaMarsh, the first woman in a Liberal cabinet, took on the difficult and pivotal portfolio of Health and Welfare. ("I was stunned," LaMarsh recalled later, ". . . I was full of gratitude, perhaps the last time so unalloyed in my dealings with Pearson."[11]) Allan MacEachen, who was back in the House after years of advising Pearson, was rewarded with Labour. Regional and other concerns led to appointments in other portfolios by ministers who turned out to be nonentities. 'Twas always thus and would always be thus. And other factors were at work. When Pauline Jewett, an economics professor with a PhD from Harvard, asked if she might be considered for cabinet, she said Pearson told her, "But we already have a woman in the cabinet, Judy LaMarsh."[12] (It must be said that this does not sound like something Pearson would say or do.)

As cabinet met on April 22, Pearson's face was swollen from the infection that had laid him low at the end of the campaign. But he and his government were in good spirits. The Liberals were back in power far sooner than most had expected after the 1958 shellacking. Mike had successfully rebuilt the party, had modernized its policies and its electoral machine, and was now free to govern for as long as the NDP's Tommy Douglas would let him, which was likely to be quite some time. Political scientists lauded the cabinet's heavy emphasis on technocrats and former public servants and ministers. There were seven francophone cabinet ministers from Quebec and three from outside Quebec, signalling the government's determination to accommodate that province's aspirations.

"The problems are agonizingly difficult and complicated but we have a chance to do something about them instead of criticizing others for not doing anything or doing the wrong thing," he wrote Geoffrey. "Psychologically, this makes all the difference to me. It means that though I started in right after the election and have had no let up I feel fine, full of energy and without any need for a holiday, yet." Morale in the public service was high, he claimed. "We have a very efficient managerial government, and we will not lose touch—as in 1956 and 57—with public and parliamentary opinion. There will be no arrogance in this administration if I can prevent it. But there is certainly going to be unpleasantness in the House of C. D is very nasty and cannot conceal his frustrations. He misses the pomp and prestige of office greatly and obviously."[13]

The government wasn't much larger than its predecessor. Both the Prime Minister's Office and the Privy Council Office fit into an East Block that was still mostly occupied by External Affairs. "There was no bevy of deputies and assistants and principal this-and-that," Tom Kent recalled. He was effectively both principal secretary and chief of staff, though his title was "co-ordinator of programming." Mary Macdonald was there to manage constituency affairs and to keep a protective eye on her boss. A very young and baby-faced Jim Coutts, who would go on to become a powerful aide to Pierre Trudeau, handled logistics, while Dick O'Hagan took on and transformed the role of press secretary. The sharp-dressing former journalist, who had also worked in advertising, would become a senior adviser to the prime minister, helping craft a communications strategy for the government.

Pearson's first order of business was to repair Canada's strained relationship with both Britain and the United States. He flew to London the week after the swearing-in to meet with the Queen (such a visit was expected from any new prime minister in those days) and with Harold Macmillan. Diefenbaker's opposition to Britain entering the European Common Market, and his wilful misinterpretation of the Nassau Accord, had left relations with the U.K. almost as strained as with the U.S. Dief, however, had been proven right: French president Charles de Gaulle, showing little gratitude for the years in which Winston Churchill had hosted him during the Second World War, had vetoed Britain's entry in January of that year. But Dief's opposition to the deal had not helped, leaving Macmillan feeling even more bitter toward the former prime minister. Macmillan and Pearson, on the other hand, admired and respected each other as former foreign ministers who had made it to the top of their respective greasy poles. They spent two pleasant hours together, solving all the problems of the world.

The visit that mattered, though, was the meeting with Kennedy. Virtually all contact between the two governments had been frozen in the wake of the Cuban Missile Crisis, the Bomarc crisis, the incendiary memorandum from State, and Canada's decision to withdraw its ambassador. There was much that was stuck that needed to be unstuck. Rather than meeting in Washington, which would entail banquets and meetings around tables and such, Kennedy invited the new prime minister to the family compound in Hyannis Port, a signal of the respect and friendship the president felt for the new prime minister. The two men walked along the beach in the spring rain, talked baseball, and agreed to restart the Canada–U.S. relationship. This would include finally implementing the Columbia River Treaty, working out new agreements on offshore rights, lowering trade tariffs—both between the two countries and at GATT in Geneva—and, of course, equipping Canadian Forces in Canada and Europe with nuclear weapons. Pearson suggested that Canada might be willing to join the Organization of American States "if circumstances were propitious."[14] (It turned out circumstances would not be propitious until 1990.) Charles Ritchie, re-ensconced as ambassador, described the mood in his diary as euphoric: "clearing skies after the storm." Diefenbaker had tormented both men, and "there was an undercurrent of complicity between them, as if they had both escaped—like schoolboys on a holiday—from under the shadow of an insupportably tiresome and irrational Third Party, and were now free to crack jokes at the expense of the Absent One."[15] Despite that, both the prime minister and the president agreed that the defence production sharing agreement negotiated during the Diefenbaker years was working well. At the end of the visit, as the rain continued to pour, Kennedy lowered the presidential flag at the gates of the compound, folded it, and gave it to Pearson as a gift, a touching gesture symbolizing two old friends patching up a quarrel.

But the clock was ticking on the sixty days of decision, and still nothing had been decided. With the wisdom of hindsight, it's clear Pearson should have abandoned the commitment, pleading that having a minority government made it impossible to fulfill. Instead, the government decided to rush through a budget. It was Pearson's single biggest mistake as prime minister.

Walter Gordon had felt dejected when Mike Pearson gave his speech in January embracing nuclear arms, both because Gordon opposed the move and because Pearson had not consulted him first. After all, he wrote, "Mike Pearson was my closest friend."[16] But Gordon had invested a great deal in helping the Liberals return to power, and he accepted the role of campaign chair despite his misgivings over accepting nuclear weapons. After the election, Gordon was surprised when his closest friend suggested he might prefer to take on the job of organizing the new Department of Industry. Absolutely not, Gordon retorted. He had been promised Finance and he wanted Finance. Pearson acquiesced, but it placed a kernel of doubt in Gordon's mind. Would Pearson back him up if his budget got into trouble? And trouble was likely. Since the days of St. Laurent, Gordon had advocated for greater Canadian control over Canadian industry. Now he would have a chance to realize that goal.

The Twenty-Sixth Canadian Parliament convened on May 16, with a Speech from the Throne that promised industrial expansion, a new pension plan, and supports for agriculture and the fishery as well as for regional development. But the real story, everyone knew, would be Gordon's budget.

It was a rush job. The finance minister wanted Robert Bryce to come over from the Privy Council Office to serve as deputy minister, but Pearson said he needed the clerk by his side for another two months. The existing deputy minister, Ken Taylor, and senior staff were opposed to much of what Gordon proposed, so he brought in outside consultants, which the opposition later latched onto and pilloried. It also left Gordon at war with his own department. Over at the Bank of Canada, Louis Rasminsky was alarmed by Gordon's proposed 30 per cent tax on the takeover of Canadian companies by foreign firms. But after hearing the banker out, Pearson backed the minister.

The budget came down on the evening of June 13, within a little more than a week of the sixty-day deadline. It proposed raising taxes and closing tax loopholes in order to eliminate the deficit. It proposed measures to promote economic growth. But the measures to increase Canadian control over manufacturing got all the attention, and that attention was not kind.

Along with the 30 per cent tax that would be imposed on the sale of Canadian firms to foreign firms, the budget proposed that Canadians should own a 25 per cent interest in the subsidiaries of foreign-owned firms. Corporate Canada (Inc.) reacted with fury. The most damaging volley came from Eric Kierans, chairman of the Montreal Stock Exchange. "The financial capitals of the world have just about had enough from Canada," he wrote in a letter to Gordon that Kierans made public. "Last Friday, the original reaction to the budget was one of bewilderment and dismay. Yesterday, it was anger and scorn. Today, our friends in the Western World fully realize that we don't want them or their money. . . . And their reaction? If that's what Canadians want, let them have it!"[17] As if in confirmation, stock markets in Canada began to fall. Critics blamed the sell-off on the takeover tax. Graham Towers, the retired central bank governor, warned Pearson against Gordon's protectionist measures. Pearson knew as little about economics, and cared as little, as Diefenbaker, preferring to concentrate on foreign affairs. But he was learning swiftly that a prime minister must focus primarily on domestic matters or pay the price. And speaking of foreign affairs, the bonhomie of Hyannis Port evaporated the instant Washington grasped what Ottawa proposed. "Discriminatory features of budget had come as real surprise," the State Department telegraphed the embassy in Ottawa. ". . . While Pearson had indicated at Hyannis Port some consideration would be given problem of investment we had no impression any measures contemplated so directly affecting US investment. . . . Dept extremely unhappy re these [sic] budget. . . . While we recognize Canadian anxiety over foreign investment we hope there will be full recognition of advantages to Canada such investment and consideration other less objectionable ways of accomplishing general goal."[18] Pearson urged Gordon to rescind the proposed 30 per cent takeover tax. On June 19, Gordon told the House the tax was out of the budget. But he did so before the markets closed, which permitted some investors to profit from the news.

"There is no doubt that it was too hastily produced and included some rather unfortunate proposals," Pearson wrote his friend William Spencer in Chicago about the budget, "even though the objectives which they were designed to serve were admirable ones, namely the reduction of our deficit through increased taxation and measures to increase Canadian ownership of Canadian industry."[19] Pearson's defence of Gordon was equally tepid in public. While in his memoirs he insists he backed his friend 100 per cent, the prime minister had Dick O'Hagan quietly poll the press gallery to see whether they wanted the minister's head. When Gordon did offer to resign, Pearson told him to stay on. But criticism of the budget continued, and Gordon was forced over the coming weeks to withdraw one measure after another. The finance minister was politically crippled, and never fully recovered. His friendship with Pearson never fully recovered, either. "Walter Gordon's pride was part of the collective pride of a complaisant and overconfident cabinet," wrote Denis Smith in his biography of Gordon. "But when the crisis came, most of its members, including the Prime Minister, neglected to share the Minister of Finance's humiliations."[20]

Canadian nationalists have lamented the failure of the 1963 budget in the same way British loyalists—those few that remain—lamented Diefenbaker's defeat over the Bomarc missiles. For the next two decades, progressives would warn against increasing American domination of the Canadian economy. Gordon's ideas would live on and find at least partial fulfillment in the governments of Pierre Trudeau, which introduced the Foreign Investment Review Act and the National Energy Program. The debate peaked in the political fight of 1988 over a proposed free trade agreement with the United States. But that agreement is no longer controversial, having been subsumed by the later North American Free Trade Agreement and by the onrush of globalization. Today, American domination of the Canadian economy no longer registers as a major concern for most Canadians; instead, governments fight to preserve access to the American market despite waves of protectionism from both Democratic and Republican administrations. In the struggle over the 1963 budget, Walter Gordon and his allies lost. They lost in the long run as well.

IV

Mike Pearson, like most of the rest of the world, learned of the assassination of John F. Kennedy through television. He went immediately to the House to inform its members. The House adjourned in silence. In a televised statement later that day to Canadians, the prime minister called the assassination "one of the great tragedies of history," a tragedy that was "heartbreaking, personal."[21]

John Diefenbaker was in his office as the television broadcast the news of the shooting in Dallas. When Walter Cronkite, taking off his glasses and wiping a tear from his eye, announced that the president was dead, the Chief stood silent, saying nothing. Diefenbaker had an opinion on everything, pronounced judgment on every passing event. But not this time. What was he thinking? He would not have wished such an end for any man, however bitterly they had fought. The United States was a violent society, even at the height of its power. No one had ever shot at a Canadian prime minister, though the FLQ had placed a bomb on a track his train would travel along. He may have thought that no political leader could predict their fate, or even what might happen that day.

Not many prime ministers adapt with grace to moving from 24 Sussex Drive to Stornoway. John and Olive were more successful than most, though they had to buy a washing machine and furniture with their own money. Olive got her driver's licence and John took a refresher course, although the government eventually provided a chauffeur. In a way, he was probably happier in opposition than in government. As much as he hated losing to the Grits, he could now concentrate on attacking them for their missteps, rather than constantly having to explain his own.

There were many who wanted him to step down, and with good reason. Diefenbaker had taken the party through four elections, the last of which he had lost. He was sixty-eight years old. His health was good, though his hearing loss was becoming apparent. Davie Fulton, having left the national party, was clearly hoping to return as its leader. George Hees had similar ambitions, despite having contributed to the government's defeat through his resignation. But others remained loyal and some returned to the fold. After a couple of meetings between Bassett and Diefenbaker, brokered by radio executives Ted Rogers Sr. and Jr., the *Toronto Telegram* swung back behind the Chief.

Dalton Camp also remained loyal. He had broken with his former friends, such as George Nowlan, when they conspired to bring the leader down before the election. He was convinced such a putsch, if successful, would estrange the party from government for a generation. Instead, he ran the 1963 campaign, conceiving the whistle-stop approach—speaking to supporters at stations from the back of a campaign train—that kept Diefenbaker among friendly crowds and out of hostile territory, which now included downtown Toronto. Diefenbaker's success at holding the party together and depriving the Liberals of a majority had earned him the right to continue as leader of the party, Camp believed. But Camp's mind was a subtle, baffling thing. Though he believed Diefenbaker still had the right to lead, he hoped he could be persuaded to resign. Camp was, in fact, working both sides of the street, stressing his loyalty when talking to Diefenbaker loyalists while quietly encouraging others to push for the leader's departure.

Things came to a head at the party's annual meeting in February 1964 in Ottawa. The PC student federation, led by the smart and ambitious Albertan (and future prime minister) Joe Clark, demanded a vote on the leadership by secret ballot. Diefenbaker beat back the motion with an impassioned plea for loyalty, which resulted in a near-unanimous show of hands in favour of his staying on. At the same meeting, Camp took over as national president. He was prepared to stick with Diefenbaker for one more election, for the sake of the party. But it was the party, not the leader, whom Camp served, something Diefenbaker never fully understood.

Meanwhile, Diefenbaker did his duty as Opposition leader, and opposed. He and Erik Nielsen, a fiercely partisan but principled MP from the Yukon Territory (whose brother Leslie would earn fame as an actor), eviscerated Walter Gordon and his budget. Diefenbaker kept up the pressure in the fall and winter sittings. He lambasted Mike Pearson's efforts to accommodate Quebec premier Jean Lesage's endless demands as appeasement that would lead to disunion. To forestall any accusations of francophobia, he appointed Léon Balcer as his Quebec lieutenant, seating him directly to his right in the House of Commons. The Liberals considered the Chief's attacks in the House to be excessive, wasteful, and damaging to national unity— Diefenbaker, for example, initially criticized the Liberal pension reforms, even though his own government had reformed and improved pensions. But the leader of Her Majesty's Loyal Opposition was simply fulfilling his role, and with the Liberals commanding only a minority government that survived mostly at the sufferance of the NDP, such opposition seemed prudent.

"The House was different then," remembered Jean Chrétien, many years later. Canada's twentieth prime minister arrived in the House in 1963, speaking little English, as the rookie member of Parliament for Saint-Maurice—Laflèche, which included his hometown of Shawinigan. In the years before House proceedings were broadcast, MPs debated each other based on their knowledge of the issue at hand and the subtle rules of Parliament. The Speaker permitted no notes in the House, so members were unable to parrot the talking points of political aides half their age, and instead had to think for themselves and on their feet. Diefenbaker, of course, was a natural. The courtroom lawyer had been in the House for almost a quarter century; the House was his home. He was on his feet constantly, accusing, berating, badgering. He badgered Pearson mercilessly. The prime minister, in contrast, had never been that comfortable in the House. He preferred quiet conversations to the cut-and-thrust of debate. The record in Hansard has him ably explaining his government's position in the face of the Opposition leader's attacks. The reality was different. As Chrétien remembered it, Pearson was ill at ease on the floor of the House: "When he was under pressure, he began to stutter."[22] It didn't help that Pickersgill and other members of the front bench, after so many years on the other side of the House, kept accidentally referring to Diefenbaker as "the prime minister."

For his part, Diefenbaker appeared to genuinely enjoy life as an Opposition leader. No one could bore more effectively into a hapless cabinet minister who didn't fully grasp his government's own policy, or embarrass a government tainted by the latest tawdry scandal. During one evening debate in 1964, Richard Cashin, then Liberal MP for St. John's West, tried to heckle Diefenbaker when he was in full stride. Diefenbaker turned dismissively to the chair and declared, "Mr. Speaker, when I am after big game, I don't waste my time on rabbit tracks."[23]

Still, even with his most effective rapier thrusts, Diefenbaker could not hide a truth that grew steadily more apparent in 1964. After a stumbling start, the Pearson government was starting to get the hang of governing.

V

There were a plethora of Canadian car companies at the turn of the twentieth century—mostly small outfits making a few cars at a time along with carriages for horses, though Sam McLaughlin's enterprise in Oshawa was a going concern, building cars under contract for Chevrolet. In 1918, when General Motors acquired Chevrolet, McLaughlin merged his operation with the ten-year-old company as well, creating General Motors of Canada. Ford was already established in Windsor. Canada adopted the same import-substitution model for automobiles as it had for everything else: high tariffs to protect domestic industry, which was dominated by branch plants of American companies. For a time, the Americans were happy to go along. By investing in Canadian plants, they could export into Commonwealth countries at a lower tariff rate than direct American exporters had to pay.

But by the 1950s, the model was breaking down. GM, Ford, and Chrysler now preferred to build branch plants in European and Commonwealth countries and sell directly into the markets. The gas-guzzlers that Canadians and Americans loved were impractical in Europe, so the Americans tailored their products to the local market. That left the Canadian auto industry with only the Canadian market to sell into. That market was small, the plants were inefficient, and wages were comparatively low. Canadians paid about 50 per cent more than Americans for a car, with only a limited number of makes available, unless they were willing to pay the tariff premium on an American import. Those imported American cars contributed to the country's worrying balance of payments deficit. A troubled industry contributed to a troubled economy.

In 1960, the Diefenbaker government asked the economist Vincent Bladen, then dean of the Faculty of Arts and Sciences at University of Toronto, to study the industry and recommend reforms. Bladen reached the obvious conclusion: to maximize the efficiencies of mass production, Canadian plants should focus on making only a few models of cars, and export those models to the United States. That meant lowering tariffs. The Conservatives undertook a modest reduction on certain car parts under certain circumstances. The results were so encouraging that the new Pearson government expanded the program when it took office in 1963. Another jump in exports resulted, and an improved balance of payments sheet. But now American parts manufacturers were beginning to notice. Acting on a complaint from the Modine Manufacturing Company, Treasury Department officials launched an investigation into Canadian auto exports. Those who knew the rules were certain the investigation would penalize Canada, severely damaging the industry.

At Pearson's request, President Lyndon Johnson told the Treasury Department to take a go-slow approach with its investigation while the two sides tried to hammer out a deal. The team leader on the Canadian side was Simon Reisman, deputy minister at Industry and Trade. Reisman grew up a working-class Jewish kid in Montreal, a few blocks and light years from Pierre Trudeau, who was the same age. Public high school led to McGill, a brief flirtation with socialism, and the loss of hearing in one ear after serving as an artillery officer in the war. All of this, coupled with a post-war stint at the London School of Economics (LSE), led to a deep understanding of the economics of trade, complemented by a rich vocabulary of swear words and a theatrically volcanic temper. During his years in the federal government, Reisman developed into a skilled negotiator, adept at the impossibly difficult task of negotiating trade agreements with the United States that were advantageous to Canada, a country one-tenth the size. He was mentored at the Department of Finance by the legendary economist John Deutsch, served on Walter Gordon's royal commission on foreign ownership, and by 1964 was deputy minister in the brand new Department of Industry. For the auto-industry negotiations, he headed a small team that included a young diplomat seconded from External Affairs, Allan Gotlieb.

Negotiations lasted through the summer and fall of 1964, taking place in out-of-the-way locations such as the Seigniory Club in Montebello. The American proposal was simple: Canada should drop all tariffs and embrace free trade in automobiles. But the Canadians feared the Americans would simply consolidate operations on their side of the border and Canada's automotive sector would evaporate. The solution, boiled down to its essence, permitted the American manufacturers to rationalize automobile production into a continental industry with virtually no border; in return, Ottawa secured the guarantee that at least as many cars would be made in Canada as were sold in Canada. The Canada–United States Automotive Products Agreement, quickly dubbed the Auto Pact, was a triumph for the Pearson government. Freed of tariff restrictions, automotive production soared in Ontario, practically doubling between 1964 and 1968. It would increase far beyond that in the years to come, creating a hundred thousand jobs by the mid-1970s. Canadian-owned parts manufacturers would emerge alongside and successfully compete with American-owned firms. Canada would use similar tariff-reduction inducements to lure Japanese manufacturers to Ontario as well. Ultimately, the success of the Auto Pact would lead to the free trade negotiations of the 1980s. Simon Reisman would lead those as well, with Allan Gotlieb a key figure as Canada's ambassador in Washington.

Mike Pearson let the new Department of Industry handle the Auto Pact negotiations. In general, like Diefenbaker, he encouraged his ministers to develop and implement policy in their own departments. But Pearson had advantages Diefenbaker lacked. For one, he arrived at the office of prime minister after decades in the public service as a diplomat, a cabinet minister, and finally, leader of his party. He had none of the learning curve Diefenbaker faced. Second, the Chief never had a Tom Kent: a senior adviser with a clear grasp of the domestic agenda and ambitious plans for reform. Diefenbaker derided Kent's powerful influence—"the leader of the leader," he called him—but he would have benefited from someone as able as Kent, though he likely would never have permitted an aide such influence. Pearson was happy to let Kent stickhandle relations between the Prime Minister's Office and the line departments, and between the federal and provincial governments. Finally, Pearson was a skilled negotiator, able to smooth the most difficult situation. He would need every ounce of that skill in the months ahead.

The prime minister had welcomed Jean Lesage's decision in 1958 to step down as an MP to lead the Liberal Party in Quebec. The two men were close: when Pearson was foreign minister, Lesage had served as his parliamentary secretary before becoming a minister himself (in Natural Resources and Northern Development). After defeating the Union Nationale in the 1960 election, Lesage had embarked on a broad program of social and economic reform. The prime minister looked forward to friendly relations with his former assistant: two Liberal leaders working cooperatively to guide the awakening of Quebec.

But Lesage was far from cooperative. At the urging of his natural resources minister, the former broadcaster René Lévesque, the premier vowed to nationalize electrical generation, calling and winning an election on the issue in 1962. "*Maîtres chez nous*" ("Masters in Our Own House") had become the party's rallying cry. The Liberals effectively nationalized the health and education systems as well, by stripping the Roman Catholic Church of responsibility for them. They undertook to guide development of the automotive and steel industries and directed investment through the newly created Société Générale de Financement and the Caisse de Dépôt et Placement du Québec. The latter agency was entrusted with investing pension contributions. And speaking of pensions, Lesage announced Quebec was withdrawing from the federal pension system. Pearson had proposed a major reform to the system during the 1958 election campaign, repeated that proposal during the 1962 campaign, and made it a hallmark of the 1963 campaign. It was one of the highest priorities of his new government. Now, before his plan was even ready to be unveiled, Quebec was opting out.

Prior to the Industrial Revolution, pensions did not exist. Husband and wife worked the farm, or he worked elsewhere and she in the home, until they were too feeble for work and the children became caregivers. But during the labour tumult of the late nineteenth century, a few employers began offering contributory pension plans, in part to keep peace on the shop floor, in part to convince older and less able workers to leave. By 1900, federal employees, railway workers, and workers at some banks enjoyed a form of workplace pension. Civic unrest—especially the Winnipeg General Strike—and compassion for veterans brought about the first federal pensions for the disabled and for survivors of those who had been lost in combat. Only the very poor—who had to endure a humiliating means test—qualified for the first old age pension, in the late 1920s. In 1951, the St. Laurent government convinced the provinces, which had jurisdiction over pensions, to agree to a constitutional amendment bringing about the first guaranteed payments for all seniors over seventy, First Nations excluded. While the Diefenbaker government enhanced the Old Age Security allowance, poverty remained a chronic threat for seniors, especially for the 60 per cent of workers who didn't have a workplace pension plan. Both economists and social reformers argued for a national pension plan to which both workers and employers would contribute, and which would greatly increase income stability after retirement.

The Liberal government's first throne speech promised "to establish a comprehensive system of contributory pensions" that would permit "all Canadians to retire in security and with dignity."[24] While Pearson was happy to delegate authority, counting on Tom Kent; Gordon Robertson, the new clerk of the Privy Council; and Walter Gordon to run the day-to-day affairs of government, he made it clear that crafting a new pension was one of his top priorities.

Opposition was formidable. The insurance industry, of course, fought it tooth and nail. Walter Gordon's shemozzle of a budget made their argument that governments didn't understand how the pension system worked seem reasonable. But the biggest problem was Quebec nationalism, which Premier Jean Lesage was losing any ability to constructively channel. The chain-smoking René Lévesque demanded more and more autonomy for Quebec and more and more government control over the economy. Lesage responded by demanding greater autonomy from Ottawa, even as he rapidly expanded the welfare state, which included a made-in-Quebec contributary pension plan.

In August 1963, as a busman's holiday, Tom Kent and his wife drove to Quebec City, where they met Gordon Robertson and his wife, returning from New Brunswick. The meeting between the two men and Lesage was cordial but frustrating. The premier was determined to proceed with a Quebec Pension Plan financed by contributions from workers and employers. Nothing that Ottawa proposed would stop him.

The Pearson government could have left each province to develop a pension plan of its own—John Robarts in Ontario had already announced his Progressive Conservative government's intention to do just that. In the meantime, Ottawa could simply have boosted payments to Old Age Security to protect the most vulnerable. But such an approach appealed neither to Ottawa nor to many provinces. The poorer jurisdictions wouldn't be able to count on workers and employers having the resources to finance their plans. A patchwork of provincial plans would raise questions of equity and portability. And raising taxes to pay for increases to the OAS would make the fiscal imbalance between the federal and provincial governments even worse. Before the war, Ottawa and the provincial government each accounted for about half of all taxes raised. During the war, Ottawa acquired almost exclusive taxing authority. After the war, despite the arrival of equalization and other measures, Ottawa still collected better than 60 per cent of taxes and the provinces less than 40 per cent. But the needs—from sewers to public transit to subsidized housing to you-name-it—were in provincial jurisdiction.

Pearson favoured an approach based on what he called cooperative federalism, in which the federal government would assist the provincial governments in delivering services. In the case of the new pension plan, Quebec would have one plan, the rest of Canada another, which Ottawa would administer. The Canada Pension Plan would be pay-as-you-go, with premiums meeting only the needs of existing retirees. The premiums would increase as the number of retirees increased. (American Social Security operates in this way.) The first ministers would negotiate the details at a federal–provincial conference slated for the first week of April 1964 in Quebec City. That week, Tom Kent later remembered, was "the most miserable week I ever experienced."[25]

Protesters—students and others—besieged the Quebec capital with placards denouncing Lesage as "Ottawa's valet" and "the Queen's fool." The police presence was oppressive. Federal and provincial politicians and officials felt as though they were trapped in the building where the conference was being held. And the tension inside was scarcely better.

On his own turf, Lesage became not so much host of the conference as chief prosecutor. In every conceivable way, the Pearson government was infringing on Quebec's jurisdictions, he fumed. Student loans! Family allowances! These were Quebec responsibilities! What had become of the British North America Act? And then, behind closed doors, he delivered the *coup de grâce*: a detailed outline of the Quebec Pension Plan, which had not yet been submitted to the National Assembly. The Quebec plan delivered appreciably larger pensions than the federal plan. It included survivor and disability benefits that the federal plan lacked. Rather than relying on pay-as-you-go, pension contributions would be vested in a fund, which would generate large surpluses for many years that could be used by governments to pay for schools and hospitals and the social infrastructure of the new welfare state. The federal plan was a pale shadow in comparison. Other provinces said they would only go along with the federal plan if Ontario joined. But Premier John Robarts was inclined to opt for a made-in-Ontario plan. The conference was a failure, the federal plan was toast, and more Quebecers were asking themselves what practical good it did to remain part of a broken country.

The Liberals returned to Ottawa in a dismal mood. Lesage was now certain to introduce a Quebec pension plan independent of any Canadian plan. He would also be forced to hike taxes to pay for the expensive commitments of the Quiet Revolution. That could lead to his defeat in the next election, and who knew what might come after that? The federal Liberals also faced defeat, having compounded the failures of Walter Gordon's first budget with the failure of the Canada Pension Plan.

But there was a way forward. Even as Lesage flayed the Liberals in public over federal interference in Quebec affairs, he was privately pleading with his former federal colleagues to find a way out of the impasse. As soon as they got back to Ottawa, Gordon Robertson and Tom Kent set to work. They needed both to provide Quebec and the other provinces with the resources needed to carry out their social infrastructure programs, and to rescue the pension plan. The two men quickly put together a memorandum and brought it to Pearson. First, Ottawa would begin a series of tax point transfers: reducing federal taxes while inviting the provinces to raise their taxes by an equivalent amount. The taxpayer would notice no difference, but the provinces would have greater resources to spend on social programs. Second, to overcome Quebec's objection to new federal programs, such as student loans, Ottawa would "contract out" administration of the programs to provincial governments. Third, the Liberals would scrap the federal pension scheme and adopt Quebec's plan, which was better designed, more generous, fully funded, and which offered reserve funds for public investment. Kent and Robertson urged Pearson to give them permission to return to Quebec City with the new proposal. Pearson, though skeptical, told them to go ahead.

When he saw the new federal proposal, Lesage embraced it. Federal and provincial teams went immediately to work, grafting bits of the federal program onto the Quebec program until the two pension plans were so identical that Quebec eventually used the English version of the Canada Pension Plan as the English-language version of the Quebec Pension Plan. That was the easy part. The hard part would be overcoming opposition within the federal government to the erosion of federal control over taxation, while convincing the Ontario government to buy into the federal scheme. This is when Lester B. Pearson became a great prime minister.

First, he convened his inner cabinet: Walter Gordon, Guy Favreau, Maurice Lamontagne, Paul Martin, Allan MacEachen, and Mitchell Sharp. (Jack Pickersgill was out of town.) He told them he was completely convinced that adopting the Quebec Pension Plan was the only way to save the Canada Pension Plan; that Ottawa had to surrender some of its taxing power to the provinces, who needed the money more; that Ottawa had to become more the servant and less the master of the provinces; that hold-ing on to the status quo could wreck the country and, incidentally, their hopes for re-election. They would be attacked for selling out to Quebec. They would be attacked for selling out to the other provinces. But there was no other way.

He convinced them. Most important, he convinced Walter Gordon. The finance minister was still recovering from the self-inflicted wounds of the 1963 budget. He would bear the brunt of the criticism of the plan from within the government itself, from officials who would consider the sur-render of taxing authority a betrayal. But Gordon also wanted a national pension plan, and he wanted the government to survive. After a brief period of reflection, he gave the plan his full support.

The next obstacle was John Robarts. The Ontario premier was leaning strongly toward creating a provincial pension plan. Because of its manu-facturing strength, an Ontario pension plan would be more generous, and produce larger reserves, than the Quebec plan. At the least, Ontario expected to play a major role in shaping the national plan. Now Robarts was being offered a federal *fait accompli*, a clear rebuff to the largest and richest prov-ince in Confederation. The other provinces would follow Ontario's lead. But what would that lead be?

With his square jaw, clipped moustache, and aura of energy and com-petence, Robarts resembled a corporate executive, a breed he greatly admired. "I'm a management man myself," he once said. "This is the era of the management man. . . . I'm a complete product of the times."[26] He was part of a generation that had been raised in the Depression and tested by the Second World War, a generation of big ambitions that embraced big busi-ness, big government—even, reluctantly, big labour. Robarts understood the advantages of a national portable plan, and the threat to national unity if that plan failed. But Ontario premiers were used to being first—or tied for first with Quebec—among equals in federal–provincial relations. Now it was clear that Ottawa and Quebec City were dancing alone.

For months, he refused to commit himself, as the pension plan came under assault from the Diefenbaker Conservatives, who accused the govern-ment of selling out to Quebec. Robarts was a Progressive Conservative premier, so there was political pressure as well to align with his federal cousins. But the premier of Ontario is as important to preserving national unity as the prime minister, and Robarts knew the obligation he bore. On November 5, he and Pearson met. The prime minister used every art of persuasion to convince the premier to hold fire on an Ontario pension plan. The result was a non-aggression pact. Robarts would not support the federal plan, but he would not reject it either. Instead, he would watch the implementing legislation's progress through a parliamentary committee in which the opposition parties would hold the majority, and which would feature extensive testimony from witnesses. Then he would decide.

As it turned out, the bill sailed through the committee. The idea of a national pension plan was so popular that the Conservatives on the committee ended up switching from complaining the legislation went too far to complaining it didn't go far enough. It was soon clear that Robarts didn't need to wait for the committee to complete its work. In January 1965, he announced Ontario would support the Canada Pension Plan, removing the final obstacle. The legislation cleared the Senate on April 3.

Jean Lesage became the inadvertent architect of the Canada Pension Plan by agreeing to work cooperatively with Ottawa to harmonize that plan with his province's own. John Robarts deserves great credit for putting the national interest above parochial considerations in signing on to the plan. And Lester Pearson deserves to be known as the father of the CPP, for his relentless championing of it during the years of opposition, for his determination to preserve it after the debacle in Quebec, and for the skilled diplomacy at which he excelled that brought it home.

He only put one foot wrong, though the results were nearly disastrous. Pearson failed to consult health and welfare minister Judy LaMarsh, even though pensions were the responsibility of her department. When LaMarsh first learned of the agreement between Ottawa and Quebec City, through second-hand sources, she was so furious she prepared a letter of resignation, which could have wrecked everything. As Tom Kent entered her office, she recalled, "I was so angry I picked up the autographed photo of Pearson that stood on my desk and slammed it face down. The long shards of smashed glass skittered across the desk, reflecting back the angry glare I turned on the innocent Kent."[27] But Kent, after profusely apologizing, convinced her not to resign, and LaMarsh soon became an effective public champion of the accord.

Had the Pearson government achieved nothing else, it would have been well remembered by posterity for giving Canada a national contributory pension plan. That plan did not emerge from the ether. It built upon pensions first implemented by Robert Borden, expanded by Mackenzie King, given real scope by Louis St. Laurent, and made more generous by John Diefenbaker. Further, the move to transfer tax points to the provinces to help them fund social programs built on equalization and revenue-sharing agreements established and then expanded by the St. Laurent and Diefenbaker governments. It does not in any way diminish Pearson's accomplishment to remember that he was building on the work of others. They made it possible, but it was Mike Pearson who took the chance, who persuaded the cabinet, who kept John Robarts from quitting the game. That took courage.

VI

Quebec transformed from a cloistered, Catholic, and closed society to one more secular, open, and confident with astonishing speed. But for the rest of Canada, there were worrying signs. Polls showed a solid minority of Quebecers were inclined toward some form of sovereignty for Quebec. Donald Gordon only made things worse. The president of Montreal-based Canadian National Railways was asked during testimony before a Commons committee why there were no francophones in the railway company's senior management. French Canadians didn't have the requisite skills, he replied. Université de Montréal student union president (and future premier) Bernard Landry led the storm of protests that followed. Lesage, with a cabinet that now contained separatists, tried to stay on top of the tumult. He demanded that Quebec be allowed to opt out of any federal program that intruded into Quebec's jurisdiction, with full federal compensation. Could the federation survive such an accommodation?

In one sense, Pearson was in his element; in another, he was lost. Negotiating with foreign governments had been his life's work; if the province of Quebec was hardly that, it was distinct enough to be treated like one. The reconciliation of English and French Canada would be a fitting final achievement for the architect of the Food and Agriculture Organization of the United Nations and the hero of the Suez Crisis. But as Pearson himself ruefully admitted, he couldn't conjugate *avoir*. He had been raised in Ontario and had spent much of his adult life outside the country. External Affairs, especially in its early years, had behaved like a private club for English gentlemen. How could Pearson, a man now in his upper sixties, hope to understand what was driving the Québécois?

Like Diefenbaker, Pearson first responded to a public policy challenge by studying it, in this case through the Royal Commission on Bilingualism and Biculturalism—the B&B Commission—chaired by *La Presse* editor-in-chief André Laurendeau and Davidson Dunton, a former journalist and chairman of the CBC. Although the commission didn't publish the final volume of its report until 1969, a preliminary report in 1965 sounded an alarm: "Canada," the commissioners wrote, "without being fully conscious of the fact, is passing through the greatest crisis in its history."[28] Quebec's future within the federation was uncertain, unless all Canadians moved meaningfully to embrace the foundational principle that the country was an equal partnership between French and English, with the former accorded the respect they deserved.

Many, including Mike Pearson, accepted this core assertion, but many others did not. In Quebec, people like René Lévesque and Bernard Landry were increasingly convinced that the only realistic future for Quebec included sovereignty. In the rest of Canada, soon to be known as ROC, many objected to the sudden elevation of Quebec as a unique presence, and of French as equal to English in political and social status. For them, the result of the Battle of the Plains of Abraham had been conclusive. Canada was a predominantly English-speaking nation, and Quebec was a province like any other. Turning the aspirations of the Québécois into the dominant political issue of the day offended them. What was Quebec to Saskatchewan, or Saskatchewan to Quebec?

While the B&B Commission got underway, Pearson's more immediate concern was to find a Quebec lieutenant, someone who could speak to the province on behalf of the government and interpret the complexities of Quebec politics to the prime minister. At first, he relied on his old friend Lionel Chevrier, who had been a good and faithful servant for many years. But Chevrier was a Franco-Ontarian, and almost as old as Pearson himself. Beyond that, Chevrier represented and protected the Liberal Party in Quebec, an interconnecting web of patronage and political protection whose activities did not always bear close scrutiny. Pearson eventually sent his friend to London as high commissioner. Maurice Sauvé was eminently qualified to replace him as Quebec lieutenant, with his PhD from Université de Paris, his background in labour relations, and his close association with the economic architects of the Quiet Revolution. But Sauvé's pugnacious demands for immediate reform, combined with his relentless self-promotion—especially through leaks to the press—rendered him unpopular within caucus, especially among the Quebec old guard. Kent quite disliked him. Maurice Lamontagne, a distinguished economist and federal public servant who won the riding of Outremont—St. Jean in 1963, should have been in the running. Both intellectual and sophisticated, he had bravely fought the Duplessis regime at a time when such opposition entailed risk. But he had shown poor political instincts; had alienated the Lesage government by pushing the new Canada Student Loan Program, which provided financial assistance for university students from low-income families; and had managed to lose the confidence of both the Old Guard and reformers. That left Guy Favreau.

A brilliant Montreal lawyer, Favreau entered the public service in 1952, ultimately serving as Davie Fulton's assistant deputy minister. But he was a Liberal at heart, part of the new generation of Québécois who sought to wrest greater powers for the province, in part by patriating and amending the Constitution, which still could be amended only by a British act of Parliament. Favreau won a seat in Parliament in the 1963 election in the Montreal riding of Papineau. (Decades later, Justin Trudeau would represent the same riding.) Through a March 1964 cabinet shuffle, Pearson decided to make Favreau the face of the Liberal Party in Quebec, appointing him as justice minister, House leader, and Quebec leader.

The early months seemed promising. After slightly tweaking the work of his Conservative predecessor and former boss, Davie Fulton, the new justice minister proposed an amending formula for the Constitution that quickly became known as the Fulton-Favreau formula. Under the formula, Parliament would require the unanimous consent of the provinces before it could amend the Constitution in areas that affected their powers, or that involved areas of education or official languages. Any other amendments would require the consent of seven provinces representing at least 50 per cent of the population. Amendments that affected some but not all provinces would require the consent of the provinces involved. Favreau and Pearson secured unanimous consent for the amending formula at a federal–provincial conference in the fall of 1964. For a brief and shining moment, it looked as though Fulton-Favreau might carry the day. A century after the original agreement in Charlottetown to form a federation, that federation would have its own Constitution, one that protected and advanced the rights of Quebec within Canada, and of the English-speaking provinces as well.

It was not to be. Though the formula was almost identical to the one Davie Fulton had proposed three years earlier, John Diefenbaker decided to oppose it. Tommy Douglas was also offside, fearing that the need for unanimity would stifle future reforms in social policy. Some critics thought the amending formula gave the provinces too much power; some French Canadians feared the other provinces would gang up on Quebec to thwart its efforts for increased powers in the areas of taxation, pensions, and immigration. Lesage, initially supportive, withdrew his support, effectively killing the proposal. Fulton-Favreau would ultimately become the basis of the amending formula incorporated into the Constitution Act of 1982. But by the winter of 1965, it was clear that the Constitution would not be coming home anytime soon. And by then, Favreau and Pearson had bigger problems to contend with.

It started with the Hal Banks affair. In 1949, the American union leader had been invited to come to Canada—most likely with the blessing of the St. Laurent government—with a mission to break the power of the communist-controlled Canadian Seaman's Union, which was causing shipping companies on the Great Lakes endless grief. As the new head of the Canadian district of the Seafarer's International Union, Banks quickly expelled the communists, and if some heads were busted in the process, people looked the other way. The cure, however, turned out to be worse than the disease. Banks exercised corrupt and dictatorial control over his union; anyone who crossed him ended up roughed up, or worse. He also began challenging other unions, bringing him into conflict with the Canadian Labour Congress. By 1962, intra-union violence and labour strife had both shipowners and union leaders demanding that Banks be reined in. The Diefenbaker government responded by appointing yet another inquiry, this one led by B.C. Court of Appeal judge T.C. Norris. His report, which accused Banks of a raft of indictable offences, landed in the Pearson government's lap in the fall of 1963. The government moved to have Banks fired and the union placed in trusteeship. But now Diefenbaker was accusing the Liberals of having a longstanding cozy relationship with Banks. It didn't help that, after being charged and granted bail, Banks skipped the country and efforts to extradite him went nowhere—proof, the Tories claimed, that Banks and the Grits were in tight. The accusation was outrageous, but it did the government's reputation no favours.

There was a problem with the Liberal Party of Canada in Quebec. It was, in essence, a machine, charged with delivering votes during elections and sending Liberal members of Parliament to Ottawa. It was quasi-independent of the federal party and had no connection, formal or ideological, with Jean Lesage's Quebec Liberal Party, whose reformist bent the federal Grits in Quebec found off-putting. Their main aim was to use their powers of patronage to reward themselves and those like them. This got them into trouble.

Postmaster General Azellus Denis retired to the Senate after revelations he had appointed a bevy of defeated Liberal candidates from Quebec as "consultants." Yvon Dupuis, made secretary of state in February 1964, resigned in 1965 after being accused of accepting a bribe related to the licensing of a racetrack in his riding. Both Maurice Lamontagne and Immigration Minister René Tremblay took possession of furniture from a dealer who never bothered to charge them. (The dealer subsequently went bankrupt, and no wonder.) The government, it seemed, lurched from petty scandal to petty scandal, all of them involving Quebec ministers, all of them embarrassing the government. Then came the Rivard affair, which destroyed Guy Favreau and almost brought down the government.

In the summer of 1964, Lucien Rivard languished in a Montreal jail as the United States government sought his extradition on charges of smuggling heroin. The charge was grave, but not unexpected. Squat, brawny, possessed of a zest for life and a wry sense of humour, Rivard had been in trouble with the law since he was convicted of breaking into a storage shed at the tender age of seventeen. He worked his way up the criminal food chain in the 1940s, then hightailed it to Cuba, where he operated casinos and ran guns for Fidel Castro. By the 1960s, he was back in Montreal, back in trouble, and back in jail. Then the strangest things started happening.

Pierre Lamontagne, the lawyer representing the United States government in the extradition proceedings, received an urgent message from his friend Raymond Denis, executive assistant to Immigration Minister René Tremblay, to come to Ottawa immediately. That evening, Denis offered a bribe of twenty thousand dollars if Lamontagne would not oppose the granting of bail for Rivard. The reasonable assumption was that Rivard would skip bail, *à la* Hal Banks. When Lamontagne asked why Denis cared so much about Rivard, the political aide explained that the gangster had been very generous in his donations to the Liberal Party, and that if he were released on bail, he and several of his associates would be more generous still.

After Lamontagne refused the bribe, he received a call from Guy Lord, a twenty-five-year-old special assistant to Favreau, who said he was acting on behalf of the minister, wanting to know why there was a problem with Rivard's bail. André Letendre, Favreau's executive assistant, called as well. Guy Rouleau, a Montreal MP whose brother was a friend of Rivard, also got into the act. Rouleau happened to be one of Pearson's parliamentary secretaries. The message for Lamontagne was clear: a great deal of government work might or might not land on his desk, depending on whether he opposed Rivard's bail request.

Lamontagne went to the RCMP. By the middle of August, Denis was being interrogated by police. Favreau, once he was informed of the allegations, ordered a full investigation of everyone involved, including his two assistants. But the justice minister waited until September 2 to tell Pearson of the investigation, even though that investigation involved Pearson's own parliamentary secretary. When police presented their report to Favreau in late September, he concluded that the uncorroborated word of Lamontagne was insufficient grounds for criminal charges. Favreau made that decision without having read through and considered all of the evidence placed before him, and without consulting Crown attorneys or other advisers in his office.

He was, in his defence, grievously overworked. Pearson should never have asked a rookie MP to take on the onerous task of being House leader as well as justice minister and Quebec lieutenant. "We thought he was a superman," Judy LaMarsh recollected. "I've never heard anyone as brilliant as he was around the cabinet table on almost any subject. . . . He lifted the whole cabinet. He was the heart and soul of it. And you could just see him over the years getting beaten down with too much work and too many problems."[29] Did the stress of his many duties lead to a rash and premature judgment? Or was he simply trying to protect his staff, a member of his caucus, and the Liberal Party? Whatever his motives, Favreau should have known that word would leak out.

On November 23, Tommy Douglas asked in the House whether Favreau was aware of any allegations of impropriety surrounding the extradition case of one Lucien Rivard. Clearly the NDP leader had some of the goods. Erik Nielsen had all of them. That same day he told the House of the alleged bribe by Denis, of pressure from all quarters on Lamontagne, of Favreau's solitary decision not to prosecute. Nielsen was offering some of the most explosive and incriminating evidence ever submitted to the House of Commons. "These tentacles of this international cartel dealing in narcotics extended to the very offices of two ministers of the federal government," he declared.[30] The House, the press, the country were in a furore.

Pearson immediately convened a judicial inquiry headed by Robert Dorion, chief justice of the Quebec Superior Court. It took Dorion seven months to reach his conclusion. The testimony riveted the political class, exposing the close and seamy connections between the Liberal Party in Quebec and organized crime. To make matters worse, Pearson told the House he had only heard about the allegations surrounding his now-fired parliamentary secretary in November. In fact, Favreau had mentioned it to him briefly in September, and so Pearson had, however inadvertently, misled the House. He waited until the middle of December to correct the record, which only fuelled the accusations of a cover-up and left Favreau twisting in political agony, unable to tell the House and the world that he had informed his prime minister of the situation much earlier than Pearson had let on.

And that wasn't the half of it.

The weather was unseasonably warm on March 4, 1965, when Rivard asked for and received permission to flood the jail's skating rink. He and an associate used the hose and a ladder to climb over the fence and escape. It took police four months to find him. In the meantime, Rivard wrote letters to public figures, including Pearson—"Life is short, you know. I don't intend to be in jail for the rest of my life"—deriding their futile efforts to send him to the United States.[31] The Conservatives crucified the Liberals over the Rivard affair. In sweltering meeting halls that summer, Diefenbaker, eyes gleaming, jowls quivering, would say while removing his suit jacket, "You know, it was on an evening much like this that Lucien Rivard was sent out to flood the prison rink."[32] This episode, coupled with the raft of resignations and scandals all involving Quebec ministers, led Peter Newman to conclude, "The Ministers Lester Pearson relied on to represent French Canada inspired, both within and without the Province of Quebec, disappointment, disbelief, despair and, not infrequently, laughter."[33]

No one was laughing when Dorion produced his report on June 28, 1965, which minutely chronicled every misdeed surrounding Rivard's bail application, leaving no doubt that, in his opinion, many crimes had been committed, including the crimes of perjury by several witnesses who had appeared before him. As for Favreau: "The Honourable the Minister of Justice, before reaching a decision, should have submitted the case to the legal advisers within his Department with instructions to complete the search for facts if necessary and secured their views upon the possible perpetration of a criminal offence by one or several of the persons involved."[34] Pearson accepted Favreau's resignation. But he kept him in cabinet in a largely ceremonial role and kept him as Quebec lieutenant. It didn't matter. Favreau's reputation was shattered. He died of heart failure in 1967, his health and spirit broken. "Guy Favreau was the most brilliant Quebec MP of the time," said Jules Deschênes, who had represented Favreau during the inquiry. "I'm certain the scandal killed him."[35]

The blindness of Liberals, then and later, to the seriousness of the Rivard affair seems astonishing. Jack Pickersgill accused Erik Nielsen of turning "a trivial matter into an apparent scandal."[36] Tom Kent in his memoirs dismissed the affair as a "sordid little matter."[37] From the vantage point of the present, the remarkable thing is that the government survived. Senior ministerial aides in the Justice and Immigration departments and the prime minister's own parliamentary secretary had sought to bribe and pressure a lawyer into letting a mobster out on bail—on the implicit understanding that he was likely to skip that bail—because he contributed generously to the Liberal Party in Quebec. Forty years later, a scandal involving payments to the Liberal Party in Quebec linked to federal sponsorship of events that never occurred contributed to the defeat of Prime Minister Paul Martin Jr.'s government. Allegations in 2019 that Prime Minister Justin Trudeau had pressed his attorney general to agree to a deferred prosecution of the engineering firm SNC Lavalin helped reduce that government from majority to minority status in the next election. And what were either of those two scandals compared to the Rivard affair?

The real problem was with the Liberal Party itself in Quebec. While the provincial party, having broken completely with its federal counterparts, pursued an aggressive program of modernization and reform, the federal Liberals continued in the tired, often corrupt, old ways of exchanging patronage and other favours for votes.

The Liberal scandals in Quebec alienated English-Canadian sentiment. To many, it seemed that Quebec was making extraordinary demands for something approaching self-government, even as the province's political culture wallowed in corruption. This wasn't fair or true. But it made Pearson's job of reconciling Quebec's demands with his own government's reformist ambitions even more difficult.

VII

"Your government is weak and disorganized, because it depends on you and you are making it impossible for yourself to be a good Prime Minister," Tom Kent wrote his boss in June 1964, in a scathing memo that urged a thorough reorganization of the Prime Minister's Office.[38] That reorganization should perhaps have included the resignation of an aide who was becoming destructive in his criticism. Walter Gordon believed the low morale inside the government could be blamed on Pearson's habit of changing policies after they had been announced, and on relying too heavily on Kent and Robertson, while ignoring his ministers. "This lack of team spirit has led and could continue to lead to trouble," he warned.[39] Diefenbaker was a relentless critic in the House, centring both on corruption and on what he saw as Pearson's pandering to Quebec interests, at the expense of a united Canada. It was true that the Liberal government, once a powerful force for centralization within the federation, was sloughing off jurisdiction and revenue in an effort to accommodate Quebec's aspirations. Lesage told Pearson that he had a bear by the tail and couldn't let go. Some members of the Quebec cabinet, especially René Lévesque, had become outright separatists. Pearson himself seemed to proceed from one cold to another, and spent an increasing amount of time in Florida, far from the Canadian climate and his tormenters, especially the leader of the official opposition.

In the midst of the internal criticism, the succession of scandal-forced resignations, the tortured negotiations with the provinces, the prime minister clung to one determined goal: a new flag for Canada. He had advocated for one for decades, had seen Nasser prohibit Canadian peacekeepers because they wore the British ensign, had committed to a new, national flag in the 1962 and 1963 election manifestos. On May 17, 1964, in Winnipeg, he announced his intention to introduce a new national flag. In his resolve to act, Pearson showed a courage and strength of will for which his own advisers gave him too little credit.

He wore his service medals on that day as he stood before more than two thousand Legion members, the most hostile audience he could possibly have chosen. Millions of Canadians were not of British descent, he told them, and felt no emotional commitment to the Union Jack on the Canadian Red Ensign, the red flag with the Union Jack in the upper left and the coat-of-arms of Canada on the right that had been increasingly in use as Canada's flag. Five million and counting were neither British nor French in origin, he reminded them. All Canadians, from wherever they or their ancestors hailed, deserved "a Canadian flag as distinctive as the maple leaf in the Legion badge" that would "make us all better and more united Canadians."[40] Some shouted "No," some booed, some jeered, a few applauded politely. But he persevered. "It is time now for Canadians, in the course of our national evolution, to unfurl a flag that is truly distinctive and truly national in character," a flag that was "Canada's own and only Canada's."

He favoured a design that included three maple leaves on a white background, with vertical blue bars at each end representing the Atlantic and Pacific oceans. Cabinet was skeptical about the need to take on the challenge, but after the Winnipeg speech there was no turning back, and on June 15, Pearson rose to defend the new flag legislation in the House of Commons. In "these restless, soul-searching days," Canada needed a "symbol of national identity, national pride, national loyalty," he told the House. A flag based on the maple leaf would provide that identity, would "say proudly to the future and the world, 'I stand for Canada.'"[41]

Diefenbaker, in response, accused Pearson of "trying to separate this nation from the past" and called the new design "innocuous and insipid." "A flag cannot be something that is ordered by Parliament," he maintained. "A flag must be something to evoke the emotions of the heart, a rallying point for the finer sentiments of the people joined together in a nation."[42] He demanded a plebiscite before any flag was adopted.

Pearson had no intention of submitting the flag to a referendum, and no intention of bowing to the filibuster that the Conservatives promptly launched. If they wanted to paralyze the House of Commons, so be it. The House would sit through the summer. The lack of air conditioning could make the chamber insufferable on hot, humid days, but the Conservatives persisted. There were divisions in the Tory ranks, though, as Léon Balcer searched for a compromise. The general feeling in Quebec toward the flag debate was one of indifference, with the single proviso that if a new flag were adopted, the Union Jack must be nowhere on it. The Créditistes were with the government on the flag issue, while Tommy Douglas's NDP urged moderation and delay.

By September, it was clear that the determination of Conservatives—at least those outside Quebec—to continue the filibuster had defeated the Liberals. It was also clear that the Pearson Pennant, as Diefenbaker derisively referred to the prime minister's preferred design, was dead in the water. So that Parliament could continue its work, all sides agreed to assign the flag question to a parliamentary committee, which was given six weeks to come up with a satisfactory design. The committee looked at thousands of suggestions, by artists ranging from schoolchildren to Group of Seven painter A.Y. Jackson, but nothing appealed to both Liberals, who insisted the Union Jack be off the flag, and Conservatives, who insisted it be on it. The committee was heading toward gridlock, until John Matheson, a Liberal MP who had advised Pearson on the flag and who sat on the committee, remembered a letter he had been sent by George Stanley, a military historian who was dean of arts at Royal Military College (RMC). Back in March, Stanley had argued for a flag with a single maple leaf flanked by red bars. Red and white were the sole colours of the maple leaves on the

Canadian coat of arms, while the RMC flag included two vertical red bars. "The one-leaf design with the vertical red bars had an elegant simplicity that pleased Matheson," Rick Archbold wrote in his history of the flag debate. "Here, he thought, was a compromise that a majority of committee members might accept."[43]

On the morning of October 20, the exhausted committee members met to vote on the finalists: a collection of three-leaf designs; a collection of one-leaf designs; a collection of designs that included symbols from other countries (the Union Jack and fleur-de-lis). After a series of votes, the finalists were the Pearson Pennant, Stanley's one-leaf design, and a third that included the maple leaf, the Union Jack, and the fleur-de-lis. The Conservatives, determined to sabotage what they thought would be the Liberals' choice of the Pearson Pennant, voted for Stanley's design. To their chagrin, the Liberals voted for the Stanley design as well, and so did Social Credit and the NDP. It was unanimous. Four furious Conservatives switched their vote, and so the committee sent an unrefined version of the flag we have today back to the House on a vote of ten to four. Designers spent November working on the final look—reducing the number of points on the maple leaf from thirteen to eleven; fixing on the right shade of red. On November 30, final debate on the legislation on the flag got underway. Diefenbaker was determined to prevent its passage, and so were many, though not all, MPs in the Conservative caucus. The language got ugly and personal, with the Speaker unable to control the House. But Diefenbaker had overestimated the loyalty of his caucus, many of whom had become sickened by the fight. Léon Balcer brought that mutiny out in the open when he urged the Liberals to invoke closure. That's exactly what the government did. On December 15, in the early hours of the morning, the legislation passed the House, while MPs sang "O Canada" and "God Save the Queen" in competition.

Two months later to the day, on a cold and damp February noon hour, the Canadian Red Ensign was lowered from a flagstaff in front of the Peace Tower, as politicians, dignitaries, and a surprisingly large crowd looked on. Three non-commissioned officers, representing each service, bore the new standard, and raised it. At the end of the twenty-one-gun salute, a gust of wind sent the new flag snapping in the breeze against the blue sky. John Diefenbaker wouldn't look at it. He lowered his head and wept.

TWELVE

Swings and Roundabouts

(1965–1966)

I

A thol Murray was a good man. The Catholic priest had established Notre Dame of the Prairies College, which gave an education to any boy or girl whether the family could pay or not, and which became a hockey powerhouse. (More than a few of the Notre Dame Hounds have gone on to play in the NHL.) But like many Catholics of the time, Father Murray believed that charity began at the altar—that the church should provide social services, not the state. He fought so fiercely against the introduction of "socialized medicine" in Saskatchewan that during the 1962 strike by doctors opposing medicare, he warned, "This thing may break into violence and bloodshed any day now, and God help us if it doesn't."[1]

The strike lasted twenty-three days before the doctors gave up and went back to work. The agrarian province had a deep tradition of communal welfare—each looking after the other in a hard, forbidding land. As far back as 1916, the provincial government had passed legislation enabling municipalities to pool resources to hire a doctor. The province extended what became known as medicare to pensioners and widows in 1945 and introduced universal public hospital care in 1947, a decade before the Diefenbaker government made the program national. Despite a big-money campaign to defeat him—American as well as Canadian insurance companies and medical associations poured money into the campaign—the province's voters returned Douglas to office with a solid majority on June 8, 1960. A little over two years later, on July 1, 1962, Saskatchewan became the first jurisdiction in North America with universal public health care, which prompted the doctors' strike.

That strike was undermined by hostile public opinion, doctors who stayed on the job, and doctors who were brought in to provide services. (A socialist government employed strike-breakers!) Even the *Globe and Mail*, voice of the commercial and professional classes, condemned the strike, to the surprise and consternation of many. The paper had resolutely opposed violence and intimidation during strikes, the editorial board reminded its readers. "The doctors have not indulged in acts of violence in Saskatchewan, but the passive resistance they have instituted is the worst form of violence that could be perpetrated," the paper declared. "Except for the emergency staffs of thirty-four hospitals, they have left the sick and the injured without medical care, they have exposed those people to permanent disability and death."[2] The doctors asked for negotiations; the province made some concessions; the strike was over. Medicare was secure in Saskatchewan. When Ross Thatcher's Liberals confronted the tired CCF government in the next election, they won by promising to leave medicare intact.

Fear of socialized medicine sweeping the country prompted the Canadian Medical Association to ask the Diefenbaker government for a royal commission on health care. The commission, the doctors hoped, would study the issue to death, as so many royal commissions had in the past. But Diefenbaker had cannily appointed his friend Emmett Hall to chair the commission, knowing full well where the judge's sympathies lay. In June 1964, the Supreme Court justice and his fellow commissioners released their bombshell of a report.

The Royal Commission on Health Services (known as the Hall Commission) described "the enormous gap between our scientific knowledge and skills on the one hand, and our organizational and financial arrangements to apply them to the needs of men, on the other."[3] The quality of care people received depended on "geographic area, population structure, socioeconomic status, occupation, and ethnic background and similar environmental characteristics."[4] Which province you were born in, how much you made, whether you lived in town or country, whether you were an immigrant or native-born, the colour of your skin, all influenced how healthy you might be. Infant mortality, for example, was much higher in impoverished Newfoundland (37.5 per thousand) than in affluent Ontario (23.5).

While just under eleven million Canadians had some form of health insurance, many had no idea of its limitations. The commission, which held hearings across the country, heard heartbreaking stories from couples forced into poverty when a member of the family became ill and the insurance failed to cover the costs. More than seven million Canadians had no insurance at all. "What the Commission recommends is that in Canada this gap be closed," the report urged, "that as a nation we now take the necessary legislative, organizational and financial decisions to make all the fruits of the health sciences available to all our residents without hindrance of any kind. All our recommendations are directed toward this objective. There can be no greater challenge to a free society of free men."[5]

The Hall Commission envisioned a truly universal system that included not only primary and hospital care but dental care for children (and eventually for adults), optical care, prescriptions, prosthetic devices and home care, increased public funding to treat alcohol and drug addictions, and the end to any distinction between physical health and mental health. The Hall Commission was not only ahead of its own time, it was ahead of ours.

Although an enthusiastic supporter of medicare, Tom Kent wanted to hold off on legislation for two or three years while he negotiated the details of an agreement with the provinces. Federalism had come a long way since the days of Louis St. Laurent, when Ottawa dictated the terms and conditions of shared-cost programs. The Canada Pension Plan negotiations and fiscal transfers occurred in a new environment, which required both provincial participation and consent. Kent wanted time to work out an agreement with the greatest possible provincial buy-in, something that might not be cemented until 1966 or 1967. But Pearson was increasingly leaning toward calling an election, and he needed something to put in the window.

From today's distant perspective, the desire among senior figures within the Liberal Party for an election in 1965 seems strange. Although the environment in the House of Commons was toxic from the Winter Scandals, as *Toronto Star* reporter Richard Gwyn called the Grits' serial embarrassments, the government was having no trouble getting legislation passed. Along with the Canada Pension Plan, the Liberals had given a major boost to existing pensions, increasing the monthly benefit from sixty-five dollars to seventy-five and lowering the age of eligibility from seventy to sixty-five. The Liberals had also advanced a major electoral reform by establishing impartial election commissions that set the boundaries for ridings in each province, a move that eliminated the discreditable practice of gerrymandering. John Diefenbaker, who had Lake Centre gerrymandered out from under him, had made a similar proposal to the House but had lost power before his proposal could be implemented. Electoral commissions were another example of a reform initiated by the Diefenbaker government and implemented by the Pearson government. The Pearson government had also built on Diefenbaker programs by investing heavily in regional development, especially in Atlantic Canada, and in job training for adult workers.

A new labour relations code, authored by Allan MacEachen, Pearson's former aide and now labour minister, consolidated and modernized labour relations in federally regulated industries, such as transportation and banking. The code also introduced the first federal minimum wage for such industries: $1.25 an hour. And then there was the new student loan program for the vast numbers of baby boomers attending college or university. An education revolution was underway in Canada and throughout the developed world. Prior to the war, education ended for most students in their teens, once they had learned the fundamentals of reading and writing and calculating. Many families needed their children as workers, and could not see the need for them to study arcane subjects such as Latin and geometry. Post-war, parents and governments were determined to provide all children with the best possible education, which led to a tripling of enrolment. New universities, technical schools, and community colleges proliferated. Curriculum requirements became more accessible. To ensure everyone would be able to take advantage of the new classroom spaces, the Pearson government's Canada Student Loans Program guaranteed bank loans for students, with the loans to be repaid after graduation.

Internationally, Canada earned the gratitude of the United States and the United Nations when Mike Pearson offered to send Canadian peace-keepers to de-escalate the conflict between Greeks and Turks on Cyprus. Defence Minister Paul Hellyer had begun the process of integrating the armed services—a policy that the military hated, but one that would remain in place until Stephen Harper restored the *status quo ante* in 2011. Under the Liberals, Canada had extended its maritime offshore limit from five kilometres to nineteen kilometres to protect fish stocks. And of course, the flag. Along with the new national medicare program, the 1965 agenda included a proposed Canada Assistance Plan (CAP), which would partially fund and partially harmonize provincial welfare programs. Because it was almost certain that a majority of MPs would vote in support of both medicare and CAP, there was every good reason to keep going.

But Walter Gordon wanted an election, and so did Keith Davey, who was still the party's national campaign director, and they pressed the idea on Pearson relentlessly. The Liberals blamed the unending scandals not on themselves but on a House of Commons they could not control. "Everyone was tired and discouraged and existence in Ottawa was anything but pleasant," Gordon recalled.[6] The economy was booming, thanks in part to the Conservatives' devaluation of the dollar and to unparalleled economic growth, but also thanks to Walter Gordon's sound management of federal finances after the unpleasantness of the 1963 budget. Unemployment had virtually vanished, the books were balanced, and despite all the new social spending there was enough money for a tax cut. It was the right time for an election. And then there was the Diefenbaker factor.

Pearson wanted to rise above the bear pit that the House had become, but Diefenbaker dragged him down there anyway, as Lamontagne followed Tremblay followed Denis followed Dupuis followed Rivard followed Banks. Mike could seem mesmerized by Diefenbaker, unable to cope with his relentless attacks in the House, his political theatrics, his disregard for fact and logic. The fight over the flag had been singularly vicious. Pearson could envision no worse fate for the country than for the Conservatives to return to power under Dief. An election that produced a majority government would not only ensure that the rest of the Liberal agenda got through, it would minimize the political impact of any future scandal while guaranteeing that Diefenbaker would never become prime minister again. Polls showed that the Liberal government was very popular, Pearson himself was somewhat popular, but Diefenbaker was quite unpopular. Why not go while the going was good?

But Pearson hesitated. He wanted to wait for the Dorion report on the Rivard affair before pulling the plug. Then came a nasty seventeen-day wildcat strike by postal workers in July, which led to a significant wage increase and which fuelled the determination of public service workers to win the right to strike (they would win it in 1967), but which also delayed the election. The main reason for delay, though, was the prime minister's exhaustion. He had turned sixty-eight in April, and he was not aging well. A trip to Western Canada in the summer of 1965 had left him wrung out. He hated campaigning and hated the thought of going up against Diefenbaker one last time. If people had wanted him to retire, he would willingly have agreed. But there was no obvious successor, and Pearson's sense of duty compelled him to carry on. Winning a majority government would be a highly attractive proposition, he agreed, but was it worth the effort of another election campaign?

Gordon met with Pearson on August 30 and again the next day. The polls indicated that if an election were held soon, the Liberals would win a solid majority. Pearson threatened to resign if the election failed to deliver that majority. I'll resign with you, Gordon promised. Pearson took the matter to cabinet. Most were eager to go. The Liberal leader decided to give it one last shot. Parliament was dissolved on September 8, with the election set for November 8. Mike would fight an autumnal campaign in search of a majority government, despite his own weariness.

Walter Gordon blamed the electoral debacle that followed on Jean Lesage. The Quebec premier had decided to tour the West. Gordon begged him to put it off, but Lesage refused. He wanted to project the image of the new Quebec to Westerners, to take the temperature of the country west of Superior, and perhaps to gauge his chances of eventually replacing Pearson as prime minister. He was greeted with a mixture of curiosity and hostility, and returned the same. For Gordon, Lesage undermined what should have been a comfortable Liberal majority government. But that seems unlikely.

The Liberals lacked a proper platform. Medicare had already been announced. The same was true of the tax transfers and welfare reforms. The only reason for the election was that the Liberals wanted a majority so that they could be rid of the torment from the opposition. But they had disproved the need for one by securing their ambitious agenda in a minority Parliament. And as their opponents kept pointing out, with a majority government there would have been no Dorion inquiry into the Rivard affair. With a majority government, Walter Gordon's first budget would have passed. With a majority government, this impulsive, scandal-plagued Liberal Party could do whatever it damn well pleased.

Pearson kept to a leisurely pace, only campaigning part of the week, citing the need to remain in Ottawa to run the government. It made him look disengaged. The Liberals accused the Conservatives of dividing the country by harping on petty scandals. But the scandals were anything but petty and they did originate in Quebec and they pointed to serious corruption within the Quebec wing of the federal party. And truth be told, many Canadians, especially in the West and in rural Ontario, resented the Liberal obsession with Quebec. If the province had a list of demands, it should present them for the rest of the country to consider. Of course, it was far more complex than that, and what Quebec really wanted— acknowledgement of and respect for its distinct society, along with greater control over what went on within that society—many in English Canada were unwilling to grant. Plains of Abraham and all that.

But Diefenbaker himself was the key to the campaign, which in a way was remarkable. He should have been facing oblivion. His former Quebec lieutenant, Léon Balcer, was sitting as an independent because of Diefenbaker's One Canada refusal to recognize the importance of Quebec's special place within Confederation, as well as his refusal to step aside. He had fought off an attempted leadership review the previous February, but the party was weak and divided, the national organization a shambles, and the Quebec wing defunct. John Robarts had far more respect for Pearson than for Diefenbaker, and had distanced the Ontario Progressive Conservatives from their federal cousins. The election manifesto had been cobbled together from past speeches, and in any case, was a poor alternative to the Liberals' groundbreaking reforms in pensions and health care. Polls showed that the Progressive Conservative leader was deeply unpopular with voters. And he was seventy.

Election campaigns matter, though, and there was nothing that John Diefenbaker loved more than an election campaign. He returned to his whistle-stop tour, visiting towns and villages, speaking from the back of the train, walking down the main street and stopping in at the local coffee shop, with an evening rally at the local Legion Hall or hockey rink. He excoriated the Liberals over their scandals, head shaking, eyes flashing, offering an indignant scowl or wicked grin. He told delighted crowds that the Liberal slogan was "throw the bums in," and that the Liberal code of ethics could be summarized as "Be good. And if you can't be good, be careful."[7] He repeated the names of the Liberal serial offenders: "Rivard, Lamontagne, Denis, Rouleau. . . ." Yes, the names perpetuated stereotypes and stoked linguistic resentment. But the scandals were real. "We shall get to the bottom of this and assure Canadians that the cobwebs of the Mafia, the wrongdoings of the narcotics peddlers and the corruption of public officials does not make a way of life."[8] He told the Canadian people they had "an appointment with destiny." The election was nothing so grand as that. But for Dief, it was great fun.

"John Diefenbaker moved like a legend over the land," Peter C. Newman wrote. In an age of automobiles and airplanes, his venue was the train station. His devoted audiences were old, white, rural, and English. He "was the political poet who in his very being could evoke the pioneer virtues and the glories of a simpler past when the Red River carts still creaked along the Battleford Trail and buffalo bones littered the horizonless prairie. . . . He stood there, reminding them of a time when they had been at the forefront of Canadian civilization. They had won this country and now they were being pushed aside by an alien world they had never made, losing their legacy to the slick rootless generation of the big cities."[9]

As always, Olive—"Mrs. D" people called her—was there, standing stoically beside him at the back of the train; walking beside him as he main-streeted, despite recurring back pain; sitting behind him at the rallies; listening to the latest variation of the Diefenbaker stump speech; scribbling notes of advice—if only to remind him of a name—a glint of steel in her voice if speaking to or about someone who crossed her John. If Mrs. D lacked Edna's empathy, she more than made up for it in iron will.

The Liberal campaign went from misstep to misstep. Keith Davey's decision to keep Pearson in Ottawa much of the time made the Liberals appear arrogant and aloof. When the Liberal leader did venture out, logistics and other failures bedevilled a campaign that should have been better organized. A hall in Montreal had the capacity for ten thousand, but only three thousand showed up. The prime minister was jeered and heckled in Vancouver. At Toronto's new Yorkdale Mall, a chic suburban shopping centre, ten thousand came to see the Liberal leader but few heard him, because the sound system didn't work. When he decided to wade into the crowd and shake hands, the crush of bodies threatened to bring harm, until Pearson's bodyguards rescued their man. Things weren't any better with the other parties. Tommy Douglas's final crusade lacked purpose because the Liberals had enacted much of what the NDP leader had campaigned for all his life. Robert Thompson's Social Credit Party was falling apart, with Réal Caouette's Créditistes campaigning as a separate party in Quebec.

Once again, Mike and Maryon came down with the flu at the end of the campaign. Once again, they retreated to the Château Laurier to await the results. Pearson's advisers assured him that the chances of a majority government were excellent. The Liberals needed only five additional seats. They obtained three.

Liberal hopes for a sweep in Quebec were frustrated by the Créditistes. The Grits actually lost a seat in Ontario, and any surviving remnants of support in the Prairies evaporated, with two of three MPs there defeated. British Columbia was largely a repeat from two years before. Though the Liberal lead in the popular vote—40 per cent versus 32 per cent for the PCs—should have produced a majority, Diefenbaker's Conservatives increased their seat count, from ninety-five in the previous election to ninety-seven. Even the NDP were up by four seats, to twenty-one, while the Créditistes claimed nine seats in Quebec. In English Canada, Social Credit was virtually wiped out, reduced to five seats. But the real split was between rural and urban. In the fifty constituencies of Toronto, Montreal, and Vancouver, the Tories took only a single seat, but they took sixty-two of the country's sixty-four most rural ridings. From then till now, the Liberal base would be anchored in Canada's three largest urban centres; Conservatives would dominate the hinterland. Elections would be won and lost in the suburban ridings surrounding the downtowns. York Centre and York—Humber, which had followed John in 1958, followed Mike in 1962. York—Scarborough switched from blue to red in 1963. The region would stay Liberal for many elections to come. The Grits would be strong in Quebec; the Tories, in the West. Urban versus rural; populists versus elites, English versus French. The elections of 1963 and '65 created the social and political divides that define Canada today.

"I had never been so depressed in my political life as that evening at the Château Laurier," Pearson recalled in his memoirs. He had launched the election campaign reluctantly, and only because his advisers and pollster had convinced him that he would win a majority government. "We had gone through it all for nothing!"[10] After acknowledging as much to reporters, he announced: "It's been a long, hard two months. The results are almost all in. And I think I'll go to bed."[11]

The next day, Pearson told the national executive of the Liberal Party that he was ready to resign. He also told cabinet. Everyone urged him to stay on, which of course he had to do: an immediate resignation would have thrown the government into chaos. Having given bad advice, Keith Davey stepped down as national director, but he became the youngest-ever senator, not quite forty, a few months later. Walter Gordon offered his own resignation as he promised he would. Pearson, who wanted to replace Gordon in Finance with someone who was less resented by the financial community, accepted the offer. Gordon's departure marked the end of a long political association between the two men. It also marked the end of their friendship.

II

In Prince Albert on election night, Diefenbaker treated defeat as though it were victory. The Grits had been kept to a minority; the common folk were still with him. Even George Hees and Davie Fulton had returned as candidates, both successfully, in a show of party unity. The show was an illusion; both had returned to convince fellow Conservatives that they were worthy of consideration for the leadership after Diefenbaker stepped down. But the Chief had no intention of stepping down, at least not immediately. He even suggested that Governor General Georges Vanier should invite him to Rideau Hall.

"The prime minister called this election because he said he couldn't carry on without an absolute majority," he told reporters. "The prime minister has had his answer. There is a second party, a party of 101 or 102 seats, which believes that it can form an administration and a strong administration and carry on the government of this country without having hanging over it at all times the danger of another election."[12]

But Pearson had no intention of handing the government over to the Conservatives, especially after Tommy Douglas promised the NDP would support the Liberals on a throne speech. Instead, the twenty-seventh Parliament met in early 1966, and quickly descended to depths not seen even in the darkest days of the twenty-sixth.

It began with yet another scandal, a relatively minor affair involving a sunken-cheeked, sunken-chested postal clerk—"a pathetic little man," Pearson called him.[13] Accused of acting as a spy for the Soviets, George Victor Spencer himself admitted to journalist Jack Webster, "I've been a sucker all my life."[14] Spencer had been passing on information about dead people, bankrupt companies, and shuttered schools that could be used to provide cover stories for Soviet agents operating in the Lower Mainland. He was caught and fired, but not charged, because the information was so unimportant and because he was dying of cancer. Nonetheless, Justice Minister Lucien Cardin assured journalists on CBC's *This Hour Has Seven Days* that he would be shadowed by the RCMP for the rest of his life. Big mistake. Either Spencer was guilty of a crime or he wasn't. If he was, charge him. If he wasn't, then constant police surveillance was an abuse of his civil liberties. Diefenbaker tore into Cardin, Favreau's successor, in the House. The hot-tempered Cardin fought back. Pearson vacillated on whether he believed yet another judicial inquiry was needed to clear the air.

Matters came to a head on the afternoon of March 4, 1966, as Diefenbaker goaded both Cardin and Pearson over "the labyrinth of deception" surrounding the Spencer case. He wanted "a full and complete investigation" into how police had conducted themselves, what the government knew, and when the government knew it. He began speaking of a possible earlier cover-up, of actions that occurred after 1945, "something that required a smoke screen."

The Conservative leader was dredging up the accusations of disloyalty levelled against Pearson by the Congressional committee in 1951, the Hazen Sise affair. He was throwing everything he had at the wall, hoping something would stick. Had there been a failure of security in the Spencer case? Or had Spencer been unfairly maligned by the minister of justice? An inquiry, Mr. Speaker. The government must hold an inquiry!

"The great executioner is now after my political neck," Cardin declared in the chamber.

"You committed suicide yourself," Diefenbaker countered.

Cardin accused Diefenbaker of undermining trust in government with wild and baseless accusations. Diefenbaker responded that it was Cardin and the Liberals who were undermining public trust by stonewalling on the Spencer case. The House went from raucous to silent: a sign that things had become deadly.

Cardin: "The right honourable gentleman was accusing us of hiding the truth, of hiding evidence from the committee. Well, I can tell the right honourable gentleman that of all the members of the House of Commons he—I repeat, he—is the very last person in the House who can afford to give advice on the handling of security cases in Canada."

Reporters in the gallery glanced at each other. What was Cardin talking about? What had the Diefenbaker government kept hidden?

Diefenbaker noted that Pearson was applauding Cardin. "I want that on the record."

"I understand the right honourable gentleman said he wants that on the record," Cardin responded, not understanding that Diefenbaker was referring to the clapping, not the minister's allegation. "Would he want me to go on and give more?"

"Go on, he wants it," MPs yelled.

"Very well," Cardin answered. "I want the right honourable gentleman to tell the House about his participation in the Monsignor case when he was prime minister of this country."

"I am not worried," Diefenbaker shot back. "Have your commission look into it. Put it on the agenda.[15]

Reporters charged out of the press gallery to alert their editors. Something big has broken, Fraser Kelly of the *Toronto Telegram* told his desk. Cardin is accusing Diefenbaker of a cover-up when he was prime minister. Something involving a monsignor.

Blair Fraser of *Maclean's*, who knew things he chose not to report, spoke softly into Kelly's ear. "Fraser, it's Munsinger."[16]

It was out.

Gerda Heseler was born in what was then East Prussia in 1929. Like millions of other Germans, she fled west when the Russians occupied the territory in 1944. Strikingly good-looking, self-possessed, and intelligent, Heseler did what she needed to do to survive, which included petty theft and prostitution, and perhaps a bit of spying for the Communists. She also learned English and married Michael Munsinger, an American serviceman, as part of her unremitting campaign to immigrate either to the United States or Canada. Her applications were refused because of a criminal record and allegations of "moral turpitude." Finally, in 1955, she gained admission to Canada using her married name, although the couple had amicably annulled the marriage. Once in Canada, she settled in Montreal, working as a cashier in rather shady nightclubs and perhaps selling her services. By 1959, Munsinger was thirty, enjoying life to the full, and carrying on an affair with Pierre Sévigny, Diefenbaker's associate minister of national defence. She also dined with George Hees, who later insisted things never went any farther, though his grin when he made that claim to reporters suggested otherwise. With Sévigny's help, Munsinger applied in 1960 for a Canadian passport. While vetting the application, the RCMP discovered her maiden name, her previous applications, her checkered past, and the nature of her relationship with Sévigny. The police informed Justice Minister Davie Fulton, who informed Diefenbaker, who ordered Sévigny to end the affair, which he did. Munsinger returned to Germany in 1963, and that was that, or so it seemed.

In 1964, tormented by the Winter Scandals, Pearson had asked the RCMP to bring him information on any matter involving national security and members of Parliament. They brought him the Munsinger file. Pearson wrote Diefenbaker a note, saying he had been made aware of the "serious and disturbing" events involving Munsinger and Sévigny. "The material now indicates that the Minister of Justice brought the matter to your attention and that no action was taken."[17] The fourteenth prime minister asked the thirteenth to provide him with more details as to why he had not dismissed the minister. Further police investigation might be required. Rather than replying formally, Diefenbaker visited Pearson in person.

The Opposition leader was suffering from a cold. According to Pearson's diary, he went on "about the heartbreaks and difficulties of being a PM" before coming to the point: he knew about Sévigny and Munsinger, but took no action against his minister on the grounds that national security had not been compromised. He also alluded to the 1951 Senate testimony on Pearson's indiscretions. Diefenbaker, in his memoirs, said Pearson "in his most ingratiating way, said, 'We should not talk to each other like this, John,' and insisted he was not a politician, but a diplomat." We cannot know everything that was said in that room. But we can imagine the tension as the two men confronted each other.[18]

Pearson's request that the RCMP dig up dirt on previous governments was outrageous. His letter to Diefenbaker was outrageous. The meeting itself was an outrage. Pearson, tormented by scandal and by Diefenbaker in the House, had asked the RCMP to bring him something he could use against the Conservatives. When they came back with the Munsinger file, he let Diefenbaker know what he knew. It was blackmail: tone it down in the House or I'll use this against you. "This fishing expedition was a violation of cabinet convention and political decency unprecedented in Canadian history," wrote Diefenbaker's biographer, Denis Smith. "Diefenbaker's excesses were matched by this one."[19]

Years before, when Pearson was external affairs minister and Diefenbaker the opposition critic, their relationship had been respectful, even cordial. A decade and a half later, it had become utterly toxic. Pearson detested Diefenbaker. "Mike was afraid of him," Judy LaMarsh believed. "He was contemptuous of Diefenbaker and Diefenbaker was contemptuous of him. I don't think either of them was generous enough to see the good qualities in the other one. There was really bad blood between them."[20] Maryon Pearson referred to Diefenbaker as "that awful man."[21] Mike called him "a clown." Mary Macdonald said that Pearson once told her he did not believe anyone was fundamentally evil, "with the possible exception of John Diefenbaker."[22]

Pearson had more reason to fear and loathe Diefenbaker than Diefenbaker had to fear and loathe him. As Liberal leader, Pearson had played a relatively minor role in the Progressive Conservative government's defeat, which had mostly been caused by Diefenbaker's decision to cancel the Avro Arrow, to fire James Coyne, and to defy John F. Kennedy on nuclear weapons. But the Liberal government's great tormenter was the Conservative opposition. Diefenbaker regarded the ministers across the aisle as quarry to be hunted, and they provided him with one opportunity after another.

There was a reason Cardin blurted out "Monsignor." A few days earlier, Pearson had decided to permit an inquiry into the Spencer affair. Cardin, feeling he had been hung out to dry by his prime minister, threatened to resign. Other Quebec ministers, convinced one of their own was being scapegoated yet again by this Anglo prime minister, threatened to quit as well. Pearson talked them out of it, but the caucus was disintegrating, just as the Tory caucus had in Diefenbaker's final months. The difference was that the issue involved a petty scandal rather than anything as substantive as allowing nuclear weapons onto Canadian soil. Invoking the Munsinger affair was clearly a diversion aimed at deflecting attention away from Liberal troubles by accusing the Conservatives of hiding their own discreditable conduct.

Though Pearson later insisted that Cardin blurted out Munsinger's name without his knowledge or approval, the historical record suggests otherwise. In the midst of the Spencer affair, Davie Fulton had been visited by his friend Guy Favreau. The former Liberal justice minister told the former Conservative justice minister that the Spencer case was taking a dangerous turn, and that unless the Conservatives turned down the heat, there were people in the government who "might not be able to restrain an outburst and developments that we might all regret." Favreau hoped Fulton "might be able to use some influence or be helpful in calming things down." Fulton replied that he could not deter Diefenbaker from pursuing whatever course he took, even if he had wanted to. "I think it was implicit in all that had been said that there was pressure on them to expose the Munsinger thing and this pressure was mounting," Fulton later concluded. "So it was not an accidental disclosure; it was one that had been considered, and although there may have been some in the Liberal council who didn't think it should be done, the prime minister went along."[23] Indeed, Pearson vowed, "We're going to fight and fight hard, and, if we have to, use the same methods that are being used and have been used against us for the past three years."[24]

Goaded by Diefenbaker, he had been reduced to fighting on the same terms as his tormentor.

Cardin held a press conference to clear the air about his threatened resignation and to explain what he meant by the "Monsignor case." He told reporters about "Olga" Munsinger, including her affair with a certain unnamed Diefenbaker cabinet minister, adding that she had returned to Germany and reportedly died of leukemia.

It didn't take reporters long to figure out that Sévigny was the allegedly guilty party. The former minister, his wife and children by his side, denied that his relationship with Munsinger was anything but platonic, and called Cardin "a despicable, rotten little politician."[25] Meanwhile, *Toronto Star* reporter Robert Reguly, who had already won fame for tracking down Hal Banks after he skipped town in 1964—Reguly found him lounging on a union yacht in Brooklyn Harbour—located the supposedly deceased Gerda Munsinger in Munich, very much alive, working as a waitress in a night club, and happy to talk. Pearson called yet another judicial inquiry. It seemed as though Canada might be running out of judges.

In the House of Commons, Pearson pulled no punches. The Conservatives had tarred and feathered one honourable Liberal cabinet minister after another, he fumed. "Now those gentlemen who have been so free with their accusations over the last few years are getting a little of it, and they don't like it."[26] So it really was about nothing more than Liberals getting even.

The Munsinger affair quickly eclipsed every scandal that had come before it. Diefenbaker dismissed the inquiry as a "travesty of the judicial process," and disparaged Wishart Spence, the Supreme Court justice who conducted it, as a "solid Liberal."[27] In May, the Conservatives pulled their counsel from the inquiry, effectively boycotting it. In his report, released on September 23, 1966, Spence said that although there was no evidence of any breach of security, Munsinger was clearly a security risk, if only because of her ties to the mob in Montreal, and that Diefenbaker should have dismissed the minister. "Mr. Diefenbaker did not seem to appreciate the continuing security risk posed by his retention of The Honourable Pierre Sévigny in his then Cabinet post or any Cabinet post," the report chastised.[28] Diefenbaker ignored the report. When reporters asked Sévigny for his response, he said,

"The whole thing is bullshit." When told that word could not be used in print or on air, he responded, "No? Well, what about horseshit?" Munsinger herself delivered the final verdict: "I knew Pierre as a man. He knew me as a woman. That's all there was to it."[29]

In the end, the Munsinger affair probably tarnished the Liberals more than the Conservatives, by showing how desperate they were to distract attention from their own misdeeds. The prime minister admitted to Bruce Hutchison that he had raised Munsinger with Diefenbaker hoping "that if he was aware that I knew about the affair he might take it a little easier on us."[30] He must have hated what he had become. His biographer, John English, pronounced Liberal threats of doing unto the Conservatives as the Conservatives had done unto them "the nadir of Mike Pearson's public career."[31]

III

Richard Gwyn, writing in the wake of the Winter Scandals, offered this explanation for why they so offended the Canadian public: They were "the fossils of a rougher political era brought back to life in another and very different time," he wrote:

> Canada in the 1960s is younger, richer, better educated and more urbane than it has ever been . . . the new Canada expresses itself not through its burgeoning wheat sales but through the soaring curvilinear sweep of Toronto's new City Hall, not by the boom in the pulp and paper industry but by the seventeen new universities built within the last seven years. The new Canada impresses not by the bravado of its hockey players but by the brilliance of the Stratford Festival. In this Canada one person in four lives within the sprawling urban agglomeration of Montreal, Toronto and Vancouver. One person in two is under twenty-five years of age. This generation knows the Depression only from its grandparents, the Second World War from its parents and the first Sputnik from magazine articles. Lester Pearson . . . was elected to lead a country ready to face the challenges of its future but totally unprepared to see its government overwhelmed and nearly defeated by the sins of the past.[32]

Canada in 1966 was dynamic, restless, unsatisfied. Young men and women in jeans and tie-dyed T-shirts smoked pot, made love, and listened to rock that had lost the roll. Yorkville, a rundown precinct in Toronto's midtown that had traditionally been dominated by rooming houses, was now dominated by coffee houses, where rising singers Neil Young, Joni Mitchell, and Gordon Lightfoot performed and where high school students bought weed from the hippies who had taken possession of the neighbourhood. Farther south, at King and Bay, Canada's tallest skyscraper, the fifty-four-storey Toronto-Dominion Centre, neared completion. Toronto was replacing Montreal as Canada's largest city and financial capital.

Change was not limited to the east, either. The discovery of oil at Leduc in 1947 had transformed Alberta from an agricultural province to an oil producer. Calgary and Edmonton were both booming, even as Saskatchewan and Manitoba languished in Alberta's shadow. In British Columbia, decades of labour strife—in which governments and police often aided corporate interests in the face of tough union resistance in mines and sawmills and on the docks—had eased, as post-war affluence offered a living wage to almost any worker. Kitsilano joined Yorkville as capitals of Canada's hippie subculture. The federal government was busy upgrading Vancouver International Airport to accommodate the new jumbo jets that would be arriving within a few years. The Boeing 707, which eight years earlier had inaugurated the widespread use of commercial jet aircraft, was by now a common sight, often parked beside its chief competitor, the Douglas DC-8. People described the time they lived in as the jet age.

South of the border, President Lyndon Johnson had decided to go all-in to protect South Vietnam from being conquered by North Vietnam, which in turn was supported by Russia and China. Almost four hundred thousand American troops were in the country, engaging fiercely with the Viet Cong. By the end of the year, American losses would exceed six thousand. Young Americans increasingly protested being sent off as cannon fodder for a war that the Americans seemed to be losing against a determined enemy. The civil rights movement was becoming larger and more militant—Stokely Carmichael talked about Black Power, and Bobby Seale co-founded the Black Panther Party in Oakland. Closer to home, the FLQ's bombing campaign had resumed; on May 1, 1966, an explosion at a shoe factory in Montreal killed Thérèse Morin, a secretary.

The music was edgier, the movies grittier, the protests angrier, the divisions sharper. And two old men led the national governing parties, increasingly disconnected from the new sounds, the new hope, the new discontent. Both were outside their time.

IV

The second Pearson government was harder-edged, more pragmatic, less cooperative in relations with the provinces than the first. Programs and services continued to expand, though more slowly than in those revolutionary months of the first administration, but Ottawa in the mid-sixties was more likely to declare rather than to consult. Medicare and the new Canada Assistance Plan were offered to the provinces to take or leave as they chose. (They all chose to take it.) The government also paid more attention to the bottom line, partly through force of circumstance and partly because of Mitchell Sharp.

The future Liberal finance minister began life as "a poor boy on the wrong side of the Red River in Winnipeg" who had to quit school at fourteen to help support the family.[33] Sharp finished high school and university by taking night courses, which won him a job as an economist and then a one-year stint at the LSE. His extraordinary mind also revealed itself in his talent at the piano and his love for Schubert. A bit bland and colourless in public, in private he was tough, witty, and conspicuously brilliant. During the war, the government sent him to Ottawa rather than Europe; in the years that followed, he rose steadily in the ranks of the public service, until the leaked memorandum on the economy that Diefenbaker pounced on and the subsequent election triumph of 1958 sent him into the private sector as an executive at a tractor company. Pearson convinced him to run for Parliament, though he lost to Donald Fleming in 1962. After Fleming retired, Sharp took the riding of Eglinton in 1963, arriving in cabinet as minister of trade and commerce, then as Walter Gordon's replacement in Finance.

Sharp was a blue Liberal, more worried about sound finances and a prospering business sector than fighting the war on poverty or keeping the Americans out. He inherited a department that had to finance both the Guaranteed Income Supplement, which supported seniors who did not qualify for the Canada Pension Plan because they were too old or had not worked enough, and the Canada Assistance Plan. Both the CAP and the GIS were expensive, inflation was on the rise, and in 1965 the federal budget had tipped back into deficit. Sharp wanted to bring the budget back into balance, or something close to it. He wanted freer trade with the United States. He wanted to raise interest rates to protect the Canadian dollar. Although he believed in medicare, he worried about its cost and wanted the program delayed. From the backbench, Walter Gordon opposed most of these measures. Many Liberal MPs and cabinet ministers were with Gordon, including Herb Gray, Donald Macdonald, and Eugene Benson in Ontario, and the Three Wise Men from Quebec.

Though the 1965 election appeared to have been pointless, it had one momentous consequence: the arrival of Jean Marchand, Gérard Pelletier, and Pierre Trudeau, who would reshape the Liberal Party and Canada. The real catch for the Liberals, it seemed at the time, was Marchand. In 1949, he had led striking asbestos miners in their confrontation with the Duplessis government, becoming the most prominent labour leader in the province in the decade that followed. Fiery, eloquent, and popular, he championed social reform while also combatting separatist sentiment. The Liberals had tried to persuade him to run in 1963, but Mike Pearson's decision to accept nuclear weapons scuttled those plans. The party came courting again in 1965, but at René Lévesque's urging, Marchand insisted he would only run for the Liberals if seats were found for two others as well. One of them was Gérard Pelletier. The former editor of *La Presse* had covered the asbestos strike as a reporter for *Le Devoir*. In 1950 he helped found an influential journal, *Cité Libre*, which championed social reform and excoriated the Union Nationale. Its co-founder was Pierre Elliott Trudeau, a lawyer and self-proclaimed intellectual who had also supported the asbestos workers, becoming friends with both Pelletier and Marchand. The three men, often with Lévesque in attendance, enjoyed breakfast salons, spirited dinners, and late-night arguments at Pelletier's house and elsewhere. A man of intellectual elegance, Pelletier was the least political of the three, preferring to seek consensus, which could not easily be found at a table that included both

Pierre Trudeau and René Lévesque. Marchand, Pelletier, and Trudeau, dubbed the Three Wise Men—in French Canada they were known as "*les trois colombes*," the three doves, sent to bring peace between French Canada and English Canada—arrived in Ottawa in 1965, bent on containing separatism and promoting social reform. They had little time for Mitchell Sharp's worries about inflation, interest rates, and deficits.

Gordon clashed repeatedly with both Sharp and Pearson. The former finance minister preached for stricter controls on foreign investment, while Sharp welcomed such investment. Gordon told Pearson he wanted to resign his seat, but also mused about replacing Pearson when he retired. Reporters wrote with concern (and glee) about the latest split in caucus and the hapless Pearson's inability to heal it. But Pearson wasn't all that hapless; he urged Gordon to seek the leadership after his departure if that was his wont, but added that, as prime minister, he had no choice but to stand by his finance minister, which Gordon considered a bit rich. Things came to a head at the Liberal Party Conference in October 1966. In speeches from the floor, it soon became clear that Gordon lacked sufficient support for his reforms. Sharp, in control, proposed implementing medicare after a one-year delay. Moved and carried. But Gordon still had support within caucus. After bitter meetings, he, Pearson, and Sharp worked out a compromise. Gordon would return to cabinet as president of the Privy Council—in effect, a minister without portfolio. Sharp agreed to a policy of limiting American investment in Canadian banks. The government would commission a white paper on foreign investment, to put off confronting the splits in caucus. One crucial difference between Diefenbaker and Pearson was that, though both faced caucus rebellions, Pearson was better at holding things together. Decades of diplomacy abroad proved useful at home.

V

Norman Atkins kept the five of spades in his wallet; Chad Bark, the six; Patrick Vernon the seven; Donald Guthrie the nine. All were close friends of Dalton Camp. They were also accomplished professionals: Atkins was an advertising executive; Bark was a successful businessman. Vernon and Guthrie were lawyers. They and eight others called themselves the Spades.

Their mission was to counsel, advise, and advance the career of Dalton Camp, to whom they were devoted. In his wallet, Camp carried the ace.

Dalton Camp and John Diefenbaker were as different as different could be. Alexander Ross explored this divergence in *Maclean's*:

> Camp is affable, creative, tolerant, contemporary, humorous, candid, sophisticated and heavily disposed toward seeing several sides of every question. Diefenbaker is not. Camp drives a Buick Riviera, likes wine at dinner, and tries to understand Marshall McLuhan. Diefenbaker does not. Camp tries to learn from young people; Diefenbaker tries to instruct them. Camp prefers talking to individuals; Diefenbaker is at his best addressing crowds. Camp would have gotten along famously with John F. Kennedy; Diefenbaker emphatically did not. Camp's style is cool, controlled and intellectual. Diefenbaker's is fiery, impassioned and evangelical. Camp is a man of reason. Diefenbaker is a man of vision.[34]

Olive Diefenbaker told Sean O'Sullivan, an adoring young acolyte, that Diefenbaker had intended to step down after the 1965 election, but that he was forced to defend his leadership when Camp challenged it. Camp remembered things differently. As president of the Progressive Conservative Party, he visited the party leader soon after that election. At the meeting, Camp later recalled, Diefenbaker railed at the purported inadequacies of the candidates who might succeed him, such as George Hees and Davie Fulton. As for Ontario premier John Robarts, Nova Scotia premier Bob Stanfield, and Manitoba premier Duff Roblin, all of whom were considered potential successors, he declared, "You cannot become leader of this party unless you've been in the House of Commons. You cannot become leader of this party unless you have experience in Parliament." Diefenbaker had decided to stay on. Camp recalled, "I was in despair."[35]

In a way, the election result was to blame. Camp had decided to run against Mitchell Sharp in Eglinton—he lost, narrowly, in Donald Fleming's old riding—which conveniently made him unavailable to run the national campaign. Eddie Goodman, a successful lawyer and staunch Tory supporter and fundraiser, had taken on the job. Fast Eddie, as he was called, was no fan of Diefenbaker, but he saw it as his duty to keep the party intact and united through the election, after which he assumed Dief would step down. Hees and Fulton and others had returned to Parliament for the same reason. As it turned out, the party did better than expected, denying the Liberals a majority and picking up seats. Diefenbaker considered the result a personal vindication. And if he was planning to step down, why did he install James Johnston, a small-town newspaper publisher and Diefenbaker loyalist, as party director? Johnston, on instructions from Diefenbaker, fired Flora MacDonald, who had been largely running party headquarters. (Years later, MacDonald wrote, "'Dief' had the unrivalled ability to eviscerate Liberals. He was also paranoid,"[36] while he described her, once she became MP for Kingston and the Islands as "the finest woman ever to walk the streets of Kingston."[37]) MacDonald was Camp's friend, and everyone took her dismissal as a shot across Camp's bow. The Spades began to plot.

Diefenbaker had the support of nearly 80 per cent of caucus. Many of them were from the Prairies, where the Chief was still beloved; they would never openly defy him. Other federal and provincial party officials were similarly unwilling to publicly express their discontent with the leader. But Camp and his friends knew there was one area where Diefenbaker might be vulnerable. At the next annual meeting of party officials and delegates, members would vote for party president by secret ballot. Camp would run for a second term as president, and he would run on a single issue: the need for a leadership review.

Camp made his intentions clear at a private speech to 120 influential Conservatives at the Albany Club, a Tory bastion in Toronto, on May 19, 1966, six months after the election. He knew there were Diefenbaker loyalists in the room, and he knew the speech would leak, which it did. He never once mentioned Diefenbaker by name. But the speech emphasized the duty of the leader to serve the party, rather than of the party to serve the leader. The message was plain and Diefenbaker got it. But the Chief did not heed that message. Instead, he convinced Arthur Maloney—a brilliant courtroom lawyer and former MP—to run for the presidency against Camp. Maloney campaigned on a message of conciliation; many hoped that, if he won, he would convince the Chief to retire. But when it came to brass tacks, a vote for Maloney was a vote for Dief.

Camp campaigned across the country through the autumn of 1966, supported by the Spades and Flora MacDonald, who had taken a list of all 265 riding association presidents and their contact info with her when she left party headquarters. Norm Atkins, who was Camp's brother-in-law as well as his business partner at their advertising firm, served as campaign manager. MacDonald twisted the arms of delegates across the country. Lowell Murray, a former aide to Davie Fulton, monitored the caucus, about a quarter of whom might be persuaded to vote for a leadership review. David MacDonald, a freshman MP who had just turned thirty, mobilized Tory youth groups. As fall progressed, others joined the campaign, including New Brunswick MLA Richard Hatfield, who would soon be premier, and Roy McMurtry, a young lawyer and a rising force among Ontario Progressive Conservatives. (He would serve as Ontario premier Bill Davis's attorney general before going onto the bench.) But Diefenbaker had many supporters, both in caucus and among delegates who remembered when he had rescued the party from the ashes of its repeated self-immolations and forged it into a force that had beaten the hated Grits three times. Dief will go, the word went out; he knows it's time. Just let him do it on his own terms, with dignity. If he's ready to go, then just tell us, Camp supporters replied. It came down to whether you trusted the Chief to leave on his own terms when he felt the time was right, or you believed he must be made to leave.

Conservative delegates were to meet in the gilded ballroom of Ottawa's Château Laurier Hotel in the second week of November. Johnston sought to forestall Camp by arranging for a voice vote of confidence in the leader at the beginning of the conference, which would render Camp's plan for a leadership review moot. But the Camp forces were on the ascendent, and now included Eddie Goodman and Senator Wallace McCutcheon, whose fundraising efforts had been invaluable in 1965. Stanfield, Roblin, and Robarts were also known to favour change. Camp appealed to the national executive, which was stacked with his supporters, to change the agenda and the appeal succeeded. Diefenbaker would speak Monday night; election of officers would follow Tuesday; votes on motions would take place Wednesday. If Camp won re-election, he would be able to engineer a motion calling for a leadership review.

When Diefenbaker entered the ballroom of the Château Laurier Monday night, the room was stacked against him. Camp supporters had gotten there ahead of the speech, forcing many Diefenbaker supporters to wait outside. The Camp crowd sat on their hands as Diefenbaker entered the room. They stayed silent at lines that were intended to provoke cheers. The Chief had never stood before such a hostile audience, certainly not one composed entirely of Conservatives. He grew flushed, agitated. He began to attack Dalton Camp, who was seated on the stage behind him. The silence was now interrupted by jeers and boos. "Is this a Conservative meeting?" Diefenbaker said in distress. "Yes!" people shouted back. "I've had years in the service of this party and this country," he intoned. "Too many!" someone in the crowd shouted.[38] Diefenbaker wheeled around and pointed his finger at Camp. "No leader can stand if he has to turn around to find out who's tripping him from behind."[39] Camp sat stone-faced. As the boos and catcalls grew louder, Bob Stanfield, seated beside Camp, whispered, "Oh God, this is awful."[40] And it was all being broadcast by the CBC. Agitated, the leader cut short his speech and left the room. "It's not often you can feel a page of history turning," Patrick Nowlan, a young MP who was the son of George Nowlan, later recalled. "But we all felt it that night."[41] (George Nowlan, Diefenbaker's not-always-loyal cabinet minister, had died the year before.)

In all of Canada's political history, there may never have been anything so vicious as that party meeting. Fuelled by booze and rage, Diefenbaker supporters and Camp supporters confronted each other in the rooms and halls of the Château Laurier. Fist fights broke out. Someone, no one remembers who, punched Brian Mulroney, a Camp supporter, bloodying his nose. Diefenbaker supporter Jack Horner took a swing at Roy McMurtry. The former football player punched Horner out.

The two sides appeared evenly matched. It would all come down to the choice of party president: Camp or Maloney. The next night, which was for candidates' speeches, Camp gave a rambling, unfocused presentation. He may have been hungover. Maloney was at the top of his game. "The Right Honourable John George Diefenbaker, sometime prime minister of Canada, present Leader of the Opposition and the national Leader of the Conservative Party of Canada, when he enters into a room, Arthur Maloney stands up!"[42] The vote, though, narrowly favoured Camp, 564 to Maloney's 502. Flora MacDonald was elected party secretary. Other Camp loyalists held key positions. Diefenbaker was still leader of the party, but Camp controlled it.

The next day, the executive amended the wording of the motion in support of the leader to one that "directs the national executive . . . to call a leadership convention at a suitable time before January 1, 1968."[43] The Diefenbaker supporters entered the ballroom to the sound of bagpipes and cheers. But the motion, voted on by secret ballot, carried 563 to 186.

"I would have gone six months ago, if only they had left me alone," Diefenbaker told O'Sullivan, who would later serve as his aide before entering Parliament and then the priesthood. "But they began complaining and I will not go as long as they are fighting to destroy me."[44] He appeared before his excited supporters in the packed lobby of the Château. The old warrior rallied the troops, quoting the Elizabethan soldier Andrew Barton: "Fight on my men / I am hurt, but I am not slain; / I'll lay me down and bleed awhile / And then I'll rise and fight again." (Diefenbaker substituted "rest" for "bleed.")

Like a Bourbon, Diefenbaker never forgot and never forgave. Such people often come to an unhappy end. In his case, it was also very sad.

THIRTEEN

Changing of the Guard

(1967–1968)

I

For the first time since the Second World War, the Bureau International des Expositions (BIE) had authorized a first category world's fair, to be held in Brussels in 1958. Pavilions from nations around the world explored the theme of humanity in the atomic age, helping to make Expo 58 a great success. After touring the exhibition, Progressive Conservative senator Mark Drouin publicly suggested Canada should celebrate its 100th birthday in 1967 by hosting a similar exhibition in Montreal, which would be celebrating the 250th anniversary of the city's founding that same year. Drouin was fronting for Pierre Sévigny, who had conceived the notion but who had come down with the flu. As John Diefenbaker's Quebec lieutenant, Sévigny thought that winning a world's fair for Montreal would boost the fortunes of the Conservative Party in Quebec. Diefenbaker backed the idea, as did Premier Maurice Duplessis. The new mayor of Montreal, Jean Drapeau, fearing the fair would be captured by the Mob, was opposed. But the much greater challenge came from the Soviet Union, which applied to host a fair of its own in 1967 in Moscow. The U.S.S.R. won the bid, leaving the

Canadians bitterly disappointed. But then the Russians announced in 1962 that they were cancelling, perhaps because the Kremlin realized that hosting millions of visiting Westerners might inject unwelcome ideas into their workers' paradise. The BIE asked Canada to submit a new bid.

Much had changed. Duplessis was gone; *la Grande Noirceur* had given way to Jean Lesage's Quiet Revolution. Drapeau, defeated and then returned as mayor, was now a fervent supporter of the exhibition. The BIE approved Canada's bid in November 1962, leaving the organizers only four years to convert that bid into reality. There were plenty, both inside and outside Canada, who doubted they could pull it off.

But the Canadian team was determined. Drapeau decided the fair would be held on two islands in the St. Lawrence River: one would be expanded, the other created from scratch, using fill excavated to create the new Montreal Metro, among other sources. A team of mostly French designers and mostly English engineers overcame a host of challenges. In 1963, Lester Pearson's Liberal government became responsible for the fair. As Opposition leader, Pearson had been skeptical of the exhibition, whose scale he considered unrealistic and unaffordable. "I had assumed that with four million square miles [ten million km²] of land in Canada, we would be able to find a plot some place for our Centennial Exposition, but here he [Drapeau] had to make an island in the St. Lawrence," he wrote in his memoir.[1] Once in office, the Liberals came close to shutting the whole thing down. Walter Gordon, as finance minister, opposed the "fucking fair," or so Andrew Kniewasser, a senior official on the Expo team, maintained. "The whole idea of it being a Montreal fair was detested by the federal government. Mr. Diefenbaker was reluctant to do it, and his successor Mr. Pearson was dead against it."[2] But cabinet approved funding nonetheless, which suggests "detested" might have been too strong a word.

Sixty-one nations contributed pavilions that explored the theme "Man and His World," with Buckminster Fuller's geodesic dome for the American pavilion dominating the skyline. Canada contributed the most expensive and one of the most beautiful pavilions, which featured an inverted pyramid called Katimavik—Inuktitut for "meeting place." From opening day, on April 28 (workers had to paint the grass green because of the chilly spring) to closing day on October 29, crowds surpassed all expectations, as did reviews. A young country celebrating its hundredth anniversary had managed a dazzling architectural and engineering feat, impressing the world and introducing millions of Canadians to the possibilities and beauty of modern design, including Habitat 67, a modular apartment complex of prefabricated materials created by the brilliant young architect Moshe Safdie. Fifty million visitors toured the pavilions and enjoyed the amusement park La Ronde. A former British colony, then a semi-dependent dominion, then an independent but confused state that had only recently acquired its own flag and whose constitution remained offshore in Britain, presented a new face to the world: modern, urban, optimistic, hip. "For the first time in many of our lives, we felt comfortable with hyperbole," John Lownsbrough wrote fifty years later,[3] though novelist Mordecai Richler dismissed the fair as a "Good Taste Disneyland."[4]

Anxious not to disrupt the Centennial celebrations through his resignation, Georges Vanier tried to carry on as governor general, despite the constant pain from his war wounds and his rapidly weakening heart. But he was so visibly unwell that Pearson was reluctant to let him continue. Before he could decide, Vanier's heart failed him; he died on March 5. Thirty-one years later, when compiling the list of the one hundred most important Canadians in history, the editors of *Maclean's* magazine accorded Georges Vanier first place, not because of his exploits or accomplishments, but because he had served as "Canada's moral compass."[5] Pearson turned to his old friend Roland Michener, who had spent almost a decade as a Tory MP, including five years as Speaker of the House, and who was now serving in India as high commissioner, to take his place.

II

René Lévesque first made a name for himself in the 1940s as a war correspondent. After the war, Radio-Canada confined him to radio, until his big TV scoop of 1955, when he reported on Soviet leader Nikita Khrushchev's rudeness toward Canada's visiting foreign minister, Lester Pearson. He then hosted a popular Radio-Canada television program, *Point de mire*. By 1959, when Jean Lesage began putting together a team of candidates who could defeat the Union Nationale, Lévesque was a household name. "People in

Quebec were infatuated with him," wrote one biographer, because of his "mastery of the spoken word."[6] People found the chain-smoking charmer's shrug and wry grin irresistible. Women were especially attracted to him, and the feeling was mutual. Once the Liberals were in power, Lévesque convinced Lesage to call an early election to secure a mandate for nationalizing the province's hydroelectric companies. That election, in 1962, delivered an even bigger majority for the Liberals, and Hydro-Québec was born. The former journalist was now one of the best-known figures in the province. When the Liberals lost power to Daniel Johnson's Union Nationale in 1966, there was no chance that Lévesque would languish in opposition. Two separatist parties had contested that election, the Rassemblement pour l'Indépendance Nationale and the Ralliement National. Between them they had garnered only 8 per cent of the vote, but Lévesque was a master at detecting an emerging trend, and he increasingly inclined toward some form of sovereignty for Quebec. In October 1967, he walked out of a Liberal convention, taking a hundred followers with him. Within a year, Lévesque would be leader of a new party, the Parti Québécois, dedicated to Quebec achieving sovereignty while retaining an economic association with Canada.

Pearson's attitude toward federalism had evolved greatly over the course of his adult life. In the 1940s and '50s, he embraced the English intellectual consensus that the federal government needed to maximize its spending power and to acquire greater constitutional authority as it pursued the nation-building mission of developing a modern economy and welfare state. Provincial concerns were parochial concerns, to be dismissed or at least resisted.

But as prime minister, he discovered the best approach to achieving his agenda—on pensions, on welfare, on medicare, in education—lay in negotiating with his provincial counterparts. Throughout a decade in office, Louis St. Laurent felt the need to meet with the premiers six times. During almost six years in office, Diefenbaker convened four dominion–provincial conferences. Pearson held nine federal–provincial conferences, as they were now called, in less than five years in office. Virtually everyone who attended them marvelled at his use of humour, charm, and calm good will to ease tensions and achieve consensus. However much his ministers and advisers shaped the agenda of the Pearson governments, that agenda had to be sold to the premiers, and Mike was one of the finest salesmen in the world. If he showed less patience in his second term with Quebec's demands for autonomy and the demands of all provinces for more federal money with fewer federal strings, his instincts remained to negotiate rather than try to dictate.

His views had also evolved on the special status of Quebec within Canada. Launching the bilingualism and biculturalism commission acknowledged that shift. Quebec was not simply one province among others, as people such as John Diefenbaker and Donald Creighton—who had been Pearson's fellow historian at University of Toronto, and who had written speeches for Diefenbaker—believed. It was a unique society, and its government held a unique responsibility to preserve the province's language and culture. Cooperative federalism meant more than simply negotiating with the provinces; it recognized as well the principle of asymmetricality: some provinces had unique or special needs, and federal–provincial agreements with them would look different from federal–provincial agreements with other provinces. This was especially true of Quebec. Its demands for greater control over economic and social policies must be accommodated, Pearson believed, or the province might leave Canada entirely. The ultimate solution, he was convinced, lay in crafting a new amending formula for the Constitution, and bringing that Constitution home to Canada. The Fulton-Favreau amending formula made the most sense, and in the early years of his first government, there was real hope all the provinces would agree. But then Jean Lesage pulled back, and the opportunity to celebrate Canada's Centennial by repatriating the Constitution faded away.

Now Lesage was gone, and the Union Nationale's Daniel Johnson was even more obstreperous. Things were particularly complicated in the triangle of capitals: Ottawa, Quebec City, and Paris.

As part of its commitment to accommodate Quebec within a renewed federation, the Pearson government had worked to deepen relations with France, which Ottawa traditionally had neglected in comparison with Britain. Both governments welcomed closer consultations and exchanges in the arts and sciences following Pearson's visit to Paris in January 1964. But there was the French government, and then there was President Charles de Gaulle.

Like so many, Mike admired the general's courage and determination during the war. When the French government cravenly made peace with the

Nazis following the fall of Paris, establishing a corrupt satellite regime in Vichy, de Gaulle in London became the literal embodiment of Free France. Four years later, he embodied Free France once again, as he strode down the Champs-Élysées following the Allied liberation of Paris. He retired from politics, unsatisfied with the workings of the Fourth Republic, but returned to establish the Fifth Republic in 1958, preventing civil war by accepting the independence of Algeria. In 1967, he was seventy-seven years old and frustrated. His dream of a Europe renewed under Franco-German leadership, relegating Britain and the United States to the periphery, had foundered on West Germany's determination to preserve NATO. He retaliated by poking the Americans, the British, and the Canadians whenever he could, frustrating and annoying all three. In Canada's case, there were specific irritants, such as France's refusal to provide ironclad guarantees that any uranium purchased from Canada would not be used to construct nuclear weapons (Canada refused to sell the fuel), and a Franco-Quebec cultural accord that discomfited Ottawa. But the real flashpoint was Quebec's push toward something approaching sovereignty. Daniel Johnson's stridently nationalist Union Nationale government sought legitimacy on the world stage, particularly through enhanced relations with France. Marcel Masse, a minister in Johnson's cabinet (and later in Brian Mulroney's), declared that Quebec City, not Ottawa, should be responsible for Quebec's foreign policy in areas of provincial jurisdiction. De Gaulle, dreaming that New France might soon take its place beside the mother country among the francophone nations of the world, encouraged such talk, straining relations with Ottawa. De Gaulle ratcheted the tensions higher in February 1966, when he insisted Canadian NATO forces leave France as part of de Gaulle's partial withdrawal from the alliance. An angry Pearson asked a senior French official whether Canada should also take its hundred thousand war dead who were buried on French soil.

As part of Canada's Centennial celebrations, the Pearson government invited the heads of state from around the world to visit Expo 67 and to come to Ottawa. Fifty-nine agreed. Each had to be given dinner with the prime minister and lunch with the governor general, or vice versa. Pearson, despite his years as a diplomat, disliked pomp and ceremony; the endless procession of leaders walking toward him along a red carpet left him exhausted. Two visits were particularly fraught. The first involved Lyndon Johnson.

From their first official meeting, relations between Johnson and Pearson had been difficult—the president in cowboy clothes carousing around the LBJ ranch; the prime minister in a business suit watching in bemusement (Johnson even invited Pearson to join him in a piss on the side of the road), then getting Pearson's name wrong in front of reporters. The two men had different styles; Pearson disapproved of the president's overbearing earthiness. He was also deeply concerned about American intervention in Vietnam. Pearson had been uncomfortable with the United States' handling of the Korean War and had absolutely no intention of sending troops to Southeast Asia, though critics observed that Canada was happy to sell weapons to the Americans, including the toxic defoliant Agent Orange.

Matters had come to a head in April 1965, when Pearson gave a speech after accepting an award at Temple University in Philadelphia. While largely supportive of American efforts to deter Communist aggression against South Vietnam, Pearson suggested that "a suspension of . . . air strikes against North Vietnam, at the right time, might provide the Hanoi authorities with an opportunity, if they wish to take it, to inject some flexibility into their policy."[7] That, he hoped, might in turn lead to a ceasefire. This infuriated Johnson, who had already invited Pearson to come to Camp David, the presidential compound in Maryland. When Mike arrived, Johnson harangued the prime minister for an hour. Charles Ritchie couldn't hear most of it, but he watched through the window. Johnson "strode the terrace. He sawed the air with his arms. With upraised fist he drove home the verbal hammer blows."[8] According to another account, Johnson grabbed Pearson by the lapels. "You came to my living room and you pissed on my rug!"[9] Relations between John Kennedy and John Diefenbaker had plumbed the depths, but at least they never reached the level of physical assault. From that moment at Camp David, Johnson's enmity toward Pearson was almost as intense as Kennedy's toward Diefenbaker.

Now, in 1967, protocol demanded that Johnson visit Expo 67. The American president made it clear that he was simply fulfilling his duties. The entire trip lasted only a few hours. After a whirlwind tour of the American pavilion, he was helicoptered to the prime minister's summer home at Harrington Lake, having refused to visit Ottawa. Pearson was particularly incensed when he arrived at Harrington Lake to find the

American secret service had taken over the property, and one of them wanted to know who he was and where he was going. "I live here," Pearson replied, "and I am going to the bathroom."[10] After a short, tense meeting, Johnson returned to Washington.

But if the American president's visit to mark Canada's centennial proved to be brief and unpleasant, it did not begin to compare with the visit by Charles de Gaulle. From the outset, de Gaulle and Daniel Johnson sought to structure the trip as a visit by the president of France to Quebec, hosted by its first minister, a de facto recognition of sovereignty. Ottawa kept butting in, demanding final say on arrangements and insisting that de Gaulle visit Ottawa. Everything was contentious: Ottawa wanted de Gaulle to fly to Canada; he insisted on arriving aboard the French cruiser *Colbert*. Paris and Quebec City wanted federal officials largely excluded from the Quebec portion of the trip; Ottawa insisted on an appropriate presence. Should the visit start in Ottawa, Montreal, or Quebec City? The final compromise had the visit begin in Quebec City, with the governor general present, followed by a procession to Montreal and then a formal visit to Ottawa. Should the French host the opening reception on the *Colbert*, or Canada host on shore? And on, and on. The tripartite negotiations—which were mostly Quebec and France against Canada—went on for months, with Paris dangerously close to acknowledging Québécois over federal precedence. In the end, an itinerary was in place all could live with. Everyone crossed their fingers and hoped for the best, though definitions of "best" varied.

Things went well when the *Colbert* docked at Quebec City on the morning of July 23. De Gaulle's 270-kilometre procession to Montreal along the old Chemin du Roy the next day was triumphant. Crowds lined the route, and the years seemed to melt away as the old man reached out to grasp the hands of well-wishers. Tens of thousands lined the streets of Montreal and waited in front of Montreal City Hall. There was not supposed to be a microphone on the balcony, yet there was. There was not supposed to be a working sound system, yet there was. And so the president spoke:

An immense emotion fills my heart when I see before me the French city of Montreal. In the name of the old country, in the name of France, I greet you with all my heart. I'm going to tell you a secret that you will not repeat. This evening, here and all along my route, I found the same kind of atmosphere as that of the Liberation. Furthermore, I noted what an immense effort of progress, of development, and consequently of emancipation you are accomplishing here, and I must say this in Montreal, because if there is in the world a city that is exemplary in its modern successes, it is yours. I say it is yours, and I venture to add, it is ours.

That's what I have come to say to you this evening, and I'll add that I will take away with me an unforgettable memory of this incredible meeting in Montreal. All France knows, sees and hears what goes on here, and I can tell you, it will be the better for it.

> *Vive Montréal! Vive le Québec! Vive le Québec <u>libre</u>!*
> *Vive le Canada Français et vive la France!*[11]

On "*libre*," the crowd roared, Paul Martin gasped, and Mike Pearson summoned cabinet. Though everyone fastened on "*Vive le Québec libre*," the entire speech was an offence. Comparing travelling to Montreal with the Liberation, which Canadians had bled and died to achieve? *Emancipation*?

Martin was inclined to let the incident pass, to write it off as an old man's meanderings. But word had arrived that de Gaulle was talking openly about Quebec independence in private conversations and that French officials were taunting their Canadian counterparts. Anger was building in English Canada over the speech. That evening, Pearson went on television and delivered a statement that had already been sent to the French embassy.

"Certain statements by President de Gaulle tend to encourage the small minority of our population whose aim is to destroy Canada: and as such, they are unacceptable to the Canadian people and its government," he declared. "The people of Canada are free. Every province in Canada is free. Canadians do not need to be liberated. Indeed, many thousands of Canadians gave their lives in two world wars in the liberation of France and other European countries."[12] De Gaulle immediately cancelled the rest of his trip and flew back to Paris the next day.

Unquestionably, de Gaulle's speech fanned separatist flames. But Pearson's response was well crafted. He knew his words of censure would force de Gaulle to cancel the rest of the visit and return to France, whether in disgrace or in triumph depended on your perspective. But as the summer turned to fall and Expo prepared for its October 29 close, two truths seemed clear: when push came to shove, Mike Pearson had the measure of Charles de Gaulle, and Canada's relations with its allies were in no better shape at the end of his prime ministership than they were at the end of Diefenbaker's. In the case of France, they were worse.

III

Would John Diefenbaker accept the inevitable and graciously step down? He was seventy-one years old. His hands trembled such that he had to clasp them to keep people from noticing. He was getting harder of hearing. He had suffered a humiliating defeat at the hands of the party's national executive and its supporters. His chances of winning the upcoming leadership race were non-existent. The moment to declare his intention not to contest the leadership, but to serve until the party chose his successor, came on January 18, when the Progressive Conservatives had their turn to present a free-time broadcast that the CBC in those days offered to each political party on a rotating basis. But it simply wasn't in John Diefenbaker's DNA to go quietly.

In his television address he called for the earliest possible convention date, with only elected delegates permitted to vote, excluding ex-officio delegates such as MPs and party officials. And to anyone who might interpret his words as a parting gesture: "This is no swan song. Those who will interpret it that way do not know me."[13] Indeed they didn't. But he no longer controlled the national executive committee, which was determined to delay the leadership vote to September, to give potential candidates time to organize. Those potential candidates included Ontario premier John Robarts, Manitoba premier Duff Roblin, and Nova Scotia premier Bob Stanfield. The delay hurt early contenders Davie Fulton and George Hees, who had the advantage of being familiar names within the party.

By the time delegates—including ex-officio delegates whom Diefenbaker had tried but failed to exclude—gathered at Toronto's Maple Leaf Gardens in the second week of September, a slew of candidates had thrown their hats in, including former ministers Alvin Hamilton and Michael Starr. Donald

Fleming had come out of retirement to give it a shot, and Senator Wallace McCutcheon was there, too. The two front-runners were Duff Roblin and Bob Stanfield, who had both entered the race that summer. (John Robarts decided not to run.) Roblin, who had been an activist progressive in Manitoba, and who was also proficient in French, had the advantage over Stanfield in flair and charisma, and many were attracted to his claim that he could unite the bitterly divided party. But others were unconvinced. Roblin had flirted with the idea of running for the Progressive Conservatives in the 1965 election. If so, he would have been Diefenbaker's obvious successor, one for whom the Chief would probably have stepped aside. But he changed his mind at the last minute. "His indecision at the time of the 1965 election led some prominent Tories to consider him another Diefenbaker—moody, indecisive, and worst of all, unmanageable," one analysis of the 1967 convention observed.[14]

Roblin also made a serious tactical mistake. Dalton Camp had run successful election campaigns for both him and Stanfield. When the Nova Scotia premier appeared disinclined to run, Camp flew to Winnipeg to offer his services to Roblin. But the "unity candidate" wanted nothing to do with Diefenbaker's nemesis and said he probably wouldn't be a candidate in any case. With both Stanfield and Roblin out of the picture, Camp decided to run himself. But just as he was about to announce, word came that Stanfield had made up his mind to run. The Camp machine swung into action behind the Nova Scotia premier. Roblin then surprised everyone and annoyed many by announcing he was running as well.

But it was the *deux nations* resolution that ultimately did Roblin in. The convention organizers, hoping that the Progressive Conservative Party would get beyond internecine battles and actually stand for something, planned a policy forum for Montmorency Falls in Quebec, shortly before the convention. That conference adopted a resolution on Quebec's role within Confederation: "Canada is composed of the original inhabitants of this land and the two founding peoples: '*deux nations*' with historic rights, who have been, and continue to be, joined by people from many lands." The party's policy committee endorsed the resolution on the eve of the convention. Far from distracting attention from internal party divisions, the proposed policy deepened them. Diefenbaker loyalists condemned the resolution as one that pandered to Quebec and would ultimately lead to separation. Supporters said that a tacit recognition of Canada's linguistic and cultural reality would make the party more attractive to Quebecers. Roblin found himself caught between his Quebec supporters, who embraced the resolution, and his Western supporters, who opposed it.

Nonetheless, as delegates gathered at Maple Leaf Gardens in September, Roblin was the perceived front-runner, followed by the bland and laconic Stanfield, with Fulton and Hees hoping to come up the middle.

The convention opened with one question unanswered: Would Diefenbaker run? His supporters had managed to extract an important concession from convention chair Eddie Goodman and the organizing committee: the Chief would speak Thursday night; nominations would close Friday morning. That Thursday night, the old man owned the stage. Unlike his address at the party conference the previous autumn, he was at the top of his game as he savaged the *deux nations* resolution. "The theory that Canada is two nations can only lead to division and dissention in this country, to de-Confederation," he declared, adding that embracing a *deux nations* approach would "erect a Berlin Wall around the Province of Quebec."[15]

"Let's join together, let's end this business of trying to bring about a policy that will destroy," he pleaded. "Let's bring about One Nation, one that's undivided, let's join the nation in unity and heal the wounds of division." He went so far as to warn that he might not remain in the party if the resolution were adopted. "I couldn't accept any leadership that carried with it this policy that denies everything that I stood for throughout life." It was vintage Diefenbaker, and it left the delegates and the nation wondering what he would do next, which is just how John Diefenbaker liked things. "People have asked me how long it took me to prepare that speech," Diefenbaker wrote in his memoirs. "I answered 'my entire life.'"[16] The next morning, twelve minutes before the 10 a.m. deadline, one of his aides filed the nomination papers. He had no hope of winning. But he aimed to go down fighting.

Diefenbaker's entry destroyed the fading hopes of any number of candidates. Donald Fleming maintained he had been coaxed into running by senior figures in the party because he was seen to be outside the factional wars and because, or so they assured him, neither Diefenbaker nor any premiers were going to run. Now he was up against two premiers *and*

Diefenbaker. "The selfish monster," he declared, when told that Diefenbaker was going to run. "He is the most self-centred and self-seeking man I ever met."[17] Fleming now had no hope of winning. Neither did Michael Starr or Alvin Hamilton or any of the other candidates who were counting on the support of Diefenbaker loyalists. As one disgruntled MP said, "The only people to whom he is meaner than his enemies are his friends. The man does not know the meaning of the word gratitude."[18]

Duff Roblin also lost support from Westerners he could have counted on had Diefenbaker remained outside the race. Now the foolishness of his decision to reject Camp's offer revealed itself. Bob Stanfield's Maritime support remained rock-solid, even as some of the Manitoba delegates abandoned Roblin for other candidates. Roblin's team was outhustled on the floor and in the hallways, as the "unity candidate" refused to make deals that Camp's people were only too happy to arrange. The Stanfield internal communication system was so sophisticated and so secure that the convention organizers ended up using it when they needed to find a doctor quickly. In the end, the Roblin campaign was a bunch of amateurs confronting a bunch of professionals. As Bud Sherman, a pro-Roblin MP, put it, "We just failed to realize that this show was bigger than an election in Winnipeg South."[19]

"I had absolutely no intention of running to succeed myself," Diefenbaker said in his memoirs. But not one of the nine candidates was prepared to unequivocally oppose the two-nations approach to Confederation. "I was determined that this Two Nations resolution would not be accepted by the convention. . . . It would have been interpreted as gross weakness on my part to have voiced my opposition to the heresy of Two Nations and then to have refused to stand against it as a candidate."[20] We can take him at his word or we can ascribe the decision to foolish and selfish vanity. Most likely it was both. Greg Guthrie, who was serving as an aide to Diefenbaker at the time, was with the Chief at the convention. "He knew it could be nothing but a token," he later recalled. "He knew he wasn't going to win, but he also knew he had to go the last few steps to Calvary."[21]

If it truly was a sacrifice, then the sacrifice worked. Realizing that Diefenbaker's implacable opposition to the two nations resolution and his decision to enter the leadership race on the single issue of defeating it threatened to tear the convention and the party apart, Eddie Goodman had Ontario education minister Bill Davis table the motion, effectively killing it. Diefenbaker had won, at least for that day.

On Saturday, September 9, voting day, the old leader sat beside John Bracken, the even older former leader, the two men offering mute testimony to how this party treated its own. On the first ballot, Bob Stanfield led with 519 votes. Duff Roblin came in second, with 349 votes, followed closely by Davie Fulton with 343. George Hees was fourth, with 295 votes, and Diefenbaker fifth with 271. Had the old man withdrawn after the first ballot, those 271 loyalists might have migrated to Roblin. Few would have gone to Fulton or Hees, both of whom Diefenbaker regarded as antagonists.

But though Diefenbaker was visibly distressed by the result, he stayed in for a second ballot. In that round, Stanfield remained in first place, with Diefenbaker's numbers slipping to 172. At this point, the old chieftain decided to withdraw from the race and the hall, heading to the Royal York for a meal. But his aides didn't get the note of resignation to the convention chair in time, so his name remained on the ballot for the third round. Roblin desperately needed the Diefenbaker vote to jump ahead of Stanfield. Some people did come to him, but George Hees and Davie Fulton ultimately withdrew in favour of Stanfield, who won a narrow victory over Roblin, 1,150 to 969 on the fifth ballot. The powers within the party had settled on Stanfield, and Diefenbaker had stayed on the ballot long enough to deprive Roblin of momentum. When Stanfield was brought up on stage, Diefenbaker was there with him, having returned from the Royal York. He spoke briefly and eloquently, asking all members of the party to rally behind the new leader. He concluded: "My course has come to an end. I have fought your battles and you have given that loyalty that led us to victory more often than the Party has ever had since the days of Sir John A. Macdonald. In my retiring, I have nothing to withdraw in my desire to see Canada, my country and your country, one nation."[22] He now seemed completely relaxed, Guthrie noted, even invigorated. At one point, in his reedy tenor, he began to sing "When You Come to the End of a Perfect Day." Recalled Guthrie: "It was a very poor rendition."[23]

IV

The failures of the Pearson government's second term were many and conspicuous. The scandals that culminated in the Munsinger affair (the attempt to smear John Diefenbaker that in the end discredited the prime minister); confrontations with the presidents of France and the United States that left the country's foreign policy arguably in worse shape than when the Conservatives left office; cabinet and caucus revolts that Pearson was only barely able to contain; the return of Walter Gordon to cabinet that only served to reveal and deepen the divides—all this and more bedevilled the prime minister in his last three years.

One particularly contentious issue involved the purchase by Citibank of New York of the Mercantile Bank, a small and unprofitable bank operating in Canada that had previously been Dutch-owned. Citibank executives announced plans to greatly increase the size of Mercantile, which would result in a large, American-controlled bank operating in Canada. Gordon, as finance minister, had drafted changes to the Bank Act that would, in effect, force Citibank to sell its shares. Sharp, as finance minister, introduced those changes. Citibank executives howled and the Johnson administration threatened retaliation. Sharp proposed compromise; Gordon threatened to quit cabinet, again, if he did; Bob Winters threatened to quit if Gordon got his way. In the end, both sides found a way to stay in the same room together and the changes to the Bank Act went ahead with escape valves that would allow Citibank to gradually sell its shares to Canadians without taking a loss. But by the fall of 1967, Pearson's cabinet was almost as divided as Diefenbaker's in 1963. Then came the financial crisis.

Pearson had repeatedly displayed his lack of knowledge or interest in the nuances of economics. Tory times had been hard times. The Liberals responded with huge increases in government spending, which helped to virtually eliminate unemployment. But, of course, the inevitable happened: inflation surged.

To counter inflation, labour unions—some of which had lost control over their members—staged or threatened strikes in search of higher wages. Both the federal government and many large employers caved to their demands, which further fuelled inflationary pressures. Over at the

Bank of Canada, Louis Rasminsky had been trying to keep interest rates low to prevent Canada's robust balance of payments surplus over the U.S.— fuelled in part by the Auto Pact—from growing worse, which he feared would invoke American retaliation. But by the mid-sixties, the bank had no choice but to increase rates, just as Sharp felt he had no choice but to reduce spending and increase taxes. None of it was sufficient—or, more to the point, sufficiently thought through and coordinated—to convince the overseas markets. In the fall of 1967, officials at Finance discovered, to their alarm, that foreign investors weren't very interested in purchasing Canadian bonds. The government was having trouble financing itself. The Americans and the IMF eventually offered temporary assistance, but with the inevitable strings attached. The Liberals' efforts to limit foreign investment had only left the government even more dependent. The Pearson government, it seemed, was staggering from one crisis to another.

These contretemps distracted public attention from several major achievements in the second term that mattered far more than who slept with, or tried to pay off, whom. One was in the field of immigration.

As we've seen, immigration policy from the time of John A. Macdonald to Louis St. Laurent aimed to keep Canada white. Federal and provincial governments reluctantly accepted large numbers of immigrants from Eastern Europe before the First World War, and from Eastern and Southern Europe after the Second. Refugees from Hungary flooded into Canada after the Russian invasion of 1956, though that was more the work of Leslie Frost in Ontario than of Louis St. Laurent in Ottawa, and there had been times when Asians had been allowed in, mostly to do work so dirty and dangerous that whites couldn't be found to take it on. But on the whole, immigration policy imposed and maintained a firm colour bar. Ellen Fairclough, after years of effort, finally managed to eliminate race as a factor in selecting immigrants, one of the Diefenbaker government's proudest achievements. But the rules for admission remained inexact: in practice, each immigration officer decided whether the person being interviewed would make a good Canadian. Moreover, the system favoured family reunification—immigrants sponsoring their brothers and sisters, who in turn sponsored other family members, in a cascading flood of families—over those who would fit the needs of the economy. Finally, although immigration officials in the United States, Britain, and other favoured states processed applications swiftly, stacks of unopened applications piled up in Canadian offices in India and elsewhere, another unspoken method of keeping Asians out.

Tom Kent, after leaving the Prime Minister's Office (which was one reason why Gordon lost his battles against Sharp), had taken up the post of adviser to Jean Marchand at Immigration. Both of them, as well as MPs from all parties on the House immigration committee, were casting about for a fair and simple approach to admitting immigrants to Canada. Kent can't remember who thought up the solution. "It was the kind of idea that, once had, was so obvious that one wondered how it had been missed for so long."[24]

The idea was a formula that would assign points to each application, based on how well and quickly the applicant would fit into Canadian society. There would be points assigned for skills and training that matched needs in the Canadian job market. Younger people were assigned more points than older people. Proficiency in English or French earned you points, as did having a relative or sponsor in Canada. If the applicant earned sufficient points—with the qualifying number set by the government of the day, based on desired immigration levels—that applicant qualified for entry to Canada. The points system was transparent, fair, useful, and reasonably immune from abuse by biased officials or politicians. The policy received all-party support, and even immigration officials welcomed it, knowing that they would be able to judge applications with greater consistency. The points system came into effect on July 1, 1967, and it remains in place, with many modifications, to this day. Australia, New Zealand, and the United Kingdom have borrowed and adapted it for their own use. From the day of its implementation, the Pearson government's immigration reforms began to transform the country, opening Canada's doors to immigrants from India, China, the Philippines, the Caribbean, the Middle East, Africa, and elsewhere, making it one of the Pearson government's finest achievements, and transforming, over several generations, Canada's demographic makeup. Immigration reform made multiculturalism real. By bringing in immigrants from every part of the world, it prevented the creation of a racially defined underclass, sparing Canada from the tensions that too often mark relations between Latino and European Americans in the United States, or between white Europeans and those from Africa and the Middle East in Europe. It helped make Canada a prosperous, polyglot, diverse, and many-cultured country admired around the world. Not one Canadian in a hundred now knows the name of Gerda Munsinger or Lucien Rivard. But just about everyone knows about the points system, in principle if not in detail. Whoever came up with the idea gave us the Canada we live in today.

There were other successes. In foreign policy, Pearson's masterful diplomacy prevented a split in the Commonwealth, when Prime Minister Ian Smith unilaterally declared Rhodesia to be an independent—and apartheid—state. African, Asian, Caribbean, and Mediterranean Commonwealth members, many of which had only just become independent, demanded tough sanctions and even military action to overthrow the Smith regime. For Britain, force was out of the question and sanctions—which would mostly damage the British economy—needed to be limited. More broadly, the newly independent states resented continued British domination of the Commonwealth, while Britain, Australia, and New Zealand resented the militancy of the newly sovereign states. During nine days of acrimonious debate in London in September 1966, compromise seemed impossible. But Pearson, by keeping Canada neutral, was able to craft a final communiqué that contained sanctions while accepting that the Smith regime would be tolerated, though never recognized. Pearson was typically modest, acknowledging criticism that Canada had only been able to broker a deal by abandoning any principle other than preserving unity. "We have nailed our colours firmly to the fence," he said. Though his accomplishment was little noticed at home, where the Munsinger affair continued to dominate headlines, British prime minister Harold Wilson was enormously grateful for Pearson's efforts, which saved the Commonwealth from collapse. The Guardian declared that Canada's prime minister was "the lifeline that held the Commonwealth together."[25]

Pearson's reputation among developing countries might have been so high because, during his final years in office, he completed an arc of self-discovery and commitment as deep-rooted as his Methodist background. As the son and grandson of ministers, he had grown up believing in missionary work and the Social Gospel. Several of his relatives were Methodist missionaries. But he had sniffed disapprovingly at the squalor and poverty he encountered in Egypt during the First World War. In the 1930s and '40s, his focus remained firmly on North America, Europe, and the Western Alliance. But when he visited Ceylon in January 1950 for the talks that became known as the Colombo Plan, Pearson was struck by the poverty he witnessed in the region and became convinced of the need for Canada and other Western nations to support these new and developing countries, especially the fledgling democracies of India and Pakistan.

In the years that followed, Pearson's reasoning on foreign aid became both nuanced and interlocking. He believed that alleviating poverty overseas was morally the right thing to do: the Methodist legacy. It was also in Canada's interest, since bolstering the economies of developing countries also bolstered their ability to trade with Canada. He saw foreign aid as a bulwark against communist expansion. In the 1960s, with the arrival of the space age, he became convinced that a global civilization might be emerging. Finally, as prime minister, he directed foreign aid to newly independent francophone countries in Africa, perhaps with an eye to placating Quebec.

For all these reasons, federal spending on foreign aid almost tripled on Pearson's watch, reaching 0.33 per cent of GDP, a level it had never achieved before and has rarely equalled since. "He started his career as an Atlanticist and ended it a globalist," one analyst later observed.[26]

In Pearson's second term, the government laid the groundwork for both the International Development Research Centre and the Canadian International Development Agency. Weary and distracted by scandals and alarms, the prime minister let Paul Martin handle much of the spadework. But that work sprang from Pearson's own commitment.

In its final months, the Pearson government proposed one of the most sweeping reforms of the justice system in the country's history. It died on the order paper, but a similar bill would be passed two years later. The author of these landmark reforms was Pearson's new justice minister, Pierre Elliott Trudeau.

Lithe, cool, performative (the rose in the lapel, the cape, the Mercedes convertible); Jesuitical, witty (when introduced to the members of the *Globe and Mail*'s editorial board, one of its members said, "I write the short funny ones." Trudeau, without missing a beat, asked, "Who writes the long funny ones?"[27]); mischievous, arrogant and condescending, handsome (ridiculously high cheekbones, startling blue eyes); diffident—*that shrug*—charismatic, infuriating, charming on his best days, cruel and sarcastic on his worst; a wearer of many masks, all of them impenetrable, Pierre Trudeau is the most complex and fascinating figure in Canada's political history.

Pearson and others in the party leadership brought the Three Wise Men to Ottawa because they wanted to infuse the Quebec caucus with new blood, untainted by generations of patronage and corruption. Jean Marchand, the big catch, went straight into cabinet. Trudeau also had a positive reputation in Quebec, though more as a public intellectual than as a social reformer. He also had been scathing toward the Liberals when Pearson reversed his position on accepting nuclear-tipped weapons, calling him "the defrocked prince of peace."[28] But Pearson shrugged off the insult and made the member for Mount Royal his parliamentary secretary.

The two men were as different as could be, and yet there were synergies. Pearson was beginning to think he had given too much away to Quebec in his fruitless quest for agreement on a constitutional amending formula. "Between 1965 and 1968, Pearson's views on Quebec hardened," Andrew Cohen observed.[29] The years of devolution and accommodation were over. Trudeau stoutly opposed special status for Quebec: he fought right-wing nationalism under Duplessis and left-wing nationalism under Lesage. Nationalism in any guise, he believed, sacrificed individual liberty to collective will, which was obnoxious. Instead, he favoured greater integration of Quebec within Canada through policies that promoted bilingualism and greater participation by Quebecers in the federal government and public service. Pearson sent Trudeau to the UN and to Africa to gain some foreign-policy experience, though Trudeau already had some of his own, having visited Russia and China and Cuba. Most of all, Pearson gave Trudeau an insider's look at how a prime minister exercises power: the competing interests, the opportunities, the constraints. And in a move that shocked people within the government and without—they were expecting the popular solicitor general, Larry Pennell, to replace the hapless Lucien Cardin—on April 4, 1967, Pearson appointed Trudeau attorney general and minister of justice.

The new minister gave early warning. "This should be regarded more and more as a department planning for the society of tomorrow," Trudeau told a reporter not long after his appointment. ". . . Society is throwing up

problems all the time—divorce, abortions, family planning, LSD, pollution—
and it's no longer enough to review our statutes every twenty years."[30] Still,
few paid attention as Canada celebrated its Centennial year. But at the end
of that year, the new justice minister brought forward the most profound
changes to criminal law since the Criminal Code was enacted in 1892. One
major reform concerned abortion and family planning. Birth control had
been prohibited in Canada until that time, though people could buy con-
doms "for the prevention of disease only." The new legislation legalized
their use and permitted abortions if a panel of doctors felt a woman's
physical, mental, or emotional health might be at risk.

The legislation also decriminalized homosexual acts between two con-
senting adults in private. Pressure to legalize homosexual acts had been
growing ever since Everett Klippert, who was serving his second multi-year
sentence for gross indecency, was declared a dangerous sexual offender—in
effect given a life sentence—because the Calgary bus driver repeatedly
engaged in masturbation with other men. Tommy Douglas raised the matter
in the House, saying Klippert was mentally ill, not a criminal, and deserved
treatment, not jail. (Such attitudes were considered enlightened at the time.)
Trudeau lifted a line from a *Globe and Mail* article when he declared, "There
is no place for the state in the bedrooms of the nation."[31] He told journalists,
"I want to separate sin from crime," adding, "you may have to ask forgive-
ness of your sins from God, but not from the Minister of Justice."[32] There
was much more in the bill, which also legalized lotteries, imposed limits on
gun use, and introduced Breathalyzer tests to assess alcohol impairment.

The legislation was condemned from many pulpits and in some editorial
pages. But it fit the times, and Trudeau's diffident but confident defence of
the reforms—the slow careful explanations, the shrugs, the intellectual
drawl, the occasional hint of a smile—registered powerfully. Almost overnight he went from being one of the lesser-known figures in the Pearson
government to its most popular and compelling. And the timing was perfect.

Pearson was wearied in body and spirit. His doctor worried about the
condition of his heart. The constant entertaining of foreign dignitaries
throughout Centennial, not to mention the Johnson and de Gaulle affairs,
had left him wrung out. Under their new leader, Robert Stanfield, the
Progressive Conservatives had leapt ahead in the polls. On December 14,

having already told his family of his decision, which Maryon greeted with delight and relief, Pearson announced he was stepping down as leader of the Liberal Party. When the few questions from reporters petered out into embarrassed silence, he sighed, raised his hands, and with a wry grin declared, "*C'est la vie*." And that was that.

V

The Liberal leadership convention was set for April 6, 1968, at Ottawa's Civic Centre. Whoever won would be prime minister, at least until after the next federal election. Paul Martin was the apparent front-runner: the best-known minister in cabinet, the runner-up to Lester Pearson in 1958, and the one who wanted it the most. But he was sixty-four, had known Laurier, and polls showed that Canadians sought a new generation of leadership.

Finance Minister Mitchell Sharp—cerebral, elegant, always viewed in profile, it seemed—was willing to defy the Liberal convention of alternating between French and English leaders. He had the support of the business wing of the Party, as did businessman and cabinet minister Robert Winters until Winters ruled himself out of contention. John Turner, a young lawyer who at thirty-eight was already in cabinet, sought the votes of the next generation of Liberals. Paul Hellyer had stared down the wrath of the generals as he unified the armed forces, which he felt qualified him for the highest office in the land. Eric Kierans, who had attacked Walter Gordon's first budget as head of the Montreal Stock Exchange, had joined the Quebec Liberal government and now sought to lead the federal Liberal Party. So did Allan MacEachen, who could count on the Maritime delegates. There were several other candidates who became also-rans on the day they announced.

And Pierre Trudeau? Would he seek the leadership? Though Peter Newman and Richard Gwyn had started to pay attention to the justice minister, Blair Fraser didn't even mention him in his assessment of possible contenders. Dalton Camp put the odds of Trudeau winning the leadership at seventy-five to one. Old men seated around the white linen tablecloths of the Rideau Club scoffed at the notion. Trudeau had paid no dues, hadn't fought in the war, was friends with Fidel Castro, had even called himself a communist after visiting Russia, China, and Cuba. Loosening abortion restrictions and legalizing homosexuality did not endear him to older Liberals. Rumours circulated that Trudeau was secretly gay. (When Trudeau heard people were suggesting he was homosexual, he angrily replied that any man who thought so should leave him with that man's wife for a couple of hours.) They all underestimated Charlie Trudeau's son.

Charlie had made serious money building gas stations and creating an auto club, and then investing wisely, though his death at forty-seven scarred his teenage son for life. Pierre Trudeau gave himself the best education, studying political economy at Harvard with Joseph Schumpeter and at the LSE with Harold Laski. He also attended the Instituts d'Études Politiques in Paris, travelled widely, and picked up a law degree. He was writing for *Cité Libre* and teaching law at Université de Montréal when the Quiet Revolution that he had encouraged arrived. But to Trudeau's alarm, the movement threatened to veer into separatism. This brought him to Ottawa in 1965, into cabinet in 1967, and into contention for the leadership in 1968.

He belonged to the generation that had come of age after the war. He embraced the civil-liberties values of the baby boomers, the oldest of whom could now vote. He had brought forward groundbreaking legislation that codified the sexual revolution and had defended that legislation with a cerebral sang-froid never before seen in Canadian politics. He was, in a word, cool. And he had a very powerful patron: the prime minister.

Pearson had initially sought out Jean Marchand as his successor, but the former labour leader knew himself well enough to say no. He wore his emotions on his sleeve, his health was uncertain, and his English was uncertain as well. He urged Pearson to consider Trudeau, whose goal of integrating Quebec into the federation while not pandering to nationalists increasingly coincided with Pearson's own views. The prime minister signalled his preference when he sent Trudeau on a heavily publicized tour of the provinces, to consult with the premiers in advance of a February constitutional conference, all of it orchestrated by Marc Lalonde, Pearson's young aide and something of an unofficial Trudeau campaign manager. (He would become one of Trudeau's most trusted advisers and cabinet ministers.) At the February first ministers' conference on the Constitution, Trudeau sat directly beside Pearson, and it was the justice minister's clashes with Daniel Johnson that defined the three days, all covered live by CBC.

The B & B Commission had issued the first volume of its final report only weeks before, repeating its preliminary finding that Canada was passing through the greatest crisis in its history. Johnson had come to power on the rallying cry of *Égalité ou indépendance*. Now he and Trudeau were in the room together ready to have it out. Johnson demanded new constitutional authority for Quebec. That would mean the end of Quebec's influence in Ottawa, Trudeau replied. The justice minister pushed for constitutional reform and greater integration of and respect for Quebec within the federation. "If Mr. Trudeau's policies are followed it will mean the end of Canada," Johnson told reporters, to which Trudeau replied, "If Mr. Johnson's policies are followed, it will mean the end of federalism."[33] But viewers not following the dialectic, or just catching snippets on the evening news, noticed something else about Trudeau, as the historian Paul Litt wrote years later:

> The conference chamber was full of white men in dark suits. Many of them were smoking. He was not. Most of them had grey hair. His was brown. Many of them had moustaches. He was clean-shaven. Practically all of them were fleshy, with jowls, a grey pallor, and suits tented over sagging bellies. Trudeau was lean, taut, and tanned, an action hero in an old folk's home.[34]

It was also clear to those watching live coverage of the conference that federalism had a new champion, a Quebecer who opposed special status for Quebec.

Trudeau made no visible effort to put together a leadership campaign. He didn't have to. In Montreal, in the boardroom of Power Corp. on the top floor of Place Ville Marie, a group of young and high-powered Liberals, including Lalonde and the radical firebrand MP André Ouellet (he would serve in the cabinets of both Trudeau and Jean Chrétien), had been gathering regularly for months to consider the future of the Liberal Party in Quebec. Marchand had brought them together to advise him in his role as Quebec lieutenant. When Pearson announced he was stepping down, they quickly decided to throw their support behind Pierre Trudeau. At the same time, in Toronto, several MPs and political aides organized themselves to promote a Trudeau candidacy and campaign. There was also a cabal of academics at the University of Toronto and York University, including the historian Ramsay Cook, dedicated to the Trudeau cause. Organizers rented an office in Ottawa with their own money to advance the campaign, which alarmed the still-ambivalent Trudeau when he returned from a Christmas vacation in the tropics. Marchand arranged for Trudeau to speak at a meeting of the Quebec Liberal Federation in his capacity as minister of justice. His rousing defence of federalism brought them to their feet. At a similar meeting for the Ontario wing of the party, he was carried through the room on people's shoulders, while young women in miniskirts clapped and cried. There was a word for this accelerating adoration: *Trudeaumania*. Lubor Zink, the fiercely anti-communist columnist for the *Toronto Telegram*—he considered Trudeau a fellow traveller for Moscow—coined the term in derision. Little did he know.

There was strong resistance internally. The Liberal Party of Canada was one of the most storied and successful political institutions in the democratic world, having governed a medium-sized industrial nation for most of the twentieth century. Trudeau hadn't even joined the party until 1965, and two years earlier had called Liberals idiots for supporting nuclear weapons on Canadian soil. Where was the loyalty? Where was the commitment? Paul Martin had devoted his life to the Liberal Party. Was his richly deserved reward to be stolen by this upstart?

Finally, on February 16, a mere seven weeks before the leadership convention, in his typically off-handed way, Trudeau called a press conference to announce he was a candidate for the leadership of the Liberal Party, offering an explanation for that decision no one seeking high office had ever offered before. "It seemed to me . . . as though many of you were saying . . . 'We dare the Liberal Party to choose a guy like Trudeau. Of course, we know they never will.'" And then when someone else was chosen, he continued, the press and public would say, "'Oh well . . . they didn't have the guts to choose a good guy,' because the good guy in your hypothesis really wouldn't be running, and in mine too. . . . And what happened I think is that the joke blew up in your face and in mine."35

As well as being the political beneficiary of this movement to draft him as a candidate (spontaneously generated, though with Marc Lalonde helping behind the scenes), Trudeau got lucky. Two weeks after his February 6 announcement, Robert Winters decided he had been wrong to stay out of the race, and jumped in. Had Winters joined the campaign earlier, and organized better, the establishment and business wings of the party might well have coalesced around him to prevent Trudeau from capturing the party.

Trudeau also benefited from a terrible mistake by Mitchell Sharp. On the evening of February 19, the finance minister was shepherding a tax bill through its final stages in a sleepy House of Commons. Liberal leadership candidates were travelling across the country, chasing delegate votes. The Pearsons were in Jamaica. Sharp fell into the old parliamentary trap of allowing a vote to go ahead on the bill, not realizing that the opposition MPs outnumbered his own. The government lost the vote on third reading, eighty-two to eighty-four. By longstanding parliamentary tradition, a government that loses a vote on a money bill is deemed to have lost the confidence of the House, and must resign. Sharp had inadvertently brought Parliament to the brink of dissolution and the country to the brink of an election, in which Mike Pearson would have to lead the Liberal Party, probably to defeat. When he learned that night of the vote, "I was not only flabbergasted, I was furious," Pearson wrote in his memoirs.[36] The next morning the prime minister rushed back to Ottawa, as did the missing Liberal MPs. Pearson tore a strip off Martin and Winters for being out on the campaign trail instead of tending to their parliamentary duties. With his fingers crossed, he asked Robert Stanfield for a twenty-four-hour adjournment. Stanfield could have refused, as Diefenbaker was urging, insisting instead that the House be dissolved. But the Progressive Conservative leader was too decent a man for such chicanery, or perhaps too gullible; he agreed to the adjournment. A few days later, Liberals secured the support of the Créditistes on a motion that stated the House did not consider the vote of February 19 to be a vote of confidence. The tottering Liberal government survived. But that leadership convention could not come soon enough. And Sharp's reputation for managerial competence was fatally impaired.

The weather was unseasonably warm for the first week of April as delegates gathered at Ottawa's Civic Centre, which quickly became an oven. Who would prevail at the convention was anything but clear. Pierre Trudeau was riding a wave of surging popularity. With the Conservatives ahead in the polls, he seemed the logical choice for a party that needed to regain a sense of momentum. The media were now obsessed with him, virtually to the exclusion of the other candidates. But the Liberal Party was also an institution, and Trudeau stood apart from that institution. Many delegates were opposed to his views on divorce, abortion, and homosexuality. His campaign team, led by Gordon Gibson and Jim Davey, were more enthusiastic than experienced. But on the eve of the convention, that team received a huge boost when Mitchell Sharp dropped out of the race and endorsed Trudeau. He brought a hundred or more delegates with him, along with a campaign team that included Jean Chrétien, the savvy young Quebec MP who was clearly going places. Team Sharp was now part of Team Trudeau.

Still, victory was anything but assured. Paul Hellyer had run a skilful campaign that even included a newfangled computer to keep track of delegates. Paul Martin had criss-crossed the country, calling in every political favour from more than three decades in public office, though his campaign seemed to be fading. Robert Winters, who was vowing to privatize Crown corporations if made leader, had the support of the business wing of the party. Allan MacEachen had solid support in the Maritimes, though Newfoundland premier Joey Smallwood had endorsed Trudeau, and Agriculture Minister Joe Greene, the dark horse, could count on support from delegates in Eastern and Northern Ontario. As the result of the first ballot approached, the question was simply whether establishment Liberals would coalesce around a candidate to prevent the outsider Pierre Trudeau from capturing the Liberal Party.

The free world was in a dark mood that week. On April 4, as delegates gathered to pay tribute to Lester Pearson, Martin Luther King Jr. was assassinated as he stood outside a motel room in Memphis. The resulting riots would burn the inner core of Washington D.C. and other American cities, with Black neighbourhoods the worst hit. The delegates set that aside as they paid tribute to Pearson, watched the throngs that gathered around Trudeau everywhere he went, listened with dismay to Paul Hellyer's wooden speech Friday night (if he had any chance of becoming leader, he lost it with that speech), and were moved to tears by Greene's barnburner invoking the sacrifices of those who, like him, had served in the Second World War. Some delegates shifted from Hellyer to Greene, but that only served to further split the Anyone But Trudeau vote. After the first ballot, Paul Martin, realizing the cause was lost, withdrew with a grace that redeemed him in the eyes of many, including Pearson, who thought he should never have run. Trudeau was in first place. Could anyone catch him?

Robert Winters might have, had Paul Hellyer or John Turner dropped out early and thrown their support to him. But Turner, though he had no hope, stayed on the ballot. Hellyer, though he had no hope, stayed on the ballot. Judy LaMarsh was frantic. "Paul, don't let that bastard win it," she pleaded with Hellyer. "Paul, he isn't even a Liberal."[37] A CBC microphone caught every word. But Hellyer would not be swayed. He and Turner and Winters split the vote ballot after ballot—the standoff dragged on for seven hours, thanks to IBM punch-card machines that repeatedly jammed—until on the fourth ballot, with Hellyer finally out, Trudeau crept over the line, with 51 per cent of the vote. The leadership was his. The modern era of Canadian politics had arrived.

FOURTEEN

Twilight

(1968–1979)

I

In his brief acceptance speech at the Liberal leadership convention on April 6, 1968, Pierre Trudeau declared: "Canada must be unified; Canada must be one; Canada must be progressive and Canada must be a Just Society."[1] What did "Just Society" mean? He never quite spelled it out, but people just seemed to know.

The new prime minister could have met the House of Commons, at least for a few days, in order to allow members to pay tribute to Pearson for his four decades of service in government as public servant, minister, and prime minister. But Trudeau and his team were determined to send a strong message: the Liberal Party under this new leader was something very different from anything that had come before. And so on April 23, three days after Pearson's old friend, Roland Michener, swore in the new prime minister, Trudeau asked the governor general to dissolve the twenty-seventh Parliament (few lamented its passing) and issue writs for an election to be held June 25. It was Mike Pearson's seventy-first birthday.

There has never been, and will likely never be, an election to compare with the coronation of 1968. Though they denied it, most members of the media campaigned energetically for Pierre Trudeau, who left them agog. In the later 1960s there was a certain sort of man—in early middle age, perhaps—who desired a society that was socially progressive and sexually permissive. For them, Pierre Trudeau was not so much a politician as an icon: the literal embodiment of social and sexual utopia. He appealed to Quebecers of all stripes, who saw in him the literal manifestation of the Quiet Revolution. Many voters in English Canada hoped a Trudeau government would confront Quebec separatism head-on, though they may not have fully understood that the bargain would entail the expansion of French as a fully equal official language across the country, at least to the extent that the federal government could make it so. The party platform promised a new constitution that would include a bill of rights, along with expanded satellite service, a foreign and defence policy review, a task force on urban issues, and so on. But the platform wasn't important. Trudeau was important, and nothing else. Women reached for him, tried to kiss him. Television cameras followed his every move. In the wake of Expo 67, and as people bitterly remembered the scandals and shemozzles of Lester Pearson's governments, "his non-involvement in politics became his greatest asset," as Pearson shrewdly observed, "along with his personal appeal, his charisma."[2] This was no longer the Liberal Party of King and St. Laurent and Pearson. This was something entirely new.

Bob Stanfield travelled around the country in a turboprop plane, in contrast with the modern Liberal jet. His campaign was lacklustre, and frankly dumbfounded by Trudeaumania. As John Duffy later observed, "Where Trudeau embodied the go-go spirit of Expo, Stanfield felt like a visit to the Royal Agricultural Winter Fair."[3] The Progressive Conservative leader was photographed eating a banana. It somehow made him seem ridiculous.

There was one issue of substance: The Liberal platform promised "equal treatment and equal rights for all Canadians."[4] But the Conservative platform emphasized the notion of "two founding peoples with historic rights to maintain their language and culture."[5] That sentiment contradicted everything John Diefenbaker had stood for. His party had abandoned One Canada. The leader of the Liberal Party was now its champion.

If anything were needed to seal the Liberal triumph, and probably nothing was, it came on June 24, Saint-Jean-Baptiste Day, the eve of the federal election. Trudeau was at the front of a Montreal reviewing stand when protesters began throwing rocks and bottles. Officials tried to get him to leave, but Trudeau angrily waved them off, defiantly returning to his seat. The whole country witnessed that iron-willed resolve to confront the anarchism of separatism.

Election night smothered, at least temporarily, the regional divisions that increasingly beset the country. The Liberals wiped out the Progressive Conservatives in B.C., tied them for seats in Manitoba, and even claimed five seats each in Alberta and Saskatchewan. In Ontario, they took sixty-three seats to the PCs' seventeen, and in Quebec, fifty-six seats to four. The Tories were strong in the Maritimes and in rural parts of English Canada, and nowhere else. The NDP held firm to its seat count, but Tommy Douglas was defeated in his own riding. The last of the old triumvirate of leaders retired from the stage. While Réal Caouette captured fourteen seats for the Créditistes in Quebec, Social Credit was extinguished in English Canada.

Pearson watched it all with bemusement. "Who needs speeches when you have all the women, who have over 50 per cent of the vote, swoon very time you appear?" he wrote his friend Bill Spencer. "In any event, he now has a good majority. The Tories have been 'dished' so he will have what I never did have, five good years of security in parliament."[6]

Pierre Trudeau would discover, as John Diefenbaker had before him, that a strong majority government can be as much a curse as a blessing. The wave of victories in the West was just that: a wave, which would quickly recede. The sky-high expectations for his Just Society could never be met. But all that was for the future. June 25, the apogee of Trudeaumania, was wondrous to behold.

II

Canada seemed an oasis of calm in the stormy year of 1968. Not only Washington, but Chicago, Baltimore, and other American cities burned in the wake of Martin Luther King's assassination. On June 5, in the midst of

Canada's Trudeaumania election, Bobby Kennedy, John's brother, was shot by Sirhan Sirhan, hours after he won the California primary in his bid for the Democratic presidential nomination. He died in hospital on June 6. Senator Hubert Humphrey ultimately won the nomination, but that victory was overshadowed by the violence surrounding the convention itself, as Chicago police viciously attacked anti-war protesters. Lyndon Johnson, broken by the failures of his armies in the jungles of Vietnam and rage against the war at home, had not sought a second term. Former Republican vice president Richard Nixon won the election in November, on a promise to end the war and to restore peace at home. Support for the war in Vietnam had plummeted among Americans, as the fighting and bombing dragged on without resolution. Poor young men, many of them Black, did much of the fighting, while the sons of the affluent often found a way to avoid the draft, or headed north to Canada.

In France, students protesting capitalism, consumerism, American power, whatever, occupied university campuses in May. The heavy-handed police response prompted trade union leaders to call for worker solidarity, which prompted wildcat strikes that merged into a general strike that brought the economy and even the government shuddering to a halt. With the Communists emerging as a possible alternative government, de Gaulle fled the country on May 29 to confer with the general commanding French forces in Germany. Convinced he still had the backing of the army, the French president returned, dissolved the National Assembly, and called for parliamentary elections. That and an agreement among employers, unions, and politicians to raise wages, calmed the situation. The protests dissipated and the Gaullists were strengthened in the elections that followed. Things did not go so well in Czechoslovakia, where Communist Party first secretary Alexander Dubček sought to deliver greater political and economic freedom. Soviet tanks crushed the Prague Spring in August, leading to another generation of darkness for the captive peoples of Eastern Europe.

If Canadian students lacked the ideological fervour of their American and French compatriots, they did share the growing concern over a degrading environment. Rachel Carson's 1962 bestseller *Silent Spring* had alerted the world to the environmental harm caused by pesticides. In Canada, pesticides were heavily used on farms and in gardens, raw sewage contaminated the Great Lakes, and fumes from industry and automobiles fouled city air. Environmental groups sprang up in British Columbia, Ontario, and the Maritimes. Long-established conservation groups and new environmental organizations were pushing for limits to pesticides and curbs on industrial emissions. The federal and provincial governments moved slowly, but by 1968 most had established departments of the environment and were beginning to draw up regulatory codes. Ontario would become a leader in the struggle to protect endangered species.

The women's movement was transitioning from the Voice of Women's opposition to nuclear weapons to a younger and more militant concern with the place of women in society. In organizations such as the Company of Young Canadians, established in 1966 by the Pearson government to emulate the U.S. Peace Corps (the enterprise was short-lived), women demanded an equal role and voice in decision making. They demanded greater respect for the equality of women in education and called for new programs that would study their unique and disadvantaged role in society. Pearson had responded in February 1967 with the Royal Commission on the Status of Women. (It was telling that the order establishing the commission referred to the journalist who chaired it not by her professional name, Anne Francis, but as Mrs. John Bird.) Métis Canadians were forming provincial organizations to push for rights and services, while First Nations drew lessons from rising Native American militancy south of the border. "Lament for Confederation," a speech delivered by Chief Dan George in 1967, signalled the arrival of a new generation of Indigenous activists unwilling to accept the self-congratulatory bromides of the Centennial and determined to secure rights that they had long deserved:

> I have known you when your forests were mine; when they gave me my meat and my clothing. I have known you in your streams and rivers where your fish flashed and danced in the sun, where the waters said 'come, come and eat of my abundance.' I have known you in the freedom of the winds. And my spirit, like the winds, once roamed your good lands.
>
> But in the long hundred years since the white man came, I have seen my freedom disappear like the salmon going mysteriously out to sea.

Pierre Trudeau came before a restless people who were unwilling to burn or to occupy (in any serious way), but who were questioning, aspiring, hoping. He promised to fulfill those hopes, while unifying an increasingly fractured country. He would fail, at least in part. But 1968, the most tumultuous year for the United States and for many others in the world, was for many Canadians a year of impatient hope.

III

Mike Pearson surely knew and understood that Pierre Trudeau found it politically necessary to discard him. Voters needed to believe that the scandals, the parliamentary embarrassments, the slipshod way of doing things were being replaced by a new generation of Liberals and a new method of governing. Pearson had studied history at Oxford; Trudeau majored in political economics at Harvard and the LSE. Systems analysis and management theory replaced personal diplomacy and the management of getting by. Keen observers had noted in the 1950s that the powers of Parliament were being supplanted by a cabal of powerful cabinet ministers under the beneficent chairmanship of Louis St. Laurent. Now, in the late 1960s, cabinet itself was being supplanted by a burgeoning and increasingly powerful Prime Minister's Office. Government by the Centre had arrived; its growth over the next half century and beyond would be relentless.

But for the departing prime minister, all of this was tomorrow's news. If it wounded Pearson that he had been so visibly kicked to the curb—virtually ignored after the first night of the leadership convention; no tributes in the House of Commons; an election in which Trudeau effectively if wordlessly repudiated the previous Liberal administration as much he did the Conservatives—he never let on. During the election, he went to any riding the campaign team wanted him to visit, put in a good word for the local candidate and the party leader, did his duty, and when it was all over, went home.

He became increasingly unhappy, however, with Trudeau's foreign policy. The new prime minister thought Canada had been for too long a good and faithful servant of the United States, which was a bit much, given the Bomarc missile crisis and the Pearson government's public questioning of the war in Vietnam. In any case, the Trudeau government searched for an alternative path that kept Canada within the Western alliance while also strengthening ties outside it. Canada didn't have a foreign policy, Trudeau told his associates; it only had a defence policy. "Canada's present military establishment was determined not to impress our enemies but rather to impress our friends," he told cabinet.[7] The new PM appeared inclined to withdraw all Canadian forces from Europe, but, faced with a cabinet revolt, he settled for a 50 per cent reduction, to about five thousand men. A 1970 white paper on foreign policy rejected the Pearsonian role of Canada as "helpful fixer" and ally of the United States, focusing instead on a narrow definition of national interest and progressive values, "the extension abroad of national policies," as its guiding philosophy.[8] Pearson was quietly furious. "Foster social justice—baloney!" he scrawled indignantly in the margins of his copy. In a private memorandum that he circulated among friends, he wrote, "We will never get a world of peace, security and international relations by the pursuit of national self-interest as the principal objective of foreign policy. The promotion of national interest in the narrow, traditional sense merely evokes resistance from other nations, also in the name of national interest, and this inevitably leads to confrontation and conflict." Far better, he insisted, to pursue "a national interest which expresses itself in co-operation with others."[9] But he stayed quiet in public, even though Trudeau only consulted him once on foreign policy, and then only briefly.

In any case, he had other irons in the fire. The BBC invited Pearson in 1968 to give the celebrated Reith lecture, which he devoted to personal reminiscences of a life in foreign affairs during interesting times. His primary interest, however, was in promoting foreign aid, and he willingly took up the invitation of Robert McNamara, who was now president of the World Bank, to chair a commission on the subject. The commission was criticized for being largely composed of members of developed countries, but Pearson insisted its primary purpose was to convince the North to invest more heavily in the South. In its report, the Commission on International Development, universally known as the Pearson Commission, asserted that developing countries were making much more rapid progress than developed countries had made at a similar stage of their evolution, and could achieve developed status relatively quickly with sufficient support from the developed world.

Pearson and his colleagues failed to grasp the fragility of democratic institutions in many of those countries; the depth of corruption and nepotism; conflicts among ethnic groups brought about by illogical, colonially drawn borders; destabilizing measures effected by foreign powers—especially the United States and Russia; and the will to power of strong men. But McNamara said the report was useful as a way of getting affluent states to increase their contributions.

Through all of this, he was teaching a course at Carleton University, while he worked on his memoirs. Mike and Maryon, who had become deeply affectionate toward one another in Pearson's retirement, had moved out of 24 Sussex to a comfortable home in Rockcliffe Park, where they greatly enjoyed the visits of children and grandchildren. Pearson recalled that one night, after attending the press gallery dinner party, he was dozing in the back of a cab when it passed the driveway to 24 Sussex Drive. Startled, he called out, "In there. In there." The driver looked back, smiling sadly, and replied, "Mr. Pearson, you don't live there anymore."[10]

The Second World War had taken its toll on the Ottawa men, those charged with mobilizing the Canadian economy and sustaining a navy, air force, and armies in the field. Mistakes cost lives, and failure was intolerable, with the very survival of democracy at stake. They worked punishing hours under unrelenting stress. To compensate, many of them chain-smoked and drank too much. Years later, they paid the price.

Hume Wrong, Norman Robertson, and Mike Pearson had forged the very deepest bonds of friendship. The three men agreed to be buried side by side at a cemetery above the town of Wakefield, a serene field that overlooks the Gatineau Hills. Hume Wrong went first, and too soon. By 1953, he was clearly unwell. Mike moved his friend back to Ottawa from Washington for three months of medical leave. But only two weeks after he took on his new duties as undersecretary, his heart began to fail. Mike stayed close, trying to find a place where Hume and his wife Joyce could rest peacefully. But it was too late. At the Wrongs' home, Mike convinced his friend to go to the hospital, carrying him to the car himself. Wrong was gone the next day, at fifty-seven. The two men had served in External together for a quarter century. They had been rivals, at times, but more often co-conspirators, and always friends. Mike missed him deeply for years. Norman Robertson died in July 1968, at sixty-eight, four months after Mike stepped down as prime minister.

In 1970, Pearson told friends he was having eye trouble. It was more than trouble; it was a cancerous tumour. One eye was removed and replaced with a glass one. Through it all, he worked steadily on his memoirs. In the fall of 1972, the first volume arrived, becoming an instant number-one bestseller. Its pages are filled with grace, humour—almost all of it self-deprecating—and insight. Sadly, the two remaining volumes do not measure up, for Pearson was unable to complete them. Soon after the first volume's publication, followed by a punishing book tour, his health began to fail. Word went out to the inner circle that those who wanted to see him should see him soon. Walter Gordon decided to visit. The half-hour conversation was friendly, with Pearson expressing regret that they had "drifted apart." But though Gordon believed that Pearson would "go down in history as not only a witty, humorous person, and in many ways a lovable human being, but as one of Canada's great men," he was not prepared, then or later, to forgive his old friend for what Gordon thought was a string of personal betrayals, from the 1963 budget to his second, fruitless, return to cabinet.[11]

Pearson made as many notes as he could for the second and third volumes, but cancer had returned and chemotherapy was not working. (Aides, historians, and his son Geoffrey completed the task posthumously as best they could, based on his diaries and notes.) He faced the end stoically, joking with Keith Davey that at least he wouldn't have to endure watching the Leafs fail to make it into the playoffs. Trudeau finally had him over to lunch, and offered a government plane to fly Mike and Maryon to Florida for the Christmas holidays. But a few days later they were back in Ottawa, as Mike's liver cancer advanced rapidly. He fell into a coma on December 26, 1972, and died the following day.

In all the pomp of the state funeral at St. Andrew's Cathedral—the solemn tones of the CBC commentators; the procession of mourners past the casket; the representatives of governments who came to the service, including British prime minister Edward Heath; the honour guard; the firing of cannons—one thing stood out: the Canadian flag draped over the coffin. His flag.

IV

Robert Stanfield stepped in it by saying after he'd won the leadership, "personally, I'm determined to get along with that fellow Camp," and by appearing to suggest he'd like to move into Stornoway sooner rather than later.[12] In a personal meeting with Diefenbaker after the convention, he tried to make amends. But in truth there was nothing Stanfield could have said or done to soften Diefenbaker's rage. Dalton Camp had stripped him of his party's leadership, had publicly humiliated him. Bob Stanfield was simply Camp's agent, or puppet.

The Diefenbakers found a home in Rockcliffe Park, in which the basement rec room was converted into a shrine to John, with all the doctoral robes he'd worn on display. He moved into a relatively small office across the hall from the Prime Minister's Office—trading space for proximity to power—which he crammed with photographs and memorabilia, including the mounted marlin, in memory of his wars with Kennedy. He kept away from caucus, and even remained silent in the House for a few months, only breaking that silence in November. In the Trudeaumania election of 1968, he stayed in his safe-as-houses riding of Prince Albert, agreeing to appear only briefly with Stanfield in photo-ops that were so clearly uncomfortable for both men that the events probably did more harm than good. Not that anything could have helped the Tory cause in the election of 1968. "The Conservative Party has suffered a calamitous disaster," Diefenbaker told the CBC on election night, more in joy than in sorrow.

The election results left Stanfield in a difficult spot. There were more Diefenbaker loyalists than Stanfield loyalists in the backbenches behind him. Alberta MP Jack Horner led an unofficial opposition to the leader of the Opposition. Things turned ugly in early 1969, when the Trudeau government introduced the Official Languages Act. The act established French and English as equal languages in the federal government and created a commissioner of official languages charged with promoting bilingualism. Diefenbaker called the commissioner a "commissar" and joined sixteen Conservatives who voted against the bill on second reading. Fourteen abstained, while Stanfield was able to bring only forty of his own MPs with him in supporting the bill. The next day, the Conservative leader laid down the law, castigating MPs who forced a recorded vote. "Their stupidity was exceeded only by their malice," he told caucus. "There are some things in a political party one simply does not do to one's colleagues."[13] The rebellion petered out, and the bill passed on third reading on a voice vote. Horner continued trying to stir up trouble, but for the most part, Stanfield was able to keep the Conservatives together leading up to the election of 1972.

Diefenbaker and Trudeau got on well at a personal level. Both men rejected the two-nations theory of Confederation. Trudeau admired Diefenbaker's championing of the Bill of Rights. The thirteenth prime minister was delighted when the fifteenth invited him to Sussex Drive for lunch. "We were friends because we understood each other," Trudeau told reporters after Diefenbaker's passing.[14] Diefenbaker, like Pearson, supported Trudeau when he invoked the War Measures Act in the wake of the FLQ kidnappings of British diplomat James Cross and Quebec cabinet minister Pierre Laporte, though the Chief couldn't see the need for soldiers wearing helmets. The kidnappers murdered Laporte but released Cross in exchange for safe passage to Cuba. The October Crisis darkened the mood of a country that seemed to be tearing itself apart. The mood darkened further when Quebec premier Robert Bourassa rejected Trudeau's constitutional proposals, known as the Victoria Charter. By 1972, Trudeaumania had long since vanished; the Liberal prime minister came across as arrogant and disdainful to many voters, who were also feeling the effects of a troubled economy. Central bankers in Canada, the United States, and Europe had decided in the 1960s to combat unemployment by permitting a reasonable level of inflation. But by 1972, inflation had reached 5 per cent, unemployment was at 6 per cent and climbing, and the federal government was running chronic deficits. In the general election of 1972, the Liberal campaign slogan, "The Land Is Strong," was both inane and, on its face, untrue. People had started to warm to the modest and moderate Bob Stanfield. On election night, the results were so close there was no apparent winner. After recounts, the Liberals crept ahead, 109 seats to the Conservatives' 107. Almost half of those 109 seats were in Quebec. The Liberal Party was once more virtually banished from the West. For Diefenbaker, the results were perhaps ideal. Whatever he felt for Trudeau personally, he opposed most of his government's policies, complaining that improvements to the unemployment insurance program would simply encourage people not to work, and despairing at the Liberals' ongoing program to diminish the importance of the monarchy in Canada. Canada Post? Whoever heard of such a thing? On the other hand, Robert Stanfield as prime minister would have vindicated the machinations of Dalton Camp in 1966 and 1967. All in all, the result for Diefenbaker was probably just about perfect.

He still rose early for a brisk walk and was in the office before eight, mostly to respond to correspondence handled by a team of devoted secretaries and executive assistants who failed to make sense of his typically disorganized files. He greeted staff with the query "News, views, interviews?" which was his way of soliciting gossip.[15] Tales of Liberal incompetence, infighting, and confusion were welcome; tales of Conservative incompetence, infighting, and confusion were better still. If the news was particularly juicy, he would phone Ollie to tell her. The two of them fed off each other, a bitter brew. Olive felt her husband had been cruelly betrayed by Dalton Camp and his henchmen, and by the party as a whole. While deeply loyal to John, she helped darken his world view to the point that he started to become a caricature of himself. Or, as one wag put it in 1967: "John Diefenbaker is a madman who thinks he's John Diefenbaker."[16]

But there were many good days as well. He loved to regale schoolchildren with his stories while taking them on tours of Parliament Hill. He accepted just about any speaking invitation. He was still the best quote a reporter could hope to find, and a bit of a folk hero to the younger generation of Hill correspondents. And he could still be a lethal antagonist in the House, as Liberal cabinet ministers discovered to their discomfort. Trudeau, however, sometimes got the better of him; when that happened, Dief would return silently to his office and was best not disturbed.

He began working on his memoirs, which were where he could and should have reconciled the contradictions of his self-narrated life, a life of virtually unlimited achievement, in his mind, marred only by the craven betrayals of enemies, from T.C. Davis in Alberta to the power brokers of the Conservative Party in Ottawa to John F. Kennedy in Washington to Mike Pearson and his henchmen across the aisle to Dalton Camp, his Iago. But the Chief, as loyalists still called him, had always been disorganized in his habits, and writing an autobiography requires discipline. A bevy of aides and academics did their best to help him get his thoughts down, but there was always a phone call to take, a speech to give. The first volume, which deals with his youth on the prairie and his rise to leadership of the party, has its moments; there are fewer moments in the volumes on his years in power and in opposition.

In 1974, having poured billions into social programs to secure the support of NDP leader David Lewis, Trudeau engineered his government's defeat and went back to the people. His campaign was based largely on derision of Stanfield's proposed wage and price controls. "Zap, you're frozen," Trudeau would lampoon, insisting wage and price controls were an impractical solution to rising inflation. Having secured a comfortable majority government, Trudeau then imposed wage and price controls. It was his most craven act as a politician.

Stagflation had arrived, worsened by an oil embargo imposed by Arab producers against Western governments as punishment for their support of Israel during the 1973 Yom Kippur War. The oil shocks were a shock, but the real problem was chronic inflation: people and businesses expected prices would go up, and adjusted their wage demands and price increases accordingly, fulfilling the prophesy. Not until the end of the decade would central banks, led by the U.S. Federal Reserve, take on inflation by raising interest rates. The medicine worked, though the recession that followed almost killed the patient.

On January 1, 1976, Diefenbaker received the highest honour of his later years: the Queen named him a Companion of Honour in her New Year's honours lists. There are only sixty-five such companions, who are chosen by the Queen herself rather than recommended to her by her prime minister. Diefenbaker greatly enjoyed his March trip to Windsor Castle to receive the honour, as well as his time in London, where he was hosted by Paul Martin, now high commissioner. The two men were warriors of the old school who fought it out on the floor of the Commons without ever losing respect for each other. The salons of London received the wit and wisdom of the old Prairie lawyer. The Chief told the stories he so loved to tell; by all accounts they went down well.

Diefenbaker took little interest in the Conservative leadership convention in February of that year. The front-runners appeared to be Brian

Mulroney—the former young Tory whose advice on Quebec Diefenbaker had ignored, who was now a Quebec lawyer and business executive—and Claude Wagner, a former provincial Liberal justice minister. But Alberta MP Joe Clark—"Joe Who?" the *Toronto Star* headline asked, derisively—came up the middle to win the convention on the fourth ballot. Diefenbaker could not have been happy that one of the youth organizers of the campaign to unseat him was now leader of the party and was almost certain to become prime minister. The economy was a mess and the Liberals seemed out of ideas to unite the country or to restore prosperity. That same year, René Lévesque's Parti Québécois came to power, promising a referendum on sovereignty, but promising good government as well.

For John Diefenbaker, 1976 ended in grief. Olive had been slowly failing from arthritis and a heart condition. Throughout 1976, she recovered from a previous stroke; then came a heart attack in October. Released from hospital to be with her family over Christmas, she died on December 22. Diefenbaker was inconsolable. He had loved her very much.

He'd lost Elmer five years earlier. John's letters in February 1971 expressed concern that his brother wasn't feeling well, then optimism that he would soon be better, that the stay in hospital wouldn't be a long one, that a full recovery would begin soon, that he would regain the strength to walk. "You have had a long siege but I am hopeful that you will be back in circulation without much delay," he wrote in May.[17] Two weeks later, he was pleased to hear that someone had wheeled Elmer to a window so that he could enjoy the sun. Elmer passed on June 11. William and Mary and Elmer and Edna and Ollie. All gone. He was alone.

He worked on his own funeral, casting and recasting the roster of characters and the order of events. When he had become chancellor of the University of Saskatchewan in 1969, he had announced the university would receive his personal papers, which the university accepted reluctantly, given the expense. The Diefenbaker Centre overlooks a hill above the university and includes a replica of his office as prime minister, marlin included.

In 1979, he declared his intention to run for the thirteenth time as a member of Parliament. He should not have. At eighty-three, he was beginning to show signs of dementia. He thought Olive was visiting him. He told his aide, the long-suffering Keith Martin, that when he returned to Ottawa he intended to consult with Mackenzie King on some important matter. But it was not in him to quit, and not in others to make him. Early in that spring's campaign he had a bad fall, perhaps as a result of a stroke. Party aides kept him secluded for five days as rumours swirled. On the sixth day, recovered, he went out mainstreeting. From then until election day, his friends kept his schedule light while watching over his every word and move. On May 22, he won Prince Albert one last time by more than four thousand votes, part of a minority-government victory by Prime Minister–designate Joe Clark. After the swearing-in, Clark resolved on a lengthy hiatus before recalling Parliament, which may or may not have contributed to his government's growing unpopularity, its defeat on a budget vote in November, and Pierre Trudeau's return to power in February 1980. But John George Diefenbaker was not there for any of it. Having returned to Ottawa in July, and sending off another memorandum on proposed changes to his funeral, he died alone in his study during the early hours of August 16. He was buried at the University of Saskatchewan. Olive was disinterred from Ottawa's Beechwood cemetery and reinterred by his side. She would have wanted that.

Epilogue

The single greatest difference between Lester Bowles Pearson and John George Diefenbaker was in their ability to grow. Pearson could; Diefenbaker couldn't. Pearson's views on Britain and its empire, on the United States, on developing countries, on federalism, all evolved. Diefenbaker rarely changed his mind and never admitted he had. One good example of the Liberal prime minister's flexibility was Pearson's attitude to women. He went from seeing no reason to have two women in cabinet—if indeed that was the case—to appointing the Royal Commission on the Status of Women. The governments of Pierre Elliott Trudeau and his successors implemented some, though not all, of its recommendations: the recommendation that "housewives should be entitled to pensions in their own right under the Canada Pension Plan" remains unfulfilled to this day.[1] But if later governments may take credit for implementing at least part of the commission's vision, the Pearson government deserves praise for convening the commission in the first place.

Yet the same surely applies to Diefenbaker's decision in 1962 to establish the Royal Commission on Taxation, chaired by Toronto accountant Kenneth Carter, in response to complaints from business interests that the tax system had become hopelessly complicated. Carter pursued the radical notion that "a buck is a buck is a buck," and that all should pay their fair share, including corporations and people whose income was based on appreciating assets rather than wages. The Carter Commission's recommendations were so unpalatable to business interests that, when the report finally landed in

1967, the Pearson government refused even to pay the cost of having it mimeographed. But the Trudeau government did implement one important recommendation, which is why we have a capital gains tax today. The Trudeau government is credited with establishing the tax, but the Diefenbaker government deserves praise for convening the commission in the first place.

One purpose of this book has been to attempt to dispel the false narrative that the two Pearson governments accomplished much while the three Diefenbaker governments accomplished little. In many fields, each shared in the record of accomplishment, and in some cases the St. Laurent government deserves its share of praise as well. The Pearson government implemented universal public health care in response to a royal commission launched by the Diefenbaker government. The Diefenbaker government established universal public hospital care in response to legislation passed but not implemented by the St. Laurent government. All three prime ministers share in the achievement of establishing, implementing, and refining equalization. The St. Laurent government decided to cancel the Avro Arrow project; the Diefenbaker government took the blame in implementing the decision. Diefenbaker and Pearson share credit for creating a race-blind immigration system. Both fought to preserve the Commonwealth while opposing apartheid. One of John Diefenbaker's greatest failures, his botched dismissal of James Coyne as governor of the Bank of Canada, led his government to implement important reforms in preserving the independence of that office, which the Pearson government codified. However different the two men were—however likeable Mike Pearson may have been and however difficult John Diefenbaker may have been at times—they shared many of the same values, making their governments a continuum of progress toward the Canada we know today.

On the flip side, both sought to improve relations between Canada and the United States, only to leave things in a shambles. Neither were very good at understanding, let alone managing, the economy. Neither could control their caucus.

Where the two prime ministers disagreed, it's sometimes hard to know who was closer to the truth. Diefenbaker first accepted, then refused to accept, tactical nuclear weapons for the Canadian Armed Forces. Pearson, reversing his previous position, promised to accept them if elected. His move was politically canny and successful, if hypocritical. But Pierre Trudeau later had the weapons removed. Today, most Canadians would be surprised to hear that at one time, nuclear weapons were stationed on Canadian soil, and Canadian fighters had nuclear-tipped missiles, all under American control. As historian Michael Stevenson points out, Howard Green's opposition to nukes on Canadian soil "should be viewed sympathetically, as it foreshadowed official Canadian policies adopted in the 1970s that remain entrenched to the present day."[2]

Diefenbaker was naive to believe that Canada could strengthen economic ties with Great Britain, which was shedding the very empire he sought to preserve. Pearson was far more realistic in acknowledging the reality of American power. But in seeking to increase trade with the U.K., Diefenbaker pursued goals similar to those of Walter Gordon: reducing the dangerously high level of American investment in Canada and Canadian dependence on the American economy. Diefenbaker's route was through trade diversification rather than through limits on foreign investment, mirroring the policies pursued by federal governments from Brian Mulroney to Justin Trudeau.

Similarly, Pearson understood better than Diefenbaker the ferment roiling Quebec and the need for English Canada to accommodate French aspirations. But Diefenbaker's championing of One Canada at its best (though it was not always at its best) echoed Trudeau's belief in a strong federal government leading a unified, bilingual nation. It was Diefenbaker, after all, who brought simultaneous translation into the House of Commons. And if Canada has, in fact, accommodated the *deux nations* reality—something Stephen Harper's government acknowledged in 2006 when it introduced a motion in the House of Commons that recognized that "the Québécois form a nation within a united Canada"—then that reality must also acknowledge that the federation is arguably weaker as a result, with Quebec possessing most of the tools needed for self-government and insistently demanding it be given more.

More than Mike Pearson, John Diefenbaker reshaped the political geography of the country. Doug Fisher, speaking in the 1980s from his vantage point as columnist and former NDP MP, thought that Ottawa in the Diefenbaker years became the focus of national attention in a way it had never been before but has always been since. He credited Diefenbaker for bringing the West finally and permanently into the national political debate. And he believed the harsh verdict against Diefenbaker from some historians stemmed from that fact that Diefenbaker disrupted a comfortable establishment narrative. "He ended the Golden Era that Granatstein talks about when marvellous bureaucrats ran Ottawa and the press gallery was adorned by marvellous journalists like Blair Fraser and Grant Dexter. He ended all that and opened up the whole process." Fisher also observed that many of Diefenbaker's harshest critics are ideologically to the left of centre "and most of them don't see that Diefenbaker was pretty left-of-centre himself. But he wasn't with the right party."[3] Merrill Menzies credited Diefenbaker with breaking the hold of the Bay Street business tycoons on the party, noting, "The party will never go back to the old Bay Street Days."[4] Gordon Drummond Clancy, who was MP for the Saskatchewan riding of Yorkton in the Diefenbaker years, believed that Diefenbaker was always more popular in the West than in the East, where "his welcome wore out more quickly—he was not their style of politician."[5] In this writer's experience, all of those observations remain true today.

But putting the record of the Diefenbaker government in a more favourable light does not in any way diminish what Mike Pearson accomplished. He took a sclerotic Liberal Party that was badly in need of reform and reformed it, leaving the party stronger when he left than when he arrived— a rarity in politics. Both the Diefenbaker and Pearson governments improved life for the poor and increased pensions for seniors, but it was the Pearson government that instituted the Canada Pension Plan and the Canada Assistance Plan, and that provided loans for college and university students. And Canada's fourteenth prime minister was justifiably proud of an achievement for which John Diefenbaker may not share an iota of credit: the Canadian flag. Those who would say the flag is only a symbol don't understand the power of symbols. John Diefenbaker understood their power, which is why he fought against the flag with every fibre of his being. He lost and deserved to lose.

On December 27, 2022, on the fiftieth anniversary of Pearson's death, the seven living prime ministers paid tribute to his legacy in the *National Post*. "He dreamt of, and helped build, a Canada that punched above its weight on the world stage," wrote Justin Trudeau. Paul Martin Jr. spoke of the close friendship and shared values between Pearson and his father, Paul Martin Sr. Stephen Harper recalled that his "little neighbourhood in Leaside, Ont., was consumed by the flag debate. Many neighbours stopped speaking to one another, so intense were the differences." (The Harpers, for the record, favoured a new flag.) But once the new flag was run up the pole at his local school, "very quickly peace returned to the neighbourhood." Kim Campbell may have offered the most nuanced assessment. "When he left office," she observed, "the personality that Canada showed to the world was optimistic, modern, imaginative, and free." Campbell acknowledged the scandals that beset his two governments, but remarked, "What's astonishing is that in the midst of this political chaos, measures were taken that put their stamp on Canada." She added, "He was also a hard man to know, even for his own children. Yet his influence on Canada has rarely been matched. What enabled a man in many ways so unsuited to politics to accomplish all he did? Perhaps it was the times—or perhaps the values he held so strongly. Whatever the reason, we are all Pearsonians today."[6]

Mike Pearson and John Diefenbaker were very different men. Pearson was fundamentally decent, collegial, funny at his own expense, a team player, someone people wanted to have as a friend, though it is remarkable how critical some of his colleagues—Walter Gordon, Tom Kent, Judy LaMarsh—were of him in their memoirs. Diefenbaker was vain, untrusting, indecisive, and, as the years went on, increasingly paranoid. He might have resisted, or at least curbed, the worst of those tendencies had he come to office earlier in life, or been given a chance to apprentice for the job of prime minister by first serving in cabinet or for a term as leader of the official opposition. It was not to be.

Yet if the conventional narrative praises Pearson and buries Diefenbaker, that narrative ignores the substantial achievement of his governments. It ignores, as well, a bond that Diefenbaker forged with the people, one that Pearson could only envy.

On a warm September evening in 1967, I entered the living room of my grandmother's house in Gravenhurst, Ontario, to find Grandma and my mom in front of the black-and-white television set, shaking their heads in distress. I asked what was wrong. They said the most terrible thing was happening to John Diefenbaker. Who was John Diefenbaker? He was a great leader, they told me. He had been our prime minister. Every time he spoke it was an inspiration, the equal of Winston Churchill. And now these awful men were betraying him, forcing him out as leader of the Conservative Party. The three of us watched the balloting that Saturday. I was twelve, and knew nothing about politics, but I knew how upset Mom and Grandma were over John Diefenbaker's defeat at the 1967 leadership convention, though they were no more political than typical working-class women of their time. They worshipped him. They were the sort of people who would have been thrilled had he shaken their hand while mainstreeting during an election campaign, who were inspired by his vision of One Canada, who wept with him when the red ensign was lowered, who would have stood silently at a crossing had the funeral train rumbled through their town. Perhaps John A. Macdonald had that bond with the Canadian people, perhaps Wilfrid Laurier, but no one else before John Diefenbaker, and none since. The powerful may have despised him, but common folk loved him. And he never betrayed that love.

Notes

PREFACE
1   In conversation with the author, March 2022.
2   "Diefenbaker Funeral Train," *Trackside Treasures*, 14 June 2014. http://tracksidetreasure.blogspot.com/2014/06/diefenbaker-funeral-train.html
3   Ron Base, "Hello Sweetheart . . . Give Me Val Sears," *Ron Base Writes*, 24 January 2016. (Memories differ; some believe he said it at the beginning of the 1962 campaign, or that the line ended with "a government to defeat.") https://ronbase.wordpress.com/2016/01/24/hello-sweetheart-get-me-val-sears/

ONE: The Teacher's Son; the Preacher's Son (1895–1918)
1   John G. Diefenbaker, *One Canada: Memoirs of the Right Honourable John G. Diefenbaker, Vol. 1: The Crusading Years 1895–1956* (Toronto: Macmillan of Canada, 1975), 1.
2   *One Canada, Vol. 1*, 8.
3   Ibid., 15.
4   Ibid., 16.
5   John English, *Shadow of Heaven: The Life of Lester Pearson, Volume One: 1897–1948* (Toronto: Lester & Orpen Dennys, 1989), Ch. 1.
6   Pearson, Lester B., *Mike: The Memoirs of the Rt. Hon. Lester B. Pearson, Volume One* (Toronto: University of Toronto Press, 1972), 6.
7   Ibid., 7.
8   Ibid., 9.
9   *One Canada, Vol. 1.*, 18
10 Ibid., 19.
11 Ibid., 20.
12 Summation of oral history from Esther Bradshaw, 5 July 1986, Diefenbaker Archives, University of Saskatchewan.

[13] *One Canada, Vol. 1*, 53

[14] Ibid., 76

[15] Erica Gagnon, "Settling the West: Immigration to the Prairies from 1867 to 1914," *Canadian Museum of Immigration at Pier 21*, 2019. https://pier21.ca /research/immigration-history/settling-the-west-immigration-to-the-prairies -from-1867-to-1914

[16] *Mike, Vol. 1*, 8.

[17] Ibid., 12

[18] Denis Smith, *Rogue Tory, The Life and Legend of John G. Diefenbaker* (Toronto: Macfarlane, Walter & Ross, 1995), 21.

[19] *One Canada, Vol. 1*, 91.

[20] John George Diefenbaker, War Diary, Archives, Diefenbaker Centre, University of Saskatchewan.

[21] "John George Diefenbaker, Full Service Record" (Ottawa: Library and Archives Canada). https://central.bac-lac.gc.ca/. item/?op=pdf&app=CEF&id=2514-75

[22] Letter, 9 April, 1918, from Secretary, Board of Pension Commissioners to Diefenbaker, Memoirs, Pre-1940, John George Diefenbaker Archives, Diefenbaker Centre, University of Saskatchewan.

[23] *One Canada, Vol. 1*, 89.

[24] *Rogue Tory*, 30.

[25] Diary entry, 19 May 1915, Pearson fonds.

[26] *Mike, Vol. 1*, 36.

[27] "Lester Bowles Pearson" (Ottawa, Library and Archives Canada, Personnel Records of the First World War). https://www.bac-lac.gc.ca/eng/discover /military-heritage/first-world-war/personnel-records/Pages/item. aspx?IdNumber=562397

TWO: Love and Purpose (1919–1928)

[1] Garrett Wilson and Kevin Wilson, *Diefenbaker for the Defence* (Toronto: Lorimer, 1988), 24.

[2] *Rogue Tory*, 35.

[3] Ibid., 40.

[4] *Mike, Vol. 1*, 40

[5] Ibid., 43.

[6] Robert Toombs, *The English and Their History* (London: Allen Lane, 2014), 652.

[7] T. J. Macdonald, "Memorandum by the Minister of Labour: Unemployment Position" (London: National Archives), 18 August 1921. https://www .nationalarchives.gov.uk/education/resources/twenties-britain-part-one /unemployment-situation-1921/

8   Robert Skidelsky, *John Maynard Keynes, 1883–1946: Economist, Philosopher, Statesman* (London: Pan, 2003), 239.

9   Letter from Lester Pearson to Geoffrey Pearson, October 1950, Lester B. Pearson fonds.

10   *Mike, Vol. 1*, 46.

11   *History of the Canadian Peoples: Volume 2: 1867 to the Present* (Toronto: Pearson, 2015), 176.

12   *Diefenbaker for the Defence*, 52

13   Bob Plamondon, *Blue Thunder: The Truth About Conservatives from Macdonald to Harper* (Toronto: Key Porter, 2009), 216.

14   *Rogue Tory*, 47.

15   *Mike, Vol. 1*, 102.

16   Ibid., 106.

17   Ibid., 109.

18   Ibid., 124.

19   Ibid., 122–3.

THREE: Becoming Somebody (1929–1940)

1   Simma Holt, *The Other Mrs. Diefenbaker: A Biography of Edna May Brower* (Toronto: Doubleday, 1982), 118–19.

2   Norman Hillmer, *O.D. Skelton: A Portrait of Canadian Ambition* (Toronto: University of Toronto Press, 2015), 3.

3   *Shadow of Heaven*, 146.

4   *Diefenbaker for the Defence*, 103

5   *Diefenbaker for the Defence*, 108.

6   Ibid., 81

7   Ibid., 80.

8   Ibid., 81.

9   Ibid., 85.

10   *Mike, Vol. 1*, 78

11   *Shadow of Heaven*, 195.

12   *One Canada, Vol. 1*, 170.

13   Ibid., 139.

14   Letter to supporter, 2 December 1933, "Municipal election, 1933, 1935, Prince Albert," Diefenbaker Archives, University of Saskatchewan.

15   "Prince Albert mayoral election, 1933," Diefenbaker Archives, University of Saskatchewan.

16   Summation of oral history by Orest Bendas, 6 December 1985, Diefenbaker Archives, University of Saskatchewan.

17   Oral history from Emmett Hall, 19 May 1986, Diefenbaker Archives, University of Saskatchewan.

[18] John Diefenbaker to unnamed correspondent, 10 June 1938, "Elections-Provincial-1938-Results," Diefenbaker Archives, University of Saskatchewan.

[19] *Diefenbaker for the Defence*, 234.

FOUR: Ascent (1940–1946)

[1] "None is too many," *Dictionary of Canadian Politics*. https://parli.ca/none-many/

[2] Allan Levine, "Pre-Apology for the St. Louis, a look at Canada's former determination to keep Jews out," *Canadian Jewish News*, 11 October 2017. https://thecjn.ca/perspectives/pre-apology-st-louis-canadas-determination-keep-jews-out/

[3] Letter from Lester Pearson to Annie Pearson and Vaughan Pearson, 17 March 1939, Lester B. Pearson fonds, Archives and Special Collections, Carleton University.

[4] Ibid., 205.

[5] Letter from Lester Pearson to Maryon Pearson, 1 October 1940, Pearson fonds.

[6] Letter from Patricia Pearson to Lester Pearson, 1 October 1940, Pearson fonds.

[7] Charles Ritchie, *Undiplomatic Diaries, 1937–1971* (Toronto: Emblem/McClelland & Stewart), 86.

[8] Letter from Lester Pearson to Maryon Pearson, 30 June 1940, Pearson fonds.

[9] Letter from Lester Pearson to Marmaduke Pearson, 17 March 1940, Pearson fonds.

[10] *Shadow of Heaven*, 224.

[11] *O.D. Skelton*, 329.

[12] Letter from Lester Pearson to Maryon Pearson, 30 January 1941, Pearson fonds.

[13] Ibid.

[14] Letter from Lester Pearson to Maryon Pearson, 1 April 1941, Pearson fonds.

[15] *The Other Mrs. Diefenbaker*, 208.

[16] Ibid.

[17] Ibid., 214.

[18] *Speech from the Throne* (Ottawa: Government of Canada, 15 May 1940). https://www.poltext.org/sites/poltext.org/files/discoursV2/Canada/CAN_DT_XXXX_19_01.pdf

[19] Letter from Mary Diefenbaker to John Diefenbaker, April 10, 1940, "Family Correspondence – Mary F. Diefenbaker, 1909, 1916–45," Diefenbaker Archives, University of Saskatchewan.

[20] Letter from John Diefenbaker to Mary Diefenbaker, May 15, 1940, "Family Correspondence – Mary F. Diefenbaker, 1909, 1916–45," Diefenbaker Archives, University of Saskatchewan.

[21] Letter from Mary Diefenbaker to John Diefenbaker, 1940, "Family Correspondence, Mary. F. Diefenbaker, 1909, 1916–45," Diefenbaker Archives, University of Saskatchewan.

22 *The Other Mrs. Diefenbaker,* 225.

23 Ibid., 223

24 "Pierre Trudeau," *Sources.* https://www.sources.com/SSR/Docs/SSRW-
    Trudeau_Pierre.htm

25 "Conscription if necessary . . . not necessarily conscription," *Dictionary of
    Canadian Politics.* Parli.ca. https://parli.ca/conscription-if-necessary-not
    -necessarily-conscription

26 *One Canada, Vol. 1,* 197.

27 *Mike, Vol. 1,* 232.

28 Andrew Cohen, *Lester B. Pearson* (Toronto: Penguin, 2008), 95.

29 Ibid., 97.

30 Letter from Lester Pearson to Maryon Pearson, Late July/Early August 1940,
    Pearson fonds.

31 *Mike, Vol. 1,* 195.

32 Ibid., 197.

33 *Shadow of Heaven,* 250.

34 Ibid., 257.

35 J.L. Granatstein, *The Ottawa Men: The Civil Service Mandarins, 1935–1957*
    (Oakville: Rock's Mill's Press, 1982, 2015), 121.

36 *Lester B. Pearson,* 82.

37 Oral history from Alvin Hamilton, 7 July 1988, Diefenbaker Archives,
    University of Saskatchewan.

38 *The Other Mrs. Diefenbaker,* 235.

39 J.L. Granatstein, *The Politics of Survival: The Conservative Party of Canada,
    1939–1945* (Toronto: University of Toronto Press, 1967), 155.

FIVE: Power and Grief (1947–1951)

1 Allen Levine, *King: William Lyon Mackenzie King: A Life Guided by the Hand
    of Destiny,* (Toronto: Douglas & McIntyre, 2011), 372.

2 Heather Roberston, *More Than a Rose: Prime Ministers, Wives and Other
    Women* (Toronto: Seal, 1991), 276.

3 Louis St. Laurent, "The Foundations of Canadian Policy in World Affairs,"
    Statements and Speeches (Ottawa: Department of External Affairs, 13
    January, 1947). https://russilwvong.com/future/stlaurent.html

4 *Shadow of Heaven,* 327.

5 Letter from Edna Diefenbaker to John Diefenbaker, undated, "Edna
    Diefenbaker," Diefenbaker Archives, University of Saskatchewan.

6 *The Other Mrs. Diefenbaker,* 267.

7 Edna Diefenbaker to John Diefenbaker, 5 February 1947, "Edna Diefenbaker,"
    Diefenbaker Archives, University of Saskatchewan.

8 *Rogue Tory,* 149.

9 Ibid., 169.

10 Ibid., 173.

11 "Is It Time for a Change?" *Maclean's*, 1 June 1949. https://archive.macleans.ca/article/1949/6/1/is-it-time-for-a-change

12 "Progressive Conservative Party of Canada (1949)" *Sydney Post-Record*. https://www.poltext.org/sites/poltext.org/files/plateformesV2/Canada/CAN_PL_1949_PC_en.pdf

13 Blair Fraser, "Why Both Liberals and Tories Are Ignoring Quebec," *Maclean's*, 25 May 1957. https://archive.macleans.ca/article/1957/5/25/why-both-liberals-and-tories-are-ignoring-quebec-why-lionel-chevriers-return-made-68-mps-mad

14 *Diary of William Lyon Mackenzie King* (Ottawa: Library and Archives Canada, 2 January 1945). https://www.bac-lac.gc.ca/eng/discover/politics-government/prime-ministers/william-lyon-mackenzie-king/Pages/item.aspx?IdNumber=27866&

15 *King Diary*, 17 October 1946. https://www.bac-lac.gc.ca/eng/discover/politics-government/prime-ministers/william-lyon-mackenzie-king/Pages/item.aspx?IdNumber=30112&

16 *King Diary*, 11 August 1948. https://www.bac-lac.gc.ca/eng/discover/politics-government/prime-ministers/william-lyon-mackenzie-king/Pages/item.aspx?IdNumber=32423&

17 Ibid.

18 *Mike, Vol. 1*, 282.

19 *Shadow of Heaven*, 311.

20 Walter Gordon, *Walter Gordon: A Political Memoir* (Toronto: McClelland & Stewart, 1977), 49.

21 Adam Chapnick, "St. Laurent's Gray Lecture and Canadian Citizenship in History," *The Unexpected Louis St.-Laurent* (Vancouver, UBC Press, 2020), 459.

22 Lester B. Pearson, *Words and Occasions* (Toronto: University of Toronto Press, 1970), Ch. 11.

23 Laura Neilson Bonikowsky, "Canada and the Birth of NATO," *Diplomat*, 4 April 2015. https://diplomatonline.com/mag/2015/04/canada-and-the-birth-of-nato/

24 *King Diary*, 19 March 1948. https://www.bac-lac.gc.ca/eng/discover/politics-government/prime-ministers/william-lyon-mackenzie-king/Pages/item.aspx?IdNumber=31937&

25 John English, *The Worldly Years: The Life of Lester Pearson, 1949–1972* (Toronto: Vintage, 1972), 15.

26 *Rogue Tory*, 183.

27 *The Other Mrs. Diefenbaker*, 293.

28 Ibid., 303.

29 Ibid., 323.

30 All trial quotations from *Diefenbaker for the Defence*, 274-275.

SIX: Oil and Gas (1952–1956)

1 Letter from Lester Pearson to Geoffrey Pearson, 6 June 1945, Pearson fonds.

2 *The Worldly Years*, 68.

3 Letter from Lester Pearson to Geoffrey Pearson, 5 May 1952, Pearson fonds.

4 *Words and Occasions*, 72.

5 *The Worldly Years*, 88.

6 Dalton Camp, *Gentlemen, Players and Politicians* (Toronto: McClelland & Stewart, 1970), Chaps. 15–16.

7 Letter from John Diefenbaker to Olive Freeman, 11 August 1953, Diefenbaker Archives, University of Saskatchewan.

8 Heather Robertson, *More Than a Rose: Prime Ministers, Wives and Other Women* (Toronto: Seal, 1991), 249.

9 Summation of oral history by Clement Brown, 19 July 1989, Diefenbaker Archives, University of Saskatchewan.

10 In conversation with the author, October 2022.

11 Summation of oral history from Alvan Gamble, 22 December 1987, Diefenbaker Archives, University of Saskatchewan.

12 Letter from John Diefenbaker to Olive Freeman, undated, in 1952. "Family correspondence, Olive Diefenbaker, August–December 1952," Diefenbaker Archives, University of Saskatchewan.

13 Ibid.

14 Ibid.

15 Alex von Tunzelmann, *Blood and Sand: Suez, Hungary and Eisenhower's Campaign for Peace* (New York: Harper, 2016), 1.

16 *Blood and Sand*, 398.

17 Antony Anderson, *The Diplomat: Lester Pearson and the Suez Crisis*, (Fredericton: Goose Lane, 2015), 271.

18 Patrick Nicholson, *Vision and Indecision: Diefenbaker and Pearson* (Toronto: Longmans, 1968), 2.

19 Donald Fleming, *So Very Near: The Political Memoirs of the Honourable Donald M. Fleming, Vol. One: The Rising Years* (Toronto: McClelland & Stewart, 1985), 299.

20 Canada, Parliament, *House of Commons Debates*, 22nd Parliament, 3rd Sess, Volume 4 (14 May 1956).

21 Ibid., May 15.

22 Robert Bothwell and William Kilbourn, *C.D.Howe: A Biography* (Toronto: McClelland & Stewart, 1979), 305.

23 "Episode One: Prologue to Power," *The Tenth Decade, 1957–1967* (CBC, 1971).

24 *C.D. Howe*, 316.

25 Jamie Bradburn, "How Arrogance Cost the Liberals the 1957 Election" (TVO, 27 October 2019). https://www.tvo.org/article/how-arrogance -cost-the-liberals-the-1957-election

26 Mark Maloney, "A Tragic, Shocking, Fall from Grace," *Toronto Star*, 24 February 2007. https://www.thestar.com/news/2007/02/24/a_tragic_ shocking_fall_from_grace.html

27 Ibid.

28 Grattan O'Leary, *Recollections of People, Press, and Politics* (Toronto: Macmillan, 1977), 115–116.

29 Ibid., 118.

30 Ibid., 120.

31 *So Very Near, Vol. 1*, 324.

32 *So Very Near, Vol. 1*, 325.

33 Blair Fraser, "Why the Conservatives Are Swinging to Diefenbaker," *Maclean's*, 24 November 1956. https://archive.macleans.ca/article/1956/11/24/why -the-conservatives-are-swinging-to-diefenbaker

34 Janice Cavell, "The Spirit of '56, The Suez Crisis, Anti-Americanism, and Diefenbaker's 1957 and 1958 Election Victories," in Janice Cavell and Ryan M. Touhey, eds. *Reassessing the Rogue Tory: Canadian Foreign Relations in the Diefenbaker Era* (Vancouver, UBC Press, 2018).

35 *Vision and Indecision*, 12.

36 *Players*, 241.

SEVEN: The World Turned Upside Down (1957–1958)

1   *Vision and Indecision*, 2.

2   Lester B. Pearson, *Mike: The Memoirs of the Rt. Hon. Lester B. Pearson, Volume Three: 1957–1968* (Toronto: University of Toronto Press, 1975), 168.

3   House of Commons, *Debates*, 15 March 1957.

4   *Rogue Tory*, 220.

5   *Mike, Vol. 3*, 171.

6   House of Commons, *Debates*, 12 April 1957.

7   "Vincent Massey," *Canadian Encyclopedia*. https://www.thecanadian encyclopedia.ca/en/article/massey-charles-vincent

8   Desmond Mortin, "Uncle Louis and a Golden Age for Canada," *Policy Options*, June/July 2003. https://policyoptions.irpp.org/wp-content /uploads/sites/2/assets/po/the-best-pms-in-the-past-50-years/morton.pdf

9   Liberal election manifesto, 1957. https://www.poltext.org/sites/poltext.org
     /files/plateformesV2/Canada/CAN_PL_1957_LIB.pdf
10   Quoted in: Susan Delacourt, "The Mad Men of Canadian Politics," *National
     Post*, 4 October 2013. https://nationalpost.com/opinion/susan-delacourt
     -the-mad-men-of-canadian-politics
11   Patrice Dutil, "In Search of the St. Laurent Voting Coalition," *Unexpected
     Louis St. Laurent*, 364.
12   John C. Courtney, *Revival and Change: The 1957 and 1958 Diefenbaker
     Elections* (Vancouver: UBC Press, 2022), 104.
13   Ibid., 119.
14   Dalton Camp, *Gentlemen, Players and Rogues* (Toronto: McClelland &
     Stewart, 1970), 267.
15   Cara Spitall, *The Diefenbaker Moment* (University of Toronto Ph.D. thesis,
     2011). https://tspace.library.utoronto.ca/bitstream/1807/29878/3/Spittal
     _Cara_201106_PhD_thesis.pdf
16   *Gentlemen, Players and Rogues*, 334.
17   "The Election and Democracy," *Maclean's*, 22 June 1957. https://archive
     .macleans.ca/article/1957/6/22/the-election-and-democracy
18   "Dief to Become the Chief?" CBC, 10 June 1957. https://www.cbc.ca/archives
     /entry/dief-to-become-the-chief
19   *Howe*, 329.
20   *Mike, Vol. 3*, 24–25
21   Ibid., 27
22   *The Worldly Years*, 204.
23   Robert Lewis, *Power, Prime Ministers and the Press: The Battle for Truth on
     Parliament Hill* (Toronto: Dundurn Press, 2018), 120.
24   *The Worldly Years*, 155.
25   *The Road Back*, 16.
26   *Power, Prime Ministers and the Press*, 119.
27   John Diefenbaker, *One Canada: Memoirs of the Right Honourable John G.
     Diefenbaker, Vol. 2: The Years of Achievement* (Toronto: Macmillan of
     Canada, 1976), 34.
28   Note from William Macadam to author, November 2022.
29   *Royal Commission on Canada's Economic Prospects Preliminary Report*
     (Ottawa: Government of Canada, 1956), 89. https://publications.gc.ca
     /collections/collection_2020/bcp-pco/Z1-1955-2-11-eng.pdf
30   *Rogue Tory*, 268.
31   Letter from John Diefenbaker to Mary Diefenbaker, October 1958,
     Diefenbaker Archives, University of Saskatchewan.
32   H. Basil Robinson, *Diefenbaker's World: A Populist in Foreign Affairs*
     (Toronto: University of Toronto, 1989), 31.

33 *Rogue Tory*, 266.
34 House of Commons, *Debates*, 20 January 1958. https://www.lipad.ca/full/1958 /01/20/13/
35 Ibid.
36 *So Very Near, Vol. 1*, 447.
37 House of Commons, *Debates*, 21 January 1958. https://www.lipad.ca/full/1958 /01/21/13/#1931445
38 *Mike, Vol. 3*, 33.
39 *Fights of Our Lives*, 225.
40 Peter C. Newman, *Renegade in Power: The Diefenbaker Years* (Toronto: McClelland & Stewart, 1963), 22.
41 "Ep. 3: From Victory to Triumpth," *The Tenth Decade*.
42 *Fights of Our Lives*, 227.
43 *Mike, Vol. 3*, 35.
44 *Renegade in Power*, 75.
45 "Total Triumph for Diefenbaker, Tories," CBC, 6 April 1958. https://www.cbc .ca/archives/entry/total-triumph-for-diefenbaker-tories-in-1958

EIGHT: The Chief (1958–1961)

1 Steve Paikin, *John Turner: An Intimate Biography of Canada's 17th Prime Minister* (Toronto: Sutherland House, 2022), 27.
2 *Rogue Tory*, 303.
3 Ibid., xii, xiii, 325.
4 *Renegade in Power*, xi.
5 John Ibbitson, "How Will LGBTQ Canadians Take Trudeau's apology?" *Globe and Mail*, 14 September 2017. https://www.theglobeandmail.com /news/national/lgbtq-canada-apology/article37071384/
6 Peter C. Newman, "Holding the World on a Leash," *Maclean's*, 24 June 1996. https://archive.macleans.ca/article/1996/6/24/holding-the-world-on-a-leash
7 Ellen Fairclough, *Saturday's Child: Memoirs of Canada's First Female Cabinet Minister* (Toronto: University of Toronto Press, 1995), loc. 1563.
8 Ibid., loc. 314.
9 David Matas, "Racism in Canadian Immigration Policy," *Refuge*, Vol 5, No. 2, 1985. https://refuge.journals.yorku.ca/index.php/refuge/article/view/21485
10 *Order-in-Council 1911–1324*, Canadian Museum of Immigration at Pier 21. https://pier21.ca/research/immigration-history/order-in-council- pc-1911-1324
11 William Lyon Mackenzie King, "Canada's Postwar Immigration Policy," *Alberta Online Encyclopedia*. http://wayback.archive-it.org/2217 /20101208165211/http://www.abheritage.ca/albertans/speeches/king_1.html
12 *Saturday's Child*, loc. 2042.

13 House of Commons, *Debates*, 19 January 1962. https://parl.canadiana.ca
    /view/oop.debates_HOC2405_01/11?r=0&s=1

14 *Rogue Tory*, 240.

15 "False Assumptions and a Failed Relationship," *Royal Commission on
    Aboriginal Peoples, Vol. 1, Part 2*. http://caid.ca/RRCAP1.8.pdf

16 "Diefenbaker and the Indigenous Vote," CBC. https://www.cbc.ca/archives
    /entry/diefenbaker-and-the-native-vote

17 *Speech from the Throne* (Ottawa: Government of Canada, 12 May 1958).
    https://www.poltext.org/sites/poltext.org/files/discoursV2/Canada/CAN_
    DT_XXXX_24_01.pdf

18 Letter to John Diefenbaker from Percy A. Paull, 24 February 1962. https://
    diefenbaker.usask.ca/documents/online-exhibits/the-enfranchisement-of
    -canadas-aboriginal-peoples/paull_to_dief.pdf

19 Letter to Percy A. Paull from John Diefenbaker, 9 March 1962. https://
    diefenbaker.usask.ca/documents/online-exhibits/the-enfranchisement
    -of-canadas-aboriginal-peoples/dief_to_paull.pdf

20 *The Worldly Years*, 202.

21 Letter from Lester Pearson to William Spencer, 8 April 1958, Pearson fonds,
    Carleton University.

22 *The Worldly Years*, 205.

23 Donald Fleming, *So Very Near: The Political Memoirs of the Honourable
    Donald M. Fleming, Volume Two: The Summit Years* (Toronto: McClelland
    & Stewart, 1985), 85.

24 Ibid., 81.

25 *Mike, Vol. 3*, 45.

26 *Walter Gordon*, 79.

27 Ana Gomers Sunahara, *The Politics of Racism: The Uprooting of Japanese
    Canadians During the Second World War* (Toronto: Lorimer, 1981), Ch. 6.
    http://japanesecanadianhistory.ca/chapter-6-deportation/

28 *Saskatchewan Bill of Rights Act* (Regina: Revised Statutes of Saskatchewan).

29 Bora Laskin, "An Inquiry into the Diefenbaker Bill of Rights," *Canadian Bar
    Review*, 1 March 1959. https://cbr.cba.org/index.php/cbr/article/
    view/2330/2330

30 Thomas Axworthy, "Diefenbaker's Bill of Rights Laid Groundwork for
    Trudeau's Charter," *Ottawa Citizen*, 6 August 2002.

31 *The Canadian Bill of Rights* (Diefenbaker Centre, University of Saskatchewan).
    https://diefenbaker.usask.ca/exhibits/online-exhibits-content/the-canadian
    -bill-of-rights.php

32 Paul Cavalluzzo, "Judicial Review and the Bill of Rights: Drybones and Its
    Aftermath," *Osgoode Hall Law Journal*, December 1971. https://digital
    commons.osgoode.yorku.ca/cgi/viewcontent.cgi?article=2313&context=ohlj

33 *Attorney General of Canada v. Lavell* (Ottawa: Supreme Court of Canada, 27 August 1973). https://scc-csc.lexum.com/scc-csc/scc-csc/en/item/5261/index.do

34 Interview with the author, 8 October 2021.

35 Ibid.

36 Axworthy, "Diefenbaker's Bill of Rights Laid Groundwork for Trudeau's Charter."

37 Mary Janigan, *The Art of Sharing: The Richer versus the Poorer Provinces since Confederation* (Montreal: McGill-Queen's University Press, 2020), 298.

38 *Renegade in Power*, 126.

39 *Leadership Gained*, 136.

40 *Revival and Change*, 181.

41 "Royal Commission on Health Services, 1961–1964" (Ottawa: Government of Canada). https://www.canada.ca/en/health-canada/services/health-care -system/commissions-inquiries/federal-commissions-health-care/royal -commission-health-services.html

42 *Diefenbaker's World*, 174.

43 *Rogue Tory*, 55.

44 Ibid.

45 Ibid, 61.

46 Ibid., Chapter 9.

47 Address by Nelson Mandela to the Parliament of Canada, 18 June 1990. http://www.mandela.gov.za/mandela_speeches/1990/900618_canada.htm

NINE: Cries and Alarums (1959–1961)

1   Oral history from Alvin Hamilton, 7 July 1988, Diefenbaker Archives, University of Saskatchewan.

2   John Diefenbaker, Notes to a Speech on the Anniversary of the Ukrainian Canadian Settlement in Canada and in Commemoration to Taras Shevchenko, Winnipeg, 9 July 1961. https://diefenbaker.usask.ca/exhibits /online-exhibits-content/the-canadian-bill-of-rights. php#LimitationsandPrecedents

3   Brian Mulroney, *Memoirs, 1939–1993* (Toronto: McClelland & Stewart, 2007), 65.

4   *Howe*, 267.

5   Ibid.

6   Bruce Forsyth, "Broken Arrow: The Rise and Fall of Crawford Gordon and A.V. Rowe Canada," *Canadian Military History*, August 2016. https:// militarybruce.com/broken-arrow-the-rise-and-fall-of-crawford-gordon -and-a-v-roe-canada/

7   *Leadership Gained*, 121.

8 *Vision and Indecision*, 204.
9 Ibid.
10 Ibid., 123.
11 Paul Collins, "Not a Strike but a Civil War" (St. John's: Provincial Historic Commemoration Program, Government of Newfoundland and Labrador, 2014). https://www.drpaulwcollins.com/wp-content/uploads/2017/06/Not-a-Strike-But-a-Civil-War.pdf
12 *Power Prime Ministers and the Press*, 121.
13 Peter C. Newman, *Here Be Dragons: Telling Tales of People, Passion and Power* (Toronto: Douglas Gibson, 2004), Ch. 5.
14 Peter C. Newman, "The Powerful Gifts and Glaring Flaws of John Diefenbaker," *Maclean's*, 23 March 1963. https://archive.macleans.ca/article/1963/3/23/the-powerful-gifts-and-glaring-flaws-of-john-diefenbaker
15 *So Very Near, Vol. 1*, 483.
16 *So Very Near, Vol. 2*, 39.
17 Ibid., 41.
18 *So Very Near, Vol. 2*, 302.
19 *Renegade in Power*, 301.
20 Marcel Belanger, *The Coyne Affair* (Ottawa: University of Ottawa, 1970).
21 *One Canada, Vol. 2*, 274.
22 J.E. Coyne, *Credit and Capital* (Ottawa: Bank of Canada Archives, 12 December 1959), 27.
23 J.E. Coyne, *Living Within Our Means* (Ottawa: Bank of Canada Archives, 18 January 1960).
24 J.E. Coyne, *Inflation and Unemployment* (Ottawa: Bank of Canada Archives, 12 May 1960), 10.
25 James Powell, *The Bank of Canada of James Elliott Coyne: Challenges, Confrontation and Change* (Montreal: McGill-Queen's University Press, 2009), 161.
26 House of Commons, *Debates*, 14 June 1961. https://www.lipad.ca/full/1961/06/14/2/

TEN: Things Fall Apart (1961–1963)

1 *Diefenbaker's World*, 165.
2 Ibid., 173.
3 Knowlton Nash, *Kennedy and Diefenbaker: The Feud That Helped Topple a Government* (Toronto: McClelland & Stewart, 1991), 97.
4 John Diefenbaker to Mary Diefenbaker, May 1957, Diefenbaker Archives, University of Saskatchewan.
5 Stephen Ambrose, *Eisenhower, Volume II: The President* (New York: Simon and Schuster, 1984), 559.

6   "Episode Three: The Power and the Glory," *The Tenth Decade.*
7   "Address before the Canadian Parliament in Ottawa, May 17 1961," *John F. Kennedy*, American Presidency Project. https://www.presidency.ucsb.edu /documents/address-before-the-canadian-parliament-ottawa
8   *Diefenbaker's World*, 199.
9   *Kennedy and Diefenbaker*, 132.
10   Ibid., 223.
11   *One Canada, Vol. 2*, 46.
12   *Revival and Change*, 129.
13   *Getting Things Done for Canada and Canadians* (Ottawa: Progressive Conservative Party of Canada, 1962). https://www.poltext.org/sites/poltext .org/files/plateformesV2/Canada/CAN_PL_1962_PC.pdf
14   *The Liberal Programme* (Ottawa: Liberal Party of Canada, 1962). https:// www.poltext.org/sites/poltext.org/files/plateformesV2/Canada/CAN_ PL_1962_LIB_en.pdf
15   "Remarks at a Dinner Honoring Nobel Prize Winners of the Western Hemisphere," 29 April 1962. The American Presidency Project. https:// www.presidency.ucsb.edu/documents/remarks-dinner-honoring-nobel -prize-winners-the-western-hemisphere
16   *Kennedy and Diefenbaker*, 166.
17   Susan Delacourt, *Shopping for Votes: How Politicians Choose Us and We Choose Them* (Toronto: Douglas & McIntyre, 2013), 53.
18   In conversation with the author, October 2022.
19   *So Very Near, Vol. 2*, 517.
20   Summation of oral history of Neil Crawford, 15 May 1986, Diefenbaker Archives, University of Saskatchewan.
21   Alvin Hamilton oral history.
22   *So Very Near, Vol. 2*, 526.
23   *Debates*, House of Commons, 22 October 1962. https://parl.canadiana.ca /view/oop.debates_HOC2501_01/801?r=0&s=3
24   *Diefenbaker's World*, 287.
25   *Kennedy and Diefenbaker*, 196.
26   Irving Studin, ed., *What Is a Canadian? Forty-Three Thought-Provoking Responses* (Toronto: Douglas Gibson, 2009), 6.
27   *Kennedy and Diefenbaker*, 223.
28   Ibid., 225.
29   Ibid., 225.
30   Ibid., 226.
31   *Words and Occasions*, 204.
32   "Episode Four: Treason and Transition," *The Tenth Decade.*

33 *Vision and Indecision*, 262.
34 "Treason and Transition."
35 Ibid.
36 Ibid.

ELEVEN: Mike (1963–1965)

1 George Grant, *Lament for a Nation: The Defeat of Canadian Nationalism, 40th Anniversary Edition* (Montreal: McGill-Queen's University Press, 2005), Ch. 3.
2 Ibid.
3 *Kennedy & Diefenbaker*, 273.
4 Ibid., 274.
5 Ibid., 278.
6 Ibid., 290.
7 "Liberal Party Platform, 1963," *Election Manifestos Canada* (Quebec: Centre for Public Policy Analysis, Laval University). https://www.poltext.org/sites/poltext.org/files/plateformesV2/Canada/CAN_PL_1963_LIB.pdf
8 *The Worldly Years*, 264.
9 *Mike, Vol. 3*, 81.
10 "The FLQ and the October Crisis," *The Canadian Encyclopedia*. https://www.thecanadianencyclopedia.ca/en/timeline/the-flq-and-the-october-crisis
11 Judy LaMarsh, *Memoirs of a Bird in a Gilded Cage* (Toronto: McClelland & Stewart, 1968), 48.
12 Doris Anderson, "Pauline Jewett Blazes Trails for Women," *Toronto Star*, 16 July 1988, J1.
13 Letter from Lester Pearson to Geoffrey Pearson, 26 May 1963, Pearson fonds.
14 "Telegram from Hyannis Port to the Department of State, May 11, 1963" (Washington: Office of the Historian, Department of State). https://history.state.gov/historicaldocuments/frus1961-63v13/d449
15 *Undiplomatic Diaries*, 471.
16 Gordon, *Memoirs*, 118.
17 "Letter from Eric Kierans to Walter Gordon, June 18, 1963," in John N. McDougall, *The Politics and Economics of Eric Kierans: A Man for All Canadas* (Montreal: McGill-Queen's University Press, 1993).
18 Telegram from Department of State to Embassy in Canada, June 28, 1963 (Washington: Office of the Historian, Department of State). https://history.state.gov/historicaldocuments/frus1961-63v13/d451
19 Letter from Lester Pearson to William Spencer, 4 July 1963, Pearson fonds.
20 Denis Smith, *Gentle Patriot: A Political Biography of Walter Gordon* (Edmonton: Hurtig, 1973), 178.

21 Broadcast by Lester B. Pearson, following President Kennedy's death,
    22 November 1963. CBC. https://www.cbc.ca/player/play/1243983939654
22 In conversation with the author, November 2022.
23 Jim Coutts, "Why Dome Matters," *Toronto Star*, 26 April 1987, B3.
24 *Speech from the Throne* (Ottawa: 16 May 1963). https://www.poltext.org
    /sites/poltext.org/files/discoursV2/Canada/CAN_DT_XXXX_26_01.pdf
25 Ibid., 273.
26 Jonathan Manthorpe, *The Power & the Tories: Ontario Politics, 1943 to the
    Present* (Toronto: Macmillan, 1974), 58.
27 *Bird in a Gilded Cage*, 91.
28 *A Preliminary Report of the Royal Commission on Bilingualism and
    Biculturalism* (Ottawa, Queen's Printer, 1 February 1965), 13. https://
    publications.gc.ca/collections/collection_2020/bcp-pco/Z1-1963-1-3.pdf
29 "Episode Five: Search for a Mandate," *The Tenth Decade*.
30 Robert Dorion, *Special Public Inquiry 1964: Report of the Commissioner*
    (Ottawa: Government of Canada, 1965). https://publications.gc.ca/collections
    /collection_2014/bcp-pco/CP32-114-1965-eng.pdf
31 Tu Thanh Ha, "Montreal Mobster Nearly Sank the Liberals," *Globe and Mail*,
    14 February 2002. https://www.theglobeandmail.com/news/national
    /montreal-mobster-nearly-sank-liberals/article4131433/
32 "Funny Tales from Campaign Trails," *C2C Journal*, 29 June 2015. https://
    c2cjournal.ca/2015/06/funny-tales-from-campaign-trails
33 Peter C. Newman, *The Distemper of Our Times* (Toronto: McClelland &
    Stewart, 1968), Ch. 18.
34 *Special Public Inquiry 1964: Report of the Comissioner The Honourable
    Frederic Dorion* (Ottawa, 1965). https://publications.gc.ca/collections
    /collection_2014/bcp-pco/CP32-114-1965-eng.pdf
35 "Montreal Mobster Nearly Sank Liberals."
36 *The Road Back*, 247.
37 Tom Kent, *A Public Purpose* (Montreal: McGill-Queen's University Press,
    1988), 326.
38 *The Worldly Years*, 295.
39 *A Political Memoir*, 188.
40 "Legionnaires Boo PM Pearson Over Flag," CBC, 20 November 2017.
    https://www.cbc.ca/player/play/2640087987
41 Canada. Parliament. *House of Commons Debates*, 15 June 1964. https://
    parl.canadiana.ca/view/oop.debates_HOC2602_04/944?r=0&s=1
42 Ibid. https://parl.canadiana.ca/view/oop.debates_HOC2602_04/950?r=0&s=1
43 Rick Archbold, *I Stand for Canada: The Story of the Maple Leaf Flag*
    (Toronto: MacFarlane, Walter and Ross), 95.

TWELVE: Swings and Roundabouts (1965–1966)

1   Lorne Brown and Doug Taylor, "The Birth of Medicare," *Canadian Dimension*, 3 July 2012. https://canadiandimension.com/articles/view/the-birth-of-medicare

2   Richard Doyle, *Hurly-Burly: A Time at the Globe* (Toronto: Macmillan, 1990), 146.

3   *The Royal Commission on Health Services, Volume One* (Ottawa: Queen's Printer, 1964), 18. https://publications.gc.ca/collections/collection_2016/bcp-pco/Z1-1961-3-1-1-eng.pdf

4   Ibid., 100.

5   Ibid., 10.

6   Gordon, *A Political Memoir*, 219.

7   *Distemper*, 323.

8   Craig Baird, "The Elections: 1963 and 1965," *Canadian History* Ehx.2021. https://canadaehx.com/2021/09/06/the-elections-1963-1965/

9   Ibid., 319.

10 *Mike, Vol. 3*, 207.

11 "Episode Six: No Joy in Heaven," *The Tenth Decade*.

12 Baird, "The Elections: 1963 and 1965."

13 "No Joy in Heaven."

14 Ibid.

15 Canada. Parliament. *House of Commons Debates*, 4 March 1966. https://www.lipad.ca/full/1966/03/04/12/

16 *Power, Prime Ministers and the Press*, 110.

17 *Mike, Vol. 3*, 180.

18 *One Canada*, Vol. 3, 269.

19 *Rogue Tory*, 521.

20 Peter Stursberg, *Diefenbaker: Leadership Lost: 1962–67* (Toronto: University of Toronto Press, 1976), 143.

21 "Liberal Party Wins When It's Most Liberal," *Montreal Gazette*, 24 September 1986. https://www.newspapers.com/newspage/422602122/

22 *The Worldly Years*, 215.

23 *Leadership Lost*, 147.

24 *Mike, Vol. 3*, 355.

25 "Sex and Security," Historical Society of Ottawa. https://www.historicalsocietyottawa.ca/publications/ottawa-stories/personalities-from-the-very-famous-to-the-lesser-known/sex-and-security

26 *Distemper*, 364.

27 *One Canada, Vol. 3*, 272.

28 Mr. Justice William Flett Spence, *Report of the Commission on Inquiry into Matters Relating to One Gerda Munsinger* (Ottawa: Queen's Printer,

September 1966), 21. https://publications.gc.ca/collections/collection_2014
/bcp-pco/Z1-1966-2-eng.pdf

29 Kenneth Gibbons and Donald Cameron, eds., *Political Corruption in Canada:
Cases, Causes and Cures* (Montreal: McGill University Press, 1976), 106.

30 *Rogue Tory*, 521.

31 *The Worldly Years*, 355.

32 Richard J. Gwyn, *The Shape of Scandal*: A Study of a Government in Crisis,
(Toronto: Clarke Irwin, 1965), 6.

33 Kim Lunman, "Mitchell Sharp Dies at 92," *Globe and Mail*, 20 March 2004.
https://www.theglobeandmail.com/news/national/mitchell-sharp
-dies-at-92/article20429078/

34 Alexander Ross, "The Man Who Finally Belled the Cat," *Maclean's*, 1 Feb.
1967. https://archive.macleans.ca/article/1967/2/1/the-man-who-finally
-belled-the-cat

35 *Leadership Lost*, 163.

36 Flora MacDonald and Geoffrey Stevens, *Flora!: A Woman in a Man's World*
(Montreal and Kingston: McGill-Queen's University Press, 2021), 65.

37 Ibid., 1.

38 "No Joy in Heaven."

39 *Rogue Tory*, 546.

40 *Leadership Lost*, 170.

41 "The Man Who Finally Belled the Cat."

42 *The Player*, 186.

43 Ibid., 187.

44 Sean O'Sullivan, *Both My Houses: From Politics to Priesthood* (Toronto: Key
Porter, 1986).

THIRTEEN: Changing of the Guard (1967–1968)

1 *Mike, Vol. 3*, 306.

2 John Lownsbrough, *The Best Place to Be: Expo 67 and Its Time* (Toronto:
Allen Lane, 2012), 102, 3.

3 Ibid.

4 Ibid., 5.

5 "Georges Vanier," *Maclean's*, 1 July 1998.

6 Kathryn LeBere, "Rebel with a Cause: The Rise of René Lévesque," *University
of Victoria Journal*, 2018. https://journals.uvic.ca/index.php/corvette/article
/view/19008

7 *Mike, Vol. 3*, 138.

8 *Undiplomatic Diaries*, 499.

9 The statement is attributed to Johnson by Lawrence Martin in *The Presidents and the Prime Ministers* (Toronto: Doubleday, 1982). Ritchie makes no mention of it.

10 *The Best Place to Be*, 100.

11 "Long Live Free Quebec," *Emerson Kent.com*. http://www.emersonkent.com/speeches/long_live_free_quebec.htm

12 *The Worldly Years*, 343.

13 *Rogue Tory*, 550.

14 Michael Vineberg, *The Progressive Conservative Leadership Convention of 1967* (Master's thesis, McGill University, 1968).

15 *One Canada, Vol. 3*, 283.

16 Ibid.

17 *So Very Near, Vol. 2*, 672.

18 *The Progressive Conservative Leadership Convention of 1967*.

19 Ibid.

20 *One Canada, Vol. 3*, 280–282.

21 *Leadership Lost*, 196.

22 *Progressive Conservative Leadership Convention of 1967*.

23 *Leadership Lost*, 196.

24 Kent, *A Public Purpose*, 410.

25 Quoted in: Blair Fraser, "Canada Rescued the Commonwealth—But Was It Worth the Trouble?" *Maclean's*, 5 November 1966. https://archive.macleans.ca/article/1966/11/5/canada-rescued-the-commonwealth-but-was-it-worth-the-trouble

26 Robert Greenhill and Marina Sharpe, "Lester B Pearson's Road to Development," *Canadian Foreign Policy Journal*, 1 November 2018. https://www.tandfonline.com/doi/full/10.1080/11926422.2018.1522262

27 Vivienne Lawrie "Lives Lived: Alastair Lawrie, 90," *Globe and Mail*, 15 July 2016. https://www.theglobeandmail.com/life/facts-and-arguments/lives-lived-alastair-lawrie-90/article30915628/

28 John English, "A Thirst for New Blood," *Globe and Mail*, 14 October 2006. https://www.theglobeandmail.com/news/national/a-thirst-for-new-blood/article1107285/

29 *Lester B. Pearson*, 159.

30 *Distemper of Our Times*, 401.

31 "A Thirst for New Blood."

32 *Distemper of Our Times*, 402.

33 Paul Litt, *Trudeaumania* (Vancouver: UBC Press, 2016), 16.

34 Ibid., 149.

35 "When Pierre Trudeau Finally Said He'd Run for the Liberal Leadership," CBC, 16 February 2020. https://www.cbc.ca/archives/when-pierre-trudeau-finally -said-he-d-run-for-the-liberal-leadership-1.5458170

36 *Mike, Vol. 3*, 316.

37 Bonnie Turner, "Judie LaMarsh Spoke Her Mind, and the Entire Nation Heard Her," *Kingston Whig Standard*, 24 April 2020. https://www.thewhig.com /opinion/columnists/judy-lamarsh-spoke-her-mind-and-the-entire-nation -heard-her/wcm/16a14704-0207-4c5d-be47-49055d03f3af/amp/

FOURTEEN: Twilight (1968–1979)

1   Fed Vid, *PET 1968*, YouTube. https://www.youtube.com/ watch?v=soVhEOXrpmE

2   *Mike, Vol. 3*, 326.

3   *Fights of Our Lives*, 142.

4   *Liberal Party Policy Statement, 1968*. https://www.poltext.org/sites/poltext .org/files/plateformesV2/Canada/CAN_PL_1968_LIB_en.pdf

5   *Progressive Conservative Policy Handbook: 1968 – General Election*. https:// www.poltext.org/sites/poltext.org/files/plateformesV2/Canada/CAN_PL_ 1968_PC.pdf

6   Letter from Lester Pearson to William Spencer, 28 June 1968, Pearson fonds.

7   J.L. Granatstein, *Pirouette: Pierre Trudeau and Canadian Foreign Policy* (Toronto: University of Toronto Press, 1990), 23.

8   Ibid., 33.

9   Ibid., 34.

10 *Mike, Vol. 3*, 333.

11 *A Political Memoir*, 330–331.

12 *Blue Thunder*, 261.

13 *Rogue Tory*, 564.

14 *Rogue Tory*, 575.

15 *Both My Houses*, 42.

16 Ibid.

17 Letter from John Diefenbaker to Elmer Diefenbaker, 20 May 1971, Diefenbaker Archives, University of Saskatchewan.

EPILOGUE

1   Florence Bird et al., *Report of the Royal Commission on the Status of Women* (Ottawa: Information Canada, 1970), 38.

2   Michael Stevenson, "Ch. 3: Howard Green, Disarmament and Canadian-American Defence Relations, 1959–63: 'A Queer, Confused World,'" *The Nuclear North: Histories of Canada in the Atomic Age*, Susan Colbourn and Timothy Andrews Sayle, eds. (Vancouver: UBC Press, 2020.)

3   Oral history from Douglas Fisher, 21 April 1986, Diefenbaker Archives, University of Saskatchewan.
4   Oral history from Merrill Menzies, 15 April 1986, Diefenbaker Archives, University of Saskatchewan.
5   Summation of oral history of John Dafoe, 16 April 1986, Diefenbaker Archives, University of Saskatchewan.
6   "Pearson's Legacy: Seven of His Successors Assess How He Changed Canada," *National Post*, 27 December 2022. https://nationalpost.com/news/politics/pearsons-legacy-seven-of-his-successors-assess-how-he-changed-canada

Index